Teaching
Feminist
Activism

Teaching Feminist Activism

Strategies from the Field

Edited by

NANCY A. NAPLES AND KAREN BOJAR

Routledge
New York and London

Published in 2002 by
Routledge
29 West 35th Street
New York, NY 10001

Published in Great Britain by
Routledge
11 New Fetter Lane
London EC4P 4EE

Routledge is an imprint of the Taylor & Francis Group.

Printed in the United States of America on acid-free paper.

10 9 8 7 6 5 4 3 2 1

Library of Congress Cataloging-in-Publication Data

Teaching feminist activism : strategies from the field / edited by Nancy A. Naples and Karen Bojar.
    p. cm.
   Includes bibliographical references and index.
   ISBN 0-415-93186-X — ISBN 0-415-93187-8 (pbk.)
   1. Feminism—Study and teaching (Higher)—United States. 2. Social action—Study and teaching—United States. I. Naples, Nancy A. II. Bojar, Karen.

HQ1426 .T42 2002
305.42'071'1—dc21

2002016556

Contents

Preface

Teaching Feminist Activism is designed as a resource for feminist faculty interested in linking feminist theoretical perspectives and case studies on political activism with feminist pedagogy and experiential learning. This edited collection presents diverse theoretical approaches, methodological strategies, and practical teaching tools for feminist faculty in a variety of college and university settings. Authors demonstrate the value of, and challenges faced, when feminist faculty attempt to integrate experiential learning and research on feminist activism into their classrooms. The collection includes descriptions of internship programs, relevant videos, and related teaching materials that have proven valuable in working with students to encourage their understanding of feminist political activism through experiential learning.

Contributors to the collection represent a wide range of disciplinary and interdisciplinary locations: ethnic studies, literary studies, sociology, social work, economic development, architecture, anthropology, political science, and education as well as women's studies. All but one essay (Naples, chapter 6) are original manuscripts published here for the first time. We are grateful to Ilene Kalish for her encouragement and resourcefulness in bringing this collection to life, and to Kimberly Guinta for her excellent editorial assistance. We would also like to thank Chrys Ingraham and an anonymous reviewer for their useful comments on our book proposal and selected chapters. We are also extremely grateful to Berenice Fisher and Pat Huckle for their insightful and detailed suggestions on the draft of the full manuscript.

We could not have completed this book without Jennifer Rogers's tireless efforts and commitment to the project. Jennifer read each essay, edited the chapters, and worked with authors throughout the revision process. She also collaborated with Joan Ariel, University of California Irvine's women's studies librarian extraordinare, to generate a thorough bibliography of sources that maps the field of feminist pedagogy, feminist praxis, women's community activism, and women's movements.

Teaching Feminist Activism

As editors, we collectively bring over forty years of experience in conducting experiential learning in women's studies classrooms for the purposes of teaching feminist politics. In the next two sections, we independently discuss how we came together to pursue this book project.

Experiential Learning in Women's Studies— Karen Bojar's Reflections

Working on this collection has been a rewarding experience for me. First, collaborating with Nancy has been particularly rewarding. As someone once reluctant to embrace e-mail and the Internet, I would not have believed that an online collaboration could have worked so well.

Also, the opportunity to learn about a range of models and resources for incorporating an experiential component in women's studies courses has clarified my own thinking about the sometime unexamined assumptions underlying my classroom practice. Those of us who juggle heavy teaching loads, activist commitments and family obligations often find it difficult to carve out the time for reading and reflection.

I confess one powerful response I had to working on this collection was envy. As a community-college teacher, I am lucky to teach one introduction section of women's studies each semester. Teaching a seminar on feminist activism is an unrealizable dream. On the other hand, this twinge of envy is countered by the realization that an urban community college is a wonderful base for an activist. One of the greatest satisfacttions of my teaching career is sharing my knowledge of local activist networks with my students. I have introduced them to local feminist organizations, recommended several for the boards of local community organizations, and seen some become staff members for local feminist and progressive organizations.

Despite these rewards of community-college teaching, I long for time to step back from the day-to-day struggles and explore the larger issues. I work with a wonderful group of women in the local chapter of the National Organization for Women, but we are always focused on the current struggle, the current election cycle. I once thought of suggesting a study group where we would read the works of feminist historians, sociologists, economists, and political theorists, but I know the reaction would be: "Nice idea, but who has the time?"

My community-college colleagues who also teach courses in our fledgling women's studies/gender studies program are not local activists; the meetings of our women's studies program, which I coordinate, are focused on such issues as how to enroll more students in our classes so they are not canceled and how can we get administrative support to develop new courses. Urgent matters to be sure, but not a source of intellectual stimulation and growth.

In a sense, the National Women's Studies Association (NWSA) annual conference has been a lifeline, a once-a-year opportunity to discuss recent scholarship on feminist movements and to probe some of the deeper issues underlying our choice of activist projects and the intellectual context we try to provide. For me, the idea for this book grew out of discussions of the NWSA Feminism and Activism Interest Group formed at the 1999 NWSA conference in Albuquerque. It's so easy to get caught up in the day-to-day pressure of designing syllabi, gathering resources, and helping our students design activist projects while trying to maintain our own commitment to feminist organizing (which in these conservative times is so often reactive in nature). We often do not stop to think about why we are channeling our energy in this direction, or into these organizations, why we encourage students to choose particular activist projects, or whether our students (and our own) short-term projects are connected to a larger strategy, a broader vision.

Reading these essays has me aware of the range of possibilities, helping me avoid becoming too comfortable with my choices, too certain of my analysis. This collection has also made me aware of the tension between the goal of deepening students' awareness of feminist issues and promoting activities most likely to advance a feminist agenda. Although many of us see ourselves as advancing both goals, and clearly they are mutually reinforcing, the limited time at our disposal may force us to give greater emphasis to one or the other.

Most of the students I teach are usually not in need of consciousness-raising; they usually do understand race, class, and gender oppression. What they need are the tools to combat inequality. They need to learn about the range of organizations working for social change, both explicitly feminist organizations and the range of progressive organizations advancing goals consistent with a feminist agenda. They also need to know about the possibilities for advancing a feminist agenda within the labor unions and professional organizations to which they may already belong (in the case of the older students) or to which they may join when they enter the full-time workforce.

I realize that in other institutions, raising students' awareness of race, class, or gender oppression is the first priority; several contributors to this collection have made a case for experiential education as a powerful tool for countering student resistance to an analysis of these issues. The essays in this collection demonstrate that strategies will and should vary according to institutional context.

Feminist Praxis and Experiential Learning—
Nancy Naples's Reflections

In the fall of 1999, I remember seeing an e-mail from Karen Bojar, who reported that a group on activism had been formed during the 1999 National Women's Studies Association. I wrote to Karen and asked to be included in their new listserv. Karen replied to my e-mail saying that she had used my book *Grassroots Warriors: Activist Mothering, Community Work, and the War on Poverty* (1998) and found it to be useful in teaching about women's community activism. Since she lived in Philadelphia, one of the two cities I highlight in the book, she had appreciated reading about the community activism of women in her city. Over e-mail we shared our interest in teaching women's studies students about activism experientially. We discussed how each of us tried to teach politics in our classrooms. Karen then told me of her interest in producing an edited collection that would be useful for women's studies and other feminist faculty interested in teaching feminist praxis (i.e., linking theory and practice), and thus our collaboration began.

This has been one of the most satisfying collaborations, though I have yet to meet Karen face-to-face. We have been fortunate to have the rare experience of sharing a vision of the classroom as a site for teaching feminist praxis, a belief in the value of experiential learning, and a commitment to action that moved this project along in almost record speed. Sending out a call on the women's studies listserv and tapping into our different communities, we were able to attract authors who also wish to share their experiences in activist-oriented classrooms with other feminist faculty.

The ease with which we have collaborated is especially noteworthy given that Karen and I teach in very different kinds of institutions. Karen's career has been spent at an urban, working-class community college in Philadelphia. My experiences have been primarily within women's studies programs in research universities, first at Iowa State University and then at the University of California, Irvine (UCI). However, the differences we have had in our teaching experiences served to complement what we each had to bring to this collective project. Our work has been further helped by the assistance of Jennifer Rogers, an undergraduate women's studies and sociology major at UCI who I have been fortunate to work with since she first took my introductory women's studies course as a first-year student.

I would also like to thank the Women's Studies Program at UCI, and the Department of Sociology at the University of Connecticut for providing the funds for research assistance to help complete this project. Thanks to UConn research assistant Kate Brown for systematizing the references. I am also extremely grateful to Paula Goldsmid, former director of the Center for Women and Gender Education at UCI, and Donna-Jean Louden, former coordinator of the Rape Awareness Project at UCI for sharing their time and wisdom with my students over the years. I would especially like to thank my graduate teaching assistants for their tireless efforts in the women's studies classrooms. Thanks also to DeeDee Nunez and Rosie Humphreys—the most patient and supportive program managers any women's studies program could wish for.

Nancy A. Naples and Karen Bojar

Introduction:
Teaching Feminist Activism
Experientially

Karen Bojar and Nancy A. Naples

This collection provides an overview of the relevant research and pedagogical tools for theoretical and practical use in teaching feminist praxis in women's studies classrooms and beyond. The themes for the collection include: explicating the politics of experiential learning as well as the politics of experience in women's studies, exploring the relationship between feminist praxis and women's studies pedagogy, demonstrating how feminist activism can be incorporated into introductory women's studies courses and senior seminars, providing exemplars of courses designed to teach intersectionality and critical self-reflexivity, and illustrating the pedagogical power of community partnerships for experiential education. We also include lists of resources such as websites, videotapes, reference guides, and recommended texts for use in teaching feminist politics experientially. This collection emphasizes the diversity of approaches to teaching feminist politics as women's studies faculty respond to the varied institutional, political, regional, and demographic contexts in which we teach.

Research on feminist movements and women's activism enhances our understanding of the complex dynamics of politicization and feminist politics, helps clarify feminist priorities, informs our understanding of how to organize across differences, and contributes to the development of activist strategies for progressive social change. This book links scholarship on feminist activism with experiential projects. By including both research on activism and experiential reflections by activist researchers and praxis-oriented feminist instructors, we provide an overview of the relevant research and pedagogical tools for theoretical understanding and practical use. The collection demonstrates how feminist activist scholarship can be used as part of the reflective component of experiential education courses and internships in women's studies as well as substantive courses on feminist theorizing and feminist politics.

Teaching Feminist Activism builds on several recent collections, most notably Colette Hyman and Diane Lichtenstein's *Expanding the Classroom: Fostering Active Learning and Activism* (1999),[1] Maralee Mayberry and Ellen Cronan Rose's *Meeting the Challenge: Innovative Feminist Pedagogies in Action* (1999),[2] Kerrissa Heffernan and Barbara Balliet's *The Practice of Change: Concepts and Models for Service Learning in Women's Studies* (2000),[3] and Robyn Wiegman's *Women's Studies on Its Own* (2002).[4] In addition to these important sources, there are numerous edited collections containing scholarship on women's movements and feminist activism.[5] Missing in this rich literature on women's studies teaching and feminist activism is a volume focused exclusively on linking scholarship on feminist activism with experiential projects. Our collection fills a particular need in the field for a volume that explores how this ever-growing body of research can provide resources for activists as well as academics (although we do not pose these as mutually exclusive categories). Our hope is that *Teaching Feminist Activism* will help instructors in women's studies link their feminist pedagogy with the rich literature on women's movements with attention to the diversity of feminist activism.

Our collection places its primary emphasis on experiential education and on integrating feminist scholarship with experiential activist projects in women's studies courses. In the minds of many of its practitioners, women's studies and feminist activism are inextricably intertwined. In the early days of women's studies programs, the link between the academic study of women's lives and the feminist movement was for the most part unquestioned. However, as women's studies programs became institutionalized a note of anxiety about compromising one's scholarship through political engagement was sometimes heard; increasingly, some feminist scholars began to see feminist activism as something of a career risk.

Of course, the riskiness of a public commitment to activism varies considerably depending on one's social location. A teacher in a community college might be rewarded for what is seen as laudable civic engagement; a feminist scholar seeking tenure in a traditional academic department at an elite institution might well worry that activism would jeopardize her career. Whether feminist activism is likely to reap rewards or punishment is clearly dependent on the political climate of the institution and its surrounding community. Navigating these minefields has led some of us to use more politically acceptable terminology like service learning or experiential education rather than activism to describe our activist-oriented pedagogical strategies.

Defining Terms

Experiential education is the catchall term that includes any structured learning experience outside the traditional classroom. It could include a business major interning in an accounting firm or a women's studies major interning in a radical direct action group. The term *internship* is usually applied to experiential education involving a major time commitment and preparation for a specific career area; internship is typically unpaid work. While participating in an internship may enhance a student's future career possibilities, some students may not have the time, or cannot afford to give up paid work, to engage in this form of experiential learning.

Service learning tends to be used for experiential education projects that are short-term and not necessarily connected to a career area. Service learning has proven for some to be a politically useful term since there are now national organizations, such as Campus Compact (Balliet and Heffernan 2000), dedicated to its promotion and funding. Some teachers who use the term focus on traditional service projects such as tutoring and working in homeless shelters, whereas others use the term to include projects that might be characterized as social change or advocacy work. The term *service learning*, with its connotations of traditional charitable work, has long made many feminists uneasy. Although celebrated by some strands of feminist thought as embodying an ethic of care (Noddings, 1994), charitable work has been regarded with suspicion by feminists who have seen such work as reflective of female subordination or as an attempt to prop up an unjust status quo (NOW 1973).

Activism is the term that contributors to this collection are most comfortable with, though it is clear that authors have different understandings of what counts as activism as well as very different priorities. There are also differences as to their reasons for inclusion of an activist component in a women's studies course. Is the activist project primarily intended to help students develop a deeper understanding of feminist issues? Or is it to promote the development of skills necessary for building a powerful feminist movement? Many of us would no doubt lay claim to both goals. The emphasis may shift depending upon one's students and the level of the course. A focus on expanding awareness is more likely to be the top priority in the introductory course; an analysis of strategies for advancing the feminist agenda is more likely to be the focus of a senior seminar intended for women's studies majors.

Not only does the level of our courses influence the kind of activist projects we develop; institutional constraints clearly shape the possibilities available to us. Options abound in urban areas rich in feminist organizations. Frequently in such areas, institutions are managed by liberal administrators who provide support or at least are not actively opposed to our efforts. Once one leaves the Boston–Washington megalopolis, the Pacific Coast and a few urban centers in the South and Midwest (Atlanta, Austin, Chicago, Minneapolis-St. Paul) the range of potential community partners for feminist projects dwindles.

In addition to geographical location and political climate, another powerful constraint is time. Residential campuses provide opportunities for campus-based projects not available at commuter colleges where students rush off to jobs and family responsibilities. Finding time for activist projects is an especially urgent issue for a teacher at a community college who may desperately pack as much as possible into her introductory women's studies course knowing that this may be the only such course her students will ever take. The options available to such teachers are worlds apart from those available to teachers of senior seminars for women's studies majors in four-year colleges. Every course is an unstable compromise, and this is particularly the case when we try to incorporate an activist component. Fortunately, we do get the option to refine, revamp, and recreate our courses.

Compounding the institutional constraints, we all are confronting the challenge of teaching feminist activism in conservative times. In women's studies courses that enroll large numbers of nonmajors, students are often resistant to feminism in particular and to activism more generally. Several contributors address these issues and describe strategies for combating student resistance.

Many of us have been waiting for decades for the pendulum to shift while trying to do our part to change the political climate. Student activism in the global justice, antisweatshop, and "justice for janitors" movements offers hope that we may be on the cusp of a turn to student activism. However, it's not clear how powerful these movements will become or whether they will address feminist issues.

Although we may not enjoy a social climate supportive of feminism, we do have a wealth of literature exploring feminist activism (and women's movements not explicitly feminist) written from every conceivable cultural and theoretical perspective. We have the rich intellectual legacy of second-wave feminism to guide us as we confront the challenges of the current political climate. A major goal of this collection is to demonstrate the various ways in which these textual resources can be utilized to deepen students' understanding of their activist projects.

The book is organized into five parts: "Theorizing Experiential Learning and Activist Strategies"; "Teaching Feminist Activism Experientially"; "Teaching Intersectionally: The Politics of Gender, Race, Class, and Globalization"; "Women's Studies, Experiential Education, and Community Partnerships"; and "Using the Web for Teaching Feminist Politics." We conclude with a thorough and useful overview of reference guides, additional publications not referenced by the authors in the previous chapters, and videotapes generated by women's studies librarian Joan Ariel and research assistant Jennifer Rogers. The guides to resources in the field can be drawn on for class reading, special assignments, and specialized research on feminist activism, praxis, and pedagogy.

As editors, we are aware that there are many more dimensions relevant to teaching feminist activism that we could not include. We also recognize the gaps in what we were able to identify for this collection. Among the missing dimensions are attention to the dilemmas of generational and religious differences. We also recognize that the diversity of the students we teach are not fully represented by the chapters in this book. With a few exceptions, we have not been able to include the experiences of our teaching assistants and representatives of the community agencies with which we collaborate. However, we hope that this collection will serve to inspire others to share their experiences in and out of the feminist classroom and to encourage many more to take up the challenge of teaching feminist activism experientially.

The contributors to this collection offer their research and reflections on their teaching experiences in the spirit of collaboration that makes women's studies programs among the most invigorating places to work within the university. We offer this collection as a means by which feminist faculty and students can link their commitment to social change with the activist efforts in the classroom, on campus, in local communities, and beyond.

Notes

1. *Expanding the Classroom* was one of the first collections to link feminist praxis and feminist pedagogy.

2. *Meeting the Challenge* is a wonderful collection of essays by feminists with years of experience in feminist classrooms. This anthology provides a rich overview of the frameworks that inform feminist pedagogical practice. For example, Maralee Mayberry highlights the distinction between feminist pedagogy and collaborative learning. Sandra Bell, Marina Morrow, and Evangelia Tastsoglou address the difficult issue of students' resistance to critical and antiracist approaches in the classroom. They highlight the importance of Paulo Freire's philosophy of education for feminist pedagogy. The collection also explores the dilemmas of institutionalization and technology for women's studies programs. For example, Jane Rinehart discusses the strategic use of institutional resources as well as the potential for co-optation. In her chapter in *Meeting the Challenge* (Mayberry and Rose 1999) Ellen Cronan Rose examines the dilemmas of distance education for feminist pedagogy and challenges women's studies faculty. Melissa Kesler Gilbert, Carol Holdt, and Kristin Christophersen outline their experience in implementing a capstone course that linked women's studies students with community-based organizations in a community partnership model.

3. This is one of the few resources on experiential learning. The Campus Compact (Balliet and Heffernam 2000) collection emphasizes the philosophical assumptions underlying service learning as well as the process of arranging internships rather than the integration of scholarship on women's movements with service learning.

4. *Women's Studies on Its Own* (Wiegman 2002) incorporates analytic essays on the challenges of women's studies programs in the twenty-first century, including an examination of the relationships among women's studies, ethnic studies, and area studies; discussion of internationalizing the curriculum; and an assessment of enacting interdisplinarity in the classroom. The collection also includes chapters that highlight the specific challenges of teaching the large introductory and senior capstone courses. All of the chapters grapple with the politics of teaching feminism in the contemporary women's studies classroom.

5. For example, *Women's Activism and Globalization: Linking Local Struggles and Transnational Politics*, edited by Nancy A. Naples and Manisha Desai (2002); *Democratization and Women's Grassroots Movements*, edited by Jill Bystydzienski and Joti Sekhon (1999); *Community Activism and Feminist Politics: Organizing Across Race, Class, and Gender*, edited by Nancy A. Naples (1998a); *Feminism and Social Change*, edited by Heidi Gottfried (1997); *Women's Movements in Global Perspective*, edited by Amrita Basu (1995); *Feminist Organizations: Harvest of the New Women's Movement*, edited by Myra Marx Ferree and Patricia Yancey Martin (1995b); *Women Transforming Politics: Worldwide Strategies for Empowerment*, edited by Jill Bystydzienski (1992); and *Third World Women and the Politics of Feminism* edited by Chandra Talpade Mohanty, Ann Russo, and Lourdes Torres (1991).

I

Theorizing Experiential Learning and Activist Strategies

T he first two articles of *Teaching Feminist Activism* explore the implications of feminist theory for teaching feminist activism. A core principle of feminist pedagogy has been the insistence on women's experience as a starting point for knowledge production. Nancy Naples, in chapter 2, locates the antecedents of feminist pedagogy in the works of John Dewey and calls attention to the close relationship between feminist pedagogy and critical education theorists such as Paulo Freire and Henry Giroux. Naples notes that experiential approaches to feminist pedagogy have come under attack from critics both within and outside the women's studies field. According to Naples, "Poststructuralist analyses, which call into question what 'counts as experience,' form powerful cautions against valorizing women's experience in the women's studies classroom." Yet despite such reservations, women's studies practitioners have continued to view women's experience as a starting point and have continued to teach feminist praxis through an experiential approach. Naples argues for "a critical feminist pedagogy that is open to self-reflexivity about the processes by which we produce knowledge for and with our students," and describes ways in which Dorothy Smith's institutional ethnographic approach fosters such self-reflexivity. She describes how institutional ethnography can provide methodological guidance for experiential learning and community action.

In chapter 3, Jane Rinehart analyzes the theoretical underpinnings of her classroom practice; her focus is on the classroom itself as a site for justice. Rinehart argues that "aiming for just relationships in the classroom is as important as providing students with readings about social justice." She describes her attempts to put her theoretical commitment to relinquishing authority in the classroom into practice in a seminar on women and activism. The pedagogical principles described by Rinehart and Naples inform—at least to some extent—all the articles in this collection as contributors describe their attempts to deepen students' understanding of and commitment to feminist activism.

In chapter 4, Catherine M. Orr describes her work with students who in general share her core values and perspectives. Orr describes her efforts to present students with the intersectional complexities of race, class, and gender issues. She reports, "What I was not quite aware of, however, was how my attempts to call into question the content I presented actually eroded the foundation for traditional forms of activist struggle." She discusses her students' reaction to Sherna Gluck's contention that "Women's Studies as a discipline and feminist theorizing as a practice, partakes in exclusionary discourses on race and class that limit our visions about the scope and variety of feminist activism." Orr's students saw such focus on difference as an impediment to action. Orr states that to her astonishment, "even students of color and avowed postmodernists in the class, at first timidly and eventually forcefully, argued for the importance of a cohesive narrative to activist, identity-based struggles." This observation highlights how conflicts among feminists can lead to a paralysis of action and raises the question of whether there is tension between the goal of deepening students' understanding of the complexity of feminist issues and the goal of fostering commitment to action.

In the last chapter of this section, Karen Bojar describes the challenges and opportunities provided by the political climate at an urban community college. In a city with a generally liberal political climate, there exists a wide range of feminist service and advocacy organizations. Also, with a student body and faculty with deep roots in the local community, there are numerous opportunities for sustained commitment. Bojar calls for probing the underlying assumptions that lead us to encourage some types of projects rather than others and to engage our students in the process of analyzing our choices and in developing a long-term strategy for building a powerful feminist movement.

2

The Dynamics of Critical Pedagogy, Experiential Learning, and Feminist Praxis in Women's Studies

Nancy A. Naples

As an undergraduate student I recall my excitement when I was first introduced to the educational philosophy of John Dewey. After twelve years of Catholic schooling where the ability to memorize seemed the most valued sign of intelligence, I had all but soured on the possibility that classrooms could be a place for free exchange of ideas or "engaged pedagogy" (hooks 1994b). Dewey, one of the most prominent U.S. educators to argue for experiential learning, believed that: "As formal teaching and training grow in extent, there is the danger of creating an undesirable split between the experience gained in more direct associations and what is acquired in school" (1944/1966: 9).

Decades later, feminists like Dorothy Smith also criticized the abstract forms of knowledge production that rendered invisible the experiential dimension of knowing. I see parallels between Dewey's emphasis on experiential learning and the feminist pedagogical goal of fostering critical consciousness. For example, bell hooks (1994: 61) emphasizes that when "our lived experience of theorizing is fundamentally linked to processes of self-recovery, of collective liberation, no gap exists between theory and practice. Indeed, what such experience makes more evident is the bond between the two—that ultimately reciprocal process wherein one enables the other."

After outlining some of the diverse approaches to experiential learning as articulated in theories of critical education and feminist pedagogy, I assess the institutional, political, and academic challenges of experiential learning in the feminist classroom. In the second section, I discuss different approaches to the relationship between feminist pedagogy and community action, and how the institutional ethnographic (IE) approach of Dorothy Smith (1998)

provides a framework for linking experiential learning and feminist activism to the broader pedagogical and instructional goals in women's studies.

Epistemologies of Experiential Learning

Returning to John Dewey who had been so influential in the early development of my own educational philosophy, I was struck by his attention to self-reflexivity as an essential component of the learning process. In *Democracy and Education*, Dewey notes that experience is comprised of both active and passive elements "peculiarly combined." For Dewey "[m]ere activity does not constitute experience." Experience requires a process of self-reflexivity, that is, "learning from experience" (1944/1966: 139). He concludes his chapter "Experience and Thinking" by emphasizing the danger in severing thinking from experience.

In the context of the women's movement of the late 1960s and early 1970s, feminist faculty across the United States developed innovative pedagogical strategies designed to draw on women students' personal experiences and to incorporate processes of dialogue and reflexivity into classroom interaction and course assignments (see, e.g, Maher and Tetreault 1994; Fisher 2001). Early women's studies classes used journal writing, autobiographical essays, and oral histories of family and community members among other techniques to provide students with the opportunity to explore how their personal lives were shaped by processes of oppression. The notion that "the personal is political," the central tenet of consciousness-raising groups of this period, provided the pedagogical framing for many of these classroom exercises. However, these techniques could be adopted without incorporating the group process and collective action that had been central aspects of consciousness-raising during the women's movement of the time. Furthermore, since consciousness-raising groups typically grew out of localized interpersonal networks, the political analyses developed in these groups are typically limited by the homogeneity of the group. In addition, as hooks (1994) points out, consciousness-raising strategies do not necessarily provide the context through which we can recognize how social structural dynamics such as capitalism, colonialism, or racism shape our experiences.

Consciousness-raising (CR) techniques drew from "the Chinese revolutionary practice of 'speaking bitterness' in which peasants began to reject the inevitability of their predicaments" through collective discussions about their experiences (Stern 1994:512; see also Mitchell 1971). As philosopher of education Berenice Fisher (2001:32) notes, "CR often resulted in the development of strong and deep bonds among women that could support activism. But feelings of comfort and even love of other women could lead to an exclusive coziness that discourage action or, in the case of heterosexual women who became uncomfortable with the intimacy, to homophobic panic." Despite this danger, Fisher concludes, "consciousness-raising *supports and generates women's political agency* because this process assumes that problems flowing from women's oppression are serious political issues and that women are capable of understanding, addressing, and responding to those issues" (p. 39; italics in original).

Many radical feminists of this era viewed CR as "a starting point for feminism, a place from which to begin doing more public, activist organizing, rather than an end in itself or an investigative model" (Hogeland 1998:25). Lisa Hogeland (1998) reports that while personal experiences served as the beginning for feminist analysis, CR groups were to switch their energies to political projects such as abortion rights, expansion of child care services, employment and educational equity, and fight violence against women. Therefore, radical feminist explications of CR included linking personal issues to political analyses for the purposes of political action. Furthermore, many second-wave women's movement activists viewed CR as the method through which feminist political analysis and action proceeded.

The newly defined curricula area of women's studies was initially viewed by many feminist faculty as the academic arm of the women's movement. However, with the institutionalization of women's studies, links to women's movement goals and feminist organizations began to weaken. In some cases, academic administrators required women's studies faculty to distance themselves from activist organizations and controversial issues. Sandra Krajewski (1999) reports that when the battered women's shelter opened in her community in 1978, an administrator at the university warned the women's studies director to avoid associating with the new shelter and addressing the issue of battering.

Recognizing the limits of CR as a pedagogical strategy, women's studies faculty have experimented with approaches that might produce a "more intellectually sound, more politically and theoretically sophisticated" approach to CR in the women's studies classroom (Hogeland 1998:166). For example, Hogeland highlights Estelle Freedman's (1990) "Small Group Pedagogy: Consciousness Raising in Conservative Times" as an illustration of one successful strategy. Freedman includes CR in her course as a separate component, one that takes place outside the classroom through small group processes and journal writing. However, the institutionalization of women's studies in the academy constrains the development of collective political action that characterized the CR groups of the 1970s. With power differentials between teachers and students and among students, and the surveillance of women's studies curriculum by bureaucratic bodies within the academy, feminist faculty often find it difficult to incorporate the "commitment to praxis" in their classrooms. Given the contradictions of institutionalization, what strategies can women's studies faculty employ to retain a pedagogical commitment to feminist praxis? In the remainder of this article, I demonstrate the possibilities of teaching feminist praxis through an experiential approach.

Experiential Learning and Women's Studies

Ironically, while activist strategies in the women's studies classroom are often viewed with suspicion, problem-solving learning and internship programs have received renewed legitimacy within the academy (see *Feminist Collections* 1999). Problem solving or service learning and internships can be used to promote critical consciousness among students. However, the distinctions between internships, experiential learning projects, and community action are often blurred in practice. For example, in her course on women and society at the University of Colorado, Kayann Short (1999:32) initiated a service-learning practicum she termed Why Shop? Week through which the students learned how "individual consumption practices" were linked to "women's labor and resources exploitation." (See also Short's chapter in this volume.)

While exercises like Why Shop? Week can contribute much to the feminist pedagogical goal of promoting the investigatory and political skills to complement students' growing critical consciousness, internships are typically less likely to do so. In many cases, internships are developed in response to employers' interests in training an educated workforce with employment-relevant skills. Some students, especially those from middle- and upper-class backgrounds who have not found it necessary to seek employment while going to college can gain many advantages from internships in the community. For working-class students, internships are a mixed bag. On the one hand they might provide experiences that can contribute more to the students' upward mobility than the minimum-wage jobs they often hold while attending college. These experiences, coupled with the letters of recommendations from professionals in not-for-profit community organizations, could enhance students' employability following their graduation from college. On the other hand, internships are typically unpaid, and require students to engage in volunteer work while juggling their paid jobs and attending college. Students who are parents find internship requirements even more taxing.

In contrast to internships in predominantly social service agencies, internships in feminist activist organizations provide the opportunity for women's studies students to learn about the everyday work of feminist activism. To cite one example, Bronna Romanoff, Chrys Ingraham, Pat Dinkelaker, and Jennifer MacLaughlin (1999) designed a course called Women Changing the World that is required for all graduating seniors at the Sage Colleges in Troy, New York. The faculty link students to different government agencies and non-governmental organizations to help implement community projects. The projects the students became involved in included "helping organize a Take Back the Night rally and march with neighborhood groups" and "surveying neighborhood residents' ideas for rehabilitating a dangerous vacant lot" (43).

Community action projects can be as labor intensive as internships, even though the group context can include a division of labor that could be responsive to different students' schedules and time commitments. Regardless of format, however, my interest here is how we might use experiential approaches to teach feminist praxis. This goal seems especially important given the so-called postfeminist political context of the 1990s.

Consciousness-Raising and Oppositional Consciousness

Interactive or group reflection on the connection between personal problems and political processes is the essence of the consciousness-raising strategies adopted by the women's movement of the late 1960s and early 1970s. Consciousness-raising groups broke down the isolation between women, shifted the site of knowledge creation, and built communities of resistance. With this inspiration to contest the power attributed to "experts," feminist educators argued that a process of empowerment occurs as we shift the site of knowledge creation from the institutionalized expert to women and other marginalized social actors. This analysis significantly contributed to the development of diverse and interdisciplinary feminist standpoint or "positional" epistemologies. As Dorothy Smith (1987:17–18) argues, "Being excluded, as women have been, from the making of ideology, of knowledge, and of culture means that our experience, our interests, our ways of knowing the world have not been represented in the organization of our ruling nor in the systematically developed knowledge that has entered into it."

In response to calls for "situated knowledges" (Haraway 1988) and for empowerment of women students, women's studies faculty across the United States developed innovative pedagogical strategies designed to draw on women students' personal experiences and to incorporate processes of dialogue and reflexivity into classroom interaction and course assignments (see, e.g,, Maher and Tetreault 1994). Journal writing, autobiographical essays, and oral histories of family and community members, among other techniques, were employed to provide students with the opportunity to explore how their personal lives were shaped by processes of oppression often hidden from view. These techniques could be adopted without incorporating the group process that was the context for CR during the women's movement of the late 1960s and 1970s.

The CR group process enabled women to share their experiences, define and analyze the social and political mechanisms by which women are oppressed, and develop strategies for social change. Many radical feminists of this era viewed CR as "a starting point for feminism, a place from which to begin doing more public, activist organizing, rather than an end in itself or an investigative model" (Hogeland 1998:25). In contrast to this radical feminist version, Jane Kenway and Helen Mondra (1992:156) argue that CR "can be engaged in a way that is not articulated with action: after all, one might develop a heightened awareness of pain and contradiction but may still feel powerless to resolve problems." They distinguish between CR and Paulo Freire's analysis of "conscientizacao" which they see as more closely linked to the development of critical analytic skills. Freire's (1985) conceptualization of *conscientization* was first developed in the Latin-American context to describe the process by which people come to understand how their particular situations are shaped by their culture, how they reflect on these new understandings, and how they act against the circumstances that oppress them to create a more just social world.[1]

From a feminist pedagogical perspective, the development of critical consciousness provides students with the ability to call into question taken-for-granted understandings of social, political, economic, and academic life. This process of politicization can lead them to develop an "oppositional consciousness."[2] Since the development of oppositional consciousness is not an inevitable consequence of experiential learning, my goal as a feminist educator must necessarily be more modest. However, I agree with feminist educational theorist Kathleen Weiler that we can build toward counterhegemony. Weiler notes, "The empowerment of students means encouraging them to explore and analyze the forces acting upon their lives" (1988:152). I would also like to see feminist education include lessons that link theory and feminist practice. As Nancy Schniedewind (1983:270) points out, "As long as we live in a sexist society, feminism inevitably implies taking action to transform institutions and values." This, I believe, is one of the major contributions of experiential learning for feminist educational practices.

Critical Education and Experiential Learning

Critical educational theorists have also explored the value of experiential learning for democratizing education and encouraging students to develop their critical analytic skills (see Apple 1993; Giroux and Aronowitz 1985). However, as Jennifer Gore (1993) notes, feminists in women's studies rarely reference the work of critical education theorists in their discussions of gender and schooling. Few feminists located in women's studies have been in dialogue with critical education theory with the possible exception of Freire, who argued that "both teachers and students are agents" (Weiler 1988:17) in the educational process. Some authors speculate that this lack of dialogue between women's studies faculty and critical education theorists results from the structural divisions across schools of education and schools of social sciences and humanities, where women's studies programs are typically located. However, in some locations, for example, the University of Wisconsin-Madison, the Ontario Institute for Studies in Education, or New York University, feminist faculty in the field of education, like Elizabeth Ellsworth, Dorothy Smith, and Berenice Fisher have been at the forefront of feminist pedagogical discussions on campus.

Freire provided a model of educational practice that recognizes how domination as well as resistance is possible in the classroom. For example, Rina Benmayor (1991:161) describes how researchers in the El Barrio Program in New York utilize Freire's model of "empowerment pedagogy." As students share their stories with each other, they "foster solidarity, and move the discourse from individual to collective levels." In a process similar to consciousness-raising, sharing their personal narratives provides the students the opportunity "to realize that their circumstances are not unique, accidental, or the product of their own errors or "shortcomings." At the same time, CR also has different implications for women of different racial and class backgrounds. For example, as Aída Hurtado (1996a) notes, "feminist political discourse cannot take the public/private distinction for granted, either its advantages or its disadvantages for differently situated women" (cited in Fisher 2001:43). For example, poor women who are subject to state intervention in their personal lives, or women with certain kinds of disabilities who do not have the same expectations of privacy as women without disabilities, may experience the expectations of CR groups as oppressive rather than liberatory. Furthermore, the production of certain narratives or "a certain normative subject" through a CR process may serve to marginalize or silence other narratives or subjectivities that do not fit the dominant mode.[3]

In her book *The Struggle for Pedagogies: Critical and Feminist Discourses as Regimes of Truth*, Gore (1993) brings together insights of feminist educational theory with radical pedagogy. Fisher (2001) also effectively links the work of critical educational theory and feminism in her new work entitled *No Angel in the Classroom: Teaching through Feminist Discourse*. She defines feminist pedagogy as "*teaching that engages students in political discussion of gender injustice*" and includes the goal of seeking "to understand and challenge oppressive power relations" and questioning "the meaning for differently situated women of oppression and liberation" (2001:44; emphasis in the original). Her book provides a rich discussion of how she negotiates her commitment to feminist pedagogy and the strategies she uses to engage students in feminist praxis.

With Gore and Fisher, I am interested in developing a critical feminist pedagogy that is open to self-reflexivity about the processes by which we produce knowledge for and with our students. Furthermore, Fisher (2001:63) calls for critical reflection on "the authority of experience" where both professors and students interrogate "experience for its hidden assumptions and limitations." Yet, this move also presupposes our own liberation, a problematic assertion in the context of our own institutional location within the academy, as subjects within a racist and homophobic social context, and as invested with authority within the classroom (see also Shrewsburg 1997).

Gore defined pedagogy broadly to include "both instruction and social vision" (1993:2). However, I note with interest her comment that socialist feminist thought was missing from feminist pedagogical discourse. She suggests that "this lack of attention is linked to socialist feminism's emphasis on the 'broader,' more abstract, macro questions of ideologies and institutions rather than on micro questions of classroom pedagogy and/or linked to socialist feminism's closer alliance with critical pedagogies which have posed class-based relations as the primary social relation" (1993:19). As a materialist feminist with a strong interest in feminist educational practice, I found both the absence she noted and her explanations troubling. In my view, without an analysis of the larger relations of domination and oppression that shape our everyday lives and the resistance work necessary to challenge inequalities, it is unclear how we can link our local practices to broader strategies for change. In part two of this chapter, I will demonstrate how materialist feminist perspectives, in particular Smith's IE approach, can provide epistemological tools to help students link the so-called micro social world with the macroprocesses that shape our world and illustrate this point with the community action project.

Feminist Pedagogy, Community Action, and Institutional Ethnography

As a consequence of their evaluation of feminist classrooms across the country, Frances Maher and Mary Kay Thompson Tetreault (1994:208) explore "how positional understandings are discouraged or blocked in the academic environment." Maher and Tetreault (1994:226) observed that students in feminist classrooms found it difficult to examine "their own lives as embedded in social structures of class and race as well as gender and heterosexuality." They recommend that "positional pedagogies could help them to explore those categories not as natural states, or as normal or abnormal conditions, but as different positions within a structural power dynamics, which these students could imagine challenging." Positional or standpoint epistemologies include the work of Patricia Hill Collins (1990), Chandra Mohanty (1991, 1995), Chela Sandoval (1991), and bell hooks (1994).[4] However, positional or standpoint theorizing provide insufficient guidance for feminist pedagogical practice. In contrast, I argue, Smith's everyday-world standpoint epistemology and institutional ethnographic approach can provide methodological guidance for experiential learning and community action.

Institutional Ethnography and Community Action

Smith (1992:88) describes her institutional ethnographic approach as a "method of inquiry, always ongoing, opening things up, discovering." Outside of sociology and the field of education I rarely see Smith's standpoint on epistemology discussed as methodology. Nor have feminist educators explored her approach for feminist pedagogical practice. However, I have found her approach useful in providing both epistemological and methodological guidance for my own pedagogical practice and especially in relationship to the community action project I developed for use in my introductory women's studies classes. Institutional ethnography is a research method that can be "accountable to people's lived experience" and "as a means of making visible the social relations that organize and shape our lives" (Smith 1992:190).

For feminist undergraduate and graduate students, Smith's everyday-world approach to understanding "how things are put together" offers a powerful pedagogical tool for experiential teaching. By mapping the ways institutions function to render invisible the gender, race, and class dynamics embedded in bureaucratic rules and procedures; assumptions about clients, consumers, or citizens; and organizational products and outcomes students come to recognize how inequality is produced and reproduced in everyday life. They also are given an explicitly feminist approach to help guide their investigations. Smith's (1987) everyday-world perspective does not end at the level of the individual woman as "knower" but is "directed towards exploring and explicating what she does not know—the social relations and organization pervading her world but invisible in it" (Smith 1992:91). Her IE approach to "experience" emphasizes how subjects of inquiry are "situated in the actualities of [their] own living, in relations with others" (Smith 1996:5). For Smith, "experience" is "always social and always bear[ing] its social organization"

(1996:1). Smith's mode of inquiry calls for explicit attention to the social relations embedded in women's everyday activities and can provide the foundation for a theoretically and methodologically grounded approach to experiential learning.

Smith (1990:4) writes in her introduction to *The Conceptual Practices of Power* that "the practices of thinking and writing that are of special concern here are those that convert what people experience directly in their everyday/everynight world into forms of knowledge in which people as subjects disappear and in which their perspectives on their own experience are transposed and subdued by the magisterial forms of objectifying discourse." Smith's epistemology makes it possible "to disclose to those women [e.g., in a particular institutional setting like education] how matters come about as they do in their experience and to provide methods of making their working experience accountable to themselves and other women rather than to the ruling apparatus of which institutions are part." It is this aspect of Smith's IE approach that contributes to its power for feminist pedagogy as well as feminist activism. Those who adopt an IE approach link their work to a variety of traditions, including phenomenology and ethnomethodology as well as Karl Marx's historical materialism and poststructuralism. Institutional ethnographers "examine processes of ruling in the production of texts in specific work-places (such as schools, health care and criminal justice settings, government agencies, newsrooms, professional offices, and so on) and in the uses of texts (such as official records and reports) that organize people's activities in various settings" (DeVault 1999:48). Due to the influence of phenomenology, Marxism, and poststructuralism, institutional ethnography has an inherently interdisciplinary reach. While Smith's particular project is to help construct a sociology that starts from and can speak to the everyday actualities of people's lives, her methodology for social critique, and textual and institutional analyses has much to offer interdisciplinary feminist pedagogical practice.

Smith (1999:130) resists providing content to the standpoint of social actors because, she explains, "I want it to function like the arrow you see on maps of malls that tells you 'you are here.' The metaphor of a map directs us to a form of knowledge of the social that shows relations between various and differentiated local sites of experiences without subsuming or displacing them." Smith's mapmaking strategy helps an investigator map the activities that coordinate and reproduce oppressive systems and provides a useful tool in the women's studies classroom. It also helps capture the nuances, contradictions, and less formal processes, and the institutional processes that intersect in particular social or institutional locations. This knowledge can be used as a resource for social change efforts, providing an assessment of how power operates in local practices of ruling and where activist interventions might be most successful.

This approach to social investigation also broadens "people's own good knowledge of the local practices and terrains of their everyday/everynight living, enlarging the scope of what becomes visible from that site, mapping the relations that connect one local site to others." The social maps generated from institutional ethnographic investigations are "through and through indexical to the local sites of people's experiences, making visible how we are connected into the extended social ruling relations and the economy." Since the "product could be ordinarily accessible and usable, just as a map is," it offers a guidepost for activist interventions (Smith 1999:94-95). However, as Marjorie DeVault (1999:53) explains,

> using research results effectively to promote change requires the pragmatic evaluative and strategic skills of activism, honed through more daily participation in front-line work than most researchers can manage. . . . These comments point to a final element of institutional ethnographic investigation: to be fully realized, such inquiries should be conducted with an eye to their use by specific groups.

The institutional and political knowledges that students derive from their investigation of how things are put together in order to make the changes they propose illustrates the link between institutional ethnography and feminist activism. In the context of a community action project, students are advised to explore the institutional forms and procedures, informal organizational processes, and discursive frames used to construct the goals and targets of the work the institution performs. They are also encouraged to remain self-reflective of their own assumptions and interactions both individually and as part of their community action groups. An illustration of this approach can be found in University of California, Irvine graduate student Karen Kendrick's (1998) investigation of battered women's shelters in Orange County, California. Kendrick notes how pressures from governmental officials, funding sources, and professionals in law and social welfare displaced battered women and other community members as central players—a finding consistent with other research in this field. In addition to analysis of organizational history and institutional change, Kendrick describes how her understanding of what it meant to be a feminist—strong, independent, and resistant to patriarchal control—impeded her ability to seek help as a battered woman. She felt that if she came out as a battered woman, it would signify that she was a "bad feminist." Further, when Kendrick initiated her research on the politics of battered-women's shelters, she expected to find a very vocal radical feminist perspective among the shelter staff, one that contrasted sharply with the perspective of the police and lawyers, for example. This belief, held by many students in our women's studies classrooms, often leads to their quick disillusionment as they witness the constraints placed on feminist activists in a variety of community-based settings and the depoliticization of feminist activism more generally. With the tools of institutional ethnography, Kendrick's research led her to a much richer analysis of the politics of race, class, sexuality, gender, and institutionalization as they intersected in constructing the battered woman as the target of shelter work. By drawing on Smith's institutional ethnographic approach, Kendrick and other students are provided with a feminist epistemological approach that Smith developed directly out of her activist engagement with academic knowledge production. Smith's approach also ensures that a commitment to the political goals of the women's movement remains central to feminist pedagogy and experiential learning.

Conclusion

With the development of university-based centers for women and for gay, lesbian, bisexual and transgendered students, among other organizations for support and grassroots political engagement, women's studies classrooms are no longer the only formal sites in colleges and universities where consciousness-raising and individual empowerment occurs. We now occupy the institutional location from which to further develop strategies that link the personal to the political to the theoretical in new and creative ways. Moreover, given the growth in size of our women's studies classrooms (especially at the introductory level), we need to find epistemological and pedagogical approaches that lend themselves to feminist education without marginalizing the important insights of early consciousness-raising strategies. While the institutionalization of women's studies in the academy and of women's movement goals more broadly makes it more difficult to sustain the commitment to feminist praxis within the women's studies classroom, I remain convinced of its continued vibrancy and centrality to the project of women's studies.

Through the investigatory process and activist interventions they choose for their community action projects and other experiential learning assignments, students learn about the "extralocal organization of everyday experiences" (DeVault 1999:49) or "how things work" to reproduce inequality (Smith, 1990:34). These lessons also illustrate the feminist critiques of "objectified and authoritative knowledge" as embodied in "professional, scientific, and other academic discourses" (Smith 1999, 31). In this way, experiential learning informed by an explicitly feminist epistemological framework deepens students' understanding of the themes addressed in women's studies' classrooms. Maher and Tetreault (1994) point out that despite their institutional success, women's studies and ethnic studies departments are still viewed "as 'add-ons,' whose existence is necessitated by the failure of other departments to incorporate their challenge to mainstream views" (p. 208). From this vantage point, the goal would be the elimination of such programs as evidence that feminist, antiracist, and anticolonialist academic perspectives are integrated into the traditional disciplines. This view, however, denies the unique interdisciplinary scholarship that derives from transdisciplinary sites like women's studies and ethnic studies programs within the academy as well as the unique commitment to feminist and antiracist praxis.

Notes

My thanks to Karen Bojar, Jennifer Boyle, Michelle Grisat, Robyn Wiegman, Chrys Ingraham, and an anonymous reviewer for helpful comments on an earlier draft of this chapter.

1. Friere's approach was enthusiastically taken up by feminist and critical educators. See Susan Stern's (1994) insightful comparison of feminist and critical education theorists' approaches to empowerment and emancipatory praxis. Also see Patti Lather's (1991) assessment of the limits and possibilities of critical pedagogy.
2. Drawing upon Antonio Gramsci (1971), Aldon Morris (1992) contrasts "oppositional consciousness" with "hegemonic consciousness" (or "the ideas of the ruling class") and characterizes the power of "oppositional consciousness" as residing in its ability "to strip away the garments of universality from hegemonic consciousness, revealing its essentialist characteristics" (p. 370).
3. My thanks to Robyn Wiegman for this observation.
4. Political theorist Catherine O'Leary (1997:48–49) argues that "forms of standpoint theory, such as those developed by Patricia Hill Collins and bell hooks which propose to refigure the status of knowledge and identity for political practice by employing experience as a political and interpretive category, represent alternatives which transform feminist standpoint theory in promising and empowering ways." She further asserts, "The concept of a politics of engagement and coalition provided by [Chandra] Mohanty and [Bernice Johnson] Reagon offer an answer to both post-structuralist anxiety about the power of identity claims and the anxiety of some feminists about the multiplicity of differences" (p. 51). See Collins (1990); hooks (1984); Mohanty (1995); Reagon (1992).

3

Collaborative Learning, Subversive Teaching, and Activism

Jane A. Rinehart

I am always eager to teach about social justice. I was attracted to sociology and women's studies because they promised ways of connecting academic work to progressive social activism. For several years, I was a lecture-style teacher, dedicated to making clear arguments supported by compelling evidence. I also encouraged students to disagree with the lectures and assigned readings, and some did. I found a kind of success teaching this way—that is, I received tenure. However, during the 1980s, increasing student passivity in the classroom prompted me to reassess my pedagogy. A few students seemed to dominate discussion and all of their comments were directed forward, toward me. It seemed that I had constructed in the classroom the same situation that I was criticizing in my lectures: a disengaged citizenry watching experts perform, a generalized lack of responsibility. I needed to figure out how to teach more justly.

Collaborative learning emphasizes students' responsibility for constructing classroom conversations about course texts. The interpretive work of students and the knowledge they make together is the center of the course. I was drawn to these methods because I believe that America is an unjust society characterized by deep social inequalities based on race, class, gender, and sexual orientation. These inequalities create the conditions for the lack of discussion and genuinely shared decision making in the public sphere—in workplaces, neighborhoods, community centers, political organizations, churches, and schools. The silencing and exclusion of most Americans from the creation of social policy is produced by, and contributes to, social injustice. Justice requires shared responsibilities and resources: a place at the table, opportunities to speak and be heard, and a sense of agency. The practical-evaluative quality of agency develops in situations that foster reflection and communal interpretation. Collaborative learning methods create such situations, although their outcomes cannot be guaranteed. Having practiced collaborative learning principles and strategies for the past twelve years, I have come to believe that aiming for just relationships in the classroom is as important as providing students with readings about social justice.

To *collaborate* means "to work jointly with others, especially in an intellectual endeavor," but it also means "to cooperate with or willingly assist an enemy of one's country and especially an occupying force" (Singley and Sweeney 1998:63). Both of these meanings are operative in my experience of collaborative learning as a method for creating a shared vision of a more just society and enacting it. Collaborative learning in women's studies courses is shared intellectual work, and it is also cooperation with an occupying force (composed of feminist scholars) that opposes the taken-for-granted customs. However, that cooperation does not take the form of full agreement with all of the views of the "enemy;" rather, it refuses the either/or contained in the usual meaning of collaboration as betrayal of one's country and surrender to its foe. Instead, collaborative learning frames disagreements as opportunities to raise questions about all positions, as invitations to listen and seek new understandings. Its collaboration is not tied to conquest, but to conversation that welcomes differences and the uncertainties these produce. I want my classroom to be a site where social justice is both examined and practiced. I want to be in dangerous classrooms with students who ask difficult questions leading to complex and ambiguous answers that open up more questions. I hope for questions that require critical examination of conventional concepts, theories, and methods, leading to answers we cannot predict or control.

While I use collaborative learning approaches in all of my courses, I am going to focus on one course in this essay: Women and Activism, the capstone seminar for the women's studies concentration during the spring 1999 semester. Many of my women's studies students hope for changes in the world; many also admit to skepticism about the efficacy of any form of social activism. Thus, while they do not believe in "the system" in the sense of agreeing with its principles, they affirm its power. The capstone seminar was an opportunity to challenge their resignation and encourage them to envision possibilities for making social change. My experience with Women and Activism has deepened my commitment to collaborative pedagogical practices as an essential component of an education that promotes social justice.

I realize that "experience" has often been used as a warrant for claiming unassailable knowledge, a knowledge that directly refers to reality, a knowing that disclaims its practices. That is not my intention in this essay. Instead, I operate within the approach to experience as described by historian Joan Scott (1992:37) in these terms: "Experience is at once always already an interpretation and is in need of interpretation. What counts as experience is neither self-evident nor straightforward; it is always contested, always therefore political." I will be using my experiences and reflections as a specific context that allows you, the reader, to understand my "location" as a basis for assessing my claims. My location is constructed within my interpretation; it is not its outside grounding or authorization. My account of subversive pedagogy in women's studies is not idiosyncratic or utterly personal; it is linked to the work of many other feminist educators (hooks 1994b; Lather 1991; Luke and Gore 1992). But it is particular, shaped by my specific circumstances, resources, commitments, and temperament.

Subversion and Collaboration

Subversive teaching aims to communicate an "oppositional imagination:" an ability to think past received habits of thought and action. Teaching about justice and practicing classroom justice contest acceptance of gross social inequalities and abdication of citizenship. Subversive teachers invite students to consider what they believe, what evidence can be used for and against this position, and what the alternatives look like. When this invitation takes place within classroom collaborative learning groups, the traditional classroom structure and process is destabilized. The students' voices are heard more often than that of the teacher, authority is dispersed, and knowledge is regarded as socially constructed rather than grounded in something independent of human practices. Practicing subversion means constructing the classroom as a public space in which serious conversations take place about society, culture, policies, and responsibilities, and requiring students to participate in these.

Student participation has to be required because most students do not volunteer for this activity. Most fear exposing themselves—bringing their confusions and questions into the open—and they doubt the value of doing this. Their fear and doubt are often based on inexperience; many have not had the opportunity to engage in serious, continuing conversation about complex topics with their peers in which they are responsible for constructing an understanding together. Collaborative learning subverts the cultural ideals and social practices premised on a lack of genuine participation that maintains the status quo. That kind of work is more likely to occur when I stop talking so much and require the students to talk with each other about the course material. If I want students to learn how to think for themselves and talk with others about how gender is constructed, the inequalities it creates, and how it could be changed, then I have to get out their way. I have to get over my notions that time invested in process is *wasted* time and that my responsibility as a teacher is to *give* students knowledge, even to convert them to my perspective. I am often uncomfortable with collaborative learning; admitting that to myself and to the students has been helpful because it is something we have in common.

The tension between subversion and conversion is basically about how "authority" is constructed and the effects of its different constructions. In a traditional understanding of education, authority belongs to the teacher who uses it to present students with expert knowledge. Such knowledge is obtained by examining the world carefully, using the procedures of a particular discipline. Teachers transmit what is known and an established set of procedures for knowing. In foundational classrooms knowledge comes to the students as a ready-made object or thing, and learning is the process of comprehending that object. What is correct is discovered by overcoming one's biases and closely following the rules of disciplined inquiry. Within a foundational conception of knowledge, students can participate in the classroom, but their participation is shaped by firm limits.

In nonfoundational knowing and teaching, the project is not "getting it" but "doing it." This doing is not about an individual grasping an object, but about individuals (teachers and students) building relationships with one another and negotiating agreements about what makes sense. Such knowing is deeply subversive of established practices in schools and in society that disqualify most people from active participation, and treat knowledge as a thing produced by a few experts whose proficiency depends upon their disconnection from relationships and commitments. In collaborative learning, the activity of knowing—"what knowers do"—is brought into the center. Knowledge is the consensus of a particular community; it has no grounding apart from communal agreements. Teachers represent both their disciplinary departments and the network of the university, and these communities are neither stable nor in full agreement. Students enter the classroom as representatives of a variety of interpretive communities—their families, friends, neighborhoods, and other social groups to which they belong—making communication more likely to be troublesome because translation is necessary. In collaborative interpretation, the traditions that individuals bring with them to the conversation are honored and employed as resources for understanding. In this way, students often recognize that their views are more complicated, inconsistent, or limited than they had previously believed. Groups can help members to interrogate their perspectives, to identify the strengths and limitations within each position, and to shape more comprehensive approaches. The "big" labels, even that of "feminist," mask the complicated mixture of ideas and feelings that each of us brings to our conversations. A nonfoundational approach is not necessarily a shift to different content, but a shift in what we understand as knowledge that involves seeing authority and truth as dependent on communal human effort.

Further, such communal efforts depend on a sense that the work of shared interpretation matters, that this is how people come to know, rather than just a way of killing time until the teacher is ready to tell us what to write on the exams. One cannot urge students to socially construct knowledge and then play the spoiler: "But here's what is *really* true." Yes, some students will say things that I wish they would not say or think. Collaborative learning means that I do have opportunities to voice my criticisms and suggest other interpretations, just as everyone else does. It also means that I have to work at listening to what everyone else is saying, listening with an ear for the best insights or the openings for the next question.

These contrasting versions of how teachers exercise authority create very different experiences of learning about feminist scholarship and activism. When I construct my role as the expert on feminist inquiry and action, students are able to watch feminism, write feminism down in their notebooks, and present feminism in their papers while maintaining their distance from it. This is difficult to do when a course is designed to encourage thinking with feminist perspectives rather than thinking *about* feminist knowledge. Practicing feminist interpretations and criticizing these undermines passivity and fosters a sense of agency. The oppositional imagination has to be practiced rather than just received. The practices of collaborative learning subvert ingrained habits of detached watching. Further, these same practices make the goal of subversive education—fostering a critical awareness in students of received ideas and habits of behavior—more likely. As bell hooks and Tanya McKinnon note, "So much intellectual thought in our culture does not try to engage people where they are; instead, it tries to push people to move from where they are to some other place. This is not an effective means of educating for critical consciousness" (1996:825). Collaborative learning produces effective engagement with ideas. This engagement offers opportunities for movement that are not generated by my pushing, but instead by the choices students make to explore and test what they know and want to know.

In addition to being an effective strategy for fostering critical thinking, collaborative learning is a practice of citizenship. The theory that guides my teaching choices describes American society and culture as fostering a withdrawal from public life. This withdrawal can be explained in a variety of ways. The kind that I see in most of my students is based on a sense of their power-lessness to make any significant difference in the public realm. It is not that they believe America and the rest of the world are fine just as they are—when asked, many express serious doubts about various public policies and estab-lished institutions—but at the same time, they cannot imagine changing what they dislike. Their fixation on pursuing individual occupational success and consumer satisfactions reflects a refusal to believe that they have any power to change the rules of the game; they can only hope to be successful players. So, while they may have many questions about current social arrange-ments, many of my students seem paralyzed. They do not fully trust their own interpretations of social issues (even while they are often skeptical about what politicians, pundits, and professors say), and they seem unable to envision possibilities for collective action. Many refer to social movements entirely in the past tense (e.g., as in the 1960s), and have no knowledge of continuing activism on the part of neighbors, workers, or churches.

It is not enough to present students with ideas about how America might become a more just society because its lack of justice includes the belief that such ideas have no practical import. Teaching about justice requires classroom practices that challenge the sense that we cannot make any difference. The connection to practice means that the theoretical characterization of individu-alism and a retreat from public life are continuously examined and contested through classroom strategies to create relationships, conversations, and class-rooms that are not incidentally or occasionally participatory but thoroughly collaborative in principle and action. Collaborative learning is both a fragile and promising path for subverting the dominant forms of social organization and cultural ideals that foster paralysis—the sense that social problems are too complicated and ordinary people too powerless for significant change to hap-pen. These ideas seemed to be the best place from which to begin my course, Women and Activism.

Women and Activism

I doubt that I could have continued to teach for over thirty years without the subjects, texts, methods, and support of feminist scholars and teachers. Feminist education has provided me with reasons to stay at my university. It has given me courage and resources for sustaining commitment in the midst of continuing obstacles. It has also offered me opportunities for activism on campus. I have been both amazed and humbled by the message from my women's studies students that they find it difficult to imagine translating their knowledge and enthusiasm to the world beyond school. They wonder what they can "do" with their passion for ending gender inequality. Even more sadly, some have expressed a sense of despair about making social change rather than accommodating themselves to changes they would not choose. As hard as I have tried to make my women's studies classrooms sites of connection, collaboration, and empowerment, many students have told me that their experiences there do not translate in a larger world where powerful people speak another language of disconnection, hierarchy, and adjustment. Students taking the full concentration in women's studies have identified a need for course material that relates what they are learning to action, especially the action that promises change in individuals and social patterns. It matters to them that women's studies be a hopeful project linking scholarship to transformation. I have acted on their need in different ways: encouraging internships, developing a community service component for the introductory course in women's studies, and advising the women's studies club to create opportunities for activism. This essay describes another effort: a version of the capstone course for the women's studies concentration that incorporates several methods for promoting student awareness of the ways that social activism and research enrich and challenge each other. I will describe pedagogical decisions about seminar design, course materials, and requirements, and evaluate how these worked out in one "real life" semester of good and not-so-good moments.

At my university, the symposium in women's studies is led by rotating faculty members. Thus far, faculty members belonging to three different departments have taught it; this year, a fourth department will join the rotation. The focus of the course varies in relation to the faculty leader's interests and expertise; we've had one capstone built on the writing of Toni Morrison, another on the topic of epistemology. Several months before the spring 1999 semester I started talking with the students that would be taking the course about possible themes. The interests that came up repeatedly were practical: How does feminism make a difference? How can feminist ideals influence social change? What are women doing to bring about changes? Although I had proposed several different topics for our seminar, the focus on activism was the one that grabbed their attention.

When it began in January 1999, the seminar had eight regular students and one auditor, all women. Four were political science majors, and one each majored in biology, criminal justice, English, physics, and religious studies. All except the auditor (a graduate student) were traditional college-age students taking the full 21-credit concentration in women's studies. We met once a week for three hours. We used a regular classroom and arranged the student desks in a small circle on one side of the room. It was important to me to be a seminar participant, rather than the teacher up in front. I sat in the circle, facilitated specific classes, wrote a seminar paper each week that was read and commented upon by a different student reader each time, and contributed to the discussion. I was a one-of-kind participant, however, because I was the only one who read all the students' papers, commented on them, and graded them. I also made several of the key decisions about the course: selecting the possible texts, deciding on the required written work, and committing us to the collaborative discussion format. What I did not do was organize the syllabus.

One of the impediments to developing a shared sense of ownership about a course is the syllabus, usually fully constructed and ready for students on the first day of class. So, this time I did not have one, and my anxiety taught me about how I use syllabi as my first line of defense; distributing a syllabus on the first day of a course helps me to establish who is in control for the semester. I think that teachers do control many aspects of a course, but I am dismayed at my appetite for it. In Women and Activism, I did not surrender all teacher prerogatives, but, without a syllabus, I felt somewhat undressed and vulnerable. We spent the first class meeting doing these things: We introduced ourselves. I asked each seminar participant to write on a large index card the answers to two questions: What do I want everyone here to know about me? And what do I want to learn in this seminar? After about 15 to 20 minutes, we went around the circle and shared what was on our cards. For the most part, the answers to the first question focused on personal habits in discussion: "I tend to interrupt or talk too much, especially when I really care about a subject"; "I prefer to listen for awhile before I jump into a discussion." The answers to the second question revealed considerable consensus along the lines of, "The topic is completely new to me and I am ready to learn anything about it."

I talked about the decisions I had already made. I explained my reasons for requiring interviews with activists (stepping outside our books and listening to the stories of women in our community might bring us closer to identifying our own gifts and options) and research projects (providing each of us an opportunity to develop our own individual interest and enrich the class with our insights). I gave a brief description of each of the ten course books available in the bookstore;[1] I explained that all of them addressed women's activism, highlighting different agendas, contexts, and difficulties. I invited each seminar member to look over these books and come back to class the next week with her own list of preferences of topics and readings. I emphasized that we would set up the syllabus together, deciding on topics, readings, and order. I distributed copies of the guidelines for the seminar, which focused on preparation of a short paper for each meeting. Lack of preparation is one of the bad habits that can mar collaborative learning; in a small seminar, it was vital that everyone come prepared. The guidelines emphasize close and careful reading of the text, individual responses and questions, and making connections to personal experiences and ideas in other women's studies courses. I cannot remember any seminar meeting for which each member did not have a paper, but I suspect that some students may have used their two allowable absences for the purpose of avoiding coming unprepared. I gave an interactive lecture about social change, activism, and feminism. My principal goal was to draw out the seminar members' conceptions of each of these, and also to suggest connections among them. We worked together to identify questions that we hoped to explore during the semester. The questions clustered around the relationship between feminist and activist identities, such as, When women act together to address inequalities and injustice is this necessarily feminist action? Does feminist consciousness develop out of such activity? If it does, how does this happen?

During the second meeting of the seminar, we spent most of our time discussing the results of the first assignment: putting together a schedule, exploring ideas for the research projects, and brainstorming about the interview with a woman activist. I was somewhat apprehensive about the schedule, wondering how we might deal with significant differences in priorities, but this proved to be unfounded. It was obvious that the students had already talked with each other about the books, despite my suggestion to the contrary, and made some decisions. Everyone agreed about reading the first two books in their entirety (*Holding the Line* by Barbara Kingsolver and *A Tradition without a Name* by Mary Field Belenky, Lynne Bond, and Jacqueline Weinstock), and when we moved into considering the anthologies, consensus about issues and themes helped us to select specific chapters. It took us about 75 minutes to come up with a list of readings for each class meeting, as well as the dates for reports on the interviews and research projects. We also identified a facilitator for each meeting.

As we took a 15-minute break, some of the students suggested that we play music during our breaks—women's music that inspired and nurtured their commitment to feminism. A few volunteered to bring CDs or tapes for the next several weeks, and I promised to bring a portable stereo. I should not have been surprised by this idea, but I was. I remember that music was a big part of my own student years, but long ago I surrendered the stereo in my home to my children (mostly male), and had learned to pay more attention to what was offensive rather than to listen for encouragement. The seminar members said that Ani DiFranco, the Indigo Girls, Tracy Chapman, and others had made a big impact on them. I was curious, and grateful for their willing-ness to share their favorite songs.

The last thing we did on our second night of the seminar was to watch *The Women of Summer* (1985). This videotape, about the reunion of participants in the Bryn Mawr Summer School for Women Workers from the 1920s and '30s presents a vivid and moving portrait of women activists in the university, in the labor movement, and in international development. In the discussion that followed, the students mentioned that everything in the video was news to them. They seemed amazed that women had been so involved in organiz-ing unions and criticizing capitalism. Again, I was reminded of how little exposure my students have had to women's contributions to the American story. The video also introduced students to the music of Holly Near and Ronnie Gilbert.

Since describing each class meeting is impossible, I will confine myself to selected highlights that convey some of the triumphs and struggles during the rest of the semester. Let me begin with something that was a mixture of both: rotating facilitator responsibilities. As might be expected, students brought different levels of skill and ease to this role. On our best nights, the facilitator was highly prepared, confident, and able to keep everyone involved in the conversation. On the not-so-good nights, one or more of these qualities was missing. However, the class had enough camaraderie and commitment that the difficulties were overcome by shared effort and goodwill. The students seemed to recognize when a peer needed help, and how to offer this tactfully.

I recorded their weekly grades in my book, but did not put them on their papers during the first half of the semester. I explained that they could ask me for their grade, if they wanted to know it. Restraining myself from writing a letter grade on their papers had the good effect of encouraging me to write more commentary in the margins. I also wrote a general message to all of them after their first papers. In retrospect, I think that the most important message in that handout was that I expected passion in their writing and oral discussion. Women and Activism is the only course in our women's studies curriculum that is not cross-listed and that is reserved for those taking the concentration. Therefore, it is the one place where it is okay to be *invested* in women's stud-ies—not simply exploring its ideas. I think the students in the seminar needed to acknowledge this, to realize that they could be unabashed feminists in our class. As the semester went on, I deliberately aimed to write conversational comments on their papers; that is, I wrote responses and suggestions in a manner that conveyed that these were part of a continuing dialogue between us about their interests and their development as readers and writers.

The interviews with activists were a positive ingredient in the course. The students chose diverse subjects including a labor union leader, a nun who founded a downtown drop-in center for women, a breast cancer survivor active in promoting awareness of the disease, a peace and justice activist, an environmentalist, and a lesbian committed to gay and lesbian rights. I provided them with some general directions for the interview and the report, but what was most striking was how individualized the reports were. The students were excited about the experience, and full of details about the lives of the people they interviewed. The reports also led to a thoughtful consideration of the difficulties of describing and explaining the complexities of activism as personal identity, activity, commitment, and struggle. For me, the interviews were designed to move the students beyond the university and books, but they moved further and deeper than I had expected. This was a firsthand experience of understanding and conveying the quality of an individual's life story, and it produced many questions about choices and their consequences—both their subjects' and their own in shaping a report about what they learned.

The timing of the class meant that many students waited to have dinner until after class. A few weeks into the course, I discovered that a group was regularly going out together to a nearby restaurant. Everyone was invited, but there seemed to be a core group of four to six members who made this a habit. They told me that seminar discussion continued over dinner, that going out to dinner was a way not to have to stop talking. After they had gone a few times, they asked if I wanted to come, but I sensed that this would change the dynamics and I was reluctant to do that. It seemed important that they have their own time with each other that was connected to the seminar, but more informal. I know the dinner companions well and enjoy them; I think they would say the same about me. But I think undergraduates and a middle-aged teacher are separated by differences that add to the teacher/student gap. My intuition was to stay out of the dinner ritual, and I haven't second-guessed this decision.

I had not anticipated (although it seems like I should have) that the class might become a springboard for activism, but this did happen, with mixed consequences. During one class break, some of the students hung around in the classroom and talked about what needed to be changed at our university. Their conversation quickly centered on experiences they had shared as students with a particular professor. I spoke up quickly and said that I could not encourage them to have such a discussion. This did not deter them; they agreed to talk about it outside of class. They must have done a lot of talking because they eventually prepared a 12-page petition to the dean that included interviews with students outside of our class. They selected two representatives to talk with the administration about their issues, and they reported to me their frustration about the reaction to their complaints. Their activism did not succeed in the sense of accomplishing their goal, which was to have the administration agree that the problems they identified merited further investigation and possible sanctions for the professor. Nevertheless, they said they were proud of themselves for trying and were able to appreciate that their short foray into protest helped them to empathize with the obstacles faced by the women we read about.

Evaluations

I strongly disagree that a teacher's evaluations are best expressed in the grades students receive and that the students' evaluations are best expressed in the numerical rankings they give a course on a university form. My disagreement is based on the belief that these are limited and distorted ways of understanding what has happened in a semester. The limits are revealed by the focal point in each type of evaluation: grades are given to individual students and students evaluate the teacher (with perhaps one question that asks them to rate the course). Neither type of scoring or ranking acknowledges the experience of the course as a whole and neither emphasizes what was learned. I agree with bell hooks's point that it is vital to recognize the difference between learning and enjoying, between learning and feeling safe, between learning and liking the teacher (1988, 53). It does not seem to me that standard course evaluations encourage students to make these distinctions. Assigning letter grades to students, even with plus and minus distinctions, does not satisfy my desire to say more than a single symbol allows me to say about a student's performance. Still, I am stuck with both kinds of evaluations and have had to find ways to shape them for my own purposes. In the Women and Activism course I was less stuck than usual because the fact that it is not cross-listed meant I could choose to use only the women's studies program evaluation forms and avoid the other university forms. The women's studies forms are qualitative and assume that collaborative learning will be a key dimension of the course. They invite students to reflect on their contributions to class discussions, rather than focusing solely on a professor's performance. This is subversive of the standard university acculturation into passivity and lack of responsibility, which is manifested in course evaluations that are only about what the teacher did or did not do.

In Women and Activism, all of the students had previous experience with collaborative learning and the seminar format reinforced this as a key dimension of the capstone course. Even though they were familiar with collaborative learning, the student evaluation responses emphasized that this seminar was their fullest experience of it. Their answers also revealed their readiness to take responsibility for their own learning: "I appreciated Dr. Rinehart's participant rather than professor role because it meant we seldom fell back on her when we didn't feel like talking;" "I like the idea of students having a voice in the development of the syllabus." Signs of change are all over the student evaluations for the course: "It made me think for the first time about what activism looks like. I have a new understanding of my life goals"; "I feel a strong combination of confidence, responsibility, and desire to change the world through feminist activism."

Even though the seminar ended in the usual fashion—with me figuring out final grades for the students—that work felt different to me for this course. I had been a partner in the work of the seminar. As partners over the course of the semester, each of us had developed a particular role. Part of my role was to give constructive feedback, and letter grades eventually became a part of that—a way of letting students know where I would place their written and oral contributions on a familiar yardstick. But the grades weren't everything because there was a great deal of commentary given, by me and by their peers, on their ideas and expression. Women and Activism helped me to put letter grades into better perspective as one of the ways that my specific skills might be useful to students, rather than as the sole measure of their work in the course. They did much of that measuring themselves.

In that context, the activity of filling out grade boxes on a form assumed smaller proportions for me. It also helped that on the last night of class I distributed to the students my summary of what I was taking with me from the course. Although I had done something similar before in a different women's studies class, this time the act of harvesting the fruits of the semester was especially empowering. It allowed me to remember what was genuinely important.

Mary Rose O'Reilly (1989:142) has written, "Indeed the Heart of Darkness strikes me as an appropriate metaphor for the classroom in more ways than one. It's here we confront chaos and misrule, savage silence, chills, fever." I wouldn't choose such dramatic words, but I agree with her that "nothing ever works, perfectly, with students. They aren't always ready to center, nor are we" (p. 145). Still, Women and Activism came close to satisfying even my perfectionist soul. I do not claim that collaborative learning and readings that reveal the work by women to change the conditions of their lives can transform students and universities, but I believe that they are significant elements of the changes envisioned by philosopher Jane Roland Martin (2000): a woman-friendly academy based on equality that connects theory with practice, the university with the community, teachers with students and with each other, and mind with heart. This vision helps me to talk about women's studies in a different voice, one that is not defensive but celebratory. Striving to make better decisions about how and what to teach in women's studies courses, and appreciating how this can affect students in their ability to work for justice is good enough work for me.

4

Challenging the
"Academic/Real World" Divide

Catherine M. Orr

Experiential learning, service learning, community service, and activist projects are the categories of pedagogical practice that we use to turn the theories of our classrooms into practices in the "real world." This is surely not a controversial claim. Nevertheless, I always cringe a bit when the academic/real world divide is evoked, whether in the classroom, in journals, at conferences, or even in casual conversation. It is not that I disagree with the need to demand that students think about how what we do inside the classroom has effects outside the classroom; nor do I think that there are not important differences between the academy and other institutions and locations in our society. Rather, the cringing comes from my discomfort with the dichotomy itself, our tendency to see activism as, in Sonita Sarker's words, the "constructed Other" of our theoretical selves (cited in Bart et al. 1999). Like any act of "othering," separating our activist selves from our theoretical selves endangers our abilities to see connections and promotes the importance of gaps. It emphasizes difference as a fact rather than encouraging investigation into its inception. And it invites oversimplified ideas where subtle and complex perceptions would serve us better. If our disciplinary mandate of making positive changes in women's (and men's) lives is to be advanced, then the othering of our activism needs to be investigated.

Specifically, I want to address the need for historical, theoretical, and emotional reflection on the construction of the academic/real world divide in our classes that require experiential learning. More than just saying that such divides are problematic or must be transcended—claims that permeate our discipline's discourse—I want to focus on *how* we can go about doing such work. In this essay, I discuss the ways I have attempted to provide my students with content and structure to promote such reflection as they embark on their experiential learning and activist projects. I concentrate on three undergraduate courses I have taught that utilize experiential learning or activist projects: a course on welfare reform, an advanced feminist theory course, and a first-year seminar on global issues and local politics. As the extended illustrations of these courses will attest, some attempts have been more successful than others. However, the explicit focus on the "nuts and bolts" of struggling across and through differences has provided some of my most rewarding teaching moments. In addition, I believe that the implications of this struggle for students are crucial to both their understandings of and practices around issues of difference.

To be clear, when I say difference, I am speaking of particular understandings of social, historical, and cultural landscapes and the positions that my students and I occupy in such landscapes. These differences, of course, include gender, race, class, sexuality, nation, region, and so forth. But our understandings require an awareness that we are experiencing such differences through a particular location and point of view—through, in other words, an academic lens. This is why I think it crucial that we see the academy as an institution that is very much part of the "real world" as demonstrated by a number of issues: the increasing corporatization of colleges and universities, the related tendency to see students (and encouraging them to see themselves) as consumers and/or products of the academic industry, the ways in which academic careers are made and perhaps unmade by the promotion and fetishization of certain theoretical discourses and research foci, and questions about what colleges and universities can offer and can take from the communities in which they are located. Higher education is and has always been a business that uses and exchanges both material and cultural commodities. And the institutions in which we are located are part of a much larger economic new world order, one that is wreaking new forms of havoc for already impoverished communities around the corner and around the globe.

Viewed from this perspective, the work of experiential learning or activism in our courses must become more than sending students out into the community to encounter "the other." Rather, in "working to construct . . . a terrain of coalition and cooperation," argue Inderpal Grewal and Caren Kaplan (1994a:5), "we have to rearticulate the histories of how people in different locations and circumstances are linked by the spread of and resistance to modern capitalist social formations even as their experiences of these phenomena are not at all the same or equal." The rearticulation of these links in classroom settings can help both instructors and students move beyond the static construction of the academic/real world, theory/practice, and self/other divides.

Teaching Feminist Activism

With this rearticulation in mind, I see the goals of my pedagogical practice around experiential learning as: (1) helping students reflect on their place in a world based on differences that include gender, race, class, sexuality, nationality, and so forth, as well as economic power that manifests itself in a very complex politics of domination and subordination; (2) asking students to critically interrogate how such differences can easily lead to "othering" and lack of mutuality in their activist struggles, especially in off-campus communities; and (3) using these reflections to assist students in working through strategies and potential pitfalls as they attempt to affect positive social change.

"Welfare Reform" through the Lens of Race, Class, and Gender

Through the common women's studies course rubric of women, race, and class, I decided to teach a course focused on the then recent state and national shifts in the collective policies known as welfare reform. The stated purpose of the course was as follows:

> Using historical texts, fiction, social theory, feminist analyses, and speakers from the [off-campus] community, the origins of, interests in, and attitudes about sexism, racism, and poverty will be explored. As a kind of case study, special attention will be paid to the assumptions behind the most recent version of "welfare reform," how it was packaged and sold to voters, and the often devastating effects it is now having on impoverished families throughout the nation.

My overall aim for the course was to demand that students think about the historical foundations and political investments in our nation's class stratification, and about how this stratification makes abundant use of gender, race, regional, and ideological divisions. To accomplish this, I utilized a variety of course content including short essays on various intersections of race, class, and gender by Paula Gunn Allen, Barbara Ehrenreich, bell hooks, June Jordan, Audre Lorde, and Cherríe Moraga. In addition, we read Stephanie Coontz's *The Way We Never Were* (1992), Linda Gordon's *Women, the State, and Welfare* (1990b), and Toni Morrison's *The Bluest Eye* (1970) to provide more nuanced and historically informed understandings of divisions not just among but within the categories of race, class, and gender. Finally, I brought in a number of guest speakers from local community organizations and social service agencies to talk about their work. I chose the course content to function as the theoretical backdrop for the major fieldwork assignment, which required that students "participate on a regular and ongoing basis with a particular community outside of the college setting. This community must be in some way—directly or indirectly—braving the effects of current welfare reforms." These communities were not difficult to locate. Beloit, Wisconsin, the small city of 35,000 where Beloit College is located, once thrived with factory jobs that attracted many African-American families, and more recently Latino immigrants, to the community. Now it suffers from high unemployment, increasing poverty, and thus rising incidences of social stress. I worked hard in the weeks and months before the class making contacts and developing relationships in community centers, youth organizations, health centers that target low-income populations, and the local job center.

While most of the required writing for the course was based directly on their fieldwork, one set of three short papers assigned early in the semester instead pushed students to reflect on their position within the larger categories of gender, race, and class. Taking Jordan's "Letter from the Bahamas" (1985) and Moraga's "La Güera" (1981) as models, I asked students to analyze themselves "as historical subjects." In other words, students were required to consider some precipitating event(s) in their lives as a means of "dis-covering" their current attitudes, assumptions, and understandings about the assigned topic (gender, race, or class). Like Jordan and Moraga, I wanted students to regard their own experiences as "texts" to be unpacked and revealed as part of larger historical and cultural trajectories that fostered division from those with whom feminist political ideals demanded that they should be allied. Although the Introduction to Women's Studies course was a prerequisite for this class, I knew that what I was asking students to do was well beyond the typical insights into how various social institutions—family, media, the state, and so on— shape and idealize, for example, particular gendered identities.

The first round of papers (on gender) was disappointing. While most students seemed to be able to name and explain some illustrative precipitating event that threw into relief cultural assumptions about gender and even articulate those assumptions using readings and discussions from the course, their analysis tended to be abstract, distant, and lacked any kind of struggle to get at how they themselves were positioned advantageously or disadvantageously compared to others. Because this was my first attempt to build a course around experiential learning, I panicked a bit as to my own and my students' ability to pull together theory and practice at the very moment they were embarking on their fieldwork. Swallowing my own fears of inadequacy to lead them, I decided to grade the papers according to the standard of work I envisioned (in other words, harshly) and speak to them openly about my concerns. We went back to the Jordan and Moraga essays, studied particular passages that illustrated the kinds of self-interrogation I expected, and agreed that a deeper analysis of their own positionality was necessary to inform the kinds of work they were undertaking in the off-campus community.

Subsequent essays were much better. For example, one student who immigrated at the age of 12 from El Salvador because of the war wrote about his consternation with how his national identity was interpreted in the United States. It started as soon as he, his mother, and his sister arrived at the airport:

> We had to fill in a form that asked for race. There was Mexican, Puerto Rican, Asian, Pacific Islander, White—Non Hispanic, Black and Latino. I did not know what to mark. I was looking for Salvadorian. I asked my mom. She told me to check Latino, so I did. I did not know what I just signed up to become. For the first three years that I spent in California and other states, I learned how to be Latino (read: Mexican). . . . I memorized information about other Latin American countries, but mainly Mexico, because that is where people (read: whites) thought I was from. . . . I acquired knowledge that became worthless to me because I did not want to be Mexican. I decided to be Salvadorian instead, but I just did not know how.

For this student, the importance of specific contexts in shaping otherness came to the fore. He wrote in the final essay (on class) about how the various experiences that mark his race and nationality within the United States played out along class lines. In his first semester of college, he grew weary of once again being thought of as Mexican, but at the same time he "still wanted to share an aspect of being Latino." He claims he was being a "cultural classist":

> "Mexican immigrant" has connotations of what I was not supposed to be. The insults and stereotypes my friends and I used to describe the lower-class Mexican included *mujado*, or wetback, lazy, lots of children and one welfare check to feed them, soccer fanatic, bean eater, etc. . . . We were immigrants who came from a different intellectual background. Some of the Mexican immigrants in my neighborhood were richer than we were, but my mom implanted the idea that I should think of myself [at] a higher cultural level than the one they were in because I understood American culture better.

Throughout his fieldwork, this student was able to use these short paper assignments, fieldwork journals, and the final project to move between theory and practice, discourse and experience, and self and other in the analysis of his own particular positioning in contemporary race, ethnic, class, gender, and national identity politics. It was fortuitous as well that this student chose to be a tutor to the son of one of the college's janitors (who happened to be Mexican). As a tutor and eventually as a mentor, this student actively engaged his young pupil in these discussions. Thus, for this student, the demographic categories of gender, race, and class took on richer and more complex renderings so that it was increasingly difficult to say that he or anyone else was simply "other." By the end of the course he was able to articulate where some authors fell short in accounting for his particular situation or the situations of others he knew.

For many of the white, middle-class students, Barbara Ehrenreich's *Fear of Falling: The Inner Life of the Middle Class* (1990) became a touchstone in assessing their own assumptions, values, and goals in relation to those they encountered in their fieldwork. Ehrenreich's easy-to-access prose and concrete examples, especially from popular culture, challenged students to consider the investment they had in rendering their own class and race positions as "invisible" while those they worked with seemed so obvious and even "overexposed." After struggling to define and limit what she means by the middle class, Ehrenreich injects:

> But the very things that make this class so hard to talk about also make it urgent that such talk begin. Nameless, and camouflaged by a culture in which it both stars and writes the scripts, this class plays an overweening role in defining "America": its moods, political direction, and moral tone. If we hope to see ourselves with any clarity, we have to begin to make the effort to step back and see the middle class as one class among others, and as a class with its own peculiar assumptions and anxieties. (1990:6)

One consequence of this middle-class invisibility for some students was their assumption that middle-class values are universal values, and that what they saw as important or worthy of sacrifice (self-reliance, formal education, "good" taste) should be regarded the same way by those they encountered in their fieldwork.

After attending a community organization's holiday party for adolescent parents, for example, one of my students wrote in her journal that she was irritated by these young mothers' parenting practices:

> It was very frustrating to me to see the children (all five years old or younger) run around with reckless abandon and to see a mother walking around every so often asking people where her baby was. . . . I wondered what the women were doing since they weren't watching their children. . . .

It occurred to me that the nature of these young women's lives just may not be compatible with child raising.

After inquiring as to whether any child really was in imminent danger at this gathering, I asked this student in the margins of her paper to think about where exactly she was getting her ideas about child rearing. I pointed to the course readings by historians Stephanie Coontz (1992) and Linda Gordon (1990) that documented various and shifting assumptions about parenting—not to mention culture, race, and class—that have existed across time.

Building on Ehrenreich's thesis, it became quite easy for me and eventually other students to quickly recognize and challenge each other on these class-based assumptions that so thoroughly permeated their work with community members. They even began to recognize how such assumptions were operating among administrators and volunteer coordinators in the very community organizations in which they worked—organizations that claimed to be client centered and even client driven. These insights meant that our class discussions often included multilayered analyses of the ways in which differences were reproduced by institutions claiming to assist people in transcending those differences. By the end of the semester, for instance, the student who earlier expressed such anguish at the young mothers wrote an excellent final research paper on the effectiveness of grassroots community organizations that foster and encourage mutually supportive networks among parenting teens as opposed to more bureaucratic organizations that emphasize independence and self-reliance. Apparently, these young mothers did a fine job at "schooling" my student on her narrow class assumptions as well as alternative approaches to parenting.

Feminist Theory and Community Activism

Some of the women's studies students who braved my first attempts to build a course around experiential learning in the Women, Race, and Class course showed up in my advanced feminist theory seminar the next year. They were full of expectations—for which, of course, I must accept some responsibility—of how women's studies as a discipline is and should be inherently different from other approaches to knowledge production because of its activist origins. Although pleased with their ambitions to make theory "do" something, I have to confess to some irritation at the time in being asked to orient the most intellectually demanding, and thus for me fulfilling, course I teach toward time-consuming "outside projects." Yet, throughout the semester I came to realize that their demands were immanently connected to the content to which I exposed them. For example, I cast the course, borrowing from Katie King's terminology, as a *conversation* that has taken place (most intensely at least) over the past 35 years or so. In this conversation, some topics have been taken up to the detriment of others, some discussants have been included or excluded based on a number of concerns, and some stories make it into the larger narrative whereas others are seen as peripheral to the issues at hand. This conversation, however, is necessarily based in and draws from a larger context of activist struggles. How, then, could I ask them to become a part of the conversation while at the same time resisting their need to create for themselves part of that larger context by becoming activists?

Although in this particular course we worked the activism into gaps in the syllabus, the last time I taught the class I explicitly structured the course to work through the theory/practice divide by requiring an activist project that involved the entire class. My goal was to allow students who were becoming more historically informed and theoretically sophisticated to bring their knowledge to bear on the various intricacies of working for social change through a single project that involved the whole class. This seemed straight-forward enough. However, I now understand that the relationship between how I presented the content and what I asked for in the activist assignment was something that I did not think through to the extent I should have. As a preliminary analysis, I think the shortcomings of this approach actually pro-moted the activism-as-other phenomenon. In other words, unlike the course on welfare reform, the feminist theory course took on a number of issues central to feminism theorizing (experience, essentialism, difference, identity), and I focused much of our time on thinking about the practice of theorizing itself. Although interesting and thought-provoking for students, this approach proved to be too disparate and unfocused to allow them to structure an activist project in which they saw themselves as a cohesive group with a common purpose. Missing, then, was an awareness on my part that offering students a series of conflicting perspectives across time did not necessarily provide them with the grounding and support to act on their convictions. In fact, as I detail below, this course was all about questioning and even under-mining their convictions to the point that they experienced near paralysis when it came to the activist project.

Now, I'm quite aware of my own method for teaching theory. On a varia-tion of what Gerald Graff calls teaching the conflicts, what I present on the one hand I quickly call into question on the other. I focus on the presentation of clashing perspectives in the hopes that students will develop critical think-ing skills and come to their own conclusions, or perhaps understand that conclusiveness itself is inevitably based on the position of the thinker involved. Positionality, in other words, is key. The dialectic in my courses is constant and, as some students have indicated, relentless: "After this class, I question everything!" one student bemoaned with a smile. At the time, I took that as a compliment in that this student was conveying to me the powerful effect this course was having on her ways of thinking about the world. What I was not quite aware of, however, was how my attempts to call into question the content I presented actually eroded the foundation for traditional forms of activist struggle. And without offering alternative ways of thinking about activism, I left my students in a conceptual vacuum. Thus, what we experienced was a kind of object lesson on how historicizing ourselves in various discourses of domination may be necessary, but it certainly is not sufficient.

Along with the larger theoretical conversation that dominated the course, I included some time to discuss the history of second wave feminism so that students would have a grounding in how ideas relate to the context from which they emerge. Using Ruth Rosen's *The World Split Open* (2000) as the basic primer, they learned about the relationship between activism and knowledge production in the history of the women's movement. What I noticed early on was how the women's movement *as history* seemed to distance students from their own agency; they became passive recipients of Rosen's activist narrative. The movement, in other words, became a magical moment in time that was lost to them through the bad timing of their birth. As an attempt to question the "naturalness" of Rosen's history (or any other history of the women's movement for that matter), I asked that students read Sherna Gluck's "Whose Feminism, Whose History?" (1998). Gluck questions the cohesiveness of the history of the women's movement by pointing to various activist groups of women who worked for positive social change within their respective communities of color but did not think of gender as their only or even their primary unit of analysis. Thus, Gluck presents us with a powerful illustration as to why the "common" history of the women's movement, and by extension women's studies as a discipline and feminist theorizing as a practice, partake in exclusionary discourses that limit our visions about the scope and variety of feminist activism. I find Gluck's insights to be exciting and inspiring. My students, however, seemed to find them disconcerting and anxiety-producing. To my astonishment, even students of color and avowed postmodernists in the class, at first timidly and eventually forcefully, argued for the importance of a cohesive narrative to activist, identity-based struggles.

The conversation about theory often shifted from considering the very concrete ways in which their ideas are shaped by discourses of difference to ideals of activism. What they were seeing (and I was not accounting for) was how their mandate to be activists was getting more and more complicated.

For example, we had seemingly endless conversations about the possibilities or impossibilities of working across and through the "town/gown" divide. This a very palpable dynamic in our community given the differences between most of my students' class and race backgrounds in comparison to the largely working-class and "minority" populations that make up the small, recently deindustrialized town in which Beloit College is located. We often pointed out to each other how the very things that the college claims to strive for as an institution (excellence, exclusivity, achievement) play into the all-too-powerful dynamics of social and institutional structures that foster the divides of race, nationality, region, gender, and class. These conversations too often led to static conclusions about guilty privilege. "The community," then, was a term shot through with longing and nostalgia for the times when feminists were not concerned with questioning their place in the academy but instead marched in the streets, and, in the parlance of the students, "fucked shit up." So, as we read and discussed, say, Barbara Smith's call for an activist struggle based on gender, race, and class oppression in "Racism and Women's Studies" (1998) or Cherríe Moraga's (1981) claim that feminism needs to actively engage the diversities that make up the category "women," students wondered aloud about their "feminist credentials" and interpreted their lack of concrete and vigorous activism as personal failures. They fretted, in other words, that they—and by extension, women's studies—were part of the problem instead of part of the solution.

My approach to addressing this nostalgia and feelings of personal failure was to, once again, go back to the history of the institution in question. The academy, I explained, is a social institution, which among its many functions, almost universally reproduces the middle class of each generation. In other words, higher education is not a neutral space that exists outside of "real world" interests or that just happens to attract certain kinds of people. Rather, the academy is heavily invested in promoting difference. It is no wonder, I assured them, that their participation in this institution makes them feel isolated. The university was and is, then, intricately woven into the needs of for-profit corporations and expanding state bureaucracies. Thus, I attempted to recast the students' personal feelings of longing and failure into a political context and reconnect them to the "real world" from which they felt so sequestered.

With this history in place, the students and I then could begin talking about these feelings of separateness from "the community" as more than just personal failures to be "activist enough." We identified the academy as a socializing institution imbedded in a much larger and complex historical trajectory, one that was and still is invested in maintaining, not transcending, class and race divides in particular. In doing so, the practices and priorities of our academic lives (reading theoretical articles and books, learning the history of the discipline, conceptualizing applications for what we study in our discussions and our writing) could be transformed from guilty pleasures of the privileged into analyses of how we are positioned in this institution and thus how we can resist such positions through activist endeavors. Yet, as I soon discovered, the students' investment that students had in fortifying women's studies as the origin from which the resistance to elitist discourses must be launched raised the stakes of any form of activist intervention. The analysis seemed to always already trump their desire to act. In other words, their knowledge about the power of institutions such as the academy to shape understandings of various class, race, and gendered positions became so overwhelming that paralysis began to set in. They saw the shortsightedness and contradictions of so many of the various contributors to the conversation on feminist theory and began to doubt their own abilities and even motivations to intervene in the practices of domination and subordination that pervade people's lives, including their own.

It should not have been a surprise, then, that choosing the topic for the activist project proved more than a little problematic. Because the stakes seemed so high and because the need for some resolution was precipitated by the time constraints of the semester, they (to use a sports metaphor) punted. They chose abortion rights. In picking a topic that few of the students felt strongly about in any personal sense, the project became a compromise of sorts and something quite separate from the issues that dominated our classroom conversations. And instead of talking across their own differences (gender, race, and sexuality, in particular) as they related to this issue, they decided to break off into pairs so that they could work with those with whom they felt most comfortable. They put together performance pieces that were acted out in the cafeteria during the lunch hour, constructed ominous signs using coat hangers and hung them in the trees around campus, organized discussions about reproductive rights, and, in an attempt to involve "the community," developed fliers with provocative literature about abortion and distributed them on cars at a local church and at Walmart. The results were less than satisfying to them. They reported that events were poorly attended or ignored altogether, they had no way of knowing if their actions had effects, and they wondered whether what they had done constituted activism at all.

Their final papers, in which they were required to pull together some theoretical components of the course with the activist project, were full of self-flagellation and remorse based on an ideal of activism that was created over the course of the semester. One student recounted the general theme of disappointment she encountered from her classmates:

> What we did was not enough for what we had envisioned this "activism" to be . . . [N]o one seemed to say, "Hey, we did a good job on this. We tried our hardest." Would this have been different if we did not already have assumptions based on what we thought "activists" on campus and in the world did? Would it have been different if we had not read *The World Split Open* in class and seen pictures of the Second Wave marches and protests?

Another student admitted that the contradictions I presented made it too painful to even attempt activism:

> I guess I'm destined to stall out in my feminist thought and be forever designated The Immature Feminist. I refuse to embrace my contradictions. I acknowledge that I have them, but will work to disown them. I refuse to believe that there is no category *woman*. I believe that however the category was and is being constructed, there was a common denominator before it got hyper-constructed. It is essential to my mental well being that I believe this. I believe that for now it is best for me if I do not engage in activism. It is in my ten-year plan to find a group that espouses cultural feminist beliefs and go live among them. I realize that criticism will follow. Some might ask what a plan like that does for the greater good. I'm thinking that the utopia is a while off yet, and until then, I'm punching out.

Reading these papers was bittersweet for me. In my students' defense, these conclusions are not as cynical as much as they are reflective, and consequently despairing, about the very contradictions within the conversation to which they opened their hearts and their minds. They worked hard and took their assignments seriously. But clearly in doing so, activism became more than just an encounter with "the other." For some, it became something that could not be encountered at all, something utterly untouchable.

So what happened here? I don't think that the response to that question is simple, but I do think that possible solutions would involve, first, a restructuring of the activist assignment to be narrower in scope and topic. I might choose a particular article or set of articles from the course and ask students to break up into groups to design and implement a project based on those readings. This more limited approach would force students to consider the rewards and pitfalls of activism without being responsible for the entire conceptualization process that poses nagging questions as to whether their chosen topic is even "activist enough." Second, the inclusion of concrete examples of contemporary and local activism that attempts to work through various conflicts around difference by building coalitions must be a part of the course content. In other words, we would use some local issue as a case study and not only look at specific and local histories, but also study strategies and talk to the people involved. Although I included such "role models" in other, less-advanced courses, I assumed that theoretically savvy and historically informed students would somehow know how to extrapolate specific lessons from abstract ideas and distant events. Perhaps because the questions that surround difference and othering can be discussed at more length and depth in a feminist theory course, pointing to activists who understand the pitfalls of working with others to accomplish social change *and* continue their work in spite of them becomes even more important.

Teaching Activism in "Global" Contexts

During the same semester that I taught feminist theory, I also taught a course entitled Global Issues/Local Politics for my college's First Year Initiatives (FYI) program. The program is designed to increase retention of first semester college students by providing a bonding experience within an academic context as well as impressing upon them the ethos of the college. For me, this meant that incoming first year students would be exposed early to the idea that a primary goal of their college education was to learn how to affect positive social change from a theoretically informed perspective. As I stated in the syllabus, "the overall goal of the course is to promote students' understanding of themselves as change agents in our increasingly complex and interconnected new world order." Although not explicitly a women's studies course, I included a number of readings written from feminist perspectives. Once students realized my background and position as a women's studies professor (in choosing among about 20 FYI seminars, students were given a course description but were not told the name or discipline of the instructor), they soon settled into the idea that gender, race, and class were foundational components of the course. The key understandings that I wanted to convey to students included a broader and deeper sense of the tumultuous economic shifts that have occurred during their lifetime, some insight into how those shifts connect them to very complex issues of injustice and poverty on a worldwide scale, and some exposure to activist theories and strategies used to address such issues.

Not surprisingly, this course had more potential to confirm my anxieties about sending students out to effect social change. After all, I was asking students in their first semester of college—before they had a chance to take a course in women's studies, sociology, twentieth-century American history, political theater, or anything else that oriented them toward a college-level, disciplinary context for understanding activism—to reflect on their positions in the world. I worried about the maturity level of 18-year-olds and their ability to take the material seriously and to conduct an activist project in a community that was new to them while they were simultaneously making the transition from adolescence to adulthood. Working in my favor, however, was their almost universal enthusiasm to see college as the place where they were suppose to think in new ways, to have their old ideas challenged, and to work harder than they did in high school. These are the values that my college's recruitment literature promotes, and now I know that many students come to the college looking for experiences based on these values. In addition, I was careful to word the description of the course to appeal to students who saw themselves as (or at least wanted to learn how to be) social activists.

The biggest graded assignment for the course was what I called a community intervention project. It asked students to "conduct thoughtful investigations and undertake specific interventions in some specific local/global relationship with the goal of making a positive change in people's lives." The four topics decided on by the class at the midpoint in the semester were living-wage campaigns, Walmart and unionization, "female genital mutilation" (FGM), and homelessness. The projects were carried out in groups of four and varied in quality and "success" according to their stated goals. All projects nevertheless offered concrete situations in which to reflect on the more theoretical aspects of the course material. What worked particularly well in this course was the ways in which reading materials fostered frameworks that led students to quite profound insights into their relationships to the "others" they were attempting to "help" through their activism. Thus, despite my early concerns about the students' naïveté, I found that most were remarkably open to taking new perspectives on their own race, class, gender, and national locations in a very serious manner.

For example, the group concerned with FGM floundered around for quite a long time before deciding on a course of action: an information session at the Womyn's Center of Beloit College as part of a larger campaign to raise awareness among their peers about the practice. As drafts of their individual research papers trickled in, I found myself writing harsh comments and conveying strong warnings in student conferences about taking into account, among other things, the long history of Western imperialism in the areas of Africa, where much of their research focused. "You cannot simply assume that your ideas about what constitutes a human rights injustice are free from notions of Western moral superiority," I railed. "You are setting up the cultures that engage in these practices as some primitive 'other' that can only benefit from your condemnation." I argued that they must account for their own particular position as white, American college students and perhaps reflect on their own interest in the practice. In other words, I asked them to consider how they, as individuals or members of larger social/political/ national groups, might reinforce their own sense of who they are through comparisons to nameless and faceless "others."

Two sets of readings in the course proved particularly useful in making my point. The first was the short unit I included halfway through the semester on representation. The point of this unit was to cover the basics of cultural studies' postulations about the differences between "reality" as a fact versus reality as a cultural construction. My intent was to ask students to not only reflect on their positionality but to think about how that positionality actually determines their understandings of what's "wrong" with the situations they are attempting to alter through their activism. This unit included a chapter from Susan Moeller's *Compassion Fatigue* (1998) in which the author details how our interpretations of international events such as war and famine are shaped by corporate news sources that value spectacle and economically efficient reporting over comprehension and in-depth, historically informed, nuanced accounts of events in Africa, Latin America, and Southeast Asia in particular. This reading was complemented with the two-part film titled *Consuming Hunger* (Ziv 1987) which chronicles the media construction of and Western response to the Ethiopian famine of 1985. I wanted students to be aware that the information they consume about other people and places in the world, especially through the media, is always already filtered through very interested discourses embedded in colonial legacies, racial prejudices, and cultural biases.

Most beneficial in this endeavor was Uma Narayan's "Cross Cultural Connections, Border-Crossings, and Death by Culture" (1997), an essay that points out the way in which the focus on U.S. feminists' readings of other cultures' women-hating practices can obscure the women-hating practices woven into our own cultures. Specifically, Narayan takes up dowry murders in India and compares Western feminist understandings of this gender-based violence to deaths of U.S. women from domestic violence. She investigates "the 'effects' that national contexts have on the 'construction' of feminist issues and the ways in which understandings of issues are then affected by their 'border-crossings' across national boundaries" (p. 84). One of the students in the FGM group wrote a paper on and gave a report to the class on this article. Thus, in talking with group members about their approach to their project, I was able to demonstrate how Narayan's questions applied directly to the assumptions under which they were operating in positioning themselves in relation to women who underwent FGM. In her final paper, one student acknowledged the difficulties that inhere in grounding activism in moral indignation: "Even by calling this an 'African' custom, we blame and generalize the identity of a culture separate from our own. Self-righteousness allows us to trivialize cultures outside of the U.S."

A second unit of reading that proved particularly useful in asking students to consider how "othering" manifested itself in the context of the community intervention projects was Robert Rhoads's *Community Service and Higher Learning: Exploration of the Caring Self* (1997). Using postmodernism's "unabashed questioning of all that we have come to know" about knowledge, identity, and community as a starting point, Rhoads asks "how . . . we build community in spite of the cacophonous strains" of difference and power that characterize our experiences of those we encounter in our activist work (p. 1). Rhoads's own accounts of his students' experiences of community service illustrate well his contention that "higher education must play a crucial role in this struggle." Although my students found some of the narrative illustrations tedious and "boring," they respected greatly Rhoads's insights into the concept of "mutuality," a relationship based on equality and collaboration between the 'doer' (providers of a service) and the 'done to' (receivers of a service)" (p. 8). "Too often," Rhoads argues, "community service is structured as a one-way activity in which those who have resources make decisions about the needs of those who lack resources" (p. 127). Most importantly, Rhoads's confessional style and his reflections on class and race differences in particular functioned as a surrogate for expressing my own anxieties about how they were conceptualizing and executing their respective intervention projects. In discussing Rhoads's approach to mutuality, I pushed students hard to think about whether they felt it necessary, important, or even possible to foster it in their own projects. "Or," I asked, "is what you're doing simply, as Rhoads describes, charity?"

Because the Rhoads reading came at the time of the semester when they were all immersed in the completion of their projects, the students had a number of concrete experiences from which to draw. They discussed their projects in groups and then returned to the larger group to reveal their responses to the readings. Some students were extremely hard on themselves and others, claiming that their race (white) or economic level (middle class) precluded almost from the outset any hope of mutuality. As one student from the homelessness group confessed, "I'm sorry, but even now when I see a homeless person, I just go 'eeww' and am afraid that he's going to ask me for something or get violent." This very honest and risky comment to the class allowed me to push students into a very productive series of conversations about the fear of difference. Most students, because of their self-proclaimed liberal or even radical political orientations resisted talking about feelings in relation to their activism at first. Their fears of encountering difference, they eventually admitted, felt like a failure to be sufficiently "political" or "activist." After gently affirming their fears as common and quite understandable given their various backgrounds and lack of experience, I pointed back to Rhoads's characterization of this kind of work as *struggle*. With their anxieties out on the table and now part of the course content, subsequent class discussions and student conferences focused a significant amount of attention on fostering mutuality with the off-campus communities they encountered in the course of completing their projects. Their emotional reflection, in other words, became a significant and legitimate part of their community intervention projects.

This conversation had a particularly strong impact on the group investigating the viability of a living-wage campaign in the community. They immediately understood, for example, that interviewing janitors and food service workers on campus about their wages and working conditions and expecting trust and cooperation was not likely to be the best first step. "Why should these people trust us with that kind of information?" one student wondered aloud during a group meeting. "We're just a bunch of middle-class white kids doing a school project." Instead, the students turned their attention to a local labor coalition already at work on gathering information on the viability of a living-wage campaign. In doing so, these students were pleasantly surprised to find that the president of the labor coalition encouraged their presence and participation in not only helping to conduct research for the local campaign, but in asking that they be present at upcoming city council meetings on the topic. As they reported to me, he felt that the college has clout in this community and people would listen to the students. In addition, one of students involved in the project shifted the focus of her final research paper to the importance of involving community members in community development work.

What I have attempted to illustrate in the above descriptions of my courses is the importance of providing students with classroom structures designed to help them reflect on activism, not just as the application of the theory learned in the classroom, but as a practice that engenders power and makes use of particular understandings of difference. To accomplish this, students must be encouraged to account for their own positionality, both in terms of identity (based on gender, race, class, sexuality, etc.) and institutional location (i.e., the academy, with its interests in both economic and cultural capital). In addition, these classroom structures have to move beyond historical and theoretical explications of the academic/real world divide to make room for emotional reflection as well. The differences that permeate our experiences of the world, in other words, are not just encountered cognitively.

Women's studies, more than most other disciplines, draws students who want to not only think about their place in world, but who want an outlet for their political passions in the world outside the classroom. This is not an easy negotiation. I see my job as one of helping students navigate the difficult and complex terrain of difference in such a way that makes the "real world" more about access and engagement than about encountering "the other," whoever that other may be. Working with students who want to be effective social change agents on the nuts and bolts of struggling across and through differences has proven to be one of my most difficult yet, at times, rewarding pedagogical practices. For this, I feel very lucky.

5

Teaching Feminist Activism: Probing Our Assumptions, Analyzing Our Choices

Karen Bojar

For the past 25 years I have been involved in service learning at the Community College of Philadelphia, and have developed a service learning course and an Introduction to Women's Studies course that incorporates a service learning module. I am not completely comfortable with the term *service learning*, with its connotations of noblesse oblige, of charity rather than social change. However, I have found it politically useful. When I wrote a grant that provided initial funding for our Community Involvement Center, I used the term *service learning*. It is a term with which funding agencies and college administrators are generally comfortable and which I generally use when referring to my courses. I often use the term *activism* to refer to projects developed within these courses or in connection with the student women's issues club, for which I am the advisor. I have tended to avoid the term *activism* if I am seeking funding or administrative support. Is this pragmatism or opportunism? I'm not sure.

Under the pressure of heavy community-college teaching loads, I usually find myself more focused on the nuts and bolts of arranging placements and projects and less on the terminology I employ or my rationale for course design and choice of placements. In this essay, I have taken the opportunity to analyze my sometimes unexamined assumptions about these courses, my unease about the choices I have made, and my anxiety about the extent to which I may be imposing my own political priorities and sense of social possibility on my students. I would like to argue for critically examining our own assumptions about what constitutes activism, how these underlying assumptions shape our curricular choices, and the importance of sharing our interrogation of our own activist values with our students. I would also like to argue for including participation in electoral politics among the options for fulfilling service-learning requirements.

Special Challenges and Institutional Constraints

Before probing my own assumptions and attempting critical analysis of my practice, I would like to describe some of the special challenges and constraints faced by service learning practitioners at community colleges. First there is time—we never have enough. I envy the luxury of time which teachers and students at four-year residential colleges enjoy. At community colleges everything seems to be done on the fly; we're all (teachers and students alike) rushing around, always behind. We waste endless hours standing in line at our understaffed copying center; most of us do not have computers in the tiny offices that we share with one, sometimes two or three, other faculty members. Many of us are low-salaried adjuncts dashing frantically from job to job. And, of course, there's never any money to fund the books, videotapes, or honoraria for speakers that we want. Administrators have accused us of fostering a culture of complaint, but we have reason.

The time bind faced by the faculty pales in comparison with the intensely pressured lives of many of our students, who are desperately trying to juggle school, job, and family responsibilities, often on very limited incomes. For many students, civic engagement is a luxury they cannot afford. For this reason, I keep the minimum requirement for volunteer hours quite low (twenty hours for the Community Involvement course, ten hours for the experiential option in women's studies). The volunteer project is an option rather than a requirement in the women's studies course as I would not want students to decide against taking Introduction to Women's Studies because they could not meet the volunteer requirement. Although my minimum requirements may seem very low, when transportation and time to arrange child care is factored in, 20 hours can easily become 50 hours. Many students give much more time than this, but for some, this is all they can manage. Better this minimum involvement than none at all.

Although I strongly believe in service learning, I have been reluctant to require it of our students. I have not pushed for the community involvement course to be anything other than a highly recommended elective in our women's studies program. Similarly, the service-learning module in the Introduction to Women's Studies course (involving a minimum of ten hours and an analysis of the experience in lieu of a significantly longer paper) is an option. This option works best when students are taking both courses concurrently, but once again the students' tight schedules often do not allow this.

In addition to the time bind, many students are further handicapped by inadequate high school preparation. Although they bring a wealth of life experience and sometimes a history of involvement in women's organizations, many have not had the opportunity to read widely and build an extensive knowledge base. The capstone course (which often includes an experiential component) taken after several semesters of women's studies courses is a luxury few community college programs can afford. And of course many of the students in my introductory course are not enrolled in the women's studies concentration but are simply picking up an elective that fits their schedules. (I realize this situation is hardly unique to community colleges.)

Opportunities

Our diverse student body is surely one of the great joys of teaching at a community college. My students include African Americans, Asian Americans, European Americans, and Latinas; they range in age from their late teens to their late 70s. Contrary to stereotype, not all urban community colleges students are from low-income backgrounds; some are middle-class students taking advantage of low tuition.

Most of my students have lived in Philadelphia all their lives and are very likely to stay here. Thus, they are well-positioned to maintain the organizational ties developed as a result of service-learning programs. They may lack familiarity with the academic literature on inequality, racism, and sexism, but in general they understand these issues; they often have an intuitive skepticism toward authority and "establishment" institutions that students from more privileged backgrounds frequently lack.

In addition, we have a rich array of feminist service and advocacy organizations in Philadelphia, including local chapters of national organizations. We are well positioned to help students get involved in local progressive politics and to forge connections with local organizations working to advance a feminist agenda in the electoral arena. There is a great deal of local knowledge that we can help students acquire.

Community-college faculty are more likely to be life-long residents of the area than are teachers at four-year colleges and universities. (Increasingly, long-term residence in one place is becoming a class marker.) Thus, community-college faculty are more likely to be in possession of a good deal of knowledge about local organizations. Like the students, faculty are more likely to be from working-class backgrounds and have attended non-elite schools. (I fit this pattern as a product of row-house Philadelphia and graduate of Temple University.) Students' (and in many cases the faculty's) deep roots in the community can be a powerful advantage in designing service learning programs.

Another advantage is that the power structure of the city in which I work (the college is funded in part by local government) is on the moderate to liberal end of the political spectrum. This means I can bring in guest speakers from National Abortion Rights Action League (NARAL), place students as volunteers in NARAL and not suffer any consequences. Quite a few years ago, a student saw a flyer for my courses that listed NARAL as a participating organization and wrote a letter of complaint to the college president. The president (not our current president) immediately fired off a letter defending my right to include an organization that advocates for abortion rights. In a city in which the political leaders are generally pro-choice, this was not a high-risk strategy. In other parts of the country, such a strategy could be very high-risk indeed.

Different institutions face different challenges and constraints. Many campuses do not have women's organizations (let alone feminist organizations) within easy reach. Traditional four-year colleges that draw their students from around the country will not have the opportunity to engage students in long-term efforts to build local feminist communities and organizations. Their students leave after (approximately) four years with skills and insights but without ongoing connections. In these cases, I believe it is critically important to build ties with national organizations such as the National Organization for Women (NOW), NARAL, the Feminist Majority, the National Coalition of 100 Black Women, the Coalition of Labor Union Women, and the National Women's Political Caucus, among others. In short, I find myself increasingly focused on organization and movement building, in addition to consciousness raising and skills development.

We all struggle for some enduring impact, something that remains when the semester ends. I think my students and I achieve something of this with our ongoing connection to local organizations. Our Students for Women's Equality club has a continuing relationship with the Philadelphia NOW chapter. One student commented that NOW functions as the alumni group for our club. If students stay connected with NOW, they can continue with the projects they worked on for my classes and can stay in touch with each other.

Underlying Assumptions and Political Values
That Shape Our Activist Projects

Although my practice is certainly shaped by the special challenges of teaching at an urban community college, my own values and history as a feminist activist also inevitably influence the way I design my classes. In both my women's studies and service-learning courses, my students have a wide choice of placements. In the service-learning course (Community Involvement: Theory and Practice), students may choose any organization as long as it is a registered nonprofit (501c3 or 501c4) providing a service to the community. I define service to include traditional charitable organizations and advocacy organizations, including those involved in partisan politics. In the women's studies course, the organization must provide service to women or advocate for women's issues.

Most of my students show a marked preference for direct service over advocacy, and frequently note the intense satisfaction they derive from working directly with individuals in need. My students in both courses have been overwhelmingly female, and they frequently report that their commitment to community service has been a lifelong pursuit, in many cases growing out of deeply rooted family tradition. For most, community service has meant traditional volunteer work rather than political activism. I want to honor that tradition, but also to encourage students to explore other options. I try to do this by exploring the relationship between traditional volunteer work and political advocacy, and the ways in which feminist unease with service-oriented volunteerism is intertwined with conflicts in feminist thought. No student is obligated to participate in social change projects. A student might choose a more traditional placement such as volunteering in a shelter for homeless women.

In addition to these individual projects, my students and I develop group projects; here the possibilities I suggest usually reflect my own priorities. Students can become involved in these group projects as part of (1) the optional service learning project in my Introduction to Women's Studies course; (2) the required service learning project in my community involvement course (many students take this course and Introduction to Women's Studies concurrently); or (3) as one of the projects undertaken by the Students for Women's Equality club, to which I am the faculty advisor.

Given my students' very pressured lives, the limited time at their disposal, the limited time frame of the semester, and in some cases students' total inexperience in community activism, I feel I have no choice but to play a role in designing group projects. The special circumstances of community colleges increase the likelihood that teachers will be involved in project design, unlike teachers in four-year residential colleges where students generally have ample time for such projects. Yet even in courses at residential colleges, where students presumably have more time to design their own projects and the teacher functions as a consultant, a sounding board, she still inevitably plays some role in shaping the project by virtue of advice she gives or chooses not to give. No matter how nondirective the teacher, her assumptions and values play a role.

In organizing the group projects, I have become especially anxious about the ways in which my own political values and priorities influence my choices. Many of these projects involve electoral politics; I am heavily invested in this area, have many local contacts and can easily set up such projects. I always try to give students a sense of other avenues, other strategies that might be equally effective in widening opportunities for women. Yet my personal investment in certain strategies and my own role in our local NOW chapter must in a sense stack the deck.

Because of anxieties I have about pushing my politics and priorities on my students, I always spend time interrogating my own activism. Would time spent participating in electoral politics be better spent in social movements or in building alternatives to the two-party system? Those who are also taking my Community Involvement course have an excellent resource for thinking through these issues. The basic text for this course, *Organizing for Social Change* (Bobo, Kendall, and Max 2000), analyzes a range of approaches to social change. Also, many of the guest speakers I regularly invite to my class have had experience in direct-action organizing, in electoral politics, and in a range of government and nonprofit agencies. Those students who are taking only the Introduction to Women's Studies course that covers a range of topics in addition to feminist activism have far fewer resources to assist them in sorting out their own priorities as activists or potential activists.

In the interest of making my biases clear, I share my activist history and my doubts about my current choices with my students. As a long-time grassroots activist now in my mid 50s I have been forced by dwindling energy and greater family responsibilities to reassess how I am going to spend the limited time, energy, and money I have to devote to social activism. Although I have devoted energy to a range of progressive causes over a lifetime, at this stage in my life I want to focus solely on feminist issues. And I have decided to focus on electing more women to political office and encouraging more women to become involved in grassroots politics.

As a young woman, I disdained working within the two-party system; I did not want to settle for piecemeal reform and engage in the messy compromises that are part and parcel of participation in the electoral arena. For me the wake-up call came in the early 1980s with the election of Ronald Reagan. I realized it did matter who won elections. This may not seem like a major revelation to most citizens, but it led to a major about-face for me. As I watched the Reagan administration build up the military budget and starve social programs, as I began to realize that *Roe v. Wade* was in danger due to Reagan's appointees on the U.S. Supreme Court, I decided I could no longer afford to vote for protest candidates. I now serve as a Democratic committeeperson, chair the Philadelphia NOW Political Action Group and serve on the board of the Pennsylvania NOW Political Action Committee. The major focus of my activist work is electing progressive women to political office. As I saw many of my low-income women students' lives ravaged by social policies developed for the most part by affluent white men, I decided to focus on helping these students get involved in grassroots politics.

Thirty years ago I would have found such projects appalling. Instead of participation in electoral politics, I would have encouraged participation in social movements or in building alternatives to the two-party system. (This is the tragedy of 1960s activists; we spent our youth in a time of social possibility and our middle and probably later years during a time of reaction.) At this stage in my life, I do not see a viable alternative to the Democratic Party emerging in the near future and I do not see any powerful social movements on the horizon. To my aging eyes, the young protesters I met who were engaged in the direct actions projects at the Republican convention held in Philadelphia do not seem to have the kind of coherent philosophy, clear agenda, and organizational savvy that could lead to such movements. Yet I realize that just because I don't see the potential doesn't mean it doesn't exist. Many people have been taken by surprise by social movements, which seemed to appear out of nowhere. Ruth Rosen (2000) begins her history of second-wave feminism with sociologist David Riesman's remark made on July 21, 1967: "If anything remains more or less unchanged, it will be the role of women." Could I be as blind to what might be on the horizon as Riesman was in 1967?

As my sense of social possibility has diminished, slow gradual change is all I can imagine. There is a reason that revolutions are always made by the young. As a middle-aged woman with a secure (although not particularly high-paying) job, health care benefits, a house, and a pension, I have to admit I would find the prospect of revolutionary social change threatening indeed. Of course, my age is not the only possible explanation for my drift to a more conservative, work-within-the-system approach. The political climate in the United States has shifted dramatically to the right in the past thirty years; although I have become much more conservative in my sense of social possibility and in my political practice, I am still way out in left field.

I worry that, by the choice of projects I encourage, I am teaching my students to view the social landscape through the lens of my own diminished sense of social possibility. I realize of course that while I worry that I've become too conservative, in some parts of the country my teaching would be viewed as a dangerously radical project. I share my doubts and political history with my students and present my current choices as problematic; yet so far none of my students have challenged my choices. It's a little voice from my past that raises questions about my focus on electoral politics within the two-party framework.

A Case Study: The Committeeperson Project

One of the most ambitious of our group activities was a project to encourage low-income women to become involved in grassroots political activity by running for committeeperson, the entry-level political position in the Democratic and Republican Parties. With the assistance of our local NOW chapter and a grant from a local foundation (the Bread and Roses Community Fund), my students and I organized workshops at four campus sites. (The Community College of Philadelphia, like many community colleges, has campuses in different areas of the city.) Although our primary goal was to encourage women—particularly low-income women—to run, the workshops were open to everyone. We encouraged teachers to bring their classes and attracted a diverse audience: women and men; African Americans, Asian Americans, European Americans, Latinas; an age range from teenagers to senior citizens.

This project seemed very timely; with the draconian approach to welfare reform in Pennsylvania, many of my students were being pushed out of higher education by male legislators with no understanding of the difficulties involved in raising children while struggling to climb out of poverty through higher education. We wanted those hurt by these policies to have a voice in the political arena. Also, running for committeeperson is a very easy entry point into electoral politics. You do not need to raise money; all you need is to be willing to ring doorbells.

We developed literature explaining the local party apparatus and the role of the committeeperson in recommending candidates to constituents and serving as community liaison with elected officials. Committeepersons also elect the ward leaders; electing women committeepersons might help us elect more women as ward leaders, a position which is often a springboard for a race for local office (city council, state legislature, etc.).

We also explained how to run a successful campaign: how to get street lists of registered voters in the candidates' division, and how to find out who the incumbent is. In many divisions there is no incumbent, and thus the task is much easier; if an incumbent is in place we explained how to analyze the relative strength of the incumbent and evaluate whether a race is feasible. We also explained how to obtain voter registration forms in order to register neighbors and potential supporters. We provided information about a range of city services, women's service and advocacy organizations, and the telephone numbers of essential departments and elected officials, as well as suggestions on how to get information about candidates' and elected officials' voting records.

Measured by the number of women who attended the workshops who actually ran for committeeperson, our project was a dismal failure. (Several considered running, but no one actually followed through.) Measured by the information we disseminated and the interest generated in grassroots politics, the project was at least a partial success. All participants—the students who helped to organize the workshops, the local NOW volunteers and staff— agreed that it was a valuable learning experience.

However, we had seriously miscalculated the amount of time the women who attended the workshops would need to become comfortable with the idea of running for office. We ran the workshops in January and early February. The filing date for candidates was in mid-March. Prospective candidates would have had to make the decision within a four- to six-week period. I had thought that since the committeeperson races were so small scale, so low-profile, they wouldn't be terribly threatening; therefore, no one would need a lot of lead time to get used to the idea of running. I was wrong. Several women said they would probably run next time, but just were not ready to plunge in.

Unfortunately, local party officials changed the term for committeeperson from two years to four years; thus, we will have to wait until 2002 for our next series of workshops. Most ward leaders do not want many new people coming into their parties. New committee people—not those chosen by the party structure—tend to recruit new voters. In general, politicians prefer to stay with the predictable electorate and the party activists they know. This change in party rules was an educational experience for many students, bringing home to us all the extent to which most politicians prefer to try to carve out a larger slice of an ever-dwindling electorate rather than expand the pool of potential voters.

Yet many students did report that, despite the frustrations, they wanted to get more involved in electoral politics and try to make the system more responsive. My students and I may never have economic power; we will not sit on the boards of directors of major corporations that have such a powerful influence on our lives. However, we do have the power of the ballot box and the pressure we can put on politicians.

A new generation of activists is challenging this notion—rejecting participation in electoral politics and advocating direct action just as I, and many of my generation, did in the 1960s. I had the opportunity to meet some of these activists during the protest activities in response to the Republican convention. Many of them don't vote, and if they were teaching my courses and advising the Students for Women's Equality club, they certainly would not be helping students organize anything along the lines of the committeeperson project.

I hope to bring some of the young women activists into my classes to learn more about their activist values. I hope to engage my students in that always ongoing debate among progressives: to what extent do we work within the system while we at the same time challenge its fundamental premises? I want my students to learn how the existing power structure works, but I also want them to learn about alternatives to the two-party structure, alternatives to working within the system. I want them to make informed decisions if they choose the path of political activism. Above all, I want them to have a greater sense of social possibility than that which I myself can muster at this stage in my life.

I am encouraged by the role of young women among this generation of radical protestors. At least from the perspective of my city, it is clear that young women are in the leadership of these *networks*—a perhaps more accurate term than *organizations*. I am impressed by the young women I have met although I have some questions about their tactics and am disappointed that feminist issues do not appear in the foreground; nonetheless, they certainly appear to have assimilated feminist lessons about gender roles. I come from that generation of 1960s women activists who in retrospect were little more than groupies—file clerks for macho new leftists. My own feminist consciousness developed relatively late—too late to avoid some major mistakes. I cannot imagine the young women I've met in our local activist network making the mistakes that many of my friends and I have made.

I suppose all young activists make their own mistakes—mistakes that can become a valuable learning experience. Although the group projects that I have encouraged and secured funding for have tended to focus on electoral politics, I want my students to explore the many pathways to social change and to decide for themselves which pathways are most congruent with their needs and concerns. I want to encourage them to clarify their own activist values before making decisions about strategies and organizational affiliations.

Some of the other group projects I have helped students design have included working with NOW and other local women's organizations to interview candidates for local office. In 1999, we held a mayoral candidates' forum on women's issues to try to forge a women's agenda for the city of Philadelphia. This race posed some very difficult issues for feminists: what do we do when a male candidate takes stronger positions on women's issues than does a female candidate? (One of the leading candidates was a woman with a good track record on women's issues; however, the best candidate on women's issues—in the sense of his sensitivity to issues affecting minority and low-income women—was a male candidate.)

Last year students were involved in the process of planning an educational forum: What is the feminist stake in local judicial elections? Our goal was to educate feminists on the kinds of issues that come before our local courts and to explore obstacles women candidates face when they seek judicial office. We interviewed candidates for local judicial office and developed a feminist slate. Since these elections are generally low turnout elections, this is an area where a small, well-organized group can make a real difference.

One theme I emphasize repeatedly is the importance of picking battles that are winnable, goals that are achievable. I sometimes wonder if this pragmatic emphasis discourages students from thinking in more ambitious ways about possibilities for social change. Yet as long as I continue to raise hard questions about the value of these projects and explore the merits of organizing within the two-party framework versus organizing outside of traditional electoral politics, I believe I can justify my emphasis on such projects and such pragmatic themes.

How I Will Do It Differently Next Time Around

One of the wonderful things about teaching is that there are second chances. If we don't get it right the first time, we can try it again and again. Next time around I will definitely focus on integrating scholarship about feminist activism and grassroots political movements, to help students better understand the deeper implications of the committeeperson project, and more generally, their own activist projects.

When I organized the committeeperson project in 1998, students discussed it in the context of NOW statement about volunteer work and the 1970s debate about the efficacy of traditional volunteer work versus activism. Students analyzed the 1973 statement from the NOW Task Force on Volunteerism, which argued for political activism as opposed to the "Band-Aid" approach of service oriented volunteerism:

> Essentially NOW believes that service oriented volunteerism is providing a hit or miss, band-aid, and a patchwork approach to solving massive and severe social ills which are a reflection of an economic system in need of an overhaul. More than this, such volunteering actually prevents needed social changes from occurring because with service-oriented volunteering, political energy is being used and will increasingly be used to meet society's administrative needs. ("Report of the National Organization for Women Task Force on Volunteerism," 1973)

Using the NOW material struck me as particularly appropriate, as my students and I had organized the project in conjunction with NOW. Yet it became clear to me that the relevant material for this project was not the exploration of service versus advocacy but the exploration of working within traditional electoral politics versus working to change the system from the outside. Since no student was required to participate in the group project but could pick another community service activity consistent with her needs and interests, there were students who participated in the discussions who saw involvement in electoral politics as a waste of time. They saw all politicians as having no interest in serving the community, but only in serving themselves.

I hope students will be interested in the committeeperson project in 2002, and if we organize it again, I intend to have students read Nancy Naples's *Grassroots Warriors* (1998c) which analyzes in-depth interviews with women community workers in New York and Philadelphia who were initially employed in the 1960s and 1970s as part of the war on poverty. Naples explores such questions as: What motivates women to undertake community work in low-income neighborhoods? How do community workers ensure that the next generation will continue the struggle? Many of the women were combining service with advocacy and achieved powerful positions within their communities, but were deeply suspicious of any involvement with electoral politics. These are attitudes I know many of my students share and, despite my own involvement in politics, I also, at times, share their distrust.

Much of the literature on women's grassroots activism, such as Temma Kaplan's (1997) *Crazy for Democracy* reports similar distrust on the part of community activists. One of the activists Kaplan profiles, Dollie Burwell, sees no contradiction between electoral politics and community organizing. Burwell worked on political campaigns, registered voters, joined the Congressional Black Caucus, and served as country register of deeds. Kaplan reports, "Unlike most of the other activists in Warren County, North Carolina, Burwell maintains her optimism about working in organized politics. And she becomes very angry when she recalls that some people say she can no longer speak as a grassroots activist because she once held political office" (pp. 89–90). Many of my students share this idea that "authentic" grassroots activists must stay above the fray of electoral politics.

The service-learning movement itself is on every level shot through with the notion that politics is dirty business. Tobi Walker (2000), who is one of the few service-learning practitioners to argue for encouraging student involvement in electoral politics, cites numerous examples of leaders of the movement (a director of a student-run national service organization, government officials at the Corporation for National Service) who exalt service over politics and reflect "a troubling tendency within the community service movement to conclude that politics is evil" (p. 31).

In addition to the literature on feminist movements and grassroots activism (so often characterized as the "good kind of activism" versus the "suspect activism" of electoral politics), I hope to include analyses of the impact of second-wave feminism on the political system. When we organize the committeeperson project again, I intend to use Harriet Woods's *Stepping up to Power* (2000). Like the careers of the women Naples describes, Woods's career as an activist began with something close to home. When the local government refused to act on her demand to fix a manhole cover on her street, telling her they'd "have to think about it, they had many other priorities" (p. 19), she organized her neighbors, going door to door to collect signatures. Her first run for political office was an election for Democratic committeeperson. So began a political career that led to her election as lieutenant governor of Missouri, two (unfortunately unsuccessful) races for the U.S. Senate, and a stint as president of the National Women's Political Caucus.

Woods makes a powerful case for the importance of getting more women to run for political office. She reports "an amazing match between between the numbers who run and those holding office. . . . When women run, women win" (2000:197). Woods's book is a useful tool for exploring the question of why so few women are in fact running. One reason she cites is women's discomfort with power—which may be particularly true for women from non-elite backgrounds. Woods argues that it is important

> not to create a stereotype of the ideal woman candidate. Fannie Lou Hamer was a black Mississippi sharecropper with minimum education who gained confidence to speak for her people and had the courage to run for public office. There are single mothers with limited education who rise out of hopelessness to sit on community boards to make decisions on their neighborhoods. . . . We have no idea who might be ready to move up the political pipeline. (2000:197)

Clearly many women, my students among them, need this kind of encouragement. Not every one in public office needs to have an advanced degree. Our goal with the committeeperson project was to get more women from nonelite backgrounds to see running for office as a possibility for them.

I am currently looking for a text that explores participation in third-party movements (e.g., the Green Party) from a feminist perspective. Opportunities (albeit limited ones) for feminists do exist within the two-party system, but I certainly want to encourage women, especially younger women, to think outside this framework. I am also searching for a study of what campaign finance reform (in those few pockets where some semblance of it exists) has meant for women candidates; I am convinced that it is a feminist issue and that framing it that way might be a way to get it on more women's radar screens.

As I develop all sorts of ambitious plans for linking the committeeperson project with the literature on feminist activism, I keep bumping up against the reality that I am teaching an introductory women's studies course, not a course on feminist activism. Most of the students in this course are not concurrently taking the community involvement course, which provides opportunities to reflect on the implications of their choices and the various strategies for achieving social change.

Yet hopelessly incomplete as my courses are, I am committed to exploring with my students the kinds of projects most likely to contribute toward building a powerful feminist movement. Johanna Brenner, director of the Women's Studies Program at Portland State University, noted in her speech at the 1999 National Women's Studies Association conference that we used to try to identify the kinds of short-term reformist projects that would be most likely to lead to a movement for long-term change. Her comment made me realize that so many of us no longer struggle to balance short-term goals with long-term strategy. We need to encourage our students (and ourselves) to think strategically rather than responding in ad hoc fashion to the crises of the moment. I do not mean to imply that every project needs to be linked to strategy for long-term change, but when we encourage our students to critically analyze their activist projects, we should encourage them to take the long-range view, to try to place their work in the larger context.

In conclusion, whether we characterize our work as service learning, experiential education, or activism, we are all limited by the constraints peculiar to our institutional settings, by the constellation of organizations and political forces in our geographical locations. We are also inevitably influenced by our own, sometimes not fully examined, assumptions about what counts as feminist activism. If our projects fail or fail to meet our expectations, we can view them at least as partial successes if they encourage our students to think though the deeper issues and decide for themselves what strategies best advance a feminist agenda, what organizations are most worthy of their time and energies.

II

Teaching Feminist Politics Experientially

Experiential learning can be incorporated into all the phases of the women's studies curriculum, from the introductory course to the senior seminar. The challenges to teaching experientially are greatest in introductory courses, which often enroll large numbers of students not concentrating in women's studies. In chapter 6, Nancy Naples highlights the challenges she faced when she incorporated an experiential project in a large introductory women's studies course. Students were expected to develop a group project that would leave a legacy beyond the ten-week framework of the course. With a class of 210 students and a team of teaching assistants, each supervising approximately 26 students, the task resembled managing an organization more than teaching a class. Naples explores student resistance and the dilemmas of implementing a group community-action project in such a large course. Yet despite these logistical difficulties, Naples argues that the group project is valuable in that it "challenges the privatization of academic knowledge production. Students begin to recognize how the individualized approach to higher education inhibits the development of certain kinds of knowledges, privileging self-interest and competition among students rather than cooperation and group learning."

Although the classroom management issues described by Naples tend to be confined to the large introductory course, there are challenges which surface at every level. For example, the debate about whether or not to require "action projects" is relevant to the introductory course as well as to the senior seminar or capstone course. In chapter 7, Jennifer Rexroat describes an upper-level course in which the major assignment is a historical analysis of a local women's organization. Rexroat does not require her students to become actively involved in the organizations they study. She notes that many students at the University of Illinois at Chicago are low-income students working full-time jobs while taking full course loads in addition to caring for extended family and children. Given these con-straints, Rexroat argues that "requiring students to become active partici-pants in the organizations that they study, in many cases, constitutes a hardship for students who already have extremely limited time for aca-demic requirements." Instead, she encourages her students to maximize the research time that they are able to spend with the organizations, and hopes this might lead to active involvement in the future. Senior seminars such as the one Rexroat describes have the advantage of small size (in Rexroat's case 10 to 15 students per semester) and the further advantage of students with background in and a commitment to women's studies. Thus there is the opportunity for in-depth analysis of organizations students choose.

Conflicts and unresolved questions as to what counts as feminist activism is a recurrent theme in the essays in this section. In chapter 8, Ellen Cronan Rose describes a capstone course in which students are required to complete a semester-long individual or group project that embodies their conception of feminist praxis. Rose describes various projects students design and probes their underlying assumptions as to what constitutes fem-inist praxis. The essays in this section highlight how students take advantage of experiential learning projects to address issues of special concern to them. At the same time, experiential learning provides students with an opportunity to learn the lessons of feminist theory and feminist practice. As Rose points out, even action projects in organizations that are not explicitly feminist can equip students to become agents of social change. As the three chapters in this section also demonstrate, experiential learning offers an exciting opportunity for feminist faculty to learn from their stu-dents in a more collaborative learning environment than is typically avail-able on college and university campuses.

6

Teaching Community Action in the Introductory Women's Studies Classroom

Nancy A. Naples

D rawing on lessons from the community action project, an experiential class project I developed for use in a large introductory women's studies course, this chapter explores the continued significance of experiential learning in women's studies. My goals with the community action project are twofold: first, to teach lessons in politics, collective action, and feminist analyses; and second, to help students develop investigatory and political skills that can complement a developing critical consciousness. From a feminist pedagogical perspective, the development of critical consciousness provides students with the ability to call into question taken-for-granted understandings of their social, political, economic, and academic life. In this chapter, I demonstrate how community action as a pedagogical strategy permits us to move beyond the early consciousness-raising approaches in women's studies classrooms while retaining some of the valuable lessons derived from experiential learning.

The community action project (CAP) serves as a semistructured exercise in identifying sites of intervention and strategies for social change that can be implemented within the time frame of a ten-week course. Students, who rarely come to the course with experience as self-initiated political actors, have the opportunity to move from individual-level personal concerns to collective action while simultaneously developing a sense of how patterns of inequality circumscribe their everyday lives in ways that are often invisible to them.

The CAP forms part of the requirements for the second in a three-quarter-year-long introductory women's studies series. The first quarter course is Gender and Feminism in Everyday Life and the third is Gender and Popular Culture. The second course, entitled Reproducing and Resisting Inequalities, demonstrates how inequalities of gender, race, class, sexuality, and colonialism are embedded in institutions generally thought to be "value free." In the first part of the course we examine the institutional formations of science, medicine, agriculture, the capitalist economy, citizenship, and the state through a historical and international lens. In the second half of the course we emphasize how women's community-based and international organizing challenge local, national, and global processes of inequality. The CAP gives students the experiential base from which to understand how to link local community actions with broader struggles for social change and feminist theorizing about these processes.

I draw on my own research and experiential learning about community activism, as well as the rich body of feminist literature that explores the construction and reproduction of inequalities and resistance strategies, to help guide the class project. For almost twenty years I have been exploring the processes by which diverse women develop their commitment to community-based activism and how this relates to a process of politicization. My research affirms the important relationships among positionality, constructions of community, the development of oppositional consciousness, and willingness to engage in political action that have been implicit in many feminist theoretical perspectives, especially materialist feminist frameworks. These lessons led me to consider the ways in which I might provide my women's studies students the opportunity to learn how to "do politics," and in the course of this activity discover firsthand how inequality is reproduced in institutions that shape our daily lives as well as how they can effectively challenge these patterns of inequality.

Experiential Learning, Politicization, and Community Action

Women's studies students are often disappointed when they observe firsthand how professionalization and bureaucratization interfere with feminist practice within women's organizations like battered women's shelters, women's health centers, or women's counseling centers. Furthermore, as a consequence of the success of feminist activism, some women's shelters and related organizations have now been established by professional groups or through government initiatives without a feminist analysis of the issues they address. In addition, with demands for service often outstripping resources, even staff who retain a feminist vision have less time for political activism.

Not surprisingly, as I reviewed the CAPs completed for my course, I found that students encountered similar dilemmas. Many wanted to jump quickly into a service mode in response to specific needs they identified. Through a process of politicization, which sometimes requires a painful recalculation of their taken-for-granted beliefs about gender, race, class, and sexuality, students began to recognize the broader conditions and institutional practices that contribute to the specific problems they targeted. The process of politicization parallels consciousness-raising in some ways, but it explicitly directs attention to the political actions that are necessary to challenge inequality. The CAP provides a context through which students explore how dominant ideologies and organizational practices obscure systemic patterns of oppression. It also incorporates the goal of political action directly into the learning process.

Community action projects can be conceptualized as class-initiated problem-solving strategies or linked with targeted internship programs. In either form, CAPs can facilitate teaching the investigatory and political skills that can complement students' growing critical consciousness. The CAP begins from the students' personal concerns but quickly moves them outward to the larger context of their social, political, economic, and cultural lives. The CAP provides a site in which students can experience a process of politicization through group interaction and political analysis of a problem or issue they choose (although there is no guarantee that this will occur). Although "working the steps" and completing weekly reports on their group's progress does not leave much time and space for discussion of personal experiences related to the projects as is more typical in a consciousness-raising group context, personal experiences do provide the foundation for a number of CAPs.

For example, Bahareh Myers (1995:1–2) helped initiate a group entitled How to Make the Most of your Research Experience, which developed guidelines for students and faculty in Biological Sciences field research independent studies (known as Bio 199):

> This community action project caught my interest as a result of the negative experiences I have had, in the past, with Bio 199 research. When I started doing the research, I had just assumed that the professor had the authority to make you do whatever he/she wanted. This incorrect assumption has caused me much grief. For instance, on my first days at research, the professor took me to a small, dark isolated stock room and placed me in front of a paper shredding machine. He then told me that my job for the next few hours would be to shred stacks of paper. . . . On my second week at research, I was placed in front of a photocopying machine and then told to copy a stack full of death certificates. Being trapped in a small photocopy room for four hours copying people's death certificates overwhelmed me with anxiety and depression. I will always remember the tears of anger and frustration each day as I left the research facilities.

Myers subsequently quit her research job and did not pursue another assignment because she thought that other jobs would be just as tedious.

The next year, Myers's roommate returned home to complain about her research assignment. She told Myers (1999:3) that her professor "constantly yells at her and calls her useless. In addition, when time came for her to leave for the day, he would complain about her to the other students in the laboratory." After hearing about her roommate's experiences, Myers understood that she "was not the only person to go through this deeply degrading and dehumanizing experience doing research. I realized that, in this situation, the personal is political. What I first thought was only my problem turned out to also be a problem for countless others."

She brought up the issue in her discussion group and found that several other students had similar experiences. Myers and her CAP group found that, rather than gain research experiences, many students complained that they are primarily asked to do clerical or other nonacademic work. Some students also complained of sexual harassment. This CAP group developed an information sheet explaining what students should expect from their research experience and how to protect their rights. It was specifically addressed to women students, although both men and women students find this form useful. They approached the Dean of Biological Sciences to request that the form be included with the Bio 199 application. The Dean agreed that this was an important step to ensure that the students would have a meaningful research experience. This two-page form detailing the rights and responsibilities of students and teachers is now included with the Bio 199 application form at UCI.

Students who were drawn to address violence against women sometimes explained their motivation to create a CAP on this topic as a consequence of personal experiences of abuse. In the final reports from individual members of these groups, a number of students described their personal experiences of acquaintance rape or of growing up in a household where their father abused their mother. While few of these individual stories are shared in the large lecture course, they are often brought up in the small discussion groups or with other CAP members. Since we have developed a close working relationship with the Center for Women and Gender Education, which sponsors groups for survivors of sexual assault, those dealing with eating disorders, and adult children of alcoholic parents, among others, we encourage students to seek out these avenues of support if needed.

As in many women's studies classes, the topics we discuss often trigger memories or emotional responses that cannot be dealt with effectively in the classroom. However, the CAP offered students an activist strategy for dealing with these issues. As Myers explained in her final report, when she recognized that her personal problem was collectively experienced, she understood that it could become the focus for political action. This process was empowering for her as she was able to help improve the situation for other students. The "personal" and "political" were analytically linked in both theory and practice because the experiential project was embedded in a larger pedagogical context in which we read and discussed feminist activism and the reproduction of inequality from a social structural perspective. In this way, the CAP as implemented in a group context retains some of the features of consciousness-raising. The CAP used as a requirement for the introductory course propels the students to action, even if their only initial motivation is a grade. In addition, many students emphasize the importance of finding their "voice" through their participation in the project. As one student explained in her final report, "This class experience made me aware of my potential to voice my opinion and make a difference if I am willing to put forth the effort" (Au 1994:8).

Implementing the Community Action Project

Despite the contradictions of the CAP as an assignment in a required course for which a grade is given, reviewing the projects from 1994 to 2001, I recognized that they continually reinspired my own sense of political possibilities for a new generation of women's studies students. The first course I taught in women's studies at the University of California, Irvine (UCI) was titled Social Perspectives on Gender. It was the second of the three-quarter introductory series in a new interdisciplinary women's studies major established in the fall of the 1992–1993 academic year. My job was to teach feminist perspectives in the social sciences. The first course was intended as an interdisciplinary overview and the third highlighted humanities perspectives on gender. My initial goal in introducing women's studies students to community action through the CAP was to teach them the skills of political and institutional analyses in order to enhance their effectiveness as agents of change in their everyday lives. Furthermore, since most of the students had little understanding of what "doing politics" entailed, I offered the CAP as an experiential means by which they could begin to learn what constitutes political action and from there see how gendered, racialized, and class-differentiated processes were often hidden from view in the institutions that pervade our everyday lives.

The students are asked to conceptualize a project that will leave a legacy beyond the ten-week quarter. From the start, they must consider how to ensure the continuity of their work and what political strategy would help them accomplish this goal. The CAP is implemented through a series of specific steps. Although the CAP is a group project, each student submits a short weekly report on the progress made by the group for each step as indicated in the outline. The final report on the CAP is a comprehensive narrative of the history of the project including (1) evaluation of group process and the project itself; (2) incorporation of assigned readings as appropriate; and (3) integration of the comments provided by the teaching assistant or instructor on the progress reports.

The students encounter difficulties at four junctures: (1) defining the problem that will be the focus for their CAP; (2) constructing a project that can be implemented in the course of ten weeks; (3) identifying the relevant actors in different institutional sites who have power to make the changes they envision and getting these actors to respond; and (4) working in groups. In the next section, I will describe how the students, teaching assistants, and I deal with these dilemmas. I also discuss how we negotiate relationships with other units on campus, especially the Center for Women and Gender Education, which are involved in the students' projects. I then outline the diversity of themes that emerged from the projects over the last eight years and illustrate how these were linked to class content. I next discuss the legacy of certain projects on campus and in the wider community and conclude by exploring the limits of community action for teaching intersectional, cross-cultural, and transnational feminist praxis.

Defining and Coordinating Community Action Projects

At the first meeting of each discussion group, students are asked to identify issues of concern to them that affect women on campus, in the communities in which they live, or in the broader social environment. A list of themes for projects is then compiled. Between the first and second meetings of the discussion group, students write a short statement that describes why they believe it would be important to address a particular issue. These statements are used to facilitate the formation of small groups. Students read their statements in an attempt to encourage other students to join with them. When all students feel that their issues have been raised and considered and a defined number of projects have been outlined, small groups of five to eight students are formed where the specified issues chosen are further clarified and the specific action steps are developed. Before reaching consensus on a particular action plan, group members gather information about the feasibility for each plan proposed.

In some cases, a number of students quickly see that they have overlapping interests and agree to join together. Sometimes, however, only one or two students are interested in a particular topic. When this occurs, we usually work with these students to see how they might refocus their interests to choose a group that has a sufficient number of members to proceed. Since many tasks are involved to produce a CAP in such a short time frame, groups of four or less are typically unable to effectively implement the project. If the concern expressed is a broad one, such as racism in the community or sexual harassment on campus, the group may decide to construct a series of actions that could be implemented over an extended period of time, but one specific aspect of the plan must be implemented within the ten-week quarter.

The teaching assistants (TAs) assigned to the course are charged with the responsibility for ensuring effective coordination among CAP projects, campus programs and administrative staff, and community groups. With the current class size of 210, each TA supervises three sections, with approximately 26 students and at least five CAP groups in each section. In some cases, students in different sections come up with the same topic for their CAP. The TAs must then work together to make sure that these separate groups coordinate with each other to develop somewhat different foci for their interventions. During my weekly meetings with the TAs, we identify which groups are working on similar projects and attempt to put the groups together in order to encourage them to differentiate their CAPs or to coordinate their community actions. While it is possible, broadly speaking, to identify and prevent duplication among groups in different sections, it is not possible to avoid contrasting views of similar issues.

By way of example, during the winter quarter of 1998, groups in two different sections defined their CAP in terms of campus safety. One group focused on testing the effectiveness of the campus Safety Escort Service and determined that the long response time posed a problem for women who needed to use the service. They investigated further and found that one explanation for the delay was the lack of available escorts. Furthermore, due to lack of escorts, the service stopped in early evening. Working with the student government and the Department of Campus Parking and Transportation, they developed strategies to increase the number of escorts and to extend the hours of service. The second group decided to explore the availability and effectiveness of pepper spray to counter sexual assault and to increase awareness and access for UCI students. This group's final presentation prompted a heated discussion among class members about this strategy since the first group had also investigated its effectiveness and came to the conclusion that it was relatively ineffective since it had to be directly sprayed into the eyes and could be easily avoided by the attacker.

Providing students with the space to identify and specify their community actions does require giving up some control. In a private discussion with a member of one group who was working on establishing a support group for incest survivors, and as a consequence of what she was sharing with me, I decided to inform her that I was also an incest survivor. I had, in fact, written about it (albeit without much detail about the abuse) in a chapter that appears in *Feminism and Social Change*, edited by Heidi Gottfried (Naples with Clark 1996). The last week of classes I have each group briefly describe their project and what they accomplished or learned from it. This student was the presenter for her group and in the course of her presentation enthusiastically told the class that I too was a survivor of incest. Now, to be fair, she had asked me just before class if that was okay. If I had more time I would have explored with her why she thought this was necessary for her presentation, but after coming out to her about it and in an effort to support her decision to come out to the class about herself as an incest survivor, I felt I could not withhold my consent.

Although I want students to be in control of their projects, there have been instances where I have felt obligated to intervene in order to prevent dissemination of erroneous information. To cite one example, a group working on breast cancer seized the opportunity to educate men on campus about their risk for the disease. Misreading the statistics on the extent of the problem, they created a flyer and distributed it throughout campus with the following statement: "It is estimated that out of 1,400 men, 200 will be diagnosed with breast cancer." The report they took this statistic from actually said that in a study of 1,400 men diagnosed with breast cancer, 200 died from the disease. When I attended the group to hear their CAP presentations, I read the flyer and noticed the error. After a brief lesson in reading statistical information, I asked group members to retrace their steps, go through each flyer, and cross out the sentence with the erroneous statistic.

The most difficult challenge faced by the TAs was negotiating conflict and uneven division of labor within groups. In some cases, TAs were unaware of such problems until the end of the quarter. As one member of the 1999 class wrote in her final report, "Our group lacked cohesiveness and direction from the very beginning. I came to dread each group meeting. . . . I was frankly disappointed at the lack of maturity and communication skills of my fellow group members, [but] I also take blame on myself for not handling the situation more effectively" (Tarbell 1999:6). She went on to detail the problems as, (1) lack of focus ("We never clearly defined and limited our project—its title, goals, or the activities necessary to accomplish it"); (2) lack of commitment (the entire group was present at a meeting only two times); (3) lack of leadership ("when no one stepped up to the task, I should have provided more direction"); and (4) lack of communication ("people in the group did not clearly express their opinions and goals and did not clearly understand the concerns of other members").

In addition to the challenges of coordination across the projects and within each group, we have also found even more difficulties managing the relationships that are forged by students with other units across campus. When I first began using the CAP at UCI, Paula Goldsmid, director of the Center for Women and Gender Education, called to tell me that women's studies students were descending on the center and asking its staff to help with their CAPs. The Campus Assault Prevention Program coordinator Donna-Jean Louden was especially swamped with requests for assistance.

After discussing possible solutions, we determined that the students needed some guidelines to help negotiate how and when to approach the center for help. First, center staff would only meet with groups as a whole. Initially, students from the same group would approach them individually, unaware that another member of their group had already done so. Second, they needed to explore a number of other options before going to the center. There were websites, community groups, and other sources of information the students need to identify before making an appointment with center staff. Third, groups needed to be clear about what they wanted to do for a CAP before their meeting with a staff member. Center staff were then invited to speak to the class at the beginning of the quarter to discuss the procedures that would protect their time while retaining their role as consultants for relevant CAPs.

While the Center for Women and Gender Education is the most important site on campus for students to turn to for assistance with their projects, each year I receive calls from one or more other campus units who have been targets for different community action projects. These include the campus police, student health services, and campus housing departments as well as the *New U* (the UCI student newspaper) and academic schools and departments. As the size of the class grew from 70 in 1994 to 210 in 2001, it became increasingly difficult to coordinate the frequency with which individual groups contacted these and other programs on campus. However, since the CAP has been implemented for eight years, most relevant units now understand the purpose of the project and have typically been very supportive even when they are the target of the proposed actions.

Working the Steps

The first time I used the CAP in a women's studies class, I met with resistance from the students who felt that it took too much time, that they didn't know where to begin, and that it was too hard working in groups outside of discussion period, which is scheduled for one hour per week. When I explored their resistance with them, it became clear that they had, in fact, spent little time outside of class on the project. In fact, the main problem was that they felt burdened because the CAP made them uncomfortable. It required skills that they had yet to develop, including working in groups, finding information outside of the library, and researching through interviewing and other interpersonal strategies. Once I realized the source of their resistance, I began to provide more specific guidelines. For example, I included the following in the CAP outline for the first step:

> Tasks for this step include identification of relevant community groups established to address the issue, phone calls to these groups to clarify the current status of work on this issue, interviews with key individuals who are employed by these groups. The groups and individuals may be identified through phone books, resource guides, networking with resource people who are knowledgeable about the area. The broader the search, the better. All this information is needed for you to move effectively to the next step. Providing more specific direction for CAP members also helped the TAs since many of them had never engaged in community action.

For those students who begin the CAP with a lot of enthusiasm, the process of defining a specific project usually takes them through a period of disillusionment. As Lisa Ross, a member of a group concerned with women and AIDS, wisely reflected,

> In the beginning everyone talked as though we were going to save the world, but I had my doubts. I think a lot of community action fails because they set unreachable goals for themselves. Workers all have a dream that they want to see come true. That is what promotes community action. But these dreams are huge; if it were not a huge dream, then it would not require social reform to make it into reality. If social action groups would set smaller goals for themselves instead of trying to change the world all at once, then there would be more positive social reform because movements would have more of a foundation. (Ross 1994: 3)

She described the first meeting of the group as follows: "[W]e wasted a lot of time discussing the impossible. Our first meeting consisted of everyone sitting around and discussing our TV broadcasts and our celebrity endorsers while I sat quietly and tried not to destroy their fantasies" (p. 5). After a series of discussions about forming a "doable" project, Ross reported that the group realized "that we are four students" and "AIDS is a worldwide epidemic. We could not make a difference on a big level, but by making our community the University, then we as students managed to get something done" (p. 6).

At the next step (designed for implementation during the third and fourth weeks of the quarter), students are asked to analyze the community and institutional context for the problem they are addressing. This step usually poses the most difficulty for the students in that they are asked to move from a general definition of the problem to a more focused framework through which to determine the institutional and political forces that contribute to the problem they have defined. To provide some guidance for the group work process necessary to successfully complete this step in the action plan, I instructed the students to "brainstorm alternative strategies to reach the desired outcome, and indicate top strategies. Remember, this is a group project and all group members points of view must be evaluated before moving ahead with a specific strategy."

The third step (which ideally should occur during weeks four and five) takes the students into a more detailed analysis of the institutional and political context for their action plan. Here they must consider who occupies positions of power (both formal and informal decision makers) in the institutional arenas that are the target for their interventions. The group then decides how they will contact each person and what strategies to adopt in order to influence that person. A parallel goal for this step is to identify likely obstacles and opponents as well as to discuss how to negotiate the resistance. Another aspect of this step in the action plan is to determine who might be likely allies in the political change effort. After identifying which individuals or organizations will most likely benefit by the action, group members determine how they will be contacted (e.g., by letter, phone, or in person) and which member or members of the group will make each contact.

Once the group has assessed the institutional and political context, considered who are potential allies and what are potential hindrances, the group must develop its specific strategy. During this step, group members develop a time frame for implementation of the specific action and consider what resources they will need. This step is often linked with the next one, which involves broadening the constituency for the action plan. Students are expected to complete this step by the fifth week. The targeted date for implementation of the CAP (the seventh step) is the sixth or seventh week of the quarter.

If the CAP group is successful in keeping to the time frame (and many are not for one reason or another), the next two weeks can be devoted to evaluating the project (the seventh step) and the group process (the eighth step). For the seventh step, the group members assess what they have achieved, what they would do differently if they were to implement a similar project in the future, and what new community actions might follow the one they just completed. The eighth step involves a critical assessment of the group process. In addition, while the students have been asked to consider their work in light of the class readings, lectures, and discussions through the quarter, this step formalizes this exercise. They are asked to analyze their project in terms of the themes and concepts discussed in class—for example, understanding how "relations of ruling" (Smith 1987, 1990) are embedded in different organizations (e.g., science, medicine, agriculture, land policy, politics); how colonialism, sexism, racism, poverty, and homophobia can be challenged in everyday life; and the difficulties of coalition building.

The separate reports generated for each of the steps are then used by the students to construct their final report. They are also asked to identify ways to publicize the results of their CAPs. Depending on the focus of the CAP, students can consider sending announcements to local newspapers and radio stations. Copies of selected reports are kept on file in the Women's Studies program office for other students to use for reference. In this way, the students in future classes will benefit from the work done by the students who came before them. In a few cases, students have used these reports as jumping off points for their projects, thus extending or following up on the work that has already been accomplished. In some cases, strategies chosen by previous groups were used by students in the next cohort. The overall list of topics and issues addressed is also shared with each new cohort.

Themes Emerging from the Community Action Projects

Since the students are required to identify topics of interest to them rather than assigned by me or the teaching assistants, the CAPs illuminate which issues or concerns are the most salient for them and, as importantly, how the students understand what counts as politics. Here the lessons of politics and feminism are given meaning in the context of where the students are in their learning process. There is a great deal of continuity from year to year in the topics that students identify for the CAPs (which may be partly a factor of their knowledge about the topics and issues addressed by previous cohorts). The most prevalent area of concern is violence against women. This includes preventing sexual harassment and acquaintance rape, increasing safety on campus, multicultural sensitivity in battered women's shelters, self-defense, and antistalking measures. For example, after researching the problem of stalking and identifying how to reach students with this information, one CAP group developed a brief description of stalking and the steps students could take to protect themselves. They gained approval from the relevant administrators to insert the text in the *Student Survival Guide* given to all incoming students.

The next set of concerns relates to health. CAPs focused on college women and eating disorders; increasing the awareness of breast health among younger women and women of different minorities; stress management for university women; raising awareness about the risk of dioxins in high absorbency tampons; prevention of cervical cancer; teenage sexuality; women and AIDS/HIV prevention; HIV testing; and HIV prevention in a local high school. One group was interested in promoting anonymous HIV testing for women on campus, noting that many women resisted getting tested because they felt that there was a stigma attached to testing and were afraid that their parents or others would find out that they had been tested. As one student explained in her final report, "it was not until I enrolled in a women's studies class at UCI that I became aware of the differences between confidential testing and anonymous testing for HIV." Along with four other students, she decided that they wanted "to identify and address the barriers that may exist" that "could prevent women from taking advantage of anonymous on-campus testing." As a consequence of their investigation, they developed a series of recommendations for the health education office on campus and a flyer titled "What You Should Know about Anonymous HIV Testing at UCI."

The third theme is contraception. For example, several CAPs worked to increase the awareness, education, and accessibility of both male and female condoms on campus. Many of these groups produced flyers for distribution through the campus health services and the Center for Women and Gender Education that continue to be used by staff and peer educators.

Education was the next most popular topic for student projects. I define this category broadly to include projects that encouraged women students to enter the sciences as well as a campaign to place the Equal Educational Opportunity Initiative (EEOI) on the November 1998 ballot. The initiative was designed in response to the passage of Proposition 209, which ended affirmation action in admissions to the University of California. The EEOI read, "In order to provide equal opportunity, promote diversity, and combat discrimination in public education, the state may consider the economic background, race, sex, ethnicity, and national origin of qualified individuals." In addition to educational forums and a petition drive, the students contacted UCI's assistant vice chancellor for enrollment services, assistant vice chancellor of counseling and health services, and director of the counseling center to explore what strategies UCI was adopting in order to ensure racial/ethnic diversity within the student body.

The next set of issues concerns parenting, childcare and gender socialization. CAPs were organized to address a variety of concerns including the lack of quality day care for UCI students who are parents. One of my favorite projects in this category involved working with the managers of South Coast Plaza, a large and popular shopping center in Orange County, to challenge the distribution of gender stereotyped toys at the carousel, an amusement ride in the mall. Students investigated who managed the carousel and who made the decisions about which toys would be given out. After a series of meetings with relevant managers and submitting a petition that outlined why they thought that this practice was ill-conceived, the students convinced store managers to change their toy distribution strategy. Now if you take your child to the carousel at South Coast Plaza your child can choose which toy she would like rather than automatically receive a gender-stereotyped toy.

The next topic that drew the students' attention was the negative images of women in various media. Several groups challenged sexist images in advertising. For example, one group focused on a local health club that used a very sexist depiction of a woman in their advertising campaign. As part of their CAP, students investigated previous campaigns against sexist advertising, noting that in 1971, the National Organization for Women protested National Airlines for an ad campaign that featured an attractive woman saying, "Fly Me." They discovered that the company mandated that flight attendants wear buttons with the slogans "Fly Me" and "We Make You Feel Good All Over." As one student reported, on the picket line outside the ticket offices of National Airlines, "they carried signs like, 'Haven't you heard, I'm not a bird'" (Tran 1993:2). As in this example, the students were regularly teaching each other about different feminist issues, historical events, and political strategies they uncovered through their CAP-related research. Consequently, the students' research enriched the educational content presented in the course and contributed to building a learning community that engaged them in the educational process.

There are always two or three groups each year who choose a topic related to promoting women's studies. For example, one group targeted a local high school and worked with teachers to help develop a feminist studies curriculum; another group designed and implemented strategies to recruit male students to women's studies; and a third group worked to counter negative stereotypes of feminism among students at UCI. The later group developed a flyer entitled "Who Are Feminists?" that is now used by staff and peer educators at the Center for Women and Gender Education. Less frequent topics include equal promotion and representation of women's sports on campus. These projects are often initiated by women athletes enrolled in the class who emphasize how little support and visibility women's sports are given in the student newspaper and by Cheers, the group that promotes attendance at sports events.

A number of groups have focused on discrimination in employment and housing. One group, which called itself Live and Let Live, targeted the UCI apartment complex Verano Place for its discrimination against lesbian and gay couples. The strategy to persuade Verano Place housing authorities to reconsider their rental policy (which precluded gay and lesbian couples from living together unless both were enrolled as students) included a position paper, a petition drive, and a staged homosexual wedding on campus.

As this brief overview of selected projects reveals, students initiated research on a variety of topics that could not be covered on a ten-week syllabus. Since they identified the topics of most interest to them, they frequently brought a lot of enthusiasm to their research and analysis of the problems and institutions that were the focus of their projects. Of course, since the course attracts a large number of students who are more interested in fullfilling a campus-wide breadth requirement than in a class titled Resisting and Reproducing Inequalities, it would be misleading to claim that every student approaches the CAP with tremendous energy and enthusiasm. I have, however, found that after a short period of frustration and resistance at the very beginning of the course, the majority of the students do come to appreciate the value of the CAP for their own learning process and political development.

Legacy of the Community Action Projects

Beyond the pedagogical value of the CAPs there have been a number of projects that have made a lasting impact on the campus and in the community. One of the main topics of concern for the students over the years has been rape awareness and safety on campus. During the first year of the CAP (1994), a group came together with a concern about sexual harassment. As part of the process through which the group was attempting to define a specific action, they discovered that the annual orientation manual, the *Student Survival Guide*, did tell students not to walk dogs on campus, and did note where to get discount tickets for shows at the university theater, but failed to provide students with information on something as noteworthy as sexual harassment. The group investigated who was responsible for producing the *Survival Guide*, met with the relevant people, and proposed including a paragraph on sexual harassment. Following review of university publications on sexual harassment, and in consultation with Paula Goldsmid of the Center for Women and Gender

Education, they drafted a paragraph that was subsequently inserted into the *Survival Guide*. One of the students expressed her enthusiasm for their success in her final report as follows: "It was really exciting that as students we could influence and motivate faculty members into action!" (Mitchell 1993).

In 1995, another CAP group, inspired by the success of the first year's group, developed a paragraph on acquaintance rape that was inserted into *The UCI Residents' Guidebook*. Another group concerned about rape prevention and calling itself Dare To Be Heard, worked in collaboration with Joan Ariel, then academic coordinator (and women's studies librarian) of the Women's Studies Program and Donna-Jean Louden, the (Campus Assault Prevention Program coordinator), to develop a proposal for a feminist self-defense course. This course is now regularly taught at the Center for Women and Gender Education. A 1999 CAP successfully changed the telephone number for the Safety Escort Service from one that was difficult to memorize to 824-SAFE.

The following year a CAP group reviewed the processes by which students were informed about rape prevention and determined that first-year students needed more information. The group titled their project, "Could You Be Next?" They developed a proposal that they submitted to two housing complexes where first-year students were assigned, and called for annual rape awareness/prevention workshops for dorm residents. Working closely with Donna-Jean Louden, the group successfully obtained approval for their proposal.

Obviously, not all efforts to work on campus or with community groups have been successful; but, regardless of the outcome, students come away with a great deal of knowledge about the intersection of race, class, gender, and institutional politics. Since UCI's population is over 50 percent Asian American, a number of projects focused on advocating for the rights of Asian-American women in a variety of settings. One CAP group discovered that Interval House, a shelter located in a predominantly Vietnamese community in Westminster, served a predominantly white European-American population. This group worked with shelter staff to identify obstacles preventing Vietnamese-American women from utilizing the shelter. Drawing on readings from the course, they developed a proposal for the establishment of a bilingual and multicultural community board that they presented to the staff. Their proposal was met with "mixed responses." The shelter director explained that they could not initiate such a program without approval of funding agencies, including the California Department of Social Services. In her final report, group member Hanh Nguyen (1995) acknowledged that the group might have achieved more success if they had the time to gather support from others in the Vietnamese community.

Groups have increasingly turned to the Internet as a site for their political actions. I have been somewhat cautious in my support of this strategy since webpages must be updated regularly and need to be linked to other relevant sites that are also subject to change. Other concerns I have include the risk of duplication; the difficulty, in some cases, in constructing this intervention as political action; the extensive time needed to gather the data and source materials; and the technical expertise that often prohibits many members of the group from participating. One group created a webpage to promote women's sports on campus, and reported that in the first ten days the page was available they received 300 "hits," and that almost a dozen people had signed up to the e-mail listserv connected to it. This group optimistically said they would keep the page going after the course. Given time constraints, the diversity of projects, and the problems tracking students after they leave the course, it is difficult to access how many CAPs live past the term and to determine, for those that *do* continue, *how* they continue. My general sense is that few CAPs continue, even when students express an interest in keeping them going, since students encounter other demands on their time or lose track of fellow group members as they graduate or move on to other classes.

However, some students individually continue to demonstrate a commitment to community action or other forms of community-based work while at UCI, though it would be difficult to determine how long that involvement continues after graduation. Ranu Mukherjee (1999:6), whose project concerned addressing the problem of eating disorders among UCI students, wrote, "Even though my project is over, I really want to continue doing something about this problem that affects so many young women. . . . I am really interested in this subject and I want to make sure that I am constantly involved in something that I feel so strongly about." Hanh Nguyen explained why she expected to continue her work on behalf of battered women in the Vietnamese-American community, writing in her final CAP report,

> I have a personal stake in continuing this effort because this is my community. Domestic violence is never talked about in the Vietnamese community because it is sanctioned for men and shamed for women. However, my social location as a middle class student provides me with opportunities to tap into resources such as [English] language [proficiency] that will aid abused women. (p. 10)

Unlike many, who bemoan the loss of a commitment to political activism, I have witnessed firsthand among the younger generation of feminists an energy and enthusiasm for challenging patterns of inequality in diverse institutions and social practices. As students uncover how corporations test and market certain products, or as they examine the practices of certain professions, they empirically test some of the premises of the feminist analyses presented in class. Therefore, the experiential approach reinforces the instructional content of the introductory course Reproducing and Resisting Inequalities, which explores the social organization of knowledge and the processes of inequalities that are woven in and through institutions.

Teaching Feminisms Experientially

Over the years, students have expressed a variety of positive and negative feelings about working in groups to accomplish a project's goals. Among the problems they report are the difficulty scheduling meetings outside of class time, determining an effective division of labor, negotiating the different degrees of participation (which causes some group members to perform a disproportionate amount of work), and achieving consensus. UCI and, consequently, the women's studies introductory sequence draw a diverse student body. In some cases, this diversity poses some challenges for the process of group concensus-building; in other cases, it serves as a resource. Nayomi Munaweera (1995:8), who worked on the project concerned with increasing Vietnamese-American women's access to services for battered women, wrote, "The fact that we were of diverse racial backgrounds was really more of an advantage than not. We really represented a multicultural slice of American since we were a Vietnamese, an African American, a Causasian, a Latina, and a Sri Lankan." For students who did not achieve the level of consensus or cooperation that Munaweera reports, they often agreed that, despite their difficulties, working in groups is a necessary part of fostering change.

Experience working in the CAP groups highlighted many themes of class discussion, sometimes providing painful lessons. Shadi Aryabod (1998:5), who worked on the EEOI campaign, remarked on the gender division of labor that occurred within her group. She wrote,

> With one exception, the division of labor in the group was delineated according to invisible rules about gender appropriate tasks. For instance, men were reluctant in helping with poster making since they believed that our "pretty, female hand-writing" [was] more appropriate than their "manly hand-writing"! In addition, they practically monopolized our "public relations" activities by not sharing the information with the others. If any contacts were given out, they tended to be the less influential ones. Finally, all the letters and flyers that went out in the first part of our project contained the signatures of the two male co-organizers, in spite of the fact that one of the three founding co-organizers was a female.

Once Aryabod recognized the pattern of gender inequality, she developed an alternative strategy to ensure her active participation in outreach and group decision-making:

> Hence, after a short period of disillusionment, I realized that I could not afford to sit back and hope that they would consider my opinions. Therefore, I took it upon myself to change my approach. I began to make plans and to seek the assistance of other women in the group. Moreover, I started to make contacts with prominent members of the University and the community . . . . These contacts proved to be, not only of great importance to our efforts, but helped me learn more about myself and activism.

In her final report, Aryabod (1998:6) reflected on this experience and recognized her own process of politicization; she wrote, "I came to experience first hand how the valuable knowledge women have is commonly subjugated and not taken into consideration."

By researching their chosen topics and discovering certain information on their own, the students developed a deeper understanding of the issue than if they only heard it discussed in class or in assigned reading. For example, Tenisha Powers (1999:5), whose group focused on date rape, reported in her final paper,

> This was a total learning experience in so many different ways. First of all was the knowledge I received just studying date rape. I knew date rape happened but I was unaware of how frequently it occurred. I myself held some of the misconceptions about date rape, for example, believing that most rapists were strangers to the victim. It is amazing how many women are raped by someone they knew. . . . Once people know what date rape is more women would be more willing to come forward with their stories and more men would think twice before pressuring a woman into sex.

Many students expressed frustration in their final reports about the limited time frame for the project. In considering why her other two group members were less enthusiastic about the CAP, Anna Vasquez (1994:7) wrote, "I feel that many students felt rushed and arranged to have workshops for the sake of getting the project done and over with. I feel that these people could be capable of so much more given ample time." However, despite their frustrations regarding the limited time they had to implement the CAP, many other students came to view it as a valuable experience.

Most students were able to draw connections between the CAP and feminist theorizing. In my first introductory women's studies class at UCI in the winter of 1993, I remember introducing students to the different "feminisms": liberal or reform feminism; socialist and Marxist feminism; radical feminism; lesbian feminism; "third world" feminism. Various other categories of feminisms appear in women's studies texts. These include (1) historical categorizations, such as "first-wave" (up to 1950) and "second-wave" (1950–early 1980s) feminisms (Humm 1992); (2) labels that refer more to specific theoretical frameworks, such as psychoanalytic feminism (Tong 1989; Humm 1992); and (3) designations connected to the racial and ethnic identities or social locations of the authors, and/or that center race, postcolonial analyses, or gendered processes of globalization such as black feminism, multicultural feminism, and global feminism (Collins 1990, Shohat 1998; Basu 1995). To further add to the complexity, Terry Haywoode (1991) analyzes dimensions of "working class feminism," and Maxine Baca Zinn and Bonnie Thornton Dill (1996:323–24) describe "multiracial feminism," which locates both men and women "in multiple systems of domination." African-American women and Latinas have created terms that self-consciously reject the feminist label, such as xicanista and womanist (Walker 1983; Castillo 1995). In a recent effort "to contribute to the creation of multi-centered, women-affirming, and transformative politics," Angela Miles (1996:x–xi) demonstrates how "types of feminism usually perceived as absolutely different, even opposing, share important integrative principles." Her articulation of "integrative feminisms" further challenges rigid distinctions among liberal, radical, and socialist feminisms.

For students in an introductory course in women's studies, such complexity of feminisms is often confusing, to say the least. While presenting the variety of feminisms does contest the very limited constructions of feminism that circulate in the media and popular discourse, teaching multiple feminisms as typologies could also undercut the students' ability to appreciate the complex political traditions, theoretical debates, and historical factors that contributed to the articulation of the diverse feminist approaches. Given the short time frame for the class, it is also difficult to give the students a more textured historical, comparative, and international introduction to diverse women's movements' relationships to different feminisms. However, in the context of the CAP, political interventions that the students identify for their change project become resources for more grounded discussions of different feminist strategies.

For example, one CAP group this past year was interested in finding a way to address the educational needs of students in other parts of the world. They discussed the factors that contribute to illiteracy and determined that lack of resources was a key factor. From this recognition they decided that they would mount a campaign to raise funds from local businesses to send school supplies to a rural community in Kenya that one of the students was familiar with through her neighbor, who founded the Center for Indigenous Knowledge. When I discussed the proposal with them, I asked them to consider how this intervention would challenge the system of inequality that underlay the problem of illiteracy and how the action they proposed would address gender inequality. The group then continued their discussion without me to revise their CAP in response to the issues I raised. They returned a week later to tell me that they would revise their project to target the sororities on campus to see if they would be willing to sponsor an annual drive to raise funds for school supplies for schoolchildren in Kenya.

This left me with another dilemma. When do I use my authority to veto a project if it does not reflect a more complex understanding of politics? I have learned that while I can provide some structure and guidance, I cannot tell a group that they need to find another type of community action. I do use the process of topic selection and discussion of possible interventions to teach about the theoretical differences in political actions. However, in the course of ten weeks it is not always possible for students to redirect their efforts. Fortunately, the steps of action they do take can always be understood within different feminist frameworks. School supplies to Kenya as a strategy to fight illiteracy reflects a liberal response to inequality that continues to inform social welfare policy. A project like this one gives me the opportunity to discuss liberal, postcolonialist and "third world" feminisms in the context of a very particular action devised by members of the class. Rather than highlight the limits of their intervention, I can acknowledge the contribution that these students make to class discussion.

Through the investigatory process and activist interventions they choose for their CAP, students learn about how institutions are put together in ways that reveal the relations of ruling that shape everyday life. As they uncover how corporations test and market certain products or as they examine the practices of certain professions, they empirically test some of the premises of the feminist analyses presented in class. Therefore, the experiential approach reinforces the instructional content of the course.

The Limits and Possibilities of Community Action

Community-based activism as a political strategy is limited in a number of significant ways. These limitations apply regardless of whether the collective actions emerge in a particular neighborhood or university context. Some critics argue that community activism by definition rarely transcends the local; nor, in many cases, is it likely to continue after the particular issue and targeted problem is resolved. Even when particular actors or community organizations attempt to build linkages with others beyond their local community, limited time and resources often prevent effective coalition building.

Furthermore, issue-based community activism often contributes to a narrow focus that renders invisible the larger political and economic factors in which the particular concern is embedded. Therefore, group members often have difficulty extending their political and economic analysis beyond the immediate context. Furthermore, few CAPs focused on international issues. This is of particular concern since the course is designed to reveal the intersection of the local, international, and global in the production of knowledge, the reproduction of inequalities, the organization of women's everyday lives, and resistance strategies.

Since I began this course in 1994, there have been only three groups that addressed international issues. (Of course, this is not surprising given the strong recommendation that groups target an identifiable community that they can contact directly and attempt to influence in the ten-week time frame.) One group became interested in promoting awareness of indigenous women's struggles in Chiapas, Mexico. This group was formed after a student in the class discussed her summer trip to Chiapas and emphasized that there was a need to raise awareness about the political and economic situation there. She suggested establishing a webpage with information about the circumstances surrounding the struggle and what interested people might do to support the indigenous people. In addressing my concerns about using the web for their project, the Chiapas group was able to demonstrate how they would maximize the potential of the Internet for raising awareness of this issue. They planned to create a webpage accessible to UCI students that would predominantly serve as a link to relevant sites that already had institutional sponsorship, in order to ensure that the information on linked webpages was updated regularly.

In an effort to promote a more international and intersectional framework for the CAPs, I have explored how materialist feminist analyses and Dorothy Smith's institutional ethnography can provide epistemological tools to help students link the so-called micro social world with the macroprocesses that shape our world (see chapter 2 in this volume). Institutional ethnography is a sociological method that can be "accountable to people's lived experience" and "a means of making visible the social relations that organize and shape our lives" (Smith 1992:190); this method highlights the extralocal processes that organize everyday life. Students are asked to examine relevant texts, organizational practices, and institutional relationships to explore how things are put together in order to reproduce inequalities in specific settings. As students develop knowledges from their investigations and community action, they begin to understand the link between institutional ethnography and feminist activism.

Conclusion

As a feminist pedagogical tool, the CAP challenges some of the basic tenets of contemporary academic production. At the close of the 1990s, we find increasing pressure on colleges and universities to maximize faculty labor while raising the bottom line through large course sizes, distance learning, and computer technologies. Those of us in joint positions in women's studies and other academic units are further engaged in this process as our service commitments and curriculum offerings are expanded to serve the needs of two diverse units. On the one hand, like other problem-solving exercises and internships, the CAP serves this goal well by encouraging the students to become "self-taught" in a variety of topics that we cannot cover in a ten-week quarter. On the other hand, the CAP as an experiential group project challenges the privatization of academic knowledge production. Students begin to recognize how the individualized approach to higher education inhibits the development of certain kinds of knowledges, privileging self-interest and competition among students rather than cooperation and group learning. The project also provides a context through which students can critique the academy as a site of social control as well as discover how it is linked to other institutions to reproduce patterns of inequality. Finally, students come to recognize their own position within these institutions as well as their ability to challenge oppressive institutional practices. In some instances, they succeed in making small changes within the university or their community. In many instances, these changes are fleeting. Regardless of the specific outcome, the CAP group process offers one strategy for incorporating social-change-oriented pedagogy into the women's studies curriculum. In other words, the institutionalization of women's studies does not mean the inevitable loss of feminist praxis in the feminist classroom. It challenges us to reinvent ourselves as feminist educators as well as help our students resist the privatized and apolitical discourse and practice that accompanies life in the academy and beyond. Yet I also have to acknowledge my ambivalence about the use of such a challenging project in the large introductory women's studies class. When I first began the project, the class was limited to 70 students. Working with one TA, I was able to intervene more directly in the implementation of CAPs as well as more quickly link the specific action steps in which the students engaged the course material. However, as the class size grew to the current enrollment of 210 with four TAs, I felt a growing unease about the feasibility of effectively implementing this experiential project. Many of the TAs are themselves new to community action and are consequently unsure in their role as CAP facilitators. Ideally, I would like to see the CAP offered within the context of an upper-division course that is limited to no more than forty students. I would also like to create a related course for teaching assistants interested in linking theory and feminist practice. While we have discussed these options in our Women's Studies Program, we presently do not have the faculty time and resources to offer these courses.

Different academic settings provide different contexts for the use of experiential projects like the CAP. I offer the lessons I have learned from the Community Action Project since I believe that experiential learning is a dynamic process that can invigorate our teaching as well as feminist praxis in the classroom and beyond.

Note

I would like to express my thanks to all the students in the Reproducing and Resisting Inequalities course for their work on the CAPs. I owe a great deal of gratitude to Robin Goldberg, who taught the course for the winter quarters of 1996 and 1997, to Paula Goldsmid and Donna-Jean Louden for graciously sharing their valuable time and wisdom with the students, and to the following graduate teaching assistants for their essential role in guiding the CAPs to completion: Jennifer Boyle, Cindy Cheng, Michelle Grisat, Clara McLean, Chrisy Moutsatsos, Julie Park, Beth Quinn, Beth Rayfield, Charlene Tung, and Clare Weber. I would like to express special appreciation to women's studies student Rosalia Vassalla, who helped me systematize the CAP reports. My thanks to Karen Bojar, Jennifer Boyle, Marjorie DeVault, Michelle Grisat, Adina Mack, Chrisy Moutsatsos, Karen Tice, Charlene Tung, and Robyn Weigman for helpful feedback on an earlier draft of this article. Portions of this chapter appear as "Experiential Learning in the Introductory Women's Studies Classroom: Lessons from the Community Action Project" by Nancy Naples in *Women's Studies on Its Own*, edited by Robyn Wiegman, Duke University Press, forthcoming.

7

Bridging Feminist Theory and Feminist Practice in a Senior Seminar

Jennifer L. Rexroat

Gender and Women's Studies 390 (GWS 390) is a capstone course offered in the Gender and Women's Studies Program at the University of Illinois at Chicago. I have taught this course twice, first in 1997 and again in 1999. In this article, I analyze student experiences in this course and throughout their research processes. Based upon comments provided in student research papers and course evaluations, as well as my own synthesis of student performance, this article illustrates the various ways in which students' simultaneous accumulation of theoretical knowledge about feminist organizing, and application of this knowledge via practical research experience at a Chicago-area women's organization, helps to shape and enrich their understanding of the organizations they study.[1] This course overview and analysis stands to better inform feminist scholars and activists about pedagogical strategies that encourage gender and women's studies students to make continued connections between feminist theory and feminist practice.

Course Overview

The University of Illinois at Chicago (UIC) is an urban university that enrolls approximately 25,000 students per year.[2] UIC's Gender and Women's Studies Program, established in 1974, currently enrolls approximately 350 to 400 students per semester, and graduates approximately seven to ten undergraduate minors and six to eight graduate students per year.[3] GWS 390 is an upper-division, senior seminar topics course intended primarily for Gender and Women's Studies minors; it is a graduation requirement for those students. Occasionally, however, non-minors with previous gender and women's studies course experience enroll in GWS 390. The average enrollment for the course is approximately ten to fifteen students per semester.

The topic of the GWS 390 course I have taught twice is the history of women's organizations in the United States. Designed to acquaint students with the U.S. women's movement since feminism's second wave, it situates second-wave feminism in relation to feminist theory and to women's organizations. During the semester, my students and I explore the theoretical underpinnings of feminism and observe ways in which feminist theories have been translated into feminist activism through the formation of various women's organizations in the United States.

The course is divided into three sections. First, we consider historical accounts of feminist organizing, reading Myra Marx Ferree and Beth Hess's *Controversy and Coalition* (1995), Patricia Yancey Martin's "Rethinking Feminist Organizations" (1990), and Stephanie Riger's "Challenges of Success: Stages of Growth in Feminist Organizations" (1994). These readings provide the necessary historical backdrop to past and present women's organizing in the United States, and they also equip students with theoretical frameworks of what feminist organizations might look like. Second, we examine the ways in which feminist theories can be applied to contemporary political issues, reading Sondra Farganis's *Situating Feminism* (1994). This text allows students to gain exposure to advanced-level feminist theory, and it works well in the course because it applies that theoretical knowledge to recent legal cases involving feminist issues and organizational activity. Third, we explore the intersection of feminism as a social movement and organizations that attempt to foster collective action through the examination of feminist organizational case studies, reading Myra Marx Ferree and Patricia Yancey Martin's *Feminist Organizations: Harvest of the New Women's Movement* (1995a). This volume provides students with a wide array of perspectives about and practices of contemporary U.S. feminist organizations that espouse varying degrees of feminist identification. It is an ideal text for the course because it illustrates sites where feminist theory and feminist practice intersect, occasionally collide, and often harmoniously coexist. Each of the texts that I include in the course helps students to better understand the organizations that they study for their semester projects by providing them with information regarding trends in feminist organizing, illustrations of contemporary models of feminist organizations, and cogent examples of the combination of feminist theory and feminist action that students then apply to their evaluation of women's organizations that they choose to study for their research papers.[4]

Throughout the three sections of the course, I ask students to accumulate theoretical knowledge through their analysis of assigned course readings, brief in-class lectures, and participation in class discussions that will assist them in completing their final semester project, a historical analysis of a local (in this case, Chicago-area) women's organization. Based upon archival sources where possible, and interviews with staff and/or members of the organization, the students' papers: 1) situate the organization in terms of second-wave feminism using theoretical materials read throughout the courses as models of second-wave feminist organizations; 2) provide a throrough discussion of the organization's goals, structure, membership, clientele, modes of operation, organizational strategies, and delivery of services; 3) assess the strengths and weaknesses of the organization, both in terms of the texts read in the course and students' personal opinions; 4) evaluation of the organization in terms of feminist identity; and 5) offer conclusions and suggestions regarding ways in which the organization might develop in the future to either sustain its current organizational efforts and/or improve upon its current activist status.

The argument can be made that, because GWS 390 students are likely to share their finished research papers with the women's organizations that participated in their research, the students may be less critical of the organizations than they would otherwise be if their papers were not made available to them. I encourage students to be as objective and honest in their research and findings as possible, even if this means drawing conclusions that are not favorable to the participating organizations. Generally, the participating organizations have appreciated the students' analyses of their groups and have treated them with respect, as many organizations do not have the time or funds to devote to such comprehensive examinations of their structures and activities. On occasion, however, some students have expressed reservations, for political reasons, about sharing their less positive conclusions about the researched organizations. For example, some students have been hesitant to share negative findings with already divided women's organizations embroiled in intragroup controversies about the current status and future direction of their organizations because their findings might exacerbate tensions in the groups. In these cases, I have informed students that it is their prerogative to compile two versions of their papers, a full version that is turned in to me for the purposes of our course, and an edited version to be given to the organizations that omits any information that is of concern to the students for the above reasons. Very few students have exercised this option, and those who have done so have discussed their decisions in detail with their classmates and me as part of the semester project progress reports given by each student at each class meeting. As a group, we have talked through their rationales for making this choice so that they are aware of the advantages and disadvantages of their decisions.

At various points during the semester, I invite guest speakers who have been involved with Chicago-area women's organizations to attend the class and deliver a guest lecture based upon their activist experiences. Past speakers have been involved with the Chicago Women's Liberation Union, Lutheran women's organizations, and domestic violence shelters. I also include videotapes documenting the history of women's organizations in the course. Together, these experiences inform students of the ways in which feminist thought about women's organizations translates into feminist activism directed at the transformation of social institutions and arrangements. These pedagogical practices are in accordance with the basis of feminist pedagogy, the desire for progressive social change in our institutions, laws, and social structures that would abate the gender oppression of women (Mayberry 1999; see also Shrewsbury 1997; Lewis 1992; Maher and Tetreault 1994; Gore 1993).

Analysis of Student Performance in GWS 390

GWS 390 immerses students in an experiential setting that enables them to simultaneously learn about feminist theory and feminist practice. Consequently, students in the course are helping to build a feminist praxis. In her book, *Getting Smart: Feminist Research and Pedagogy with/in the Postmodern*, Patti Lather (1991:11–12) defines the requirements of praxis as "theory both relevant to the world and nurtured by actions in it, and an action component in its own theorizing process that grows out of practical political grounding." In "Building Feminist Praxis Out of Feminist Pedagogy: The Importance of Students' Perspectives," Kelly Coate Bignell advocates the inclusion of student perspectives in women's studies research about feminist pedagogy, because she considers women's studies students to possess their own brand of expert knowledge that can inform women's studies scholars about the successes and failures of feminist pedagogy and, by extension, feminist scholarship in general. Bignell acknowledges the potential for a feminist praxis to be built from "the experiences within the Women's Studies classroom (where feminist theory becomes action)" (Bignell 1996:315). Through an analysis of GWS 390 student comments provided in course evaluations and student research papers, I will illustrate the ways in which GWS 390 students are "doing" feminist praxis. Their experiential learning projects demonstrate the potential success of feminist pedagogies that make activism real for our students by relocating the sites for student learning about feminism from our feminist classrooms to the communities where they reside (Gilbert, Holdt, and Christophersen 1999, 332, 337).

The excerpts from GWS 390 student research papers to be discussed in this section fall into two categories. The first set of student paper comments demonstrates ways in which GWS 390 students applied their knowledge of feminist organizational theory to analyze the practices of the Chicago-area women's organizations they studied. The second set of student paper comments reveals ways in which the students themselves were transformed as a result of their research processes. Together, these student writing samples and the themes that they emphasize lend support to the creation of experiential learning environments that emphasize feminist pedagogical principles and help to build a feminist praxis both within and outside of the feminist classroom. One GWS 390 student conducted research on Artemisia, a Chicago art gallery founded to provide gallery space for local women artists. In her discussion of how she came to select this topic for her research paper, the student wrote,

> I was also interested in the role of feminism in art, specifically within the organization I was researching (i.e., are the members of the organization feminist, what role has feminism played in shaping the ways in which the organization is run, how the feminist organizational theories we studied in class [can] be applied to explain Artemisia's organization.

The student became aware, very early on in her research process, that the feminist organizational theories she was learning about in the course could be usefully applied in a practical setting. In making this realization, the student took her first steps toward the creation of a feminist praxis in her research project.

This same student provided a poignant example of the ways in which feminist theory and feminist practice can—and do—intersect in her discussion of the circumstances surrounding the founding of Artemisia gallery. She noted,

> Artemisia was founded in 1973, at a time of political awareness. Unlike the movements typical in the 1960's, which were group based, in the 1970's improvement of the self was highly valued. Instead of trying to change society as a whole, changing oneself [also] became an important form of activism. The governing belief behind this form of activism was that if each individual took responsibility for her/himself, then society as a whole would improve. The theory of Artemisia's founding members seemed to have followed along similar lines.

In this statement, the student demonstrates an awareness of historical shifts in both the form and focus of activist movements (including the feminist movement) in the United States. Here, she indicates that the founding circumstances of Artemisia tended to follow an individualized model of feminist activism that was intended to lead to collective social change. In her conclusion, this student raised the important question of the efficacy of social movements, including the U.S. feminist movement, in fostering social and institutional transformation. Here, the student applies her knowledge of feminist organizational theory to the practices of Artemisia gallery and implies that Artemisia, and other feminist organizations like it in the artistic community, may not be able to live up to their feminist missions due to the inherent difficulties of and obstacles to collective action. The student realizes that, in practice, feminist theories are not always perfect; they are abstractions that are often confounded by mitigating social forces and are, on occasion, inaccurate models of real-world activity.

Another GWS 390 student, whose semester project focused on the League of Black Women, a Chicago-area organization that provides a variety of social services for African-American women, applied feminist organizational theory to the practices of the League throughout her research paper. In an analysis of a quote from a League staff member, the student wrote that

> although [the interviewee] does not see herself as a feminist, I believe that she does indeed espouse feminist values. Feminist ideology sees women as a sex class [and] acknowledges that women are oppressed and disadvantaged as a group (Martin 1990, 191). [The interviewee's] comment indicates her awareness of gender oppression and her desire to break the paradigm of sexism that has characterized men's oppression of women.

Here the student applied feminist theory to the views and practices of the staff member, concluding that, in spite of the staff member's rejection of an explicitly feminist identification, according to some aspects of feminist thought she may hold feminist values. This assessment illustrates the student's ability to apply elements of feminist theory to a real-world interview and make inferences about the potentially feminist aspects of the respondent's viewpoints and practices.

The same student also made linkages between feminist organizational theory and the practices of the League of Black Women in her assessment of the League's organizational structure. She noted,

> Another thing that struck me was the lack of communication between the general membership and the board. It is almost as if they are from different planets. As a result of the League's highly bureaucratic, top-down characteristics, members have little control over the League's day-to-day activities. In order for the organization to stay viable in the coming century, it must reach out to a broader base of members and create a more effective way of communicating with its current members. This organization has the potential to become a real powerhouse of African-American women, but it must learn to be more inclusive so more women can partake in the knowledge, inspiration, and devotion that is so clearly reflected in the executive board of this organization.

In this evaluative statement, the student identifies an organizational problem regarding the League of Black Women's communication procedures and makes a recommendation for future action to resolve this difficulty. Specifically, the student recommends later in her paper that the League increase its efforts to become more communicative with its current members by increasing the number of meetings held with the board of directors and entire membership in order to alleviate the tensions between an active core membership and a relatively inactive group of members at large; by restarting the defunct League of Black Women newsletter and changing it from a bimonthly to a monthly publication in order to keep members regularly informed of group activities; and by implementing plans to gather demographic data about its members to better assess member needs and interests. The student proposes that, in order to promote inclusiveness in the organization, the League of Black Women consider a sliding scale for its 40-dollar membership fee and other fee-based group activities because the fees tend to exclude women of low socioeconomic status from the organization based upon their inability to pay. Additionally, the student notes an overwhelming heterosexual atmosphere within the League of Black Women, and she states that, to her knowledge, the League had no lesbian members at the time of her writing; she suggested that the organization more actively recruit lesbian members and attend to issues of concern to African-American lesbians in order to become a more inclusive group.

Another student, whose research topic was the history of the Chicago chapter of the International Association of Women Police (IAWP), a professional organization that serves women in the criminal justice community, included a powerful reflection in her paper about the ways in which her research experience has affected her life. She wrote,

> Since I was a little girl, I have felt that I had something to prove, to myself and to the world. I knew I was different, different because I was a girl. I was not less of a person, just different. Eventually, I thought about what I wanted to do with my life as I got older. I knew that I wanted to do something unconventional for my gender. I decided on the Criminal Justice field. I have pursued this work for the past three years at the University of Illinois at Chicago, and I intend to continue. I try to work as hard as I can in my criminal justice classes because it makes me feel good to know that I am succeeding and thriving in a male-dominated field of study. I feel empowered when I am able to answer questions in my criminal justice courses, especially considering the fact that I am usually one of only a few female students that verbally participates in class. It is a shame that this is the case, but that is precisely why I am grateful for discovering the International Association of Women Police (IAWP), an organization for *women* working in the field of criminal justice [*emphasis in the original*].

The experiential learning project in the GWS 390 course provided this student with early exposure to an organization which she both learned and came to care a great deal about; she was able to use her knowledge of women's organizations to make connections with a group that will likely impact her in her future. The student was deeply moved and personally transformed as a result of her practical research experience with the IAWP.

The two themes explored through the above analysis of GWS 390 student research papers—student application of feminist theory to feminist practice, and the transformation of students as a result of the research process—are instrumental to the creation of a feminist pedagogical praxis, an educational site where the ostensible gap between feminist theory and feminist practice can be bridged. Many students in the course, indeed more than can be acknowledged in this article, were successful in bridging the gap between feminist theory and feminist practice as a result of their classroom work and experiential learning projects. They gave Carolyn Shrewsbury's (1997:171) assertion that "theory can be extended to action, and action can come back to inform theory and that can again lead to action." In their field research, students in GWS 390 created feedback loops between feminist theory and feminist practice that contributed to a feminist praxis.

A review of GWS 390 student course evaluations, like passages quoted previously from student research papers, emphasize two themes that I offer as fundamental aspects of a feminist pedagogical praxis: making connections between feminist theory and feminist practice, and personal transformation through the research process. In their course evaluations, students recognized the value of doing community-based research—namely, the ability to operationalize the feminist theories learned in the classroom within a real-world setting. Student comments indicate that the particular texts chosen for the course, in combination with the structured experiential learning project, enabled them to situate contemporary women's organizations in the United States within the historical framework of second-wave feminism. As a result, the students were more easily able to identify linkages between second-wave feminist theories and current feminist practice; namely, they became aware not only of the many ways in which today's women's organizations have been shaped by theories emerging from feminism's second wave, but also of the ways in which contemporary women's organizations in the United States are building upon and occasionally departing from second-wave feminist theories in order to forge continued progress for women in our society. Students also articulated the ways in which their lives were changed as a result of their research experiences. Their comments suggest that their newfound knowledge about the history and current practices of U.S. women's organizations has provided them with a map of the struggles and victories of the women's movement that will remain with them throughout their lives. In these ways, the students' comments about the GWS 390 seminar describe their contributions to feminist praxis both within the classroom and in their communities at large.

Many students who were affected on a personal level by their research experiences in the seminar decided to continue their involvement with the organizations that they studied, or with other women's organizations, after the semester ended. Recent academic literature supports the notion that women's studies courses heighten levels of student political involvement. In their study of the effects of women's studies courses on women students' feminist identity development, Adena Bargad and Janet Shibley Hyde (1991:195) found that the women's studies students they interviewed "felt that the course had a profound impact on their thinking, expressed how much they enjoyed the course, spoke of planning to enroll in women's studies courses in the future, and commented on the fact that the course had encouraged their activism, on personal and public levels." Jayne Stake and Suzanna Rose's 1994 study of the longitudinal impact of women's studies courses on student political activism concluded that "students' feminist enthusiasm does not peak at the time their women's studies class ends but instead, that women's studies learning provides a framework for understanding women's issues that has a long-term influence on students' personal lives and feminist activism" (Stake and Rose 1994:410). These studies provide evidence that women's studies course experience is a strong predictor of future feminist activism for students; consequently, the decisions to continue their involvement with women's organizations expressed by many GWS 390 students in their course evaluations are not surprising.

The argument can be made that there are many different kinds of feminist activism, however, and that not all feminist activist projects are equally valuable. I encourage students in the GWS 390 course to examine the relative merits of various women's organizations, including those that they considered for their semester research projects, in order to better evaluate the organizations' likelihood of strategic success in advancing a feminist agenda. In order to achieve this objective, I ask students as part of their research paper assignment to evaluate their chosen organizations in the context of the theoretical materials read in the course, especially Martin's "Rethinking Feminist Organizations" (1990), which provides a typology for analyzing the ideology, values, goals, outcomes, founding circumstances, structure, practice, members and membership, scope and scale, and external relations of feminist organizations. Upon applying Martin's analytical framework to their respective organizations, many students have realized that the organizations that are the subjects of their semester research projects are doing quite well in their pursuit of a feminist agenda; others, however, have learned that their chosen organizations face continued challenges in this regard. Most students complete this exercise with the realization that while the women's movement in the United States has not attained all of its goals it is far from extinct, and many dedicated members of our society continue to work on the behalf of women for feminist change.

That several of my GWS 390 students have decided to begin or continue their feminist activism after our semester together is an outcome of the seminar is, of course, pleasing to me as a feminist teacher. I, like many feminist teachers, "share the hope for the promise of education as a political project: that through the offer of a theoretical framework—analysis and critique—students would eagerly join in my enthusiasm to work for social change in their personal and public lives" (Lewis 1992:172). If this is the case, however, the question of why I do not require my GWS 390 students to become actively involved in the organizations they study—to become member-participants rather than solely outside observers—remains. The first reason for my decision is a largely pragmatic one. UIC is an urban university whose diverse student body is composed of a large number of nontraditional students, many of whom are low-income students who often work full-time jobs while simultaneously taking full-time course loads; this is, in many cases, in addition to assuming responsibilities for extended family, caring for children, and so on. I feel that instilling a course requirement that would ask students to become active participants in the organizations that they study for their semester projects would, in many cases, constitute a hardship for students who already have extremely limited time for academic requirements. Instead, I ask them to maximize the research time that they are able to spend with the organizations, with the hope that this might spark future interest in becoming more involved with the organizations as participants.

This leads me to my second point. Some of my GWS 390 students have been involved with Chicago-area women's organizations at the same time that they were taking the course. I always encourage students for whom this is the case to examine those organizations for their semester projects, if they feel comfortable doing so as a member who would be critically analyzing the history and current development of the organization, primarily because they have already obtained a level of access to the organization that would facilitate their research. The research experiences of those students who were actively involved with the organizations that they studied for their semester research projects were, in my view, qualitatively different in certain ways from the experiences of those students who were not actively involved with their chosen organizations during their research for the course. Students who were involved with their organizations enjoyed some benefits: an easier entrée into the research process due to their existing organizational contacts; a communicative "shorthand" with the staff and members of the organization due to preexisting relationships; a degree of "insider status" due to the fact that staff and members of the organization already knew and trusted the students, allowing them to be more open in the research process than if this previous knowledge and trust were absent; and the ability to immediately see and feel the contribution that their research made to the organization, due to their simultaneous roles as both researchers and participants in the group. This does not, however, imply that all students who were not actively involved with their organizations during their research experiences had a markedly more difficult research experience than did the involved students; with few exceptions, the research experiences of those students not involved with organizations were successful and rewarding. I encourage students who are experiencing networking difficulties with their chosen organizations early in the semester, whether they are involved with the groups or not, to choose another organization as the topic of their research papers as soon as possible, as the semester time constraint requires students to solidify organizational contacts at the outset of the term in order to maximize their research time.

I feel that it is perfectly acceptable for students to research the women's organizations that they are already familiar with if they choose to do so; if not, then it is my hope that they might gain new insights and experiences as a result of their research and decide, after the semester ends, to become more involved with whatever women's organization they decided to study, or another women's organization of interest to them. Some students, as evidenced by comments made in their course evaluations, have chosen to become active participants in the organizations they studied for their research projects. I believe that the GWS 390 seminar can act as a springboard to future involvement. I also believe, however, that this should be an elective choice made by the individual student, not a course mandate; in my view, doing the observational research required for the semester projects is sufficient for an upper-division seminar research paper.

Additionally, the GWS 390 course is not intended to be an internship. The UIC Gender and Women's Studies Program offers a separate internship course that provides interested students with the "opportunity to develop knowledge and skills relevant to academic training in gender and women's studies through research and work experience with organizations in the Chicago area" (in the words of the UIC undergraduate catalog). Because the Gender and Women's Studies Program has designed a separate internship course with the express purpose of providing an intensive practicum to students interested in even greater involvement with area women's organizations than provided in the course I have taught, I do not feel that it is necessary to require this same level of activism in my course. My final reason for not requiring GWS 390 students to become actively involved with the organizations that they study for their semester projects relates to the student composition of the course. From my own feminist perspective, I do not feel that it is appropriate to require students to engage actively with these organizations since many of the students are new to feminism and to women's studies. I wish to leave the decision to participate to the students' discretion, allowing them to assert their own agency following the research-based experience that the course provides.[5]

Conclusion

The Gender and Women's Studies seminar as I have structured and taught it at the University of Illinois at Chicago offers several benefits to students, instructors, and the women's organizations that participate in students' research projects. Based on the responses of students in the course (some of which have been documented in this article) and on my own observations of their performance, it is my view that students are willing and able to participate in this kind of experiential learning project, one that is often entirely new to them and that they often initially perceive as a challenge. The GWS 390 course introduces students to conducting field research at a relatively early stage of their learning; traditionally this type of experience is reserved for graduate students. The GWS 390 students have shown that they can rise to this challenge and complete impressive research studies. By the end of the semester, students in the course learn that they can push themselves beyond their current abilities and their own expectations; at the end of the term, their research projects seem far less daunting than when class first began. Students in the course demonstrate a level of maturity as undergraduate researchers that allows them to conduct fieldwork in a manner that is often gratifying and rewarding both for themselves and for the organizations that they study.

Organizations that participate in the students' research projects often learn a great deal about their groups' histories and current activist efforts; for groups with limited staff and/or financial resources, in particular, the students' research is often the first formal analysis of their organizations. The student researchers master this same information about the organizations, and they also, in many cases, learn more about their personal degrees of feminist identity and levels of commitment to feminist activism during their research experiences. The course exemplifies ways in which gender and women's studies teachers can construct their courses to provide students with simultaneous theoretical and practical experiences that train them to bridge feminist theory and feminist practice and enable them to experience personal transformation as a result of the research process. These experiences, in turn, create a community of students and teachers who are helping to build a feminist praxis in the world.

The pedagogical emphasis on fostering feminist praxis that is incorporated into the GWS 390 course is a necessary and valuable part of the work that "conscious feminists" (Weiler 1988:54) can do in order to better utilize colleges and universities as sites for feminist, counterhegemonic teaching. If we accept Jennifer Gore's proposition that "a feminist teacher is more than a feminist who teaches" (Gore 1993:81), then it is incumbent upon feminist teachers to use and develop feminist pedagogical strategies that are dedicated to the pursuit of gender justice and overcoming gender oppression. The seminar that I have described here can be used as a model course by programs in gender and women's studies that are interested in contributing to feminist pedagogy in this way, by providing a nexus between feminist theory and feminist practice for their students and faculty.

Notes

I would like to thank Drs. Karen Bojar, Nancy Naples, and Norma Moruzzi for their insightful comments on drafts of my contribution to this volume, and I acknowledge the work of Dr. Margaret Strobel, who originated the GWS 390 course that is the focus of my chapter.

1. This study has received approval for Human Subjects Exemption from the Institutional Review Board at the University of Illinois at Chicago, IRB Protocol Number: 2000-0508, approved July 13, 2000.
2. Student enrollment figure was obtained from the University of Illinois at Chicago website: http://www.uic.edu/homeindex/prospect/prospect.html, August, 2000.
3. University of Illinois at Chicago Gender and Women's Studies Program data was obtained from Patricia Renda, Assistant to the Director, UIC Gender and Women's Studies Program, via electronic mail, August 1, 2001.
4. Throughout the course, my students and I regularly discuss issues of bias and exclusion regarding race, class, and sexual orientation in written accounts of the second wave women's movement in the United States. Chapter four of Ferree and Hess' *Controversy and Coalition* (1995), in particular, includes a section on biases in women's mobilization that serves as a point of entry for this discussion early in the semester. These issues reemerge throughout the term, especially when we read Ferree and Martin's *Feminist Organizations* (1995), which contains chapters that deal with organizational learning in the Chicago Women's Liberation Union, African-American women's organizing, conflict in contemporary feminist organizing, and Mexican-American women's organizing. I encourage students to keep these discussions of bias and exclusion in mind when analyzing women's organizations for their semester projects, and to include reports and analyses of organizational difficulties in these areas in their research papers. For more information on the omission of women of color, working class women, and lesbian women from writings about second wave feminist history, see Gluck et al. (1998). For more information on the call for diversity in feminist theorizing and organizing, see hooks (1984); Hill Collins (1991); Moraga and Anzaldua (1983); Bell and Klein (1996); and Naples (1998a).
5. For a discussion of drawbacks to forced community service in women's studies courses, see Forbes et al. (1999).

8

Activism and the
Women's Studies Curriculum

Ellen Cronan Rose

As Marilyn Boxer (1982:678) has memorably put it, women's studies was conceived as "the academic arm of women's liberation." In *Liberal Learning and the Women's Studies Major*, a 1991 report by a National Women's Studies Association (NWSA) task force for a national review of arts and sciences majors by the Association of American Colleges, the authors remind us that in the United States, "women's studies grew out of the women's movement of the 1960s and 1970s" and that although it has evolved since then into "a comprehensive intellectual and social critique," it "retains its roots in the political women's movement" (Butler et al. 1991:3). In preparing its report, the NWSA task force consulted two national surveys of women's studies programs that offered majors. Although only 38 percent of them required a "practicum or internship course applying feminist knowledge to institutions in the community or on campus" (p. 10), many women's studies programs have found ways to encourage students to apply the knowledge they gain in women's studies courses to the "real world" outside the classroom.

Although the reigning myth in academia is that one's scholarship should be pure, objective, and by no means political, many feminist academics have resisted the academic ethos that rigidly separates scholarship and activism by designing and implementing assignments and courses "that very consciously and thoroughly connect activist work with scholarly theorizing, that refuse the false dichotomy that would dismiss or minimize the importance of learning by doing" (St. Peter 1997:109).[1]

Many departments and programs that do not offer practicums require that students majoring or minoring in women's studies do an internship. At the University of Nevada, Las Vegas (UNLV), we require majors to take a minimum of six credits in either internship or independent study, thus allowing them to choose either a research or an activist focus, but we have consciously designed the senior capstone course as an exercise in feminist praxis to emphasize the social transformational aspect of feminist theory and practice.[2]

Building Praxis into the UNLV Women's Studies Curriculum

Like that of most of the programs the NWSA task force surveyed for *Liberal Learning and the Women's Studies Major*, our curriculum is composed of departmental courses cross-listed with women's studies and a sequence of core interdisciplinary courses. In designing our capstone, we were less influenced by the sample capstone course syllabi collected in *Liberal Learning and the Women's Studies Major* than by the recommendation by the book's authors that "the senior seminar should be a course to facilitate students' transition to the next stage(s) of their lives" (p. 12). Most of the sample capstone syllabi in *Liberal Learning* suggest that women's studies graduates are in transit to postgraduate study and an academic career; they are all variations on the research seminar, culminating for each student with the production of a major scholarly paper.[3] One of our program objectives is to insure that students graduating with a B.A. in women's studies "will connect women's studies scholarship and social activism and will be able to become agents of social change" (Women's Studies Program 1997). Therefore, we wanted our students, including those who go on to graduate or professional school, to make connections between theory and practice, and "to create a liberatory feminist praxis (defined by Paulo Freire as 'action and reflection upon the world in order to transform it')" (hooks 1994b:112).

The Feminist Praxis capstone has been taught twice at UNLV, in the spring of 1998 and the spring of 2000. The course's designers and both cohorts of students who enrolled shared what Liz Stanley (1990:15) has identified as a "feminist commitment to a political position in which 'knowledge' is not simply defined as 'knowledge *what*' but also as 'knowledge *for*.'" "Succinctly," Stanley says, "the point is to change the world, not only to study it." To fulfill the course's goals, each student is required to complete an individual or group semester-long project that should, as the syllabus explains, "embody a vision of feminist praxis as you define it. That is, it should put into practice formal scholarship and personal experience/knowledge in women's studies."

A Sampler of Praxis Projects

After spending several class meetings discussing what a praxis project should ideally involve (and, in the spring 2000 class, reviewing a text from the course in feminist theory that all but one of the students had taken the previous semester), most of the students divided into groups, although two of the students who took the course in 2000 opted for individual rather than group projects. In 1998, one group, composed of students with an extensive background of coursework in western (specifically Las Vegas) women's history, worked with community activists from the Nevada Women's Lobby, a nonpartisan coalition of organizations and individuals that lobbies for public policies that advance issues of importance to women and families. Together they planned and implemented a two day statewide conference, Women's Summit '98: Nevada Women United, celebrating the 150th anniversary of the 1848 Women's Rights Conference at Seneca Falls, New York. Caryll and Kay, two praxis students, attended all meetings of the conference planning committee and coordinated the exhibitors' booths for the conference. Caryll coordinated the 1977 delegate workshop, Where We Are Now: A Past, Present, and Future Look at the Women's Rights Movement. Kay directed a children's play, *The Saga of Women's Suffrage*, and gave a presentation on using feminist methodology in oral history projects. Both endorsed Caryll's sentiments, expressed in her journal: "In working with members of various women's organizations, I began my transition from student to community activist. I not only created contacts for future use, but experienced the processes utilized by these groups in planning community events."[4]

For another group of students in 1998, the prospect of collaborating on a project with community activists did not correlate with their understanding of praxis. As one student, Alexis, wrote in her journal,

> When I think of praxis I think of action in the community . . . that will effect a true change. The people involved in the Women's Summit and those who will be attending are already aware. My aim is to reach those who are not aware of what women have done and can do and what needs to be done to better the situation of women in our society.

Accordingly, Alexis, Georgette, and Nikki designed an educational outreach project "to introduce the concept of (and UNLV's program in) women's studies to local high school students:"

> As women's studies majors and minors, we are particularly conscious of the lack of diverse points of view in public school education. The accomplishments of women and minorities throughout history are generally excluded or given token mention. There are presently very few women's studies programs available in high schools across the country and none in Las Vegas. This leads to a lack of interest in it as a major, minor, or elective when these

students enter college. Many of the majors and minors currently in the program did not originally come to UNLV with women's studies as their declared course of study, but they discovered it accidentally. As majors, we see a need to introduce this program as a possibility to college bound high school students, especially those who will be attending UNLV in the future.

Although the students experienced some initial difficulty and frustration gaining access to high-school students, eventually they were invited to visit three classes at two Las Vegas high schools—a senior psychology class at Valley High School and two ninth grade general studies classes at Chapparal High School. At Valley, the women's studies students were "incredibly exhilarated" by the response to their presentation, which began by arranging the students in a circle and explaining the (feminist) pedagogical rationale for this seating arrangement. The discussion "took off," they reported, when they did some language exercises with the students (e.g., "The wedding ceremony is loaded with gender-biased language. The traditional vow of the bride was 'to love, honor, and obey,' but the groom never promised to obey. Why not? Who traditionally 'gives the bride away'? Why? Who gives the groom away? And when the marriage is sealed, the minister or official pronounces the couple 'man and wife.' Why?"). Because it was a psychology class, Georgette, who was majoring in psychology and minoring in women's studies, gathered information to present to the class about sex bias in psychological testing. The UNLV students also talked with the high-school students about why they had chosen to major in women's studies and what careers they anticipated pursuing. This presentation was slightly modified for the younger students at Chaparral (for one thing, the material on psychological testing was omitted; for another, the UNLV students talked less about themselves and invited more questions from the high-school students), but both the Valley and Chaparral students' evaluations of the UNLV students' presentation were very positive. One student wrote, "I thought learning about women's rights and how they are not equal to men was interesting. I never knew there was a class like that, but now that you came in and told me about it, I may be interested in taking the class. I thought the presentation was good; even though our class didn't have much to say, I still enjoyed it." Another said, "I like how you brought out how the world is sexist. It is brought out to be male dominated. I like how you questioned why do women have to be given away by their fathers." One of the ninth graders said she had "always thought feminists were the women who hate men and don't shave their legs, but they explained differently and now I am more informed about women's rights classes. And I never thought about some of the things they talked about."

As I mentioned earlier, the students who took Feminist Praxis in spring 2000 were, with the exception of one student who had taken the theory course in 1998, all alumnae of the fall 1999 course in feminist theory that is both required of all women's studies majors and minors and prerequisite to the Feminist Praxis course. One of the objectives of that course, announced on the syllabus, was to "encourage critiques of theories in terms of their potential ability to effect social change," and the one text from the theory course I asked the students to revisit during the first two weeks of the praxis course was bell hooks's *Feminist Theory: From Margin to Center* (1984/2000:114). In chapter 8, "Educating Women: A Feminist Agenda," hooks (1984:110) accuses institutionalized women's studies programs of isolationism and elitism, noting, "Feminist education has become institutionalized in universities via women's studies programs. While these programs are necessary and are an extremely effective way to teach college students about feminism, they have very little impact, if any, on masses of women and men." Many of the students in the spring 2000 Feminist Praxis class noted that hooks's critique resonated strongly because it spoke directly to concerns they had voiced the previous semester in the feminist theory course. Indeed, hooks (1984:109) might have been speaking for them when she wrote that "many women's studies students at universities all around the United States grapple with the issue of whether or not their intellectual and scholarly pursuits are relevant to women as a collective group, to women in the 'real' world." She recommends breaking down the wall separating town from gown: "Were these students to go into communities and discuss feminist issues door-to-door, they would be working to bridge the gap between their educational experiences and the educational experiences of masses of women. . . . As part of her or his political commitment to feminism, a positive praxis for any academic would be offering women's studies courses at a local community center, YWCA, YMCA, church, etc." (pp. 109–10).

Two of the spring 2000 projects responded directly to this admonition to take women's studies beyond the walls of the university. Celia, a student who worked as a cook at St. Jude's Children's Ranch, immersed herself in feminist and multicultural pedagogical theory as preparation for developing an after-school feminist and multicultural educational program for fifteen 11- to 14-year-old children at the ranch, who were recommended for the program by St. Jude's program coordinators. Her research uncovered what she perceived to be a fundamental conflict between two contradictory goals of multicultural education. Was the aim, as Joel Spring (1995:9) would have it (recalling E. D. Hirsch's cultural literacy project), "providing all cultural groups with an equal chance to succeed in the economic system"? As Celia saw it, this goal was diametrically opposed to "the very essence of feminism and 'liberatory' peda-gogy, as defined by bell hooks and Paulo Freire": As she noted, hooks has writ-ten that feminism "is a struggle to eradicate sexist oppression. Therefore, it is necessarily a struggle to eradicate the ideology of domination that permeates Western culture on various levels as well as a commitment to reorganizing society so that the self-development of people can take precedence over impe-rialism, economic expansion, and material desires" (hooks 1984:24). Reject-ing Spring's assimilationist model, Celia determined to develop a program whose six weekly sessions, each an hour to an hour and a half in length, would "engage" the children in "an active consideration of the social systems of their world, that they might reflect [on] and transform it."

Her lesson plans were models of careful planning. Each began with (1) a clearly stated objective (e.g., "The purpose of this first session is to introduce the students to feminist core concepts of stereotyping vs. individual mutabil-ity; how gender, race, class, etc. influence perspective; and the position and power of privilege"); (2) an enumeration of the "materials and activities" designed to realize this objective (included among the materials required to meet the stated objective of lesson one was the beautiful young woman/ancient crone "equivocal figure" familiar to students of introductory psychol-ogy classes but not, one imagines, to many eleven-year-olds); and (3) an eval-uation instrument. By the end of the six-week course, Celia had involved the students in a variety of activities—viewing and discussing videotapes, engag-ing in make-believe assembly-line and cottage-style production, conducting oral history interviews—that had required them to engage in the kind of "problem-posing" Freire (1970/1983:67) posits as fundamental to liberatory educational praxis. Even the snacks she provided were "pedagogically cor-rect." (The snack provided for the second lesson, whose objective was "to introduce the concepts of diversity and assimilation," was fruit punch, "which was like assimilation, the fruit juices all blended together so that it was impos-sible to pick out individual juice," and trail mix, whose combination of nuts, raisins, M&Ms, and pretzels is "like various cultures within a society, unique but part of the whole"). Although (as the after-class evaluation forms Celia included in her final report made painfully clear) many of the children lacked basic communication skills, they managed to convey to Celia both during the semester and after, when they visited her in the kitchen, "that they did indeed 'get it.'" Of course, the long-term effects of Celia's pedagogical experiment, like those of our more conventional institutionalized versions of feminist edu-cation, are incalculable.

Another group of students also chose to work with young people in an after-school setting. Reading and discussing feminist theoretical writings about the body during the preceding semester's theory course had raised Amy, Jo, and Melissa's concern about the mostly deleterious effect the media has on young girls' self-esteem and body image. Like Celia, they began by creating a theoretical framework for their project, drawing on resources ranging from Carol Gilligan's and Lyn Mikel Brown's work on adolescent girls' development to a website (www.about-face.com) comprising "updated feminist-critiqued advertisements, examples of body-positive ads, body image discussion questions, advice to combat poor self-esteem as a result of this type of media, links to other similar websites, [and] an extensive bibliography." Using these resources, they sketched out ideas for a curriculum and placed calls to both private and public school administrators, seeking to find a middle school or junior high site where they could meet regularly during the semester with a group of ten- to fifteen-year-old girls to conduct activities and lead discussions on a variety of subjects including but not limited to body image, self-esteem, advertising, and the media. Whereas Alexis, Georgette, and Nikki were initially frustrated in their initial attempts to gain access to high-school students, Amy, Jo, and Melissa were utterly stymied in their efforts to reach middle-school students. School principals (mostly male) objected that both women's studies, the UNLV department the students said they represented, and the topics they wanted to broach in the workshops were "too controversial." All opined that "parents would not like this sort of thing" and two "even expressed fear that a lawsuit would result." Not until the students approached the local Girl Scouts council did they find a sympathetic audience for their proposal. They were invited to speak at a regular monthly meeting of troop leaders, where they presented a detailed written proposal and demonstrated two activities they might include in one of their workshops with a troop of Cadettes or Senior Scouts, their preferred audiences.

Enthusiastically applauded by the troop leaders, the students were ultimately invited to give two presentations, to two different groups of scouts, over the course of the semester—fewer than they had originally envisaged and lacking the continuity they would have sustained with the same group over a number of sessions. Nonetheless, their first 90-minute workshop, with a troop of 12 Cadettes aged 11 to 14, was an unqualified success. The girls responded enthusiastically to a series of activities, ranging from a self-esteem-building activity called "Advertising Me" that asked each girl to write an advertisement about herself emphasizing her good qualities, to carefully crafted journal questions encouraging reflection and introspective thinking that were analyzed after the workshop by Melissa, a psychology major and women's studies minor, and incorporated into the UNLV students'—though not the scouts'—evaluation of the workshop's effectiveness.

The students' second presentation was less thoroughly satisfying to both them and their audience. They were invited to address over one hundred girls at an evening event called Girls are Great. At a planning meeting with the troop of Senior Scouts who had invited them, the students presented a sample of possible activities, but were asked to program others that would not work with such a large group, ranging in age from 8 to 17. When they arrived at the site on the night scheduled for the event, they learned that—contrary to what they had been told—they were not the "main event" for Girls are Great. Worse yet, given their skepticism about (if not downright antipathy toward) the kinds of messages about body image communicated to girls through advertising and the media, their "competition" consisted of booths on make-up, swimwear fashions, and cheerleading. Against this backdrop, and further challenged by a defective public address system that made communicating with a hundred girls almost impossible, they valiantly conducted three of the four activities they had planned and left "discouraged but definitely not defeated," because they were confident that "analysis would put the Girls are Great night into better perspective."

And it did. Bearing in mind hooks's (1984:110) assurance that "any amount of time spent making women's studies available to the public would be significant," the students chose not to dwell on the night's obvious short-comings, observing instead that even less than perfect engagement in the activities had exposed the girls to some concepts basic to women's studies. Agreeing with hooks that "the ability to 'translate' ideas to an audience that varies in age, sex, ethnicity, and degree of literacy is a skill feminist educators need to develop" (p. 111), Amy, Jo, and Melissa believed that "one way to develop this skill is to dive in and see what happens" and that "the Girls are Great night was an important example of diving in, seeing what happens, and knowing that some exposure is better than no exposure at all."

Unlike Celia and the students in the Girl Scout project, Denise did not attempt to transport women's studies content and pedagogy outside the university's walls. Rather, her project was designed to help single mothers like herself gain access to higher education and the enhanced economic opportunities it promises. A senior who was employed 20 hours a week at the Nevada Institute for Children, Denise had access to data that added special urgency to her project (namely, that in Clark County—which includes greater Las Vegas—as in the nation at large, 60 percent of all families living in poverty are headed by women). Further research persuaded Denise of the statistical verifiability of the commonsense understanding that "education is a key determinant of economic success." Her own experience of returning to school as a single mother had taught her that there are resources available to help women return to an interrupted university education—or to begin an education. Realizing the lack of awareness about these resources she decided to disseminate this information as widely as possible.

Denise began by contacting offices at UNLV and the Community College of Southern Nevada (admissions, financial aid, and student services; reentry programs; women's centers and nontraditional student unions), and agencies in the city of Las Vegas, Clark County, and the state of Nevada (the transit system, the Economic Opportunity Board of Clark County, the Nevada Division of Welfare, the Nevada Empowered Women's Project, and the Association for Children for Enforcement of Support, whose local chapter Denise chairs) that might provide resources to her target population. Using literature collected from all these offices and agencies, she assembled information packets to distribute to participants in the College is Possible workshops she planned to lead.

The next step was locating and enticing women who would benefit from attending these workshops. She designed an attractive flyer advertising the workshops and solicited the aid of family resource centers, the welfare department, and the United Way in distributing copies to likely attendees. Like the group of students who attempted to organize after-school seminars and workshops, Denise failed to gain the active support of local agencies in furthering her project. She reached fewer women than she had hoped: she was able ultimately to conduct only two seminars, reaching a total of only ten women in that fashion. But because she was tireless in her efforts to make and sustain cordial relationships with local and state agencies, she was invited to attend both a professional development seminar organized by the welfare department and a community health fair, where she disseminated her information to social-service providers who at least might convey it to those it could help. Denise also conducted a number of what amounted to ad hoc consultations with women who called to say they couldn't attend one of her scheduled seminars but were interested in returning to school. On the whole, then, Denise considered that her project had been "a huge success." And there is every reason to believe it will have an afterlife, according to the concluding paragraph of Denise's final report for the praxis course:

> I recently helped write a grant (to the United Way) for the Nevada Institute for Children (NIC), to establish a program called Learn-to-Earn. One aspect of the program, which is targeted at teenage mothers, is the College is Possible seminar. If this grant is funded, this project which I . . . created for my praxis project will continue in an effort to provide information about resources available to single parents who wish to achieve higher education. I am very excited about the prospect of having this project taken up by NIC

and, if possible, I plan to continue being a part of the project by facilitating the seminars for the Learn-to-Earn program.

Some Concluding Reflections

The students in these two offerings of our Feminist Praxis course learned a significant amount. Some of what they learned was specific to the particular activist project they engaged in—for instance, Caryll and Kay's initiation into the processes used by certain feminist organizations in Nevada to organize regional and statewide events. Whatever their chosen project, all the students learned things that will stand them in good stead no matter what forms their postgraduate community activism may take. First, except for those few who elected to work alone, they learned a lot about feminist group process. This was easier for some than for others. As their peer evaluations clearly indicated, working together on the Girl Scout project was extremely satisfying for Amy, Melissa, and Jo ("My experience with Amy was all that I could have hoped for; I learned from her and she provided support when I needed it." "Melissa is such a wonderful person on a personal level that her work ethics are outstanding! I would definitely choose her as my partner anytime." "My group experience with Jo was amazing; we worked well together, inspiring one another, and we collaborated well together.") Alexis, Georgette, and Nikki, on the other hand, had not taken a course together before, much less worked together on a specific project. There were tensions in their group, and often the lines of communication broke down, leading to anger, resentment, and frustration. But they learned they could accomplish more when they communicated their needs and mutual expectations clearly and concluded, in Alexis's words, that "the glue that held us together through the semester" was the shared goal "to help the women's studies program become more visible in the community and to simply bring awareness to a younger generation about issues that affect women and men daily." Working on the Nevada Women's Summit, or organizing a high school outreach project or a series of workshops for Girl Scouts or single parents, taught students the importance of networking. The conclusion of Amy, Melissa, and Jo's report on the Girl Scout project may stand as a summary of what all the students who have taken our capstone seminar in feminist praxis took away with them:

> We learned how to organize in the face of rejection. We learned how to come together as a group to find common ground. We learned to deal with and overcome challenges, both anticipated and unexpected. . . . We learned that there is success amidst perceived failure or disappointment. We learned

to find our voice and fine-tune our politics. We learned skills necessary for group leadership and public speaking. We conclude that we have accomplished great things.

In 1997, reflecting a national obsession with what is known as "outcomes assessment," the provost required all academic units at UNLV to develop specific "learning goals" for students majoring in their discipline and detailed plans for assessing how well the students had achieved these goals by the time they submitted their applications to graduate. As I have previously said, the first of our three stated learning objectives was, "Students completing the baccalaureate program will connect women's studies scholarship and social activism and will be able to become agents of social change"(Women's Studies Program, 1997). The method we proposed for assessing how well students had met this objective as well as the other two (confidence in expressing themselves orally as well as in writing, an understanding of how multiple systems of oppression interact) was to ask a panel composed of women's studies faculty and members of our community advisory group—many of them exemplary social activists—to evaluate oral presentations of the projects completed by students of the capstone seminar in feminist praxis. This year's panel concluded that all the projects they were asked to evaluate "evidenced a committed and thoughtful linking of scholarship to activism." Commending the students for their "excellent research skills," confidence in "their knowledge of women's conditions," and enthusiasm "in sharing this knowledge with others," the evaluation team found it "truly inspiring to see the devotion and energy with which they approached their projects" (Brents, Duncan, and Fretwell, 2000, 1).

In short, both the students who have taken the praxis course and the faculty and community activists who have evaluated their achievement agree that this capstone seminar demonstrably works to assure that students who graduate from UNLV with a baccalaureate degree in women's studies are well prepared "to become agents of social change." But how and why it works are questions that we who have taught the course are hard pressed to answer.

Before I taught the spring 2000 offering of the course, I asked Barbara Brents, who was instrumental in designing the course and was its first instructor, what she would do differently if she were to teach it again. She described a need to "work on group process [the students working on the high-school outreach project, who had to overcome serious impediments to successful collaboration, were members of Brent's class]; insist on written contracts that spell out expectations, deadlines, and criteria for evaluation; discuss a list of common readings; set up a class listserv and require students to post to it regularly."

Because all but one of the students who took the course with me in spring 2000 had worked collaboratively on a final project in the feminist theory course the previous semester, I saw no need to spend class time explicitly working on group process mechanisms and was happy to be relieved of that responsibility since I have no formal training in facilitating effective group dynamics. Having taught these students in the theory course, I also knew how resistant they were to continuing class discussion on a listserv, so I didn't attempt to set one up. Though I did not require anything so formal as a contract, I did outline on the syllabus (and go over in class) detailed requirements for the project proposal they had to submit in the third week of the semester, including explicit criteria and procedures for evaluating both their project and their overall contribution to the course. All the reading and discussion we had shared in the theory course constituted a constant if unspoken subtext of the praxis course.

Like many women's studies instructors, I suspect, Brents and I brought to our teaching of this course our own history of feminist activism in the peace, environmental, and reproductive rights movements. But perhaps the students' greatest resource in developing their own activist philosophy and modus operandi was each other. The only "weakness" in the course that students mentioned in their end-of-semester evaluations was that there were too few class meetings, although they appreciated the time thus freed for work on their individual or group projects. What they gained and manifestly valued about the class meetings—distributed strategically throughout the first two-thirds of the course—that were devoted to oral presentations of their proposals, oral progress reports, and mutual assistance and brainstorming was the intelligent, informed interest of their peers and colleagues, who invariably suggested procedures and resources the project's designer(s) had not thought of.

I think it makes a difference that students take this course as the final, capstone experience of a two- or three-year course of study as a women's studies major or minor. Its participants speak a common language based on a set of basic concepts they have all studied in a pedagogical environment that is itself the creation of self-conscious planning and correlation among the faculty who teach in our program. Though some might question whether activist projects that were not connected in some way to feminist organizations can equip students to be effective agents of social change, the students in the feminist praxis course clearly acquired both organizational and communication skills and the confidence to employ those skills to effect feminist aims.

What makes this course "work," then, is not so much a technique of teaching students how to be activists as it is the cumulative experience of studying in a program whose underlying premise—which must have a structuring effect on the design of individual courses—is that a "successful" education in academic women's studies will result in students who almost automatically make connections between women's studies scholarship and social activism and are thus eminently well prepared—given the opportunity—to become agents of social change.

Notes

1. Not all women's studies practitioners would agree with my assertion, however. For instance, in a collective interview with other scholars and activists in a 1996 special issue of *Signs on Feminist Theory and Practice*, Charlotte Bunch suggested that few women's studies students are being encouraged to relate theory and practice, and accused today's women's studies programs of having strayed "far from the origin of women's studies, which was to use the academic arena to deepen our understanding of the problems women face and to encourage women to be activists" (Hartmann, et al. 1996, 936).

2. Thanks to Caryll Dziedziak, Georgette Gafford, Amy Goldstein, Kay Long, Melissa Mankins, Celia McGee, Alexis Rajnoor, Jo Svelan, Denise Tanata, and Nikki Thompson, students in Feminist Praxis who generously shared with me their reflections on praxis and whose journals and final reports provided vital data for this essay.

3. Of the 23 students who have graduated from UNLV with a B.A. in women's studies since 1992, seven went on to graduate or professional school (in anthropology, counseling, history, law, or library science).

4. Unless otherwise noted, all quotations are taken from students' journals and reports.

III

Teaching Intersectionally:
The Politics of Gender, Race,
Class, and Globalization

The question of what counts as feminist activism is further complicated by the commitment of many women's studies instructors to "teach intersectionally"—namely, to analyze the intersection of gender, race, ethnicity, class, sexuality, and nation without privileging one dimension of positionality. This commitment often includes the goal of locating feminist analyses and feminist politics in a global context. Furthermore, experiential educators' work necessarily extends beyond the confines of particular classrooms. In chapter 9, Kayann Short demonstrates how she helped promote students' awareness of the interactions among local experiences, personal economic decisions, and global political processes. Short describes a project developed by students in her Women and Society course and maintained over a five-year period. As the project has evolved, Short and her students have rejected the notion of liberatory potential within the concept of consumerism. Short emphasizes the importance of women's perspectives and leadership in the movement against the indiscriminate global expansion of capitalism.

In chapter 10, Anna Agathangelou discusses her work on globalization and feminist student activism. She encourages her students to critically reflect on their own social locations as they engage in debates with feminist scholarship and as they contribute to community-based efforts for social change. She also analyzes the effectiveness of her work to support students' engagement in transnational struggles. Agathangelou concludes with an assessment of the connections her students make with one another and with other community activists.

In chapter 11, Simona Hill focuses on fostering student activism in student clubs and organizations. She discusses the role of the Sisterhood, an undergraduate organization that provides support for women of color at a predominantly while liberal arts college. Hill describes how, in her role as club advisor, she helped students reach out to other women's organizations on campus and build a women's alliance that cuts across racial and class lines. Essential to building such an alliance was a frank discussion and acknowledgment of the difficulty women of color faced on campus.

As Patricia Washington notes in chapter 12, women's studies "has developed into a field of interdisciplinary intellectual inquiry that necessarily investigates the impact of race, sexual orientation, class, (dis)ability, and other social markers on the quality of life for women as well as men." The essays in this collection reflect a growing consensus that experiential education, whether defined as activism or as service learning, is a powerful tool to help students deepen their understanding of the interconnection of systems of oppression. Washington finds community-based service learning particularly useful for her as an African American lesbian teaching in a predominantly white university. Here many white students (as well as some students from other racial backgrounds) are often resistant to a feminism grounded in the critical analysis of the "intersectionality" of gender, race, sexual orientation, and class oppression. Washington reports that many students think "the course is—or should be—about 'generic' women . . . and are sometimes dismayed to learn that the course they have signed up for does not focus on 'generic woman' (devoid of race, nationality, economic status, sexuality, etc.) . . . but that they will, instead, be asked to consider 'woman' in her multiple social locations—not just her 'sex,' but her race, sexual orientation, economic class, and other social markers." Washington describes community-based service learning projects that she developed to enable students to better understand an intersectional approach. Washington, Short, Agathangelou, and Hill detail the challenges and rewards of implementing community action service learning projects to help students better understand an intersectional approach to feminist praxis. Despite some similarities in their approaches, each author has tailored their pedagogical strategies to the particular constraints and opportunities afforded by their very different institutional settings.

9

Global Feminism and Activism in a Women's Studies Practicum

Kayann Short

Hey. I am worth more than 20 cents an hour. I don't deserve to be exploited.
My work should matter just as much as any man's. I want my rights and it's
time I get them. No more wasteful shopping for me.

—Why Shop? Week shopping bag

Why Shop? Week is a service-learning practicum developed by students
in the Farrand Academic Program at the University of Colorado-
Boulder. Each fall, first- and second-year students in my Women and
Society course organize a community event and media campaign to raise
awareness regarding the link between consumption practices and the transnational exploitation of women's labor and resources. Why Shop? Week locates
women as both global producers of goods and services and as reproducers
who fill social and familial needs through consumption practices like shopping. By examining how consumerism affects women specifically, Why Shop?
Week initiates an international call to action for women's rights within a
global framework.

The University of Colorado is a campus of about 25,000 students located in
Boulder, a liberal, predominantly white, middle- to upper-middle-class community of about 100,000 residents. The Farrand Academic Program is a residential hall program of 400 students that offers small sections of core courses
within the dormitory environment, part of an attempt to place all first-year students within an "academic neighborhood." The focus of the Farrand program
is community service; one of the ways students can fulfill their community
requirement is through participation in a service-learning practicum associated
with a core course. Students enrolled in my Women and Society course can

earn one additional credit hour pass/fail for participation in the Why Shop? Week project. Although the practicum for my class is optional, most of the 20 students enrolled in the class choose to participate. Service-learning practicums are intended to provide an opportunity for students to combine theory with praxis, a goal I share in developing the WS?W practicum.

Why Shop? Week begins the Sunday before Thanksgiving with a rally at our downtown pedestrian mall, and incorporates other activities and campaigns such as the International Day of Activism Against Gender Violence and International Buy Nothing Day. Besides creating a performance piece for the rally, students conduct a media campaign by coordinating a website and producing outreach materials such as shopping-bag art, videotapes, interviews, press releases, brochures, and flyers. Events in previous years have included a play, *So You Think You Had a Hard Day?*; an alternative fashion show, *Crimes of Fashion*; and a beauty pageant, *Ms. Assembly Line*, featuring industrial and agricultural women workers and a red, white, and blue-spangled Ms. Super Shopper as contestants.

In this essay, I will consider how the WS?W project helps students develop a transnational feminist approach to issues such as labor exploitation, globalization of capital, sexual violence, environmental degradation, and the growing disparity in consumption worldwide. By examining the dominance of fashion and shopping in their own lives, my students begin to analyze how their roles as both consumers and producers of what we call the 'buy it/be it" mentality position them as commodified subjects in a global marketplace. During Why Shop? Week, consumers are urged to make ethical purchasing decisions by identifying companies that exploit women and children; demanding corporate accountability for global working conditions; and consuming less during the holiday season—as well as the rest of the year. These practices can collectively begin to establish new patterns of social justice and economic development that value women's autonomy and equality, as well as environmental sustainability. I will also examine how this critique has catalyzed difficult examinations of the relationship between individual practices and social change, including questions regarding the limitations of consumer action in a corporate-"sponsored" world. In particular, my paper will outline how our original *consumerist* theoretical approach to WS?W has shifted to a concept of *ethical consumption* that challenges individualistic anticonsumer campaigns such as *voluntary simplicity*. In contrast to such campaigns, WS?W seeks to engage students—and shoppers—in a dialogue about social justice and equality in a globalized economy by focusing on women's rights through collaborative learning and collective action.

Additionally, I will discuss how WS?W faces the challenge of transnational feminist coalition amidst women's increasing economic and social disparity both within and between nations. Consumerism exploits this divide by commodifying women as either shoppers or production workers in the global assembly line, categories constituted as mutually exclusive and racially and geographically overdetermined. While women in the developed (or overdeveloped) world make purchasing decisions that have the potential to exploit or empower other women, shopping itself is often predicated on female disempowerment. Likewise, women workers' lack of wealth and bargaining power is often misconstrued solely as victimization, thus negating autonomy and agency. Calls for an idealized sisterhood may neglect women's real struggles to retain diverse identities, particularly given imperialist and colonialist histories. WS?W looks to a feminism with which women can both resist mutual commodification by corporate globalization and create a new model of economic progress that starts with female autonomy and empowerment.

In the Spirit of Beijing

I began to think about developing a service-learning practicum for my Women and Society course in the summer of 1996 after attending a conference in Denver that featured a panel of local women who had participated in the 1995 United Nations Fourth World Conference on Women in Beijing and the corresponding Non-Governmental Organization [NGO] conference in Huairou. Together with Karen Beeks, organizer for the post-Beijing conference, I initiated a project focusing on how a common female-gendered activity—shopping—links individual consumption practices to women's exploitation. We decided to focus on two strategic objectives from the Beijing Platform for Action. The first, strategic objective F.1, assigns states responsibility to "[p]romote women's economic rights and independence, including access to employment, appropriate working conditions and control over economic resources." Why Shop? Week serves as a vehicle to educate consumers about salary inequities, gender role segregation, labor discrimination, collective bargaining repression, inhumane working conditions, and inadequate legislative protections for women workers, particularly in multinational free trade zones and U.S. sweatshops.

The second strategic objective we employ, J.1, calls for an "[i]ncrease [in] the participation and access of women to expression and decision-making in and through the media and new technologies of communication." The question most frequently asked by students in this project is, Why doesn't anyone know about these problems? By writing press releases, maintaining media contacts, updating the website, and conducting local radio and newspaper interviews, they experience firsthand the difficulty of accessing media with a complex and unpopular message.

The first Why Shop? Week was actually only one Why Shop? Day, held the Sunday before Thanksgiving in 1996. That year we worked on creating the WS?W logo and message, which we refined to three main points:

1. Know the story behind the product. Who makes it? Who needs it? And who profits from it?
2. Exercise your economic power.
3. Consume less. Don't buy what you don't need.

Once we determined our message, we needed to reach the public, which meant attracting media attention. Thinking that our local indoor mall was the place for action, we asked for permission to use the community event booth, which we unfortunately discovered was in the darkest, farthest reaches of the mall. When we attempted to approach shoppers outside the community booth area, however, we were "busted" by mall security (we were also reprimanded for videotaping, which, of course, we caught on videotape), and told to remain within the area we soon dubbed the "community containment booth." We did get a small notice in our local paper, based mostly on facts from our then rudimentary website. Despite that year's limited community contact, we learned a lot about outreach and the necessity of creating a media-friendly event.

The following year we expanded the campaign to a full week and moved the rally to our outdoor pedestrian mall, again on the Sunday before Thanksgiving. Despite the cold weather, many people stopped to view our Why Shop? Bag display, sign postcards urging corporate responsibility from their favorite businesses, and challenge students about the issues. We were even featured on a Denver television news station and on local radio. A couple of days before the rally we had staged a campus presentation of a *Jeopardy*-style game show featuring categories like "Sweatshops," "Wage and Land Distribution," and "Discrimination." We also had performed a skit titled *And You Think You Had a Hard Day?* portraying a sweatshop on one side of the stage and two college-age shoppers on the other. The two scenes converged at the end as the shoppers threw "outdated" clothing out of their closets onto the heads of the exhausted workers. Although these skits were effective in both transmitting information to audiences and provoking discussion of complex issues, campus attendance and media attention were minimal, so the lesson we learned that year was that the pedestrian mall provided a more "message-friendly" venue, promising a more effective location for future performances.

The third year we staged an alternative fashion show entitled *Crimes of Fashion: Are They Worth It?* on the mall in front of the courthouse plaza. As models showcasing athletic, young executive, vacation, and evening fashions paraded down the makeshift runway to a driving beat, two announcers revealed conflicting perspectives on the fashion industry. While the first announcer hyped the chic style of an Adidas running suit, the second announcer responded, "Speaking of jogging, Adidas can jog from country to country as their workers demand more money or better working conditions, while workers in athletic wear factories get their exercise running from the riot police, who are sent in at the first sign of organizing." The performance attracted not only excellent media attention, but great crowds as well, proving the enduring appeal of costumes and music in capturing public interest.

For 1999's rally we organized a mock beauty pageant called *Ms. Assembly Line* that featured contestants from various global industries—Ms. Appliance Assembler, Ms. Produce Picker, Ms. Sweatshirt Sewer, and Ms. Sneaker Stitcher, as well as Ms. Super Shopper, a representative of overconsumption. The purpose of Ms. Assembly Line was to reveal the disparity between women's globalized roles as consumers and producers: while advertisers ask women in industrialized or "overdeveloped" countries like the United States to equate shopping with freedom or happiness, many women in the so-called developing world are working long hours at low wages in deplorable conditions to produce the goods most "first world" women enjoy. To illustrate these roles, the pageant's talent segment featured contestants from garment, athletic shoe, appliance, and agricultural businesses demonstrating their production skills while a red, white, and blue-sequined Ms. Super Shopper "swiped" a hefty credit card tab. Predictably, Ms. Super Shopper won the crown. As she sauntered down the runway in her feather boa to the familiar pageant tune, the revised lyrics mocked the notion of freedom within a consumer-driven world economy in which the only way to "win" is to shop:

> There she is
> Ms. Assembly Line
> There she is
> not quite your ideal
> With so little money her life is below the norm
> With her malnourished face and form
> She is the poorest of the poor
> Except in the U.S.
> Where she has more and more
> She's . . . Ms. Assembly Line!

Over the years we have created many resources to help consumers consider their own connection to international exploitation. We have designed brochures outlining simple steps for making purchasing decisions. We have also created a website at <spot.colorado.edu/~shortk/whyshop.html> with links to allied organizations and campaigns. The website includes a postcard that can be sent to corporations asking them to take responsibility for the conditions under which their products—and profits—are made, as well as tips for practicing ethical consumption and staging community events. The site also features media clips and a webgallery of our favorite shopping bags.

One of the most successful components of the project is the decorating of shopping bags to visually capture the attention of shoppers strolling along our pedestrian mall. Hung on large frames and strung along tables and railings, the bags prove the perfect instrument for both showcasing student creativity and inciting consumer engagement. We use ads or photos from fashion magazines to create commentary on global resource disparity, labor exploitation, and worker oppression. For example, one bag featuring a model's body with the superimposed head of a sweatshop worker bears the heading Miss Free Trade Zone and includes statistics compiled by groups like the National Labor Committee, UNITE (Union of Needletrades, Industrial and Textile Employees), and Sweatshop Watch.

Sometimes the bags comment on the ads themselves. One responds to the shoe ad slogan "All She Needs" with the question "Is This Really All Women Need?" Many of the bags connect labor exploitation in developing countries with harmful beauty standards in industrialized countries by exposing the dangers of the fashion and diet industries. For example, one bag links anorexia with resource overconsumption by juxtaposing the emaciated body of a supermodel with the words Consume Less. Umm, We Didn't Mean Food. Another features a photo of an enormous walk-in closet with wall-to-wall shoes and asks, "When is enough enough?" Each year we have expanded community support by inviting local groups to participate as speakers and at information tables. For example, one year a member of the local feminist theater group, Vox Femina, performed She-Wrecks, the story of a mother so fed up with her children's consumer demands that she turns into a giant dinosaur who devours all technological devices. Rallies have also included The Radical Cheerleaders from the Colorado University student group WAAKE-UP (World Awareness and Action Koalition of Equal United Progressives). As our rallies have become more performance based, students are challenged to use their creative skills as well as intellectual ones. Also, with increased public attention to the issues of globalization, overconsumption, and labor exploitation, particularly in sweatshops, we have more resources available to share with community members each year.

Beyond teaching the Women and Society course that introduces the issues we examine in WS?W, my role within the project is one of facilitator. While many of WS?W's aspects are established, such as the Sunday rally and the website, the students themselves must determine the messages and formats for these venues. By sharing videotape clips of earlier rallies and a scrapbook and photo album that document WS?W's history, I encourage each year's group of students to build on the work of previous WS?W organizers. Collaborating with first-year students requires a subtle balance of guidance and flexibility, an approach somewhere between "top down" and "hands off." While I set the pace and offer lots of feedback, I must be willing to follow their lead.

In 2000, for example, the students thoroughly rejected my idea to rewrite "The Twelve Days of Christmas" because "they just didn't get it." Instead, they proposed utilizing a talk show format in a segment devoted to "shopping addiction." Titled *Shop 'Til They Drop*, the skit features Cher, a teen shopper from Beverly Hills; Grandma Claus, an overly generous holiday shopper; Mikey Swoosh, a Nike fanatic; and Annie Smith, a high-school student addicted to beauty products. Experts helped guests face their addictions by educating them about their consumption habits. The show also included a choreographed chinos-style commercial and a spoof of diet ads. Without my accepting a less prominent role as each project develops, the students would never engage each other so creatively. The process really illustrates one former student's evaluation: "With more minds we were able to come up with lots of good ideas."

Where Are the Women?

With each WS?W campaign, we must reevaluate both our mission and our message in response to women's changing roles amidst increasing globalization as well as organized protests against indiscriminate growth and corporate rule around the world. As with previous resistance movements, however, women's perspectives are often absent, marginalized, or misrepresented within these debates. As Cynthia Enloe (1989:200) reminds us, "It is all too easy to plunge into the discussion of [contemporary issues] without asking, 'Where are the women?'" Precisely because many of these antiglobalization organizations do not focus primarily on women's issues, the WS?W campaign continues to develop a transnational feminist critique.

As protests heat up regarding the rapid spread of U.S.-styled consumption to other countries—or, as they're more commonly labeled, "markets"—rhetoric escalates. Language similar to that of the "population bomb" (the hysterical perception of irresponsible "third world" reproduction leading to worldwide food shortages) is echoed in statements such as "we would need the resources and absorptive capacities of four more earths for all six billion humans to live the lifestyle of the average American." The implication behind this "statistic" is that such consumption must be prevented in order to preserve what is most at stake: the continuation of "first world" affluence. In contrast, the *conundrum of consumption*, a term coined by Alan Durning in his 1992 book *How Much is Enough? The Consumer Society and the Future of the Earth*, refers to the idea that while a worldwide consumerist lifestyle is not environmentally sustainable, the equitable right to this lifestyle for all is only socially just. According to the 1998 *United Nations Development Report*, 20 percent of the world's population consumes 86 percent of the world's resources, while the poorest 20 percent consume only 1.3 percent. This "champagne glass" model, in which the resource consumption of the world's wealthiest fifth is represented by the glass's wide cup, the middle three-fifths by the narrow stem, and the poorest fifth by the flat base, strikingly illuminates gross inequality and disparity in access to goods and resources, rather than scarcity, as poverty's root cause. As Maria Mies suggests in "Liberating the Consumer" (1993:253), "If sustainability and self-sufficiency is good for people in poor countries then it must also be good for those in the rich countries: a double standard is not acceptable." Feminists, then, must critique consumerism without assuming the rhetoric of "third world" rapaciousness.

As WS?W has evolved, we have rejected the notion of liberatory potential within the concept of consumerism. In the first two years of the WS?W project, we used the term *ethical consumerism* to describe what we then thought of as "better shopping practices" that could strengthen resistance to female subordination in both cultural production and reproduction. As explained in our original brochure, *ethical consumerism* incorporated the idea that one could "vote with one's pocketbook" and that "one dollar equals one vote." Our original slogan— "Together we hold the world's purse strings"—suggested that participating in market forces could lead to women's empowerment and social change. As we learned more about the forces of global capital, however, we realized that *ethical consumerism* could only be oxymoronic since *consumerism* itself implies that purchasing products leads to economic "progress" and so-called free trade. Clearly, such a narrow definition of progress is inimical to women's equal civil and social participation. Furthermore, because free market systems are unconcerned with ending women's subordination (and are indeed predicated on the same for ever cheaper labor and expanded markets for "women's" goods such as beauty products, diet drugs, and tobacco), women's rights activists cannot look to such systems for liberatory strategies. Thus "voting" with one's "pocketbook" provides at best a compromised strategy that ineffectually confuses civic participation and political activism with consumerism.

Currently we use the term *ethical consumption* to incorporate both the demand for corporate accountability toward business practices that ensure human rights and the decreased dependence on buying products for personal and national status. This term challenges the elitist and ethnocentric view of shopping as an "American" right, as one letter to our local paper in response to our first year's event. *Ethical consumption* recognizes that everyone is dependent upon structural forces for access to goods and services, but acknowledges that possibilities for agency exist within those structures. WS?W offers operations of gender in conjunction with nationality, race, and class as criteria for evaluating how consumption practices affect women as cultural producers and reproducers, as workers and shoppers.

While WS?W still emphasizes individual consumption practices, it does so only to foreground their political and social impact. For example, by urging shoppers to "know the story behind the product" and "exercise economic power," we suggest that such actions constitute collective action toward women's global empowerment. This concept is still evolving in our campaign as we continue to inform our critique of globalization by studying historically, culturally, and geographically specific situations of women's experiences as both producers and consumers. The more clearly we can view ourselves and our actions within the larger context of women's attempts to determine their own roles in globalization, the better we can shape WS?W in effective feminist coalition. For example, while boycotting exploitative companies is generally a simple action for U.S. consumers to follow given our many product choices, we must follow the lead of factory workers and organizers regarding the advisability of targeted boycotts in order not to cost some workers their jobs without their consent.

WS?W also offers a feminist perspective missing from the "voluntary simplicity" movement. While it shares this movement's call to confront consumerism as an ecologically and socially bankrupt ideology, it does so from the basis of equality and justice, not spiritually improved individual lifestyles. By definition, the message of the voluntary simplicity concept is preached to "volunteers"—those who can afford to live more simply because they have the status and resources to do so (witness the many innovative products and cheerful catalogs geared to "self-sufficiency" and "ecological efficiency"). Obviously, "voluntary simplicity" is not readily accessible to those who are already living a life of deprivation due to poverty, prejudice, or war. This distinction is particularly relevant for women, who are more likely to experience deprivation due to gender subordination.

Sisters in Global Struggle

Feminists must work diligently to keep women's voices and experiences at the center of the globalization debates, yet we must also constantly analyze what we mean by "women's voices and experiences." Clearly, disparities of economic status, political representation, and social empowerment allow for the configuration of some women as subjects more readily than of others, at the same time that these factors account for significant differences in access to material goods and opportunities. According to Rajeswari Mohan in "The Crisis of Femininity and Modernity in the Third World" (1994:224), "In general the question of political responsibility of feminist intellectuals, the issue of theory's responsiveness to the heterogeneity of women's concerns, and the recognition of the urgent need for globally articulated accounts of women's oppression have placed on feminist discourses enormous burdens. . . . " As members of a predominantly white, middle-class, U.S. university environment, my students and I must confront both our privilege and oppression in fashioning such accounts, necessitating an uncomfortable and destabilized subject position as both oppressor and oppressed. How does one speak from this unsettled place? Does such a position lead merely to the disavowal or appropriation of critical differences or does it create the possibility of affiliation and what Bina Agarwal (1996:231) calls "strategic sisterhood"?

The epigraph at the beginning of this article—the text accompanying a fashion image of a white model on one Why Shop? Week shopping bag—remains problematic for me in its apparent blurring of worker and consumer, assuming that the "I" worth more than "20 cents an hour" and the "me" eschewing "wasteful shopping" cannot occupy the same subject position. Yet that assumption itself merely reifies a "first world"/"third world" paradigm that categorizes, in Mohan's terms, the third world as "backward" and the first world as "modern."

> The third world is seen to be ruled by religion, irrationality, superstition, backwardness, underdevelopment, overpopulation, and political chaos. . . . The first world is completely modern, running smoothly on the oiled wheels of scientific and utilitarian decision making. . . . Within this schema, traditional societies are seen as earlier forms of modern societies, awaiting their destiny of modernization.

With modernization today defined by conspicuous consumption, why wouldn't—or shouldn't—women earning only 20 cents an hour assume their place in the modern consumer world through shopping, including "wasteful" spending? At the same time, the bag alludes to the possibility of a unified struggle against sexist devaluation of women's work, including unpaid care work, which should be valued as highly as any man's. If this alliance, though, is predicated solely on gender and the subordination of women to men, any formation of sisterhood may only serve to ignore the hierarchical value of some women's work over others, as in, for example, the "work" of shopping over that of manufacturing. Furthermore, the individualistic call to "rights" marks the text again as "American" and seems to foreclose the possibility of collective action and the guaranteeing of freedoms to all women. It also implies that rights can be claimed through the individualistic action of not shopping, certainly implying the kind of "consumer choice" much revered by U.S. shoppers.

Yet even in its conflation of women's subject positions, the bag suggests how institutionalized concepts of "women's work" and "women workers" are transnationally aligned by what Chandra Mohanty (1997:28) calls "the logic and operation of capital in the contemporary global arena" and Maria Mies (1986:2) terms "a global division of labour under the dictates of capital accumulation." As Mohanty (1991:22) asserts, failure to thoroughly interrogate these conditions leads to the assumption that "the third world just has not evolved to the extent that the West has." Similarly, Laura Hyun Yi Kang (1997:417) critiques white Western feminists' comparison of "third world" women's struggles in "relation to conditions faced by American workers in earlier, darker times of their capitalist development" such as the nineteenth-century "factory girls" of Manchester, England or Lowell, Massachusetts.

A feminist critique of consumption must avoid the myth of progress that places "first world" women as potential "saviors" of their "less fortunate sisters." Mohanty (1991:58) proposes that "third world" women today form a strategic group based on "the common context of political struggle against class, race, gender, and imperialist hierarchies." Is it possible that "first world" women could be included in the "common context" of antiglobalization discourse and activism without appropriating the historically and culturally specific struggles of "third world" women? WS?W attempts to structure such an alliance through asking students—and shoppers—to analyze their roles as both producers and consumers without constructing a hierarchy of difference. In other words, all women must both produce and consume as women within their specific geopolitical locations, with those roles constituted not only by gender but simultaneously by race, class, nationality, sexuality, and ability as well. To step outside those roles is to subvert the maintenance of both male privilege and the myth of global progress. As women are increasingly commodified by transnational market interests, they must find new ways to transcend structural domination. Shoe manufacturers like Nike and New Balance, for example, advertise jobs for "females only"—and young, single women only at that—while U.S. advertisers portray the purchase of material goods as liberation. These tactics naturalize factory workers as "third world" and shoppers as "first world," a formula that overlooks labor exploitation in the United

States and the purchasing practices of women outside the United States. Both these assignments also deny the multiple forms of agency and resistance practiced by real women, from factory workers organizing for collective bargaining rights to students demanding "sweat-free" products.

My students come to an understanding of commodification most easily through their own involvement with the fashion and beauty industries. Interestingly, while they often experience beauty standards as tyrannical and omnipotent, they rarely attribute the power of those standards to the industries themselves. They critique the role of unrealistic appearance ideals in their own disempowerment but fail to attribute such ideals to institutions beyond magazines and movies or to see those media as part of the larger structures. Only after we discuss how the standards themselves, and not just the advertising of those standards, creates enormous corporate profits with ties to the pharmaceutical, tobacco, and textile industries do the students recognize how fully these standards dominate their lives.

Students are most critical of messages that focus on women's bodies—and particularly weight—as measures of women's worth. They often bring advertisements to class that feature extremely thin models and participate eagerly in discussions of eating disorders. Some have or have had such disorders themselves or have friends who are struggling with these problems. While students initially attribute the cause of eating disorders to advertising alone, they welcome discussions that place the disorders within the larger context of women's disempowerment. Here eating disorders can be understood as a kind of "self-consumption" in which a woman starves herself in a desperate, illusory attempt to control the very life that is being destroyed. Ultimately, students begin to juxtapose eating and not eating with culturally specific relationships to food and hunger.

Some of the most provocative WS?W bags feature pictures and slogans that complicate women's connections to food. One bag, for example, portrays the nude back of a thin white model and asks, "What's worse? Not eating or eating too much?" Yet does "not eating" here refer to anorexia or to hunger? Is "eating too much" a sign of addiction or affluence? When viewed through the lens of both gender and nation, the question demands a structural, rather than personal, answer. Further, advertising images are certainly racialized and increasingly globalized, as well. Mohan (1994:254) refers to Ms., an Indian cigarette for women that celebrates women who are "not subservient, not coquettish, not wily, not other-worldly pure . . . not as men have traditionally thought them to be," as a "striking instance of the recruitment of the image of feminism as an invitation to conspicuous consumption." Likewise, Virginia Slims sports a new "multicultural" campaign that features women of various cultural backgrounds (many in "traditional" dress) with the slogan "Find your voice." By developing an in-depth critique of such ads and the dangerous physical addictions behind them, students begin to theorize their own complicity in both consuming and perpetuating such disempowering norms, as well as the continued dominance of such standards in society today.

Cigarettes, fashion clothing, diet aids, and beauty products are common purchases of college-aged women. WS?W attempts to challenge the normalization of these purchases by placing them in a transnational context. To use Mies's (1986:234) example, when a corporation like Unilever, producer of Dove and Lever soaps, Vaseline Intensive Care lotion, Finesse shanpoo, Surf detergent, and Mentadent toothpaste, employs women in the jungle areas of Bihar, India to collect seeds from the sal tree for lipstick production, the women are deprived of control over what was formerly a resource for their own use. This example shows how beauty products carry human, as well as ecological, costs. Yet a boycott of lipstick may only serve to sacrifice the jobs these workers now have. One proposal may be to provide "first world" women entrepreneurial opportunities working with indigenous women in forming alternative businesses—the "trade not aid" model—while a more directly beneficial but less expedient approach may support local control of resources, along with the establishment of a women's cooperative to bargain for prices collectively.

Such differing models of development raise questions regarding how "first world" women can participate in and contribute to "third world" women's empowerment without reifying global privilege. Questions like these draw students and the public into difficult confrontations with U.S. privilege that unsettle assumptions about cultural dominance. While students may begin to realize the privileges they have enjoyed as U.S. citizens and consumers, however, they often do not feel simultaneously empowered, particularly as they worry about their futures within what they perceive as an unstable, uncaring global economy. They are especially compelled by the fact that factory workers are usually women their own age and they find the lack of opportunity afforded these women as the epitome of injustice. They are moved by the remarks of a Vietnamese Nike employee interviewed on CBS News's *48 Hours* who cannot even afford to buy a pair of the very shoes she produces. Because students are reluctant to speak for women workers in the FTZ and sweatshops, our project makes much use of secondary sources that foreground women's voices such as the UNITE and Sweatshop Watch websites linked to our site and texts like *The Maquiladora Reader* (Kamel and Hoffman 1999). We also occasionally have the opportunity to hear firsthand from the women factory and agricultural workers themselves during International Women's Week or at other speaking events. The students are understandably even more hesitant to speak *as* women workers, a situation that became evident in the differences between the Crimes of Fashion and Ms. Assembly Line performances. In the former, the script allowed them to incorporate facts and statistics about women workers within the familiar format of the fashion show. In the latter, however, the students were asked to play the roles of the workers and often seemed at a loss for material, yet the same information and testimonies were available to them for the fashion show as for the beauty pageant. The difference was all the more evident in the contrast between the contestants' portrayals, with Ms. Super Shopper an enthusiastically campy version of Ms. America that allowed for satire in a way the other roles did not. Such anxiety mirrors feminist debates over "authenticity" found in the work of critics such as Mohan, Mohanty, and Gayatri Spivak, and many others—an issue that we begin to address in the classroom and through the project itself.

What Students Gain from Their Participation in Why Shop? Week

Students' evaluations suggest that, first and foremost, they learn from WS?W that "you can make a difference." Comments emphasize "how much work it takes to put on an event like this" but that "if we put effort into it, we can make a difference or at least inform others about this issue." Other students have remarked that they have "learned how to work cooperatively as a group" to "make a project come together in the end." At the same time, students respond that they understand "more about what the women workers go through in sweatshops" and that the project "forced us to take the information that we learned about in class and then personalize it by having us look directly at the stores we buy from." They also relate lessons concerning community response: "I also learned that there are lots of supporters out there, but at the same time some people just don't care about women's rights and human rights." Finally, students remark on how the project helps them turn knowledge into activism: "Although it was hard to digest the myriad of new information concerning a world that I thought I understood, the challenge encouraged me to want to contribute my own piece to the world pie, however small it may be." WS?W requires students to consider theoretical aspects of globalization beyond anything previously encountered within their educational experiences. The project helps students confront their own positions in a system that depends upon interlocking inequities and subordination, while gaining practical organizing skills that help them challenge such injustices. Admittedly, the vision of "solidarity" projected by WS?W is both uneasy and often one-sided, a problem I will continue to address in my facilitation. At best, I hope to ground WS?W within what Caren Kaplan (1997:139) calls "a practice of affiliation, a politics of location [that] identifies the grounds for historically specific differences and similarities between women in diverse and asymmetrical relations. . . . " Such a practice of affiliation may ultimately transform not only my students' understanding of the world around them, but the world in which they live as well.

10

Globalization and Radical Feminist Pedagogy

Anna M. Agathangelou

I understood that I could feel sorrow . . . yet not confuse their sorrow with mine, or use their resistance for mine. . . . I could hear their songs like a trumpet to me: a startling . . . a challenge: but not take them as a replacement for my own work.

—Minnie Bruce Pratt, "Identity: Skin/Blood/Heart"

Globalization and Feminism: What's the Relationship?

In this chapter, I present the processes and projects that evolved in two feminist courses addressing globalization, and illustrate three organizing principles of feminist student activism. I provide an account of the processes I used in my courses to not only serve the larger community of the college but also to encourage the future social accountability and activism of my students. The research papers and collective presentations discussed here represent opportunities for students to question their own personal location in relation to the feminist scholarship they read and the communities in which they live and work. I explore the ways in which I work with students to use their transnational struggles to achieve self-empowerment through critique (self- and collective evaluation). I also describe the connections my students make with each other and other community activists that helped them forge potential alliances in the work of social change.

Feminist Knowledge Production in a U.S. Academic Context

The American college and factory engage in parallel processes: mass production, profit orientation, and a focus on the individual. College is both a site, and a set, of globalized relations. While we do not learn *all* about the transnational political economy there, we do gain insight into the history of the capitalist mode of production, especially its unevenness in the fields of knowledge and production of ideas. The main processes of the neoliberal economy are prevalent in the academic context and in our classrooms. Examples include the sexual, racial, and class division of labor, mobilities of capital that reinforce old and new oppressions, and the desire of this structure to reproduce itself by finding and exploiting "human needs that can be transformed into needs met by commodity production and exchange" (Alternative Orange 1991:1). However, globalization also brings to the academy opportunities to challenge oppressions and exploitation through individual and collective strategies of resistance.

At Oberlin College, a midwestern liberal arts college, I taught two courses on globalization and feminist social change in which I attempted to develop such strategies. The demographics of the student body were 92 percent white, 5 percent black, and 3 percent Asian and Hispanic. Sixty-five percent of the student body was female, and 30 percent were queer. Two-thirds of the students were from upper-middle-class and upper-class backgrounds, and one-third was from a working-class background, attending via scholarships and grants. Using a transnational materialist feminist lens,[1] and focusing on the "local" issues and practices exhibited in an academic site, I show that students' activism exhibits effects of globalization—dominant (neo)colonial versions of history are imposed on gendered and racialized bodies, markets, and academic sites but relations of domination are also resisted.

Gendering the Global and Local Circuits of Capital and Labor

Teaching globalization's emergence from a historical perspective and locating its implications on our present social and economic relations challenge an academic context that has focused on producing "practical" knowledges and subjectivities for the free market. Even interdisciplinary sites, like that of women's studies, which emerged out of repeated contestations of such knowledges and practices, have been colonized by this academic institutional imperative. Consequently, I divided these two courses into two parts: (1) historical development of the neoliberal world order and feminist visions about the world, and (2) feminist social change through transborder feminist solidarities. I began the courses by posing the following questions: How do we teach globalization courses in Women's Studies so that such knowledges become theories of liberation? In what kinds of liberatory or pedagogical practices must one participate in order to decolonize oneself and community simultaneously?[2]

The first section of the course was designed to prepare students for activist work they were to undertake in the latter part of the semester. The time was used to mark one's positionality (in regard to race, sex, class, ability, etc.) and the kinds of territories one comes to structurally occupy. We also tackled the questions of how globalization processes use these positionalities as the grounds on which discursive practices are translated by dominant powers and how these processes implicate one's intervention in feminist social change. Early in the course, students were asked to identify their personal understandings of globalization and feminist social change, and asked to theorize their connection to the phenomena. They were also asked to explore this relationship in conjunction with the feminist scholarship they were reading and the sociopolitical problems women and men face in a global context.

Each week students read one to three chapters from the assigned texts: *A History of Capitalism 1500–1980* by Michel Beaud (1983); *Nations Unbound: Transnational Projects, Postcolonial Predicaments, and Deterritorialized Nation-States*, edited by Linda Basch, Nina Glick Schiller, and Cristina Szanton Blanc (1994); *Patriarchy and Accumulation on a World Scale: Women in the International Division of Labour*, by Maria Mies (1986b); *Women in the Global Factory*, edited by Annette Fuentes and Barbara Ehrenreich (1984); *A Question of Class*, by Lindsey German (1996); *Feminist Genealogies, Colonial Legacies, Democratic Futures*, by Jacqui Alexander and Chandra Mohanty; *Silence: Poets on Women, Violence and Silence*, by Susan McMaster (1998); and selected pieces from a reader I designed. These texts were chosen because they historicize the development of the world capitalist system; the processes that mark this development; the relationships that emerged at historical moments, such as in particular social movements; and the emergence of resistant subjectivities against oppressive sociopolitical and economic powers. I used the readings to make connections between individual actions and their social, historical, and cultural contexts.

During the first half of each class session we would discuss the readings and the implications of such theorizations on feminism. The second half was devoted to making connections between global theories and our personal lives. Students were also asked to submit weekly journal reflections on the feminist scholarship they were reading. As a course requirement, journal writing provided students the opportunity to engage the readings, track their own development as feminists, and encourage them to envision themselves as agents within the larger global community. The first step in this process was to get students thinking about their location and their standpoint.

Anna M. Agathangelou

Demystifying One's Location and Contesting the Commodification of "Radical" Learning

Contestations emerged in the classroom especially around the issue of "who has the right to be the most radical on campus." Some students taking the course saw themselves as "radical" because they had already involved themselves in activism on campus or engaged some of these issues intellectually in their dorm spaces. A white, middle-class, Jewish female student wrote, "The other day, I was so angry at what another student said about [her] involvement in social change. She seems to imply that because she is a working class woman and a lesbian she understands all about social change. She seems to think that she is the most RADICAL of all of us in this context. I do not think so." Another student wrote, "I do not understand why we read texts like Mies (1986b). She is so difficult and does not make her points accessible like hooks ([1995] 1989). Also, I am very frustrated with my classmates who have not read texts by hooks and Malcolm X. They do not understand anything about racial or sexual politics. Why did they take the course?"

Since embodied pedagogies require us to examine the positions adopted in relation to specific bodies of knowledge and people, I asked students to engage their own frustrations with the readings. By engaging these journal entries regarding who is "the most radical," we contextualized the desire to be the most radical on campus. This desire, though useful in a context lacking social deference, reflected masculinist, racist, and classist practices that perpetuate asymmetrical social relations. If, as feminists, we were interested in actively intervening and directing efforts toward challenging dominant masculine racist structures, we could not afford to alienate ourselves from each other through commodification of knowledge, criticism, and evaluations of radicalism. Our fear of revealing the unequal distribution of privileges and vulnerabilities within the classroom made it difficult to move away from criticism of who or what was "bad" or "good."

In the classroom, I called upon students to "own" their ideas and arguments as representations of social positions. Most comparisons among students of who was the "most radical" occurred between white students and older students of color and reflected contestations among students' claims to different ideological and material identities on campus. Students of color, and some working class students, defended their "radicalness" in a multiculturalist (national identity) form, arguing that it emerged out of their social location and that white upper-class students would never understand their oppression (racism, homophobia, classism, heterosexism). This multicultural alternative with a corresponding ideology of "radical" political consciousness seemed to align itself with the ideology of the market. The radicalness of students of color became a political tool and an activist slogan to be consumed alongside other commodities that presume the individual is a volitional subject (Tumino 1993).

After seven weeks, we shifted to focus on the second aspect of the courses, entitled Feminist Social Change through Transborder Feminist Solidarities. Students were expected to move outward to create a community where they could make current social relations and the power negotiations explicit in the classroom. We moved to create a collective space outside the classroom where, through collective work, students could critique each other, communicate their ideas, and confront and negotiate their political/social positions.

Forging Collectivity: Transforming Individualism

The second aspect of the course was intended to enable students to imagine how deconstructing the familiar liberal self through mutual critique could empower each one of them as agents of change. They could learn to see themselves as agents of a collectivity who could contribute toward the transformation of not only their own communities (e.g., the social relations of the college, their home, and the market) but also their identities. I organized the class into "collectives" so that students could recognize firsthand the conflicts and contestations among feminist theorists, as well as to create a site where knowledges produced may be used to resist ideological inscriptions and the reproduction of individualism, the market logic informing the practice of various divisions of labor. The course syllabus reads as follows:

> The class is divided into five small groups of six students each, and the projects produced are expected to contribute to the whole class as a "collective" entity. Meeting once a week, the students in each small group are expected to conceptualize their interventions as feminists on the campus and the community for the semester. This labor is to be divided "equally" and expected to be done in the small groups which are to concentrate on one project (e.g., writing poetry, showing films, creating a reading group with members of the community, observing a feminist bookstore, observing the pedagogical practices of the feminist collective) and they are expected to write a collective paper (5–7 pages) on that project. The "collective" needs to figure out why and how these projects are feminist interventions and how they connect to feminist socialist democratic transformation. These projects are public and open to everybody on campus and the rest of the community.

In this course, I worked to implement feminist pedagogy as social praxis. The class decided collectively how each project intervened in a feminist way. Engaging the readings together as a class brought home the politics of recognizing one's participation in globalization and created possibilities to move outside the classroom and forge collectivities through their work projects. The collective projects were a political strategy through which students could see that ideas are not disembodied and irrelevant, but ridden with political consequences and ramifications, and that decolonization requires more than just an accumulation of knowledge about globalization and feminist theorizing on such social relations.

Feminist Agency and Empowerment:
The Collective is More Powerful than the Self

All projects were designed by the students as feminist activism. The three major processes of mutual critique, communication, and confrontation/ negotiation in the collectives became crucial in forging alliances among the different "subjects." Approximately eight collective projects were produced in each class dealing with different aspects of globalization. Project titles included "Changing Face of Citizenship in the American Society"; "The Women's Resource Center: The Dynamics of Community Involvement"; "Marketing Mystic Tibet"; "Deconstructing Disney"; "Sexual Offense Policy of the College"; "Globalization and the Media"; and "Globalization and the Environment." Students were given time in the classroom to divide the labor regarding the processes necessary to share their projects with the college and the town community. In working toward accomplishing a collective project, students were intensely involved in a process of self-evaluation. The work that was done in the classroom helped them figure out how each student was situated in the class in terms of race, class, sexual orientation; experience in feminist environments/theory; ability/disability; what sorts of assumptions people made about others' positionality; and how she might view the world because of that positionality. This also included analyzing the limitations of how each student positioned himself/herself (Lin, January 6, 2001). This work was crucial in opening up a space for them to forge connections outside the classroom to do activist work. Students were expected to meet once a week for at least an hour. There were exceptions to this "rule" depending on the needs and desires of each collective.

Through the use of e-mail, planning sessions in the classroom, and meetings outside to discuss their projects, students prepared eight final research papers and public presentations. Students also shared the labor of typing the

projects, designing fliers announcing when and where the public presentations would occur, and making photocopies and distributing the fliers to the
dorms and the rest of the community. Monies for these costs came from the
Oberlin College Women's Resource Center and some of the dorms in which
students lived. The project presentations were scheduled for the end of the
semester in the last two weeks of school. Students publicized through fliers,
announcements at campus groups, class announcements, e-mails, and in campus newspapers.

In putting together this schedule of projects, all students (i.e., both from
the working class and other classes, white and of color, queer and nonqueer)
started creating larger, diverse networks that attended and supported their
public events.[3] Even writing projects that were originally assigned as "individual" ones were pushed into the realm of collective production.

The research paper for the course was originally assigned as an "individual" paper, but two students approached me and suggested that they wanted
to collectively "write" a videotape by putting together some advertisements
about globalization, and then write independent papers reflecting on the
process of putting the video together. I saw this as resisting one way of writing (an individual research academic paper) by combining other modes of
writing (technological). This work also challenged my power and authority as
a teacher to assign a particular kind of writing. It made apparent to me my
own historical limitations regarding activism and its implementation. Through
this project, my students brought to light a tendency in academia to delineate
and fragment writing into academic research papers, and my own complicity
in that kind of practice even after I claimed that knowledge production is
always "collective." These students took themselves seriously as producers of
knowledge, and users of technology, showing how theories and ideas are not
produced only in the academic context but become concretized in other institutions like the media. One of the students, a working-class Asian-American
woman, wrote in her journal.

> Commercials that were chosen all focus on . . . several ideologies/myths in
> order to sell their product. They focus on the promises of technology—the
> power at the touch of a button, at the click of a mouse. They appropriate and
> recycle the theoretical ideas that address "globalization"—the universal global
> village, with its idiot-savant aborigine, the wise enlightened Asian man, the
> power of the mystical east, the nooks and crannies at the end of the world
> (Australian outback), the vastness of the desert where time has stopped and
> Bedouin tribes remain in perpetual travel atop their camels, those quaint
> African and Asian villages, and of course, the colorfulness of the non-

symbolic "other." Based on that premise, they expound the vital role of their product as enabling, creating, and providing for globalization. Look, with this technology, with this Internet, with these engines we are all joined, we are allowed to communicate in new, unprecedented ways across time/space.

An upper-class, white male student wrote in his research paper,

Unlike the written media, where the text is "spelled out," and the subject matter made explicit through definitional terms and verbal evidence, the visual is based on metaphors, on allusions, on bits of dreams. Thus, visual media, where images slide by you quickly, instantly, in a linear progression (not linear narrative), does not allow you the same breath of comprehension, the same level of close inspection, and the same, therefore, critical engagement. The multitude of images makes it practically impossible to decipher the full implication of each image to each image, and to decode the signifiers. . . . What does one receive in a film but what is given? Can one play with what is given, and thus become the actor of the process? To what extent can the media be used as a tool of resistance? How can its properties be used against itself to explicate its limitations and thus transcend them?

The two students moved to question the limits constituted through the globalized discourses of the media. They moved to expose the "machinations of the industry" as they juxtaposed these globalization ads and showed the potential effect (even if it is not coherent) on people who watch them. How did the students "fight fire with fire"? What was this fight about?

While producing the written text attached to the videotape, the two students were explicit about their political position. They grasped modern technologies and merged them with images of resistance to send their message and challenge the processes of commodifying life, which in turn affects understandings and practices of citizenship. Thus, we see here that the very permeability of transnational borders allows both the movement of oppressive elements and also the emergence of resistance against them through the use of the same tools. A female student also analyzed the potential effects of producing the videotape:

The images that I use are also necessarily media images, caught by the technical mechanical eye of a camera, and spouted as "truth" in an alternate context—the truth of the "third world suffering victim" in the case of the refugees, the civil rebellion in the case of the Belgrade paratroopers. These images of "resistance" thereby also lock the "third world"/other world into a representation that is problematic. Let's face it, CNN is not necessarily any less of a commercial than GE, only it claims to be news, rather than fiction.

As they bring to the fore the apparent effects of the media by juxtaposing its workings, the students' questions also point out that knowledge production through the media is a "fiction." Sometimes it is the news that produces dominant narratives in which the "third world"/other world is the peripheral victim trying to move to the liberated center of the West. Interrogating the strategies employed by the media to constitute a vision of the world, the students challenged their place, their identity, their agency in that world, and moved to claim their right to envision a collectivist community by enacting a citizenship different from the dominant one. The two students finished the paper and the videotape, which they shared with the campus, without becoming cynical about social change, in contrast to the overall reaction from another small collective. Their decision to communicate their understanding of globalization required extensive confrontation of each other, myself, and even the rest of the community. Such a confrontation through the production of this videotape pushed us (students from the whole college, and faculty) to consider our own positions in the context of globalization.

This project challenged the reproduction and maintenance of advertisements that circulate about globalization and that show that everybody can move anytime they want and buy what they want, always linked to the most "primitive" and "exotic" sites. What these advertisements silence is the fact that not everyone can move anytime or to anywhere, but this is what capital can now do. Negotiating their own power as both dominant and marginalized members of American society, the students challenged the social "fictions" or ideologies that were created to sustain particular interests—in this case, media profits—at the expense of others (poor children killed in wars). Thus, these two students, both from the U.S. Northeast, used media technology and globalization knowledges to strategize and resist the masculinist and cultural nationalists who transport their methods and specific values of power all over the world. These students were successful in their activism not in the sense of how much their minds were changed or how many other students and teachers were affected by the production of this videotape and paper, but in the way they challenged the constraints of my course assignments and critiqued the production of different ideologies and their implications for women's lives. These students were also successful not in the sense that they accumulated more knowledge but that they challenged the reproduction and maintenance of practices such as the media and the social arrangements (capitalist and racist patriarchal interests) upon which they depend and also reinforce.

Another collective, composed of a Chinese-American woman, Sarah; a white middle-class queer woman, Mary; a white middle-class woman, Rachel; an upper-class Southeast Asian–American woman, Neela; and a white working-class queer woman, decided to transform the Women's Resource Center of the college into a space conducive to a multiplicity of races, classes, sexualities, and abilities. They wanted to change its representation as a white college women's place into a space for women of all identities, including women from the town:

> Our collective project was to learn the history of the Oberlin College Women's Resource Center, which was fairly inactive and had been for several years. Our goal as a collective was to retain interest in the center because we see the need for such a space, yet we also hoped to attract those who were interested in changing the way that the center has been structured and the types of programs going on there. After talking to many of the people involved in the history (and present functioning) of the center, we came up with several basic ideas of how our collective would like to see the center move in the future. This brainstorming of ideas included the viewpoints of several people who had felt disenfranchised from the WRC, mostly Women of Color and poor/working class women, and their suggestions for creating a more productive space. At the end of the semester our collective held a public forum at the WRC to discuss its history and the possibilities for its future.

Coming from very different social locations, these four students moved beyond their comfortable spaces to enact a strategy of inclusion. Three of the students who worked on this project continue to work today with other students and women from the community to re-create this center. First, they are teaching a course—the college allows students to teach courses as part of the curriculum—on feminism. One of the white students is conducting a workshop series on white privilege, and the Chinese-Asian student brought the Chinese Students Association and the South Asian Student Association to the Women's Resource Center (WRC) for their meetings. The students stated that the course provided them with several theoretical models about forging a community that was not based on patriarchal strategies. Envisioning a community different than the one practiced at the center daily meant that they had to articulate a vision, or the stakes members of the collective saw themselves having in achieving group goals and maintaining group morale. In making their stakes explicit, the collective members were provided an opportunity to transform the center by setting up a new one through different ways of being agents. They noted that

> the vision is not given to you by higher ups or the dominant powers, but it is collectively and organically generated by the people. If it is . . . given to

you to use by the people who are already there, this space represents their political interests. So it ends up representing one vision and method of change and not others, even though the people who are doing it know they are being exclusive somehow but can't figure out how. Collectivity then is the opposite of institutionalization. It's not that there can't be guidelines that are generated, but they can't come as a given, they need to be developed from and by the people who are there, their experiences, their needs, their vision, their feminism.

The students used their memories and experiences of resistance from other contexts. For example, one of the students from Appalachia brought to this collective her memories of resistance against dominant white Anglo-Saxon America by her family and the rest of the Appalachian community; bringing to the fore these memories and experiences of resistance engendered the potential for historical change. The three students, along with another Asian-American women, are currently leading the movement to transform the WRC by confronting how the WRC was used only for the institutionalization of white liberal feminism and arguing that such a space did not meet the needs of many other women. As one student observed,

> TF is an Asian American woman who was originally welcomed to the WRC several years ago as a token Woman of Color but has transformed her own position while battling tokenization and a lack of support from other Women of Color on campus. Other women from our class collective became involved at our request as did several people from other organizations on campus. The battle to transform this space has been very difficult, and we have made many mistakes along the way.

The students came together to imaginatively arrange in new ways social relations by challenging the WRC as a space. By connecting together their histories of resistance, they moved to mobilize different desires on campus in order to transform the WRC. Their strategies can be understood as a set of transnational relations, themselves an aspect of breaking down localized/nationalized understandings of space.

A final example of an activist project follows. One collective became involved with a child pornography case that unfolded in the community (*State of Ohio v. Cynthia Stewart*; see Pollitt 1999). A mother was arrested and tried on charges of child pornography over pictures she took of her naked daughter, Nora. The students analyzed this case using the feminist readings on globalization addressed in class: How does looking at power structures from the position of the marginalized affect the agency of the more privileged in attempting to constitute trans-border alliances? To answer this question, the collective examined how the media made a spectacle of this working-class mother and constituted her as a pornographer. A worker at the store where the film was developed, and the institutions of the media and the court, made claims against this working-class woman using moralistic arguments. The students moved along with other local activists to contest the decision by the county's attorney general to prosecute a shaky case with great fervor during an election year. The five students—one Asian-American working-class woman; an upper-class African woman; a white upper-class man; a Jewish middle-class woman; and a white middle-class woman—forged a collective that coordinated efforts with local activists to systematically confront the political institutions. Negotiating their labor, the students continued to invest time to educate the rest of the community about child pornography. As they later noted, they, along with media agents and local activists, "forced negotiations and ultimately the plea bargain constructed by the county/state." As this collective pointed out,

> [T]he state defines the national self and the appropriateness of expression of that self which varies with age, sex, etc. . . . Had Nora's sexuality been portrayed in a movie like *American Beauty* or perhaps as a painting on display then the question of child pornography would not have arisen. A picture taken and then processed at a Drug Mart as opposed to a large well known professional label or person is delegitimized because of the positionality it represents. Power is not only held and defined by race and sex, but class as well.

For them, working with the rest of the activists in this case provided them the ability to look at power structures from the positionality of the disenfranchised. This case offered them insights into operations of power that they lacked because of their socioeconomic and political power in U.S. society. Recognizing that they had this power, they used it to put pressure on the local government. Their activism made them recognize and expose the intersections of state sexism and classism that oppresses working-class women who are not "officially married" (Cynthia Stewart had been cohabiting with her partner for ten years). Their participation meant a different kind of feminist intervention and alliances across positionality and privilege both within the student collectives and between them and the larger community.

Pictures of a child in a bathtub can now be seen a marketable product for personal profit, both on film and as digitized images on the Internet. The consumption of people through the creation, viewing, and selling of images now crosses borders instantly through technological advances. It is now easier for attorneys to argue, regardless of evidence or culpability, that a working-class mother is a *potential* purveyor of pornography in this globalized market. Similarly, the students in the context of globalization had to rethink their positionalities and recognize that the global and the local are always co-implicated. In adopting a location against the prosecuting attorneys' perspective the collective became "at once local and global."

The conflicts among these five "privileged" college students enhanced their awareness of the limitations of feminist transborder solidarity. The contestations that swirled around their making explicit politics of one's national/ social location were articulated between Patricia, an upper-class woman from Nigeria, and Alicia, a working-class Asian-American woman. When Patricia arrived at the collective meetings late, Alicia confronted her. As she noted, "Patricia felt that because she was/is a black woman . . . no one could understand and challenge her ideas and motives because the rest of [the group was] not black." Both Patricia and Alicia, as women of color, addressed this conflict as an issue of labor and language. "First, comes the issue of labor—we have different ideas of what labor is supposed to be. In terms of who does what, how much time we put into doing something. . . . We've realized that we had a problem with language (which partly has something to do with background and social location)." The white feminists did not want to deal with this conflict because, as they stated, it was between the two women of color. A Jewish woman in this collective said:

> I felt like if I attempted to give input or engage in the struggle it would be of no value. . . . Patricia and Alicia were doing all the labor and the rest of us were just using the information they generated but not contributing to that even in the form of support. . . . The collective experience challenges individualism and this may seem like violence but individualism is also a violence. I believe my silence is informed partly by an internalized notion that I have something that is all my own to protect. But really this limit I place between myself and others, not speaking, is the threat.

The two women of color's constant engagement, negotiation, and critiques made apparent the relatedness of the different positions in the collective, and the diverse modes of investment in social transformation. Speaking one's truth to others can open space for connections previously unimaginable. This sharing is one of the best strategies of "uncover[ing] structural inequalities between them," a starting point to understanding and recognizing the genealogy of domination as a transnational sociocultural formation.

The tensions between the politics of recognition and redistribution became apparent in the same collective when they discussed language and labor. Alicia, an Asian-American, working-class student, writes the following in her collective's paper:

> Raising the issue of identity politics both in class and the collective brought forth the problems of language and how one can be misunderstood and misrepresented as a result. This leads me to the issue of labor. Because of my social location, I have internalized the role of doing certain types of labor and doing a lot of labor. When I consciously make the effort not to do that, I feel as if that is my role and the expectation for me to do it still exists because it has been internalized within the group which causes violence in that I am unable to develop my underdeveloped self, and the same holds true for everyone else.

Alicia makes explicit the racial relations of the power/knowledge/nation nexus that enable some to speak for others. For her, these representations perform particular violences (e.g., who is supposed to do what). Within this group, attempts to forge a collective required a recognition of who has access to what power and why. Thus, as Alicia posits, the politics of recognition is not enough. What are needed are interventions to redistribute resources available within the collective, such as who does what and who shares what (i.e., labor). Usually, the liberal, white subjectivity embraces silence because she or he has internalized the ideology of individualism, which claims that one's power becomes constituted through property and access to resources. Within a women's studies classroom, a "nice" liberal subject keeps silent because the student has now become aware of his or her gendered and racial power and its implications on the lives of women of color. However, this strategy, despite "good intentions," does not transform the social relations of the collective. In this particular case, the rest of the collective described it as a problematic intervention. As this group noted,

> A means of decolonization then is confronting the barrier between individual practices and collective practices. In doing this, we must deconstruct ourselves in relation to the group and address the contradictions that arise from our own positionalities in collectivity. In respect to the Zoltan example of silencing himself, realizing this as not simply an individual action, but as representative of a specific positionality [supporting particular interests], is a practice of decolonization. So this must have been a collective realization followed by collective action.

For them, deciding on a plan of action and moving out into the community accomplished two things: it made the local community a tangible, social reality and allowed them to sustain their own struggles as they implemented their vision of the world.

Conclusion: Feminism for a Transnational Democracy and "Good Society"

In the context of a global, postcolonial world where education has been utilized as a method of colonization, albeit contradictorily, transnational feminist pedagogues can work with students to decolonize our relations and practices by producing knowledges that (de)abstract students, posit them as potential knowledge producers, and posit their activities as concrete, (de)reified, and connected to multiple sites. Moreover, such knowledges and practices demystify the globalization processes of individualism, commodification of social life, and mobility. In so doing, students of different races, classes, sexualities, and genders become activists and use their agency toward building transborder solidarities. Utilizing three major processes—critique, communication, and confrontation/negotiation—students become agents to enact their own physical, material, and discursive movements, their strategies of resistance, and their envisioning of a progressive future in which they actualize self and communities. All three activist projects described in this chapter revealed some useful insights about the larger process of globalization. Newer transnational activists are using the "master's tools" to expose the architecture of the present world order. The first project challenged the very concepts of nation, market, citizen, agency, and community by juxtaposing "fictions." The second project confronted the concepts of place, space, and community by engaging a traditionally white liberal feminist space. For this collective, transborder alliances were and continue to be constituted by transporting their own past and lived histories into (re)formulating the places they currently live and work. The third project collective moved to cooperate with other community activists in supporting a working-class mother. Recognizing a different perspective, that of the disenfranchised, this collective was forged on the strength of a history of survival other than its own, and constituted alliances that could contribute to the making of new political selves. Not only did these collectives labor to create supportive networks and work towards structural change, they also sustained a stance of seriously engaging each other's ideas "as material forces with historically determinate effects" through their selective support and/or contestation of particular interests. While there is intensity and discomfort in such practices, great possibilities exist for transforming individual relations into collective ones and politically intervening in localized spaces to create the conditions for waging gender, racial, sexual, and class struggles on a transnational scale.

Notes

1. This concept refers to a theoretical lens that explores the gendering of material structures and discourses and their affect on various people depending on their positionality of race, gender, class, sexuality, and ability.
2. Decolonization is as complex a process as colonization, generating varied responses depending on the context and struggles within that context. Rather than assuming that decolonization is a unified process, I use the classroom to show a set of varied "decolonizing" responses emerging in the classroom.
3. Composition of the one class was as follows: 27 students (five women of color, 18 white women, 2 of Jewish descent) and 4 men (a Filipino and a Vietnamese American, and 2 white men, one of Jewish descent). Composition of the other course was more diverse and its composition was as follows: 32 students (9 white women, 7 Jewish women, 3 black women, 7 biracial women (2 white-Japanese and 2 white and Southeast Asian, 1 white and Korean, 1 white and Arab, and one white and native American), 2 Chinese Americans, 3 Latinas, and 1 white male.

11

Activism and Alliance within Campus Sisterhood Organizations

Simona J. Hill

Ready to Unfold
Stand back and watch me
I'm ready to unfold!
I have decided to let my spirit go free
I'm ready to become the woman I
was meant to be
I've either been somebody's
daughter, mother or wife
And now it's time for me to take
charge of my life

—Anonymous, "Ready to Unfold"

Although the author of the above passage is unknown, the words have become an adopted spiritual motto for an undergraduate organization for women of color known as the Sisterhood at Susquehanna University. The goal of this paper is to introduce a "kitchen fights" model as one undergraduate feminist pedagogical teaching device that helps to nurture, strengthen self-identity, and build cultural diversity coalitions. (The notion of "kitchen fights" will be explained in more detail later in this essay.) The subject of this paper is the role of the Sisterhood, my experience as advisor to the group, and the development of the kitchen fights model at Susquehanna University in the academic years 1998–99 and 1999–2000.[1]

The "unfolding process" in which the Sisterhood actively engages during the academic year occurs through retreats, campus programming, community-service learning projects, mentoring of new and prospective students, some cross-cultural alliances with other women's groups on campus, and most of all friendships. For feminist educators, service-learning and community models of social interaction allow us to build "real world" concerns and connections into the overall curriculum.

Moreover, the unfolding of self (over time and through the generational information about what it means to be persons of color in a given space) becomes a successful resistance strategy, which helps members to grapple with the burdens of racism, sexism, and heterosexism in a university environment. This process benefits the university as a whole. Our experience is consistent with the findings of the collaborators of *Coming Into Her Own: Educational Success in Girls and Home*—namely that "the paradox of women-centered pedagogy is that it results in an inclusive and dynamic reinvigoration of the educational experience for all students" (Davis, Crawford, and Sebrechts (1999:21). Ana M. Martinez Alemán (2000:138) found that "women of color use female friendship as a primary site for the development of race and/or ethnic consciousness, growth that is essentially about purposeful self-definition." Friendships that help to negotiate positive self-image are cultivated and frequently flourish in the Sisterhood. Note the assessment of Alemán (2000:138): "Faced with what they perceive as a college experience that is inhospitable to or dangerous for their racial and/or ethnic identities, these women look to female friends to debate and discuss those developmental issues and questions that are critical for attaining positive racial and/or ethnic self-esteem."

Patricia Hill Collins (1998:47) reminds us that under current social conditions of racial segregation and sophisticated surveillance whereby black women's "voices" are routinely stripped of their oppositional power, "voice" is not enough. The Sisterhood is more than a social organization that "gives voice"; it is also a change agent and an intervention that promotes a positive sense of self. This is one of the most important factors in establishing a healthy identity and in enabling female students to deal with racism, sexism, and emotional and developmental challenges on predominantly white campuses.

Susquehanna University : A Brief Profile

According to the official profile distributed by its Office of Public Relations, Susquehanna University is a selective, private, residential four-year undergraduate university enrolling approximately 1650 students in the School of Arts, Humanities, and Communications, the School of Natural and Social Sciences, and the Sigmund Weis School of Business.[2] The student-faculty ratio is about 14 to 1. Degrees are offered for the Bachelor of Arts, Bachelor of Music, and

Bachelor of Science degrees. Susquehanna University is located in the heart of rural Pennsylvania about fifty miles north of the state capital, Harrisburg. It is about a three-hour drive from major cities such as Philadelphia, Washington, D.C., and New York City.

Snyder County, in central Pennsylvania, in which Susquehanna University is located, ranks as the tenth smallest county in the state, with a 1998 total population of 38,226.[3] The population is 99 percent white and the largest ancestry groups are persons of German descent (45 percent), English descent (7 percent), and Irish descent (2 percent). There is a large community of Amish living within the county. African Americans and Asian Americans constitute <0.4 percent each of the general population, and Latinos a growing 0.7 percent. The county is largely Republican and politically conservative and newcomers to the area recognize very quickly that awareness about social issues in this county is many years behind that of urban areas.

As an assistant professor at Susquehanna University, I sometimes feel that I have to tread carefully before displaying any liberal and/or feminist viewpoints. I am fortunate in being able to nurture some burgeoning ideas among some of the student population about what it means to be a feminist for the twenty-first century. As one of a few women of color, becoming an agent of diversity is almost inevitable. When I first arrived on the campus in 1998, the Sisterhood solicited me to be their faculty advisor. Sharing the belief of Barbara Gossett, Michael Cuyjet, and Irwin Cockriel (1998:30) that marginalized students need a "sense of mattering in their intellectual development as well as their personal development," I was pleased and honored to serve in this capacity. I saw an advising/mentoring role as a responsibility primarily because of the dearth of minority faculty on campus. Additionally, it was a rich opportunity to examine how students of color develop layers of solidarity in the midst of social isolation and marginality at a majority white institution.

The Sisterhood

I quickly learned about the history of the Sisterhood. The group is a constitutionally chartered organization that began in November 1994, with approximately six students and two young resolute feminist faculty of color: Tania Ramalho, a Latina who holds a Ph.D. in education policy and leadership, and Rachana Sachdev, an East Asian woman who holds a Ph.D. in British, American, and ethnic literatures. Both Ramalho and Sachdev were resident faculty, actively involved in campus women's issues. At the time, they were coteaching a course on Women in the Third World. The Sisterhood was Sachdev's original idea and she has always been credited as its faculty founder, though Ramalho wholeheartedly supported her and shared the responsibility.

The Sisterhood formed out of a need for minority women to shape an identity within an atmosphere that some would characterize as hostile, or at least not wholly responsive to their unique position on campus. At that time its membership was small yet diverse, with Native American, Latina, Asian, and African-American representation. From 1994 to 1996, the group met every week for dinner, discussion, and awareness events. During the 1996–97 academic year, however, founding members started to disappear (either because of graduation, work demands, and/or course loads). According to some alumnae, the original focus of the organization began to change in somewhat improvident ways. The Sisterhood became, for a brief time, more of a social club that excluded any consideration of political commitments. By 1998, some of the more dynamic and activist-oriented students returned, reorganized, and regained the sense of purpose embedded in the group's history. It was this new student leadership that wanted to make an impact on the university and be a viable resource for incoming students of color.

Over the years, and presently, the Sisterhood's active membership has shifted and grown to include mostly African-American and two or three Latina students. According to the group's preamble, it is a student organization whose purpose and directive is "To provide support as well as to reflect the social and political views of minority students and faculty. This organization works to create a greater awareness of the issues and concerns of minority women and to work to provide an environment in which these issues can be addressed."[4]

The Sisterhood has survived on this campus where diversity is at a premium and racism, sexism, heterosexism, and homophobia run rampant beneath a mask of politeness. The most positive aspect of the Sisterhood is that at its best it heals the fractures that erupt between itself and other organizations. This allows the group to keep its integrity without losing a sense of who it is and its power. By the time I had arrived on campus, the Sisterhood seemed poised to reach out to other women's organizations on campus and to do some collaborative programming. At the time, I was also a live-in faculty master for the Women's Studies House, where many of the other women's groups (which the Sisterhood members often referred to as the "white women's groups") were represented, including NOW (the National Organization for Women) and WomenSpeak.

It was my hope to bring at least these three groups—the Sisterhood, WomenSpeak, and NOW—together for some initial dialogue. It seemed to be the right time to work through the barriers of perception that prevented many of the women from directly communicating with each other, working on joint projects, and finding a dynamic source of empowerment by joining forces with other women's groups. Perhaps if they viewed it as a worthwhile endeavor there would be room to explore the possibilities of building a woman's alliance in which all campus women's groups, including sororities, could coalesce at a university where women are, in fact, the majority presence.

Difficult work, but not, in my opinion, impossible to accomplish because of the willingness of some key participants (both women of color and white women). It is remarkable that on a campus where most undergraduates are very unlike the members of the Sisterhood (i.e., white, from an upper-middle-class, privileged background), this organization serves as a catalyst for change. It has survived through what I call "kitchen fights" about what its direction should be—to strengthen its own sense of purpose or to reach out and embrace the larger campus community in its overall mission. In a larger parameter, these kitchen fights often erupt when, for women, the images and symbols that manufacture ideology and the ability to see themselves as women activists are in stages of transition. The goal of this paper is to introduce a kitchen-fights model as one undergraduate feminist pedagogical teaching device that helps to nurture, strengthen self-identity, and build cultural diversity coalitions.

What are Kitchen Fights?

In a 1950s report, MIT Media Lab researchers found that "the average family used kitchens more than an hour a day gathering, cooking, serving and eating food, and talking as they did" (Wolkomir 1999:58). Although today the figure on actual family kitchen time has diminished to about sixteen minutes, people continue to see their homes and kitchens as both refuge and focal points of home life. British playwright Arnold Wesker's 1950s work, *The Kitchen*, depicted the world of the restaurant kitchen as a "hellish synecdoche for capitalism where cooks, pastry chefs, dishwashers, and waitresses struggle to maintain a decent level of existence" (Conley 1998:125). The home kitchen may not have as many participants, but a university "kitchen" does, and the participants need to learn effective means of coexisting. The idea of using the kitchen as a hearth and home metaphor suggests that participants will experience some level of familiarity in their conflict. Kitchen fights are not only to be expected, but also welcomed as motivation to struggle with difficult dialogue and differing belief systems. This conflict is what bell hooks has always called "essential to the learning process" (1994:7), but more than that it leads to a level of excitement, chaos, and intellectual stimulation. The kitchen-fights model can generate internal conflict within students, and it is a model conducive to transformative learning.

The kitchen is often the center of the home environment, and it is where communication (open and closed forms), decision making, and emotional conflict take place. It is the symbolic, sometimes sacred, place within the home. It can be the locus for heated debates, and tangible forms of intimacy, power, control, warmth, and nurturing. Often, when I ask audiences to brainstorm about what they think the imagery of kitchens suggests, I get mixed responses. For example, the notion of kitchen fights can generate memories of "throwing things, bickering, fighting about private things, coming to terms with the 'nitty gritty' of life and gossip." For others, images of "waiting and patience, intimacy between kin and kinlike people, old resurrected fights, competition, negotiation, no-win situations, and noise with no one listening" come to mind. Our associations with kitchens are about territory, history, family, ideas, and preconceptions about people (socially prescribed gender roles)—often the ambiguous "other" category. One white female professor made a very telling statement when she said, "I can only cook with certain people." The kitchen holds a wide spectrum of events, shared memory, and historical commonality. It can be a safe zone to demonstrate to others our best and most familiar, and our worst and most unyielding selves. Ideally, a kitchen can represent a sanctuary of recognition of who we are, who we have been, and who we, ultimately aspire to be.

I coined the term "kitchen fights" and use it in regard to my work with women of color organizations. Over the years I have presented kitchen-fights workshops as effective tools for bringing women's groups, particularly women and minority groups, into conversation with each other.[5] Kitchen fights are: the struggle that women of color have on a predominantly white college campus, which is to nurture self-identity and shape and address social, political, and environmental concerns of people of color (students, faculty, and administrative staff) without alienating their own group or the campus community at large.

In order to discover the issues surrounding crossing boundaries of dialogue, I found it necessary to conduct some preliminary research. Sara Waite, then a senior and a sociology major, worked with me during the fall of 1999 on an independent study project entitled "Contributions of Sisterhood Organizations at Susquehanna University" (Waite 1999), exploring the state of women's groups on campus. She interviewed 25 female respondents, ranging in age from 18 to 22, solicited anecdotal remarks, and gathered recommendations from student, faculty, and administrative staff about "what needs to be done" on our campus in order to effect change among women's groups. The most significant challenge that respondents in Waite's study found was the perception of constant, subtle and overt forms of racism and sexism. At the time she conducted her interviews, the university was without a director for multicultural affairs. Students (particularly those representing diversity organizations and international programs) perceived the university's inability to find an immediate replacement for this very visible position as outrageous and a heated topic for campus debate. Students interviewed believed (on an institutional level) that "the women here at Susquehanna were not taken seriously" (Waite 1999:18). To be labeled a "feminist" or less frequently, a "womanist" group, in many of the students' opinion, put an organization at risk of being an "out-group" and thereby subject to stigmatization and marginalization on a campus of fewer than 1800 students. Whether they experienced it personally or heard it through rumor, more than 80 percent of the respondents agreed that there was some form of sexism from professors. These student perceptions were telling considering the fact that 57.5 percent of the student body is female.

When Waite asked women of color how they felt toward white students at Susquehanna University, some respondents agreed that they "did not associate with them often" or admitted that they do associate, but "not as much as they would like." A lack of understanding about white students' perspectives was deemed an important factor in determining whether students of color formed friendships with white students. Students in both categories agreed that there was not much opportunity for people to share culture and learn to understand cultural differences without feeling threatened or being threatened.

The Kitchen Fights Model

The kitchen-fights model is a threefold process. First, it requires groups to talk honestly about where one is on a college campus—that is, it elicits from interested parties (at all levels within the university) a "state of the cultural climate on our campus" conversation: Where are people of color in regard to their own perspective and that of others? Second, it discusses as fully and as frequently as possible where a group wants to be, considering, for example, the long-range goals of the institution with regard to diversity and discrimination policies. Third, it generates some definite and feasible steps of action that will ignite kitchen fights for "positive activism." The ignition may include roundtable discussions, symposia, residential hall programs, curriculum changes, new institutional practices, and, as in our case, the creation of a focus group.

To introduce this model to our college campus, I developed an Ignite A Kitchen Fight discussion, facilitated by myself, Kamika Cooper, the campus director of multicultural affairs, and Kimberly Fisher, another senior sociology major who would later continue Waite's research along with running a series of kitchen fights focus groups.

Before the Ignite A Kitchen Fight event, we received e-mail correspondence, telephone calls, and personal comments pertaining to the so-called offensive nature of the posted advertisement, which read:

IGNITE A KITCHEN FIGHT!
Beginning Campus Dialogue Between
Women of Color & White Women
Wednesday, February 02, 2000 @ 7:00pm
Bogar Hall, Benjamin Apple Lecture Hall

A white student responded, in a letter addressed to me,

> I have just received your email and I am somewhat disturbed by it. You've entitled a discussion "Ignite A Kitchen Fight." To me that sounds not only violent but sexist. Why perpetuate the stereotype that a woman belongs in the kitchen? As for the "Fight," why give such a violent term to a discussion that, I assume, is aimed towards harmony. I assume that is what your purpose was with this discussion. That is the other thing that bothered me about your email, it's a discussion between "women of color and white women." I'm assuming that the discussion is for all women. So why distinguish between women of color and white women; why separate them? The way you worded your email seemed to make it seem like there were two sides to this discussion; Women of Color vs. White Women. If the purpose of this discussion is to create a better understanding among all women in our Susquehanna community then please send out another email that says so. The email I received sent a negative, sexist and somewhat prejudice message.

Another message was sent to me and addressed "to whom it may concern":

> It seems to me that calling the dialogues advertised below "Kitchen Fights" not only promotes the sexist stereotype that the place of a woman is in the kitchen, but also promotes aggressiveness, violence, and confrontation in the place of mature debate and discussion. I have no problems with women of all races meeting to discuss any sort of issue, but I am concerned about the image that your title evokes. All women, not to mention all people of all colors, should be striving to work together for peace and mutual understanding, and I believe that your choice of title fosters the exact attitude of hostility, sexism, and inflexibility that your dialogues (I assume) are designed to combat. I appreciate your desire to increase understanding among women of all races, but the title of your program is working against you in very large ways and you may wish to consider changing it to better reflect your intentions.

As kitchen-fight facilitators, we deliberately chose not to respond to any questions or assumptions about what the term *kitchen fight* meant. We saw this as an opportunity to heighten curiosity and encourage attendance. Our silence about defining the term generated discussion among faculty and students alike about what the term could mean to university students on the edge of a new millennium.

Despite some initial negative campus reaction, evaluations of the Ignite A Kitchen Fight event characterized it as successful in terms of the numbers who participated and the level of discussion. The agenda was organized as follows:

1. Welcome/Introduction
2. Clarification
3. Why Kitchen Fights Are Important
4. "Igniting a Kitchen Fight" Group Activity/Interaction: "Stereotypes We Have About White Women/Women of Color"
5. Reflection
6. Where Do We Go From Here?
7. Building a Women's Alliance focus group
8. Conclusion

The audience was comprised of 39 women and 10 men. Out of the total number, 7 were either faculty or staff. The racial composition of the audience was 26 whites, 15 African Americans, two Latinos, two Asian Americans, and two individuals who chose not to identify themselves racially. Many of the Sisterhood members were in attendance.

The program agenda included asking the audience for their definition of the term kitchen fights, then presenting them with my own working definition. Participants who were apprehensive about using the kitchen metaphor because it seemed to suggest a pronounced bias against women spoke about their discontent. As facilitators, we made clear that we were not suggesting that women's primary role is connected to household tasks. We emphasized that we wanted everyone to use their personal experiences in order to think about the roles, rules, and associations that surround the kitchen. We conducted an icebreaking exercise to get participants to discuss stereotypes. Prior to continuing with the two-hour presentation, facilitators asked audience members to develop ground rules for the remainder of the program, particularly when discussing sensitive issues such as race and ethnicity. The rules established were as follows:

1. No foul language
2. No screaming, laughing and snickering

3. Use "I" statements
4. Group confidentiality
5. Suspend judgments about others
6. Respect the speaker
7. Come out of your comfort zone

Communicative practices across social differences and recognizing techniques of arbitrary domination over others are important, as Audre Lorde emphatically affirmed in her best-known lecture, "The Master's Tools Will Never Dismantle the Master's House" (1983). Such practices of domination include "silencing others, excluding others from public forums and rendering them invisible in the process, devaluing others' remarks when they do speak, speaking for and about others, misnaming others' practices in order to dominate them, appropriating others by treating them as tokens, using others for legitimation, or blaming others for their under-representation" (Olsen 2000:261). In this light, Ignite a Kitchen Fight participants considered the last rule, for "coming out of your comfort zone," as imperative to good discussion. In this instance, the "zone" is akin to Joe Feagin, Hernán Vera, and Nikitah Imani's concept of a racialized space that "encompasses the cultural biases that help define specific areas and territories as white or as black, with the consequent feelings of belonging and control" (1996:50). To go beyond the zone, participants must be directed toward a willingness to risk the authority they have when operating within their own localized spheres, thereby establishing a new method of communication between racial groups.

At the end of the event, questionnaires seeking volunteers for a women's alliance focus group were distributed to female audience members. Kimberly Fisher made initial contacts, recruited members, and facilitated a seven-week group. Membership consisted of 12 women—6 whites, 5 African Americans, and 1 biracial (half black and half white) woman. There were 3 seniors, 5 juniors, 2 sophomores, and 2 freshmen.

For about two hours each week focus group members discussed issues such as labeling and stereotyping, interracial dating, media portrayals of women, conflicts between whites and people of color, and fraternities and sororities on campus. They drafted a mission statement, rules for the focus group, and long-range goals of the women's alliance. Their mission was "to open lines of communication between women of color and white women by bonding and uniting through understanding in order to breakdown the existing boundaries." The focus group also established three goals: (1) to break down the myths and stereotypes surrounding women of color and white women; (2) to increase the level of interaction between female organizations on campus; and (3) to gain a better understanding of each other as women. At the end of the seven weeks, the newly formed Women's Alliance held a panel discussion as the follow-up presentation to the Ignite a Kitchen Fight program held two months earlier. As of fall 2001, no long-range goals had been achieved. However, based on students' observations that there were not many courses offered to explore the roles of women of color, I developed and implemented a new course Cultural Roles of African-American Women. This honor's seminar, cross-listed with sociology, women's studies, and diversity studies, ran in the fall 2000 semester.

Some Outcomes

Robert L. Allen comments on the Million Man March in a way that has some relevance to the kitchen-fights model. He writes, "We gain respect and self-esteem by joining with others in the collective struggle against our common oppression. When we refer to each other as 'brothers' and 'sisters' we are not necessarily speaking biologically but of a deeply felt kinship of common experience. That experience unites us all—men and women, straight and gay—into a vibrant, creative, soulful family" (1995:25). The open session of the Ignite a Kitchen Fight session provided both men and women an oppor-tunity for a common experience. It is a positive outcome of this model that the men who attended were more aware (or made aware through discussion) of women's issues related to cultural stereotypes and gender based norm expectations. Although the data collected from the focus group are subject for a larger body of work, there were some significant findings, which encourage me to continue this research.

As Lorraine Gutierrez comments in the University of Michigan videotape *Through My Lens,* women of color faculty tend to find themselves "question-ing what the current paradigms are and trying to come up with new ways of looking at things" (Aparicio 1999:23). The kitchen-fights model of self-disclosure, and the discussion of "taboo" racial, ethnic, and sexual subjects and myths, opens lines of communication between women of color and white women and creates a new way of looking at deeply held beliefs.

I admire the white women and others who volunteered for the focus group. Their willingness to discuss issues raised during the kitchen-fight ses-sions demonstrated the possibility of stronger coalitions and a movement toward embracing diversity. I applaud the Sisterhood because the members continue to learn how to implement an activist womanist model. Prior to this organization's existence, issues important to women of color were often ignored; the Sisterhood raised and acknowledged these issues in powerful ways. The Sisterhood is, by and large, a womanist group focused on women of color; this alone is a benefit to Susquehanna University because it aids in the retention of a declining minority population. The Sisterhood's participation in the focus group and its willingness to make self-disclosures to white women about what it means to be a person of color on our campus was risky, yet demonstrated the courage needed to cross boundaries. The Sisterhood's strength of character and organization has permeated the campus and has gained the respect of many of the faculty, administrators, and student peers. The double jeopardy that they face as women and as women of color makes the telling of their kitchen-fight experiences important for feminist learning both inside and outside the classroom.

Notes

1. Many thanks to editorial assistant Jennifer Fox for bringing later drafts of this paper into focus. Her sharp eye and attention to detail is much appreciated.
2. The registrar's fall 2000 summary reported an enrollment of 1682 full-time students: 57.5 percent of whom are women, 63.4 percent from Pennsylvania, 91.8 percent are Caucasian, 7.7 percent minority Americans (2.5 percent are African American, 1.9 percent are Asian American, 2.0 percent are Hispanic American, 0.4 percent are Native American, 0.9 percent are other American), and 0.4 percent are minority non-Americans. Moreover, there are more than one hundred student organizations (eleven of which fall under the diversity umbrella) and twenty-two intercollegiate sports groups.
3. Statistics were compiled from the *Municipal Reference Guide: Pennsylvania East-Central Edition 2000* (a publication of National Resource Directories, Inc.); *Editor and Publisher Market Guide 2000* (Editor and Publishers Company), and the *Sourcebook of County Demographics* (National Resource Directories), 1990 census edition, volume 1.
4. Excerpted from the 1999-2000 Sisterhood constitution.
5. Wilson College, Chambersburg, Pennsylvania, Gaudy Night Women's Conference, November 1999. The Gaudy Night presentation was most noteworthy because it was done so early in the research process. In addition to workshops given at Susquehanna University, I was invited to participate in panel at the "Women of Color and Allies Summit," sponsored by the Pennsylvania National Organization for Women in March 2000. We remain hopeful in continuing to extend alliance building beyond campus. Furthermore, continued interest in the subject matter launched the first ever Presidential Forum on Diversity. My students, the Sociology and Anthropology Department, and some of the original Kitchen Fight participants, sponsored this campus-wide event. The event was held April 18, 2001.

12

The Individual and Collective Rewards of Community–Based Service Learning

Patricia Washington

Women's studies curricula and community-based service learning have a shared tradition of educating for personal growth, civic engagement, and positive social change. As a women's studies scholar and a community–based service-learning practitioner, I find it especially gratifying to integrate the medium (community-based service learning) with the message (women's studies content). Although community-based service learning can be an effective tool for enhancing student learning in any setting, I find it particularly useful to me as a Black[1] lesbian teaching in a predominantly White university. Here many White students (as well as some students from other racial backgrounds) are often resistant to a feminism grounded in the critical analysis of the intersectionality of gender, race, sexual orientation, and class oppression.

I have found that the challenge of redirecting student resistance to the theoretical underpinnings of the courses I teach to be much more manageable when a community-based service-learning option is incorporated into the course. Specifically, it has been my experience that students who engage in a community-based service-learning project are more inclined—or, at least, better able—to recognize and articulate for themselves the interconnection of systems of oppression and the impact these intersecting systems have on women's social, economic, and political status.

While I incorporate community-based service-learning options into all of my courses, the focus of this essay is Sex, Power, and Politics, a general education course I have taught for over four years. After reviewing some of the factors that make this course a particularly rich "site" for researching the efficacy of community-based service learning in enhancing both intellectual and social growth, I provide a brief overview of standard course objectives and class format, as well as guidelines for undertaking community-based service-learning projects. Next I provide a brief methods section and descriptions of the four community partners, their projects, and the interrelationship between the academic content of Sex, Power, and Politics and the respective community service option. Finally, I present findings from a sample of student postactivity reflection papers to demonstrate, generally, how service learning can decrease student resistance to exploring the intersectionality of gender, race, class, sexual orientation, and (dis)ability as sites of oppression and resistance.

Challenges to Teaching
"Sex, Power, and Politics" Intersectionally

Students who enroll in Sex, Power, and Politics are usually, but not always, nonmajors. More likely than not, they have no particular interest in women's studies or familiarity with its pedagogical practices or perspectives, but are taking the course largely because it satisfies an all-university requirement and meets at a day and time that suits their schedule. They are overwhelmingly white, female, and—ostensibly—heterosexual, although there are usually some students of color (mostly Latina/o or Black—and, less frequently, Asian), several men, and one or two "out" lesbian, gay, or bisexual students.

Most students come to the class with predetermined, though perhaps unconscious, expectations of what a women's studies course on Sex, Power, and Politics is—or *should be*—about. To put it simply, many students think the course is—or *should be*—about "generic" women (*sex*), the discrimination they still face (their lack of *power*), and their struggle to get more power by getting into positions where they get to make the rules (*politics*). In other words, students often enroll in the class with the expectation that they will be guided through an exclusive exploration of the gendered oppression of women and the obstacles women must overcome to prevail against sexism. They are often surprised, and sometimes dismayed, to learn that the course they have signed up for does not focus on "generic woman" (devoid of race, nationality, economic status, sexuality, etc.) and her struggles to overcome oppression at the hands of "generic man" (a.k.a., "the patriarchy"), but that they will, instead, be asked to consider "woman" in her multiple social locations—not just her sex, but her race, sexual orientation, economic class, and other social markers. While students are asked to study the gendered "ways of life" that result in women worldwide being treated as inferior to men and subjected to restrictive measures based on their sex, they are also asked to explore the reality that not all women and not all men are similarly situated relative to power and privilege. In their exploration of women's subordination within various systems of power, that is, they are asked to consider how some men are also subject to the power of other men and how some women have power over the quality of life enjoyed by other women and some men. In the same vein, students are asked to adjust their thinking about what constitutes "politics." While they often expect the course to deal with formal political systems and processes (elections and governing, voting and representation, etc.)—and while some attention is paid to politics as traditionally understood—students are presented with readings, lectures, and documentaries that address a variety of informal political actions or activities, ranging from beauty pageants to rap music.

Course Objectives, Standard Texts, and Class Format

Sex, Power, and Politics examines social, economic, and political factors influencing the status of women in the United States and abroad. Topics include, but are not limited to, institutionalized systems of power and domination; media representation of women as political objects or agents; gender and sexuality socialization as they relate to political status; and women's individual and collective struggles for positive social change. Attention is steadily focused on the interrelationship of gender, race, sexual orientation, class, and (dis)ability.

I establish the framework for the course within the first weeks of the semester through lectures and assigned readings from Cathy Cohen, Kathleen Jones, and Joan Tronto's *Women Transforming Politics: An Alternative Reader* (1997). This text, which incorporates essays from women across all racial and ethnic lines (writing about topics as varied as domestic workers, disability rights, and lesbian activism) does an excellent job of representing intersectionality, as well as redefining politics as a range of both formal and informal actions situated along the continuum of power and resistance. I also provide a more "traditional" look at sex, power, and politics by assigning readings from Norris's *Women, Media and Politics* (1997), which examines the gendered roles and representations of women journalists, politicians, and activists. During the 1999–2000 academic year, I also required students to read Cathy Cohen's *The Boundaries of Blackness: AIDS and the Breakdown of Black Politics* (1999) and Elizabeth Martinez's *De Colores Means All of Us: Latina Views for a Multi-Colored Century* (1998). Cohen's (1999) text reinforces the premise of *Women Transforming Politics: An Alternative Reader* (e.g., that we need to redefine "what politics is, where it occurs, who participates in it and why"). It examines the processes whereby certain "consensus" issues are labeled worthy of the black community's attention (e.g., black male incarceration, death, and unemployment rates), whereas equally important "cross-cutting" issues (e.g., black female incarceration rates, teenage pregnancy, lesbian and gay rights, and HIV/AIDS prevention) are ignored. Martinez's text is another model of intersectionality in that it explores the author's 30 years of activism in the movements for civil rights, women's liberation, Latino/a empowerment, economic justice, and the Latino/a youth movement.

Course materials are organized around four major objectives: (1) to explore the forms of domination/control that constrain women's formal and informal political participation in the United States and abroad; (2) to understand historical and contemporary tensions between, and coalitions among, various strands of U.S. women's movements; (3) to examine some political issues addressed by contemporary feminists, especially as they intersect, or conflict, with (inter)national policies and practices; (4) to explore how institutionalized U.S. and international political attitudes and practices perpetuate systems of gender-based inequity here and abroad and to understand the role of individuals and groups in maintaining or dismantling these systems.

Class format is a combination of lecture/discussion, small group activities, and occasional guest speakers or films. Requirements include timely and thoughtful completion of reading assignments, comprehensive exams, short- to medium-length papers and e-mail assignments, and completion of a group research project or community service option aligned with course objectives.

Community-Based Service-Learning Guidelines

Community-based service-learning options from which students may select are predetermined prior to the start of the class, and representatives from the preselected organizations make class presentations during the first two weeks of the semester. An individual student and her selected agency draw up agreements, in consultation with me as the instructor, that it commit the student to an agency project for three or four hours a week for ten weeks. Agencies provide interim reports (ranging from phone calls or e-mails to typewritten reports of one or two pages) on student progress so that I may assess quality and level of involvement, and at the end of the semester students submit final reports (reflection papers) detailing the relationship between the selected community service learning option and course objectives. Because several students ultimately select the same community partner, the service-learning option may evolve into a group project, with students commuting to the selected agency or organization together, meeting in groups with the service provider, completing projects in teams, discussing their service-learning experiences in class as a "unit," and conferring with each other on their reflection papers.

Developing Quality Service-Learning Partnerships

Providing quality community-based service-learning opportunities requires building relationships (and trust) on both sides. Having incorporated community-based service-learning components in my courses for many years, I have a core group of community partners that I know will provide students with quality experiences and who are willing to work with me to ensure that students are following through on their commitments. These are partners that I can freely check in with regarding student confusion or discontent about projects, and who will freely check in with me if they feel students are not holding up their end of the service-learning contract.

Of course, not all community partnerships are successful. There have been agencies and individuals that I have discontinued working with because they did not provide the quality of experience that I wanted for my students. In one of the most disappointing instances, a candidate for local office simply doled out work assignments to students rather than engaging them in the political process. Furthermore, while the candidate supposedly promised students that they would get to "rub elbows" with certain community "movers and shakers" at an upcoming campaign fundraiser, the students were allegedly "disinvited" from the fundraiser because the host did not want "a bunch of college kids" in his home. In another instance, a community partner began to insinuate, both orally and in writing, that by providing service-learning opportunities to my students she was doing my work for me, and as such, should be hired to teach at my institution. Nonetheless, my experiences working with community partners have been overwhelmingly positive and the horror stories are rare.

Just as some individuals and agencies do not make good community partners because they fail to provide "connected" learning experiences, some students who select "quality" service learning opportunities end up either rejecting these opportunities or, seemingly, gaining nothing from them. However, as with the case of inappropriate service providers, students who sign up for, then ultimately reject or resist, community-based service learning opportunities are rare. In fact, since I have incorporated a community-based service learning component into Sex, Power, and Politics, this has been the case with fewer than ten students. There have been some "near misses," such as when a Black female student began to make disparaging remarks to me about a White female service provider whose clientele was largely black and Latina. Fortunately, because of our long-standing relationship, the service provider and I were able to communicate with each other about this matter and make the student aware of how her preexisting attitudes about the prevalence of White racism might be impacting her interactions with this particular service provider. Ultimately, the student "turned around" and became one of the most dedicated and hardworking students in this agency.

There have also been some obvious mismatches, such as allowing an extremely conservative White woman who firmly believed the myth about women on welfare (that they are lazy, Black, bear children to increase welfare payments, etc.) to work with single female welfare recipients. This student ultimately had to be removed from the project because of her disdain and disrespect toward the women who used that agency. The service provider and I learned from this, though, and since then we have included a statement in our community-based service-learning presentations regarding the need for students to be respectful of the populations they agree to work with. We stress that should students feel they cannot hold their attitudes in check, they should not elect to do a community-based service-learning option in lieu of the group research requirement. The most common form of resistance to the learning opportunities afforded by community-based service learning is lack of follow-through. Each semester I have one or two students who express eagerness to participate in one or another of the service-learning options, go through the formality of turning in a service-learning contract, and then bail out when their first interim report reveals that they have participated minimally, if at all, in their service-learning project. These students usually have a host of excuses for not following through with their service-learning commitments—often associated with some supposed lapse on the part of the service provider—and request to be released from the community-based service learning option so that they can do the group research project instead. Believing it to be to the community partner's advantage, I always allow such students to revert to the group research requirement.

Student Participants, Community Partners, and Anticipated Outcomes

There were 120 students enrolled in the Sex, Power, and Politics courses I taught during the 1999–2000 academic year. Almost two-thirds selected a community-based service-learning option in lieu of a group research project. Data herein come from a subset of reflection papers submitted by students who selected the service-learning option. For the sake of simplicity and consistency, the pool of 76 reflection papers was narrowed according to the selected community service partner. Specifically, while students had a number of different community-based service-learning options during the 1999–2000 academic year, only four agencies or organizations provided community-based service-learning projects both semesters: San Diego Lesbian and Gay

Pride (SDLGP), Supportive Parents Information Network (SPIN) of San Diego, the Women's Resource Center of San Diego State University, and the Campaigns to Elect Peace and Freedom Candidate Janice Jordan. Twenty-four reflection papers regarding students' experiences with one of these four agencies or organizations were used as the data set for this article. This sampling yielded papers from 1 Asian American male, 1 White male, fifteen White females, two Black females, and five Latinas.[2] The remainder of this chapter is based primarily on the reflection papers submitted by these students.[3]

In reviewing the selected reflection papers, I was looking for evidence that participation in community service learning had challenged preexisting (particularly stereotypical) attitudes and beliefs students held toward the constituencies addressed by a particular community organization or agency, and that students could clearly identify a relationship between course content and their activities with the community service agency they had selected. I also hoped to find evidence that working in community agencies whose service populations often included women and men across the spectrum in terms of race/ethnicity, gender, sexual orientation, class, and (dis)ability enhanced student receptivity to and understanding of the theory of intersectionality that serves as the organizational framework of the course. An additional goal was to determine from the students' own writings whether or not participating in a community-based learning experience had promoted social awareness and fostered personal growth (whether morally, educationally, or professionally).

The Four Selected Community-Based Service-Learning Partners

San Diego Lesbian and Gay Pride (SDLGP).   SDLGP is similar to other lesbian/gay/bisexual/transgender (LGBT) organizations in that it provides a quasi-familial environment for affirming and celebrating LGBT communities while simultaneously working to build bridges between these communities and the larger society. Established in 1974 as a sponsored program of the Center for Social Services, Incorporated, and developed into a nonprofit corporation in 1994, SDLGP exists to produce civic, cultural, and educational events that support and encourage a sense of pride within San Diego's LGBT communities. SDLGP is best known for organizing and producing a rally, parade, and festival that draws over 100,000 attendees each July, although it also lends support and funding to numerous other LGBT organizations and events throughout the year. SDLGP activities are overseen by a board of directors who serve three-year terms. The members of the board range in age from the early 20s to the late 60s, and include persons from diverse backgrounds, occupations, and races/ethnicities.

Students who selected the SDLGP service-learning option were required to attend meetings of the board every two weeks (totaling five for the ten-week period) in order to observe board dynamics; to become aware of issues affecting the LGBT communities in general; and to gain an appreciation for the fiscal, logistical, and public-relations efforts that go into presenting one of the largest annual public events that takes place in San Diego. Although they attended board meetings primarily as observers, students were encouraged to ask questions and to contribute their perspectives to discussion items. Since the "physical" work for Pride events (the rally, parade, and festival) takes place during June and July and I teach only in the fall and spring, students who participate in the SDLGP project specifically only attend board meetings. As described by one of this year's participants,

> Those in the class who elected to work with other organizations, such as Business and Professional Women [BPW] or Aurora Behavioral Hospital of San Diego, had specific tasks or jobs that they were to perform; on the other hand, [the SDLGP] had no such mission. My involvement with SDLGP meetings was simply that of observer. I listened, made verbal contributions to the discussions when appropriate, and observed and analyzed how the issues addressed by SDLGP intersected with our course materials. Beyond these tasks, I was on a personal mission to acquaint myself with a political identity and force that I was previously unaware of. I may not ever fully comprehend what it means to be a member of the Lesbian, Gay, Bisexual, Transgender (LGBT) community, but I am closer to understanding how they create and use their political identity.

Because the majority of students who selected this option self-identified as heterosexual, one pedagogical expectation was that, by the end of the project, heterosexual students would more readily identify heterosexism and homophobia as factors that impede both formal and informal political participation of sexual minorities. It was also expected that students who selected this option would be more inclined to view themselves as allies to lesbian, gay, transgender, and bisexual individuals and to be more willing to counter negative stereotypes regarding this population.

Supportive Parents Information Network (SPIN). SPIN is a grassroots organization founded in 1998 by an American Civil Liberties Union staff attorney whose primary focus is welfare policy and administration. Created largely to address the disconnect between legal, political, and social service systems and day-to-day realities of welfare recipients (especially after the passage of the Welfare Reform Act of 1996), SPIN's mission is to remove barriers to economic self-sufficiency by informing parents on welfare of their rights, empowering them to take proactive steps to shape policies that affect them and their families, and helping them build a power base for positive change among their own numbers and in coalition with supportive others.

When Joni Halpern, the founder of SPIN, began working with students enrolled in my courses over two years ago, SPIN had only 12 parents as members. The membership has since grown to include nearly 600 parents, and Halpern has resigned her position with the ACLU to work full-time as SPIN's director. Since the fall semester of 1998, Halpern has visited my Sex, Power, and Politics classes every semester to talk about the impact of welfare reform on families in San Diego. Over the past two years, students have been offered a range of service learning options with SPIN, including helping to arrange a two-day conference for parents on welfare regarding their rights to education and gainful employment under the CalWORKS Program;[4] developing a SPIN website with links to community service providers; creating an organizational newsletter; and helping SPIN members lobby local and federal officials regarding welfare issues. During the 1999–2000 academic year, the SPIN community service option included creating a physical space for SPIN, establishing a database of SPIN members, updating the newsletter, and christening the newly established office by arranging an open house for SPIN members and community officials.

Given my previous experience with Halpern and SPIN, I expected that most students who chose this service-learning option would experience a positive shift in attitude toward the poor in general and welfare recipients in particular. I also expected that they would understand more clearly the concept of intersectionality, especially the interconnected nature of sex and class oppression. Lastly, given the example of Halpern and the positive results achieved by SPIN members, I expected that students would more readily understand the role of individuals and groups in maintaining or dismantling systems of oppression.

Women's Resource Center.   The Women's Resource Center of San Diego State University is an all-volunteer undergraduate student organization that advocates for women's social, political, and economic equity. The center provides feminist-oriented information, resources, and support to women on campus and to the community at large. Though largely committed to educating the public about violence against women and children through such activities as the Clothesline Project, annual Take Back the Night rallies and marches, and rape awareness campaigns, the center also works in coalition with other groups to sponsor campus- and community-wide programs on hate-crime prevention, lesbian and gay rights, and intercultural awareness. In addition, the center reaches out to young women in the surrounding community by sponsoring conferences for teen mothers enrolled in local high schools to encourage them to pursue higher education. Another major outreach effort is an annual music festival that raises funds for the Andrea O'Donnell Scholarship, which is awarded each year to an outstanding female undergraduate who has actively worked to improve the quality of life for women and girls. The scholarship not only reflects the scholar activism of center members, but also honors the memory of a past undergraduate student director of the Women's Resource Center who was murdered by her boyfriend in a domestic violence incident in 1994.

Students who selected the Women's Resource Center as their community-service partner were responsible for updating informational brochures, staffing tables at events, helping to staff the center, and assisting with Take Back the Night, the Andrea O'Donnell music festival, and other events and activities associated with the center. Because of the feminist-centered nature of this service-learning option, I expected that students would learn firsthand what some of our authors meant when they referred to "sexual politics." I also assumed that, through participation, these students would understand the myriad ways in which women engage in actions that fall outside the "traditional" definition of politics, yet are nonetheless highly "political."

The Campaigns to Elect Peace and Freedom Party Candidate Janice Jordan.

During the 1999–2000 academic year, Peace and Freedom Party candidate Janice Jordan ran for a San Diego City Council seat (1999) and the San Diego mayorship (2000). In addition to attending official campaign events where she was featured as a candidate for city council or mayor, students who elected to work with Jordan were expected to orient themselves to the perspectives of the Peace and Freedom Party (PFP) of California in general and to Jordan's stand on local issues in particular. These issues included, but were not limited to, the environment, law enforcement, housing, development, same-sex marriage, the prison industry, American Indian gaming, worker's rights, public transportation, and animal rights.

One of the most compelling aspects of the community-service option provided by Jordan was that it involved student participation beyond the election period, because, in the words of Jordan's campaign materials, "Instead of disappearing between elections . . . the PFP stays active in the community." Additionally, working with Jordan's campaigns provided students an opportunity to work with a "multi-issues" feminist whose activism is grounded in understanding the intersectionality of sex, race, class, dis(ability), sexual orientation, citizenship status, and more. To cite Jordan's campaign material once more,

> As a feminist party, the Peace and Freedom Party actively supports the struggle to eliminate oppression and discrimination based on sex or sexual orientation. Sexual oppression, abuse, and violence in our personal lives are intimately related to authoritarianism and hierarchical institutions, oppression and abuse on the job, and to the violence of war. The struggle against sexism and the struggle for democratic and nonviolent human relations cannot be delayed but must be pursued actively at the same time as the struggle to eliminate oppression and discrimination based on class, race or nationality, age, or physical disability.

It was my expectation that students who worked with Jordan would not only gain an insider's view of the formal political process, but would also come to appreciate the struggles associated with third-party candidacies as well as the unique issues facing women who run for formal political office. Moreover, because of Jordan's multi-issues feminism, I expected that students would become more receptive to the concept that "women are more than their sex"—that they have multiple social locations that factor into their political, economic, and social status in the United States.

Impact of Service Learning on Stereotypical Beliefs and Attitudes

As expected, students working with SDLGP and SPIN revealed in their reflection papers a shift in beliefs and attitudes toward the groups they served as part of their community-based learning projects. For instance, one student, Jena, wrote that working with SDLGP "helped me break down some of the stereotypes that I didn't even realize I had. It taught me that gays and lesbians are as normal as I am, and that they face many of the same prejudices that I have to deal with as a Latina." Likewise, Wei wrote that his experience with SPIN "changed my negative opinions and views about mothers on welfare":

> The dominant culture tends to label welfare mothers as lazy people dependent on the government for money and other resources. The media feed this image. But through SPIN, I learned that many mothers on welfare are working part-time and going to school to benefit themselves and their children—that they are eager to get off welfare and to begin supporting themselves as a result of education and job training.

Students who elected to work with the Women's Resource Center and the Janice Jordan campaigns also showed remarkable degrees of self-reflexivity in their reflection papers. One student in particular related her experiences with the Women's Resource Center and her exposure to feminist pedagogy directly to her own values and socialization, seeing a stark contrast to the worldview she had been socialized to embrace and the alternatives offered by new information. Alta acknowledged that prior to being exposed to course materials and her activities with the Women's Resource Center, she viewed feminists as "women who were just frustrated and were against everything that had anything to do with the opposite sex." In reflecting on her work with the Women's Resource center, she discussed the challenges this experience posed to her worldview of feminists, gender roles, and cultural expectations. She described her work with the center (and for the course in general) as "eye opening experiences" for her because she ultimately came to grips with the stereotypes she had internalized about feminists as well as cultural messages that, as a Latina, she should "follow and obey the men, never talk back." In a refutation of her gender role socialization, Alta saw her work as a fundraiser for the Andrea O'Donnell Scholarship Fund as an opportunity to "help other young women like [herself] . . . get the same rights as their [male] counterparts."

Participants' Abilities to Connect
Service Learning to Course Objectives

Not surprisingly, given repeated emphasis on the importance of connecting work with service providers to what was being studied in class, students uniformly demonstrated in their reflection papers how their service-learning experiences were related to course content and objectives. One of the more creative reflection papers was a photographic essay of the San Diego Lesbian and Gay Pride event that featured "dykes on bikes," a "transfamily" (i.e., transgender) float, a six-member family unit that ranged in age from a grandmother to an infant in a stroller, and an Asian man in a T-shirt bearing the logo "Honorary Lesbian." The student, Florencia, used these and other photographs to illustrate her point that Pride is an example of what one of our assigned readings (Benmayor and Torruellas 1997:189) describes as "cultural citizenship"—"the process whereby a subordinated group of people arrive at a common identity." Applying terminology employed by Benmayor and Torruellas (1997:189) to what she saw at the Pride event, Florencia argued that "'perceived collective identities' affirmed 'cultural citizenship' by extending our perceptions of the concept of 'family' beyond the restrictive limitations of the dominant society and its 'legal canon.'"

Students who partnered with SPIN drew multiple connections between their service-learning experiences and course content and objectives. For instance, one student, Monica, stated that her experience with SPIN accomplished the general course objective that we "examine some political issues addressed by contemporary feminists, especially as they intersect or conflict with national policies and practices." With specific reference to course content, Monica stated that her experience with SPIN "drove home" Martinez's (1998) reference to welfare reform as "a terrorist war on immigrants," especially since "San Diego is a border town and there are a number of documented immigrants who live here." Another student, Karen, similarly observed, "Welfare reform should be of primary concern for contemporary feminists . . . [because] the majority of women on welfare are employed in low-paying jobs that offer no health-care benefits." Noting the disconnect between the lived experience of welfare recipients and the assumptions made by those who "made the rules" regarding government assistance, Karen stated further that "working with the SPIN office . . . helped me understand . . . how much we need to pay attention to the decisions made by policy-makers."

A number of reflection papers made mention of the course objective pertaining to media representation of women as political objects or agents; however, attention to media coverage emerged most strongly and persistently in the accounts of students who worked with Janice Jordan. Students who wrote about their experiences with Jordan demonstrated an understanding that both the party affiliation and the gender of the candidate (as well as the gender of the news reporter) will likely influence news coverage. For instance, one student, Chauncy, noted the unequal news coverage of Jordan's campaigns as compared with that of other mayoral candidates. When she compared the numerous articles written about the mayoral candidates, she found that "only [one] article focused on Janice, much less mentioned her in more than a line or paragraph. Most [articles] rarely mentioned her name, while in-depth information was provided for the other 'major' party *and* male candidates. These articles were mostly, if not all, written by men."

Another theme that emerged from student reflection papers on their work with the Jordan campaigns was frustration that—on the rare occasions there was news coverage of Jordan—she was described as a lesbian when she is, in fact, heterosexual. Four of the five student papers commented at length on the inaccurate depiction of Jordan as a lesbian and related this development to course readings and discussions concerning "lesbian-baiting" in political campaigns. One student wrote that the misrepresentation of Jordan as a lesbian was a liability to her campaign, "not only because it was inaccurate information, but also because the controversial nature of the issue [took] away from the [substantive] concerns she was addressing."

Impact of Service Learning on Participants' Understanding of Intersectionality

Some service-learning experiences lent themselves readily to increased understanding of the interconnected nature of sex, race, class, and sexuality oppression. For instance, it was very clear to the students who worked with SPIN that "women's rights can be constrained by poverty." Additionally, the photographic essay on the San Diego Lesbian and Gay Pride event served as a literal illustration of intersectionality, in that it showed participants of all sexes, sexual orientations, races and ethnicities, national origins, physical and mental abilities, and economic classes coming together as one.

As anticipated, given the platform of the Peace and Freedom Party, as well as Janice Jordan's long-standing history as a multi-issues feminist, some very strong observations regarding the importance of addressing the intersectionality of sex, race, class, disability, and sexual orientation came from reflection papers written by students who had worked on Jordan's campaigns. Students tended to gravitate to those aspects of Jordan's campaigns that most resonated with them: Louise was clearly drawn to environmental issues and public education for today's youth; Morgan focused on efforts to raise public awareness regarding nuclear waste, unemployment, and homelessness in San Diego; Chauncy raised a range of issues as she delved into Jordan's misrepresentation by the media; inequality within the criminal justice system, and the rights of racial and ethnic groups, with particular emphasis on the rights of Native Americans. The diversity of issues covered by the students is indicative of the projects they worked closely with as well as the broad-based political agenda that Jordan embraces.

Outside of the specific issues, another aspect of the Jordan campaigns that troubled many students was that while Jordan actively campaigned around a host of issues, she was often rendered invisible in news coverage of her respective political campaigns for mayor and city council. Chauncy was particularly appalled that a multi-issues candidate like Jordan could be dismissed as a serious contender for the San Diego mayorship or the city council merely because she was a nontraditional candidate—that is, a female, third-party candidate whom the press erroneously depicted as lesbian. Chauncy was also frustrated that, as a Jordan campaign volunteer, she personally worked on increasing public awareness of a host of issues—including homelessness in

San Diego, police brutality, the rights of political prisoners, and violence against women—that were ignored by the news media's singular focus (if they covered Jordan at all) on the candidate's (mistaken) lesbian identity.

Impact of Service Learning on
Social Awareness and Personal Growth

The personal and civic impact of service-learning was expressed by students in a variety of ways. Speaking of how her work with SPIN challenged her stereotypes and misconceptions about welfare recipients, Christina wrote, "SPIN, Joni Halpern, and Women's Studies 375 have been catalysts for my growth as a person. Not only have they informed me of subjects about which I was ignorant, but they have also encouraged me to seek the truth in all instances—and that is what I will take with me after the semester is over." For Cheryl, the high point of the SPIN experience was the open-house reception she and other students put on to showcase the office they had painted and furnished as part of their service-learning project. The reception followed a forum that featured policy makers, service providers, and Temporary Assistance to Needy Families and CalWORKS mothers as speakers.[5] Cheryl stated that the most meaningful part of the night came for her when she shook hands with one of the CalWORKS mothers who had spoken at the forum. When asked why this gesture was so meaningful, Cheryl explained, "Because I saw her and other people on welfare as 'real people' for the first time in my life." Speaking in support of community-based service learning in general and her experience in particular, Cheryl concluded, "Sometimes experience teaches a person more about life than any book ever could."

Working at the Women's Resource Center brought another student, Sienna, to a more somber—yet equally important—perspective. Stating that she chose to work in the Women's Resource Center in order to contribute to women's understanding of challenges they face, Sienna concluded that she "was the one who learned the most from the experience" because she came to see more fully "the lengths women are still having to go through to be treated fairly":

> It wasn't until I proposed leaving some brochures on the outside of the doors that I learned that the Center couldn't leave anything outside because other student organizations in the building would vandalize them. This was also one of the main reasons that they constantly had to lock the Center when no one was inside. . . . I came to realize that the simple fact that there exists a student organization solely for women upsets some people who do not want to see women standing up and fighting for their rights.

Alta, another student, summarized her experience with the Women's Resource Center somewhat more positively, expressing "amazement" at "how much a class and a couple of hours of volunteer work can do to change a person's worldview." Observing that "just three months ago I did not know there was so much outside of my little world," Alta wrote that by the end of her service-learning project she understood that "plenty of women suffer due to the way our society is run, that women are persecuted just for being women, [and that] . . . there are so many men and women [who] need to be educated [regarding the inequitable treatment of women]."

Service learning within the Jordan campaigns produced still other outcomes, with several students indicating that they would continue to be politically active past the community-based service-learning experience. For instance, Chauncy continued to work with Jordan and other organizations she became familiar with through the campaign even after the 1999 elections. At the end of the fall semester when her reflection paper was due, Chauncy wrote, "I now take part in as many activities as my time will allow, and then some. And, in my effort, I see a little progress now and then. That makes it all worthwhile. We all need to take part in directing where the world around us [is headed]." Morgan, another student, made similar observations. Speaking as someone with no prior formal political experience, she indicated that her experiences with the Jordan campaigns "gave her a reality check" and enabled her to make decisions about how she wanted to be involved in the government.

Conclusion

Women's studies has developed into a field of interdisciplinary intellectual inquiry that necessarily investigates the impact of race, sexual orientation, class, (dis)ability and other social markers on the quality of life for women as well as men. While community-based service learning is an effective tool for enhancing student learning in any setting, it is particularly useful for overcoming student resistance to feminism in general, and specifically to a feminism grounded in the theory of intersectionality. Well-designed and structured service-learning projects with community organizations whose missions are aligned to course objectives allow students to integrate theory with application, often with the result that students unlearn stereotypes and misinformation, gain new levels of social consciousness, and even develop a burgeoning sense of civic responsibility.

Notes

1. I self-identify as "Black," rather than "African American" because being Black allows me to embrace a broader population of people of African descent than is possible within the "African American" framework, which is based on tracing one's ancestry solely through the United States slave South and Africa. Moreover, I use "Black," rather than "African American," because discrimination against people of African descent has historically been based on skin color, not nationality. I capitalize "White" both to reclaim it from invisibility and to accord it the same status as the term "Black," which I also capitalize.

2. I taught two sections of the course both semesters, with enrollments averaging approximately 30 per section. I was fortunate to have a graduate teaching assistant assigned to me who assisted with study sessions and grading.

3. Although students complete a form granting me permission to use their written materials in my teaching and research, I have assigned them code names in this study.

4. In 1997, the California legislature established the California Work Opportunity Responsibility to Kids (CalWORKS) program in response to federal welfare reform legislation.

5. The Temporary Assistance to Needy Families program (TANF) replaced Aid to Families with Dependent Children. States received federal block grants to set up TANF programs. TANF time limits and work requirements were set up by each state, and therefore vary widely.

IV

Women's Studies,
Experiential Education,
and Community Partnerships

When feminist students begin work in women's organizations and with other politically progressive groups, they are often frustrated by what they perceive as a disconnect between the knowledge produced in the academy and the knowledge produced by (and needed by) activists. Melissa Gilbert and Catherine Sameh address this issue in chapter 3 in an analysis of the process of partnering between feminists in the academy and feminists in the community. They describe outreach projects they developed for women and girls in the course of a five-year community-university partnership that has been the basis for a series of women's studies service-learning capstone courses. Gilbert and Sameh advocate giving activists access to the university's resources and committing to an ongoing intellectual exchange between the academic and the activist communities. They delineate six principles of feminist community partnering that have guided them as they grapple with various challenges and opportunities.

In chapter 14, Isa Williams discusses a program designed to strengthen understanding and promote dialogue between the academic and the activist communities. The Atlanta Semester Program in Women, Leadership, and Social Change includes a speakers' forum with women leaders and an internship program. Drawing on Aída Hurtado's analysis of knowledge production by women of color, Williams and her colleagues emphasize the extent to which knowledge production is filtered through unequal power relations based on race, class, and gender. Through what Williams calls the "in community" speakers' forum, students become aware that groups outside the academy possess knowledge that may not fit academic paradigms—knowledge that must be respected by those who seek to partner with community activists in work for social change.

In chapter 15, Katherine Rhoades, Anne Statham, and Mary Kay Scheiter emphasize the importance of dialogue among feminists in the academy,

183

community activists, and women in low-income communities. They describe a statewide activist project sponsored by the Outreach Office of the University of Wisconsin Women's Studies Consortium, the Women and Poverty Public Education Initiative (WPPEI). The project is a collective of academic and community women working to educate Wisconsin citizens about the realities of women living in poverty, and to encourage low-income women's participation in the welfare reform debate. WPPEI has raised questions, such as: Who should appropriately take action or be an "activist"? Who are our students, those in traditional classrooms, those in the community, or both? Where are our classrooms? Who are the "teachers"? How do we interact with others as learning partners in a nonelitist, nonhierarchical fashion? The authors report that "as our engagement with the community deepens, we find it becomes more difficult to distinguish between the classroom and the community."

13

Building Feminist Educational Alliances in an Urban Community

Melissa Kesler Gilbert and Catherine Sameh

It's very much like a trapeze artist trick. Everything depends on the connection of the two trapeze artists' limbs so that one or both is not dropped. We've received a lot of instruction about how to do our community work, but that's kind of like telling a person on a trapeze how to catch the person who will be swinging towards them. It seems more like something you just have to feel and know. The other part . . . is the connection in the middle. The two artists are so vulnerable at that point, especially if one has leaped off the swing and is spinning through the air towards the other artist who is supposed to catch them.

—Capstone student

Forming partnerships between the academy and the community can feel like the trapeze act described above by one of our community-based learning students. Both activist and academic are rooted on their own platforms, having to leap from what is known and comfortable. Both of us may hang on to the bar for a long time, not wanting to let go of the world we understand, but longing to create a new connection that we know will bring important life to our work. Throwing ourselves across the divide certainly can seem risky—learning something new may force us to change our beliefs, our work, and our lives. Our prior relationships, career success, and selves may be vulnerable to dissonance and disruption. But somehow we know we have to do it. If we do not, it may mean leaving so many others behind on each platform—without the opportunity to fly.

In this essay (offered as a dialogue) we explore the process of community partnering between feminists in the academy and feminists in the community.

We share excerpts from a series of conversations between Melissa (the women's studies professor) and Catherine (the feminist bookstore founder and activist).[1] The two of us have been involved in a five-year community-university partnership that has been the basis for a series of women's studies service-learning capstone courses. Our students have participated in outreach projects to women and girls throughout our urban community. We have been extremely fortunate in that our partnership has rarely felt as personally risky or vulnerable as the trapeze act depicted above. While any boundaries between us have seemed quite permeable, it may be that the safety net below us has been the key to our comfortable connection. That net is pieced together with our shared commitment to our community, our common feminist ideologies, and similar academic and activist histories.

We suggest that our partnership has been successful for both our students and our community because of the emphasis we have placed on feminist community-building efforts. We focus our discussion on some of the key challenges we faced as partners and how this work has affected student learning, the bookstore, and our partnership. We offer a set of six principles of feminist community partnering that have emerged from our collaborative efforts: (1) building on the founding ideals, (2) reinforcing feminist community values, (3) providing feminist space, (4) encouraging inclusive collaboration, (5) enlarging the community of women, and (6) empowering community members. Finally, we explore how our partnership has helped us to personally reexamine our multiple roles as activists and educators.

A History of Community-University Collaboration

While our community does sometimes seem like a circus, we actually work in a city of bridges. Many of Portland, Oregon's bridges cross rivers and highways; in fact, a rusty iron bridge across the Willamette river geographically separates Portland State University from the In Other Words bookstore. Native American Portland activist and bookstore volunteer, Schar Freeman, identifies the need for other bridges in our metro area that are perhaps more metaphorical and stretch among neighborhoods, race and class borders, and generations:

> We can actually go into the community, get out there with the homeless girls. Be out there in the community because they're not going to come in here. So we have to find a *way to bridge* and do outreach. Those are our future women. Those are our future voices. Those are our future dreams and I feel responsible for nurturing them. . . . We can't keep thinking someone else is going to fix it. [2]

These kinds of bridges are not new to feminism. They have been at the heart of much discussion about multicultural alliances, border crossings, and academic and community collaborations.

Feminist activists Jael Silliman and Anannya Bhattacharjee (1999) present the relationship between the academy and the activist as a "crossover" and suggest that when these kinds of relationships do form that it is usually because of a single individual seeking to "bridge the divide" (1999:125). They argue that we can break down institutionally erected obstacles to our partnerships and make a commitment to developing activist/academic linkages by (1) giving activists access to the university's institutional resources and (2) making a commitment to an on-going intellectual exchange between these two communities (1999:133). While some (Hope 1999) argue that the connections between activism and education are no more than transitory and weak, many of us entrenched in the service-learning movement witness stronger and more permanent partnerships forming everyday. We believe that because there has always been a sharing of participation between the bookstore and the university that our partnership has not felt many of the tensions described by other feminists doing this work. We have been in collaboration since the founding of the store and have shared the vision of sustaining intellectual communities wherever we reside. The bridge building did not fall on the shoulders of one individual woman; it began with three, and is now shared by many.

Catherine: Our partnership between the local feminist bookstore and the university began in 1993 with the founding of the store, In Other Words, and its sister organization, the Women's Community Education Project (WCEP). Johanna Brenner, coordinator of the Portland State University's Women's Studies Program, Catherine Tetrick, a child-care and reproductive rights activist, and I founded the store together. We had been friends and had worked together as reproductive rights activists, and we began talking about opening a women's bookstore in early 1993. Johanna was looking forward to a sabbatical, and Catherine and I were exploring possible career transitions. We had been customers of A Woman's Place, the feminist bookstore in Portland that opened in the late 1970s and closed in the late 1980s. We all really missed that store, missed the community space and place for intellectual exploration. We felt certain that Portland could support a women's bookstore, and began doing research on how to open such an establishment.

We created the WCEP as a nonprofit organization because we knew that the market would never fully support our project. We knew that the sales alone of a feminist bookstore would never cover all our expenses: staff, rent, and all the programming we wanted to do. We were not in this to run a business—

although that is a big part of what we do—but to create a lasting community space where all women and their friends could discover the rich world of women's community, literature, and culture. We wanted the bookstore to be the place to go after leaving the university, or for those who never had access to the university.

Naturally, women's bookstores have a historic relationship with local women's studies departments—some feminist bookstore founders in other cities have been women's studies professors—and in our case Johanna was ideally situated to bring fellow academics on board when we started. We formed an advisory committee of 50 women (and a few men) to help us order initial inventory, plan events, and serve as ongoing advisors to the project. Many were from the Women's Studies Department at PSU and others were social workers, activists, and other feminist professionals in Portland. Today much of our retail book sales come through the academic texts we provide each quarter to PSU women's studies courses. Students from the university have also been earning practicum credit at our store since we opened. We collaborate with women's studies in many other ways as well, from cosponsoring local lectures to planning fund-raising activities. Our most recent collaborations have been part of our capstone partnership.

The Capstone Partnership

Melissa: In 1995, PSU instituted a new series of general education courses requiring each student to take a senior capstone course. The six-credit capstone is intended to be the point in each student's academic career where she puts her academic expertise to use meeting a community need, working with an interdisciplinary team of students and members of the local community in an effort to, as our university motto suggests, "Let Knowledge Serve the City." In the spring of 1996, I received a grant from the university to develop a series of long-term partnerships with area women's organizations that would provide experiential learning environments for our students. At the same time, these partnerships would help to meet the economic, health, literary, cultural, and educational needs of our city's women and girls. This program was called Women's Community Partnerships. The goal of the partnership program was to build a network of community partners who would come to learn about each other over the years, hold yearly conferences, and collectively work together as academic and activist partners. The students would be introduced to these various agencies through the capstone projects with the hope that they might be socialized into the feminist community and build lasting relationships for their future volunteerism, activism, and professional careers. We piloted two capstone projects that spring with Portland's YWCA and a local family-based service agency, Healthy Start. The next fall we worked together on an oral history capstone documenting the founding of the city's feminist nonprofit, women-run health clinic, All Women's Health Services.

Catherine: My partnership with the capstone program began in the fourth year of the bookstore's operation (1996). I was asked to participate in the All Women's Health Services capstone. I had worked at the clinic for many years, right up until the time we opened the bookstore. I participated in the capstone as a narrator, recalling my time as a health worker and clinic supervisor. In talking about that experience, I relayed what that job had taught me about building and sustaining a feminist organization, the challenges and rewards, and how that experience has carried over into running WCEP.

The next year we began developing a new one-quarter, ten-week capstone, the CityGirls project. Still relatively new in the community, the WCEP hoped to use the capstone program as an outreach tool, linking up with social service and social justice organizations that work with girls and young women.

Melissa: When we started the CityGirls capstone project we really had no idea what we were doing. We knew that we wanted to do some kind of outreach to teen girls, but I remember us struggling to figure out just what the project might look like. As our community partner for the project, the WCEP wanted lists of community advocates who might be potential liaisons for the store in years to come—schoolteachers, counselors, and agency people who might be able to help with educational programming for teens, special events, and other activities. We worked with an interdisciplinary group of senior students who also brought varied interests and community experiences to the project. Their goals helped to shape our community work that term. Half of the students in the first class spent the quarter conducting interviews with community advocates, gathering information, and creating a contact list. The other half of the class met with small groups of girls from various organizations in what we called rap sessions—spaces for identity exploration and self-exploration. Out of those sessions came transcripts of conversations, amazing artwork, teen poetry, essays, and fiction. All of these contributions from teenagers ended up being the content for the first Portland-based teen girl zine, TRIX: Drugs, Sex, and Other Pesky Things.[3] The girls, our rap sessions, and zine publishing became the primary focus of that term's work. We quickly lost site of our initial community outreach goals.

In that first capstone, we focused less on building our partnership and more on getting the CityGirls project off the ground. We were thinking about window displays and zine distribution, not about how to build a larger community that would support girls' needs today and in the future. The readings I chose for the class were about feminist bookstores and the girl zine revolution. They were very specific and were meant to introduce students only to the current project. I know I was not thinking in the long term. I was trying to meet the immediate needs of the project and find something fun and thoughtful that might turn my students on to feminism. It was my first time doing work with teenage girls, studying the literature on adolescence, and exploring zine cultures. It was not until subsequent capstones that we began to fully develop our outreach work.

Catherine: Our initial goal in working with the capstone program, particularly the first CityGirls project, was to expand our outreach to communities and individuals serving girls and young women. We felt this was a particularly important group. We had not done any serious target outreach to girls, and wanted to make them aware of us and build our teen base. Now that the partnership has grown, our goals have grown beyond outreach. Through our work with the CityGirls project, we have built our inventory for young people, increased our zine section and networked with many social service organizations. With each course we develop real working and community-building relationships with students, many of whom are experiencing a feminist organization for the first time. This has become the most rewarding result of our work with the capstone program, and goes back to our original mission of providing feminist community and education.

Melissa: After several years of collaborative work, our partnership has taken on much more meaningful directions. While the CityGirls project is still at the heart of our collaboration, our success together has been rooted in our feminist community-building efforts. We have moved beyond a project-to-project framework. We have now helped the bookstore and our university become cornerstones for feminist work in our city. Between myself and my colleagues at PSU we have collaborated with the WCEP on twelve different capstone projects. These projects have focused on sexism in children's literature, breast cancer activism, lesbian history, homeless youth, and teen girls. Through this work we have broadened our community to include advocates and activists serving grades K–12, women's health organizations, other nonprofit groups, grassroots political groups, and local government agencies. We have grounded ourselves along the way in what we have defined below as six principles of feminist community partnering.

Principles of Feminist Community Partnership

1. Building on the Founding Ideals

We have learned over time that one of the most important first steps in partnering has been to remember how and why the organization was founded.
While the history of In Other Words (IOW) is a comparatively short one, calling on its founding circumstances, foremothers, and lessons learned has been
a very meaningful process for our partnership.

Melissa: I was fortunate to learn firsthand in the second year of our partnership the value of turning toward the past for insight and vision. We designed a
capstone where students helped the store to document its history and to celebrate its five-year anniversary. The resulting historical collection, *Pages Turning*,
has become an essential document for each of my future capstone students to
read. That collection reminds all of us of the struggles of starting a nonprofit
feminist organization, but more importantly, it forms the basis for our collective understanding of the meaningful ideals the WCEP created for education
and community outreach. The collection highlighted the importance of creating a "family of women" at the bookstore, the commitment to diversity, and
the making of feminist intellectual space. Each term my students grasp on to
the history of the bookstore as a place to ground themselves. They have a circle of women in that collection who become more real to them through reading their stories. It becomes their first connection to feminists in the course,
some of whom they will come to know personally over the term. It also helps
them to recognize how effective an individual woman can be in making a difference as well as the power of a feminist collective, of women working
together. Alongside readings on feminist bookstores and feminist organizations, this collection makes the work we do each quarter pertinent to our
own city.

Catherine: This project was so important for WCEP. It gave founders, staff,
and key volunteers the opportunity to articulate what WCEP/IOW meant to
them, why they did what they did, and what the challenges and rewards were.
Articulating the history and then seeing it in the context of a beautifully
crafted collection like *Pages Turning* had a tremendous impact on all of us. We
knew we had blossomed into a really unique and vital organization, but it
helped us recommit and/or deepen our commitments to WCEP and to each
other. It was also tremendously affirming and gratifying to see all our hard
work documented and celebrated in this way. We use *Pages Turning* to orient new

volunteers to our history and mission. It brings our mission statement alive in ways that a three-hour orientation cannot do. It is also a wonderful document for founders, staff, and long-term volunteers to review—a boost on those days when we feel worn out!

2. Reinforcing Feminist Community Values

Another important aspect of our work together has been our sharing of a feminist framework in our approach to the partnership. While not so clearly articulated as they could be, we have developed a working ideology and a set of goals that are feminist and community based. These goals now move beyond one project and reflect both of our commitments to bringing feminism, an understanding of gender inequality, and antioppression strategies to our community. While as partners we share a certain set of feminist values, they are not necessarily reflected by all of those with whom we work each term. Much of the success of our partnering has been the internal reinforcement of our beliefs, coming home to this partnership knowing that we have something in common. But the more challenging work that we do together is through our outreach, where we meet the not-so-like-minded. It is at those junctures that we have to stretch and acknowledge that the differences in our perspectives may actually be able to carry us toward a new community vision. We are not just educating the community, but we are learning many lessons of our own.

Melissa: While we never sat down to write out a shared ideology for our partnership (which might be a great idea), we have over time developed a working set of principles for our projects that is feminist and community based. I see these goals as focusing on education, outreach, and diversity. I view these goals as moving beyond one project, guiding us toward social change, toward creating a more just society. In our efforts to build feminist community for the bookstore, our university, and our city we have encountered potential partners who do not share our ideological beliefs. In the CityGirls class we have met many agencies that have laid out objectionable terms for our collaborations. For example, one after-school program for girls indicated that they would not work with us if we continued to carry coming-out stories in our zines. A principal of a local middle school refused to participate unless we gave him the right to edit (read: *censor*) the material girls submitted to our zine. Most recently, we discovered after several weeks of working with a transition house for teens that the girls living there were being forced to take birth control pills without their consent.

Each of these experiences has made us return to the ideological commitments we have made in our work. While we still wanted to build community and reach the teens isolated behind the walls of homophobia, sexism, and patriarchal control, we have had to question the value of establishing relationships with these agents. To solve these dilemmas we have relied on all three of the shared goals. My students have prioritized the needs of the girls we are trying to reach and have focused on the diversity of perspective, voice, and self-expression. At the same time, the classes have each decided that we also have to stress the educational role in our work. One student set up an appointment to discuss homophobia with the agency representative. She brought with her to the meeting literature on the topic, statistics about queer youth, and more stories written by lesbian teens. A group of students went to visit the principal and talked to him about the silencing of girls in our society and the need for uncensored spaces where they can communicate. The two students working at the transition house met with the head of the house to inform her of the girls' desires not to take birth control, to have more control over their own bodies, and to receive some respect for their personal choices.

Catherine: Our ideological challenges have come mostly from within the feminist/activist community rather than from "outsiders." For example, some people feel we should do more on transgender issues or, in fact, less on transgender issues and more on lesbian-feminist issues. These challenges have not been particularly fierce, and are usually easily met by reaffirming that we are a place for all women, all feminist voices. We also encourage debates on feminist issues and the kinds of communities we are trying to build.

The stories from the students illustrate just how important feminist debate, education, and activism are, and how organizations that serve girls and women are not inherently feminist. I am so impressed that the students confronted these organizations and attempted to change minds and/or policies while following through on their commitments to the girls within the organizations. I imagine this was an empowering experience for the students, that it tested their own commitments to feminist ideals. I wonder if any of these students began to self-identify as feminists through this process and found their feminist voices of critique and resistance to homophobia, censorship, and class/race oppression (out of which forced birth control comes). I wonder this particularly because I have observed many college-age women rejecting the label of feminism even while practicing its tenets, or rejecting the notion of women's oppression until they directly experience or witness it.

Melissa: At first these issues caused a great deal of conflict within our classroom. The students are from a range of disciplines, which means they have not come to the capstone with a strong background in feminist theory or women's studies. Many have never studied oppression, homophobia, racism, or classism. Some students are angered that they have found themselves sitting in a feminist classroom, volunteering at a feminist bookstore. These students signed up for the capstone because of their interest in working with teen girls in the city, not, as one student put it, "to be indoctrinated into the feminist movement." They are resistant to the use of feminist jargon, feminist scholarship, and feminist methodologies. They write about feminism as radical, exclusionary, biased, and reactionary. Some students were "a bit embarrassed" and "taken aback" when they read the first IOW newsletter and the front page was an article about a lesbian volunteer's experience. These students thought the story was okay, but did not think it was a good idea that it was the first thing readers would notice about the store.

I also remember other issues that prompted one woman who was very new to feminism to search for as many "male-bashing" incidents as she could find in our work. She wrote one journal that shared how "unnerved" she had become when she shared her well-researched bibliography of teen books. She thought that the WCEP seemed antimale because she was asked to focus on books "that were only about girls and that did not have a lot of men in them." So, the reinforcing of feminist values within our classroom collective has not always been easy. Before those students got to the point where they were ready to take on the community's homophobia and racism, they had to struggle internally with their own. The good news is that they usually asked for help in this process. For example, the teen bibliographer ended her journal with the request, "I am wondering about why this [wanting books with female protagonists] is and would be most obliged if you could tell me."

For some students the process of developing a more critical consciousness begins (and sometimes ends) with a new awareness, a new perspective, or at the very least a new of way of seeing the world. I use many feminist pedagogical strategies to help students in the classroom stretch beyond their "comfort zones" and to grasp some of the basic tenets of feminism. At the end of each quarter most of my students describe a new understanding of the complexities of oppression, an appreciation for diversity, and a realization about the relationship between power and knowledge. While many students also start to identify as feminist by the term's end, others may at least identify with many of the ideas, beliefs, perspectives, and struggles of the feminist women and girls they have met through these capstones. Students who come to the capstone with previously formed feminist identities write about our work together as strengthening, deepening, and renewing their commitment to women. Others find themselves within a broad definition of feminism with which they feel comfortable; as one student noted, "I have come to realize that I am a feminist, where originally I would not have thought I was one. I am glad that I was able to learn new definitions of feminism and [that] my perspective of feminism has changed."

Catherine: Our commitment to working with a broad and inclusive definition of feminism and to being a space for all women is really our guiding light in all we do. One of the most delightful rewards of working with the capstone program has been to bring in students who might not have come to us otherwise, and to see students develop feminist consciousness. For many of the students, WCEP is the first feminist organization with which they have had contact. As they work with us, they see what feminism looks like "on the ground."

While many volunteers enter WCEP already self-identifying as feminists, a majority of the time they deepen their commitments to feminism and feminist activism and education as they become more integrated into the organization. They develop commitments to feminist ideals like democratic participation, collaborative work, and self-empowerment through education and activism. We founded the store with a broad definition of feminism, with the understanding that there are different feminisms, different notions of what feminism means to people. We operate each day with that assumption, and the commitment that springs from that to be as inclusive as possible in all that we do. That has been our basis for building community, and we return to that whenever something challenging comes up.

We have not had quite the same challenges that the capstone students faced, but do have times when we need to internally revisit our mission statement, our original vision, ideologies, and values. Most recently we did this at a strategic planning session with our board of directors, staff, and volunteers. We were looking at the next three to five years: what we wanted to accomplish, what our strengths, weaknesses, challenges and opportunities are. Our ongoing partnership with the university capstone program prompted many of us to question our activist role. While we all agreed that we are a community space for all women, there were some competing notions of what our emphasis is: Is our focus promoting women's literature? Is it creating a space for activists and organizers? Is our priority doing feminist education? Can we do all of this successfully? The conversation was quite dynamic and showed that volunteers are drawn to us for all of the above reasons, that we really do play a unique role in the community because we are a place for women's community, culture, literature, education, and activism. It is an ambitious project, but women's bookstores have historically played these multiple roles in their communities and still do so today. For this reason, we are well positioned to work with the capstone program. Whatever the project—breast cancer, women's health, girl power—we are positioned to support those projects and to really benefit from them.

3. Providing a Feminist Space

Many bookstore volunteers, students, and community members strongly value the intellectual, social, and community space provided by IOW. It is a place that emphasizes personal sharing and emotional ties, the socialization of new members high levels of respect and trust, and the appreciation of diversity. As Meg Daly, a bookstore volunteer, put it, "Here is where I feel at home! I think it's an invigorating place to go where your thing, what is of interest to you as a feminist or a lesbian or a woman, [is] there, present, on the table." Our partnership has worked to value and maintain that space and to bring new people into it. Providing feminist spaces has also meant introducing teen girls to IOW, making the PSU classroom feminist, and taking the ideals of feminist space out into schoolrooms, coffee shops, street corners, and agency meeting rooms.

Feminist historians have illustrated the ways in which women were segregated into a separate sphere—what Carol Smith-Rosenberg (1985) calls "a female world," where women developed a sense of sisterhood, formed networks of friendship, love, and support that enabled them to maximize their freedom and exert political and social influence. Leila Rupp and Verta Taylor (1987) suggest that through a process of female bonding these women-committed women formed relationships that were central to the success of feminist activity throughout history. Since its founding, the bookstore wanted to create what Sara Evans and Harry Boyte (1986) would call a "free space"—a setting between our private lives and large-scale institutions where ordinary citizens can act with dignity, independence, and vision. Catherine Tetrick, one of the founders of IOW, describes her initial feelings about creating the feminist space at the bookstore:

> We really felt like what we needed in this community was space by and for women . . . an intellectual space designed by and for women that was not university-based, something for women who have never had access to the university. . . . We felt that a women's bookstore was the ideal kind of place to create that kind of intellectual community, for a number of reasons. [For one,] it was a very public space and it was also an important organizing tool . . . to create a community space where women could come together to talk about contemporary issues affecting them and make those connections.

For IOW the "free space" was designed primarily as a women's space where autonomous female subcultures could articulate their individual problems, build social analyses of their own oppression, and organize communities. Our partnership has continually emphasized the necessity of this real, urban, women's space. We collect there, laugh there, and make important decisions there.

Melissa: One of the challenges we have faced as partners is that our university classrooms are not free, woman-only spaces. My students include both women and men and I try to provide equitable experiences in the community for each. At the same time, I encourage students to recognize that gender is a social process that greatly affects the potential work we can do in our communities. One particular incident reflects the different definitions of space appropriate to the bookstore and the university. During our second CityGirls capstone course there was a male student who wanted to volunteer at the store. His desire to participate at the store raised important questions for bookstore staff about the work of volunteers and the meaning of women's community space. In the classroom, this experience provided an important learning moment. Many of the women students were outraged that there was any questioning of this male's volunteerism. They felt that the store was participating in "reverse sexism." As a class, we had to work through what it means to be an outsider, how more privileged people (in this case a man) can most effectively work to end oppression, how we can be effective allies, and why many women's groups have stressed the importance of women's space. The students who felt the store was being antimale did change their minds once we discussed the incident, mostly because so many of their peers engaged with them in a very honest and painful dialogue about their own personal need for women's space in their lives.

Catherine: No man had ever asked to volunteer in the store, so we never really had a policy. We never explicitly said that WCEP was a women-only space, but only women had been interested in volunteering. This situation prompted a discussion among WCEP volunteers about what our policy should be. We do have many male customers—fathers, brothers, husbands, partners, feminist men—who really support us. Their support is critical and we welcome it. But women volunteer here because it really is a store by, for, and about women; it is women's space, one of the few places that is entirely women-run and women-focused. In this sense it is "safe" space, that is, safe from the everyday sexism encountered in integrated spaces. Our discussion

Teaching Feminist Activism

led to a consensus that we welcomed the participation of men in a more secondary way (i.e., helping with events, support of women staff, basically anything but working directly with customers/community), but that the sort of "front-line" visible IOW representatives should be women.

Some students felt it was problematic to assign men a behind the scenes role. Although many students did not initially agree with our policy, it sounds like they came to understand how this feminist model might work, how women-run organizations empower women as leaders/workers/activists. At the time, I worried that we might have alienated some women from the store.

Melissa: Very few of the students have felt alienated from the store. Quite to the contrary, these kinds of debates have moved most of them to want to be more a part of a community that builds mutual understandings. At the beginning of each term, the students do the scavenger-hunt exercise where they note items at the store that might be of interest to teenagers. That exercise gets students into the store for the first time in a very casual and fun way. Sometimes students walk in the store and it is radically different from anything they have ever known before, but they quickly find resources that speak to them. Most of them immediately want to take a friend there and are very excited about getting teenagers interested in the place. As one student just wrote to me this morning, "I've never been any place that creates such a safe atmosphere for girls to be their true selves."

The students who actually volunteer at the store describe a wide range of sentiments about their time there, from "catching the volunteer spirit" to finding enormous pride in their accomplishments. The most compelling response that I hear from many of these students is that they finally have had the opportunity to be "a part of something," "to be more connected," and "more bound to the world" through their volunteerism at the store. Others describe volunteering as helping them to establish new relationships in their city. One CityGirls' student explains that she was able to "expand that web of community involvement." While providing a space that feels safe, comfortable, and like home for my students, IOW has also opened up many doors for them as well.

Catherine: I saw students making those connections when we worked with the capstone class on our five-year history and celebration. Students were integrated into our volunteer base through their work here. They developed an elaborate window display; interviewed volunteers, board members, and staff at WCEP; and became part of the collective of volunteers here, not just for the school semester, but beyond. They saw that feminist work is social and fun, empowering and inclusive.

4. Encouraging Inclusive Collaboration

One of the key challenges of our partnership has been to work in ways that promote multiple and diverse voices in decision making, including students, community partners, faculty, and bookstore affiliates. By using consensus building, consciousness-raising, and other feminist processes we try to identify common problems and strategize about solutions. An appreciation of diversity is one of the primary learning objectives of our capstone program.

We have had to be accountable in this work to varying constituencies. As white women from two institutions perceived by the community as elite, our accountability is often called upon. Reaching out has also meant reaching in to find out who we are, why we are doing this work, and how we believe it will really benefit others. Siobhan Ring (1999:236) reminds us, "If we are going to delve into people's lives, tell their stories, mold their words, or justify theories on their backs, we owe them a lot."

Catherine: WCEP is definitely a social-change organization. We believe in the power of writing, debate, dialogue, reading, activism, and education to change lives. We reflect this in our organizational structure, which utilizes a traditional nonprofit structure board of directors, small staff, large pool of volunteers, with an emphasis on volunteer participation and leadership.

One of our main goals in founding WCEP was to provide an accessible feminist community space that would both reflect and attract a diversity of voices. Diversifying our volunteer base in terms of race and class is one of our biggest and most interesting challenges. We have always been mostly white, mostly younger than forty, mostly lesbian, mostly middle class. We are more diverse now than ever, but have room to grow. Our work with PSU students has been a great way to diversify our base. As an urban university, PSU attracts working-class students and students of color, as well as white and middle-class students who may not have had much exposure to feminism.

Melissa: Issues of diversity have also been a challenge for us both inside the classroom and as we move out into the community. One of the primary goals of our outreach is inclusivity. We work to create a group of teens that is racially and economically diverse as well as inclusive of girls with varying sexual identities. We want the zine to include and speak to a broad range of voices, experiences, and visions. However, the diversity we work toward in our project is not represented in our classroom. Only 15 percent of the capstone students are women of color. Many of the students do come from working-class families, or are currently living on welfare themselves, and there are usually several women in the class who identify as lesbians. But, while we are reaching out to diverse constituents, we do not reflect the diversity of most of the girls with whom we worked.

We have to do a lot of work in the classroom around social location and identity. While I try to provide a multicultural inclusive curriculum for my students to prepare them for community work, I have not always succeeded. I remember last year there were two students in the capstone who were disabled. They felt that the lack of readings on teens with disabilities excluded them from both the content of the course and their personal possibilities for collaboration in the classroom. One of the students who used a wheelchair asked me if she could do a quick presentation in class about her disability and invite students to take a ride in her chair. She felt that this experience would break down some of her classmates' stereotypes about her and others with disabilities and might move her to a place where she felt more included. The presentation was extremely powerful and was a turning point for our group. Another student joined her project team and together they designed a disability resource notebook for the store. Because of these students, we have now built up a series of readings and resource material about girls with disabilities and have forged partnerships with three local agencies serving disabled youth.

Community work also means border crossings for most of the students. They are very apprehensive about leaving the university. To prepare them, we do several identity assignments in class and have workshops on breaking down stereotypes and learning interruption skills (for interrupting oppressive statements). Students feel that these exercises are very difficult, but note that they have helped them to uncover prejudices deeply embodied, "close to the heart," and "something that was ingrained" in them. One white, middle-class student who had worked though many of her own biases early in the term still felt nervous about her approaching rap session with a group of diverse teens. She noted in her journal, "I feel most uncomfortable about reflecting the same institutionalized, class, and race bias I've been working a long time to combat."

Moving beyond the classroom is difficult when class and race differences are present between students and teens. We run integrated groups as well as groups where both students and teens share racial identities. But where there may be racial solidarity, there are always differences in class, power, and privilege between teen girls and university students. We experience a tension about the possibility of the girls (and the agencies representing them) feeling exploited by our work. That tension has prompted us to incorporate ally training into our preparation. We encourage the girls to set the agenda for rap sessions. When they ask the student facilitators for advice, the students turn the questions back to the girls so that they can negotiate a strategy together from their own shared experiences.

Still, students are not always welcomed or accepted by community partners. Many partners feel overstudied and previously exploited by the university. Our hope for inclusivity is often thwarted because of the agency's previous experiences with other programs, when teens were put at risk or were made to feel used. Because of these past histories, we have had a great deal of trouble forging relationships with queer youth groups and drug and alcohol treatment centers. By showing agencies that we are invested in social change, not research, and by having students participate in these agency's onsite training programs, we have been able to make some headway. But we remain suspect because we belong to an elite institution. It takes a great deal of work to reframe ourselves as trustworthy advocates and activists.

Catherine: In many ways, we experience some of the tensions that the university does, but our issues are mostly with activist groups. Even though we are a grassroots organization, we are perceived by some in the community as "not activist enough." Because we are a bookstore, located in a fairly homogenous (white, middle-class) part of Portland, some perceive us to be sort of elitist in that we are not "on the front lines" in the same ways that many activist groups are. This comes back to trying to be a space for all women, doing all things.

We organize and host activist and educational events, and support activism through our Organization of the Month program, which champions different grassroots women's organizations in our window and in the store. That is a huge commitment of ours. But of course, we sell books, too, and books are expensive, often seen as commodities of the privileged. It is a wonderful tension to work with—to try to be a community institution that serves communities of women across class and race lines, and that brings people together to explore these tensions. In that sense, we are a kindred institution to the university and our partnership benefits from a shared understanding of these dilemmas.

5. Enlarging the Community of Women

Moving beyond the bookstore and the university to strengthen and enlarge our community of women has been an essential part of our work. Four years ago, several friends of the bookstore voiced their hope that community-building would be a part of the bookstore's future. As bookstore founder Johanna Brenner suggested,

> Let's see if we can partner up with some women's organizations that are real grassroots and don't get the exposure they deserve. . . . Rather than waiting for an organization to come to us, we're going to go and see organizations to partner up with. This is a way of building our community, networking, and establishing good relationships with organizations that aren't already a part of our network.

Historically, forming networks of female relationships has strengthened political struggles. But as Ring (1999:235–36) argues, our efforts to build these relationships have needed to be flexible and "responsive to the needs and concerns of the activist group."

Catherine: One of the greatest outcomes for WCEP in partnership with the capstone program is our enlarged community as women and as feminists. Students are not just working for our organization, but are becoming part of a wider community through their work, commitments, and concrete contributions. Through the CityGirls capstone, students have created important resources for the community, like the disability resources notebook; brochures for teens on eating disorders, body image, and depression; websites for girls; and a bibliography for young women. In breast cancer capstones, students have created art projects—a quilt of breast cancer survivor stories and a bust of a woman with a mastectomy. These are permanently housed at WCEP and regularly used in our window displays and for community forums. These resources provide an important way to bring new community members into our network.

Melissa: To help meet the goals of WCEP, we have also worked to build a rich and complex feminist network of community partners in the Portland metropolitan area. One of the ways we have created this network is by strengthening the relationships that the bookstore had already established—with other local bookstores and nonprofit organizations. Most of the work, however, has been in forging new relationships in the community. This process has meant continually evaluating the kinds of new partnerships we are forming, and determining if the new relationships will mutually benefit everyone involved. Students begin these partnerships through their outreach work, and they make contacts in their neighborhoods. New contacts also come to us through our existing partners. We invite school counselors, teachers, and nonprofit advocates to work with us. We provide university resources to the partners and several students may volunteer at these sites during the term as well. We also advertise for their agencies in our zine's resource pages. Partners reciprocate by helping us to bring together teen girls for our rap sessions and zine work. Articles in our city's newspaper and radio shows help all of us to increase our visibility in the community. All of the CityGirls project partners also become partners with IOW. They are part of the constituent base and will turn to IOW when sponsoring events, conferences, and fund-raising activities.

This work introduces students to an extremely broad spectrum of teen allies, advocates, and activists, all of whom bring different perspectives to the work we do. We have partners who focus on self-esteem building, girls' empowerment, antiracist education, self-defense, therapeutic intervention, drug and alcohol treatment, pregnancy and parenting support, and traditional education.

Catherine: Our work with the Women's Studies Department at PSU has harvested many new relationships. Through the CityGirls capstone in particular, we now are connected to a coalition of scores of social service and social justice groups working with girls. Many of these groups now call on us to put up information tables at events, to provide bibliographies, and to cosponsor events. They sometimes order books for their programs through IOW. While we have always had a section of books for girls and young women, our work with this project made it possible for us to build this section and to add resources like zines and information on disability services. We became more committed to serving girls and the parents, workers, and educators who serve them. This new role became a more integrated part of our identity. We are now becoming experts in the field of girl studies and use our expertise on a regular basis in our work with girls in the community.

Melissa: At the same time, the teens—and all of our partners—are also experts who extend to us knowledge that is situated in our urban community and is informed by everyday life, intellectual work, and shared experiences. Without the mutuality of this relationship and the knowledges we share, we would only be seeing what we have discovered on our own private paths.

6. Empowering Community Members toward Social Change

In order to build trust and empower all community members we have respected and valued the multiple knowledges which inform our work. We are all experts sharing our specific knowledges, moving us toward social change.

Catherine: This partnership is successful in large part because of the very structures of our respective organizations: students are asked to work collaboratively while also being self-starters and working independently. At WCEP, every volunteer has the right to develop and implement projects. Both the capstone and WCEP encourage and support students and volunteers taking on leadership roles that help them develop as individuals. Our community volunteers offer their own workshop series at the store, sponsor special events and have editorial control of both our newsletter and window displays.

Very often, my initial ideas about how students might work with WCEP do not resonate with students, but they create ways of plugging in and working with us that speak to their desires. They take initiative, and we support their development by giving them contacts with the community, providing access to our community resources and books, and hooking them up with experienced WCEP staff and volunteers.

In our work with the zine project, students are empowered as leaders on issues that girls and young women are facing. Their hands-on work with teens through the rap groups and zines give them access to a constituency that is harder for WCEP to reach directly: teens of color, poor and working-class youth, street girls, girls in transitional houses, and girls in lock-down facilities. So while we, as a seven-year-old feminist organization, can provide leadership and support to students in their work, their work gives us more access to a larger community of girls and those advocates who work with them. Students become "ambassadors" of and for feminism, linking grassroots feminist organizations (like us) to social service agencies and the girls and young women they serve.

Melissa: Serving in this "ambassador" role helps students recognize their own efficacy in the world. They learn a great deal about social and political responsibility and begin to see how social change can take place at the community level. Many students come to understand social change as beginning with education and awareness. Almost all of the students come to believe that social advocacy and social change require a certain type of person: the "risk-taker," someone who will "put [herself] on the line for anyone," and in some cases someone who has "blind faith and a lot of luck." Some of the students come to see themselves as this kind of activist, while others move toward less risky and subtle forms of social change like community education. After going out in the community and unsuccessfully trying to rally support for the bookstore and its mission, a CityGirls student identified a new community role for herself: she now wants to inform her community about "the injustice and oppression of women, the poor, and minority groups. . . . That can be my job!"

Our empowerment work goes beyond students and bookstore volunteers. Our outreach to teens strives to empower girls by providing spaces for their self-expression. The girls see rap sessions as the foundation for raising awareness and building "girl solidarity." They come to understand the power of girls working together on issues. They turn that knowledge into art- and word-filled zine pages that deconstruct myths about girls' bodies, loves, aspirations, and experiences. They share their visions for a new society through not only their zine work, but also in the murals they paint on urban landscapes and the voices they transmit over our local KPSU airwaves. They tell us that they want their parents, teachers, and other adults to "listen up" and become advocates for their vision of social change.

Just last quarter, when a group from a boy's and girl's club was asked what new kinds of guidelines our society needs, one girl stood up, and with arms raised above her head held a poster that said STOP HITTING WOMAN, MAN! The other girls in the group joined her with cheers, one preteen girl shouting, "Yeah, boys need to form committees to figure out how to stop hurting women." Girls know how to fight violence, sexism, racism, and other forms of oppression. They tell us this all the time. Their knowledge helps empower us to get out there and "fix it" with them.

Personal Journeys toward Connection

Catherine: I became a feminist in large part because I wanted to work collectively with other women toward shared goals. My work on reproductive rights, women's health care, and founding a women's bookstore has been enriched by the connections I have made with other feminists. Making these social and personal connections has not been secondary to the larger goal of getting things done, but the very thing that has sustained my feminist work. WCEP's partnership with PSU's capstone program has enlivened our mission, fortified our resources, and enlarged our community of women and girls and those who care about them. And it has forged many new personal partnerships for me. These partnerships, framed by our shared commitment to feminist work, have made my work worth doing and sustained me over the long haul. I look forward to our continued partnership over the years and all the ways it will make life better for our community of women and girls, and for me personally. After all, isn't that what feminism is all about?

Melissa: For me feminism has been all about working with other women, hoping that they will find in our projects the same kind of passion that has come to my life through this partnership. When I moved to Portland six years ago, I did not know this city's women at all, nor could I imagine the impact they would have on my work or my personal life. A year later, I gave birth to a baby girl and found myself looking for support from places similar to those I had been familiar with in cities of my past (as an activist and volunteer)—women's health centers and feminist collectives. That is where I found a larger circle of women who became friends, colleagues, and partners in social change work. Like many of my students, it has been my renewed sense of community and a deeper feeling of belonging to a city of women that keeps me doing this work. I am now extremely fortunate to have an academic career that is a seamless threading together of scholarship, teaching, and activism. We have been able to conspire on conference presentations and collaborative writing as well. While those efforts have been especially rewarding, they have not been nearly as personally exciting as being part of a feminist community-building effort in a city that has bridged its bookstore, university, and communities of women and men working for social change.

While we may not have leaped too far from our platforms or clasped wrists in matching sequined costumes to the uproarious applause of everyone in our community, we have crossed many a divide together and have taught others how to make similar connections. I, too, look forward to continuing our "trapeze trick"—working out some of the kinks in our performance and stitching a wider safety net that makes the flight seem less risky for others to take.

Notes

1. These conversations took place over a period of several months on the telephone and via daily e-mail exchanges. We have edited our conversation here for clarity and thematic content.

2. Quotations included in this essay from bookstore founders and volunteers are taken from our 1997 oral history project, celebrating the five-year anniversary of the bookstore. Through it, capstone students conducted oral history interviews with nine bookstore affiliates. Their stories and a collective history of the bookstore can be found in our written collection, *Pages Turning*.

3. We have now published eight Portland teen girl zines. For a description of our project and sample zine pages, see our recent article in the *Women's Studies Quarterly*, "CityGirls: Learning Conversations with a City of Zinetresses," fall/winter 2001.

14

Women's Leadership and Social Change in the Atlanta Semester Program

Isa D. Williams

In 1991, the women's studies faculty (core and related) at Agnes Scott College seized a profound opportunity to create a curricular program that would recognize, value, and respond to the knowledge that women bring to the class while also encouraging them to speak in their own voice. The program's intent was to support the development and evolution of students' thinking. This program, the Atlanta Semester Program in Women, Leadership, and Social Change, brings students, faculty, and community together to create new knowledge in partnership. The Atlanta Semester Program combines "doing with knowing to empower and challenge students to lead more socially responsible lives; recognizing the interdependence of people, social institutions and communities" (Palmer 1987:109).

Agnes Scott College is a women's college with over 100 years' experience in educating women for social responsibility. Consistent with "women's ways of knowing" and experiential learning theories, the Atlanta Semester Program combines classroom learning and internships to aid students in developing their beliefs and self-confidence in order to become active and compassionate citizens. The program's mission is to provide students with exposure to both theoretical and experiential education for critical and engaged examination of leadership and social change from the perspective of women. Specific focus is on ways in which women have and are currently engaged in leadership to challenge traditional gender, race, and class arrangements that serve to systematically advantage one group over another. The program enables feminist transformation while refocusing women's studies as well as adding a gender perspective to leadership studies. The gender perspective recognizes and encourages questions regarding the privileging of traditional leadership models and theories that have often been biased by a male perspective. The program fulfills its mission by offering an interdisciplinary seminar, a speakers' forum, internships, and research projects that examine women challenging leadership and effecting social change in an urban environment. The speakers' forum consists of on-campus meetings with women leaders from, among others, community/grassroots, nonprofits, governmental, and incorporated organizations. The In Community consists of off-campus meetings with women community leaders. The Internship is a for-credit experiential learning placement affording students the opportunity to further examine women's leadership and organizational practices.

The Seminar and Speakers' Forum

Both the seminar and speakers' forum posit women's leadership that challenges traditional gender, race, and class arrangements in society as central to local and national levels of social change. The seminar introduces students to a wide array of feminist theories that serve as the foundation for understanding the social construction of differences that exist between women as well as the relationship between gender, race, and class. As a result of examining feminist theories, students are better equipped to (1) critically examine systems and structures that affect the lives of women; (2) understand their individual reaction to issues presented in the program; (3) recognize the ways in which women have been excluded from leadership and their strategies utilized to effect social change; and (4) understand the historical role of women in social change and leadership as mediated by race and class.

Women's studies core faculty, and related faculty in political science, history, sociology, anthropology, and religious studies/ethics, interact with students in the interdisciplinary seminar while women community, political, and business leaders engage the students in discussion through the speakers' forum. This interdisciplinary and integrated format allows for the examination of social change and leadership from the perspective of various disciplines defined by the theoretical foundation of women's studies as well as from an experiential perspective informed by women engaged in social and political practice. For example, a sociologist will present a theoretical discussion of welfare reform with consideration given to the economic, social, and political factors affecting women and children in poverty. Students will then meet with women community leaders engaged in advocating for social and political changes, while also meeting with the women who are daily affected by welfare reform.

The faculty and community engagement with students can best be described as "connected teaching," a form of pedagogy that acknowledges that each person in the classroom "already knows something" (Belenky et al. 1986:194–95). Theories are not afforded a hierarchical position superior to experience: students are encouraged to "find their own words, to make meaning of their experiences" through interacting with faculty and women community leaders (p. 203). Through this dynamic it becomes apparent that each person is both a student and teacher. At the beginning of the semester students and faculty discuss this form of pedagogy and its value to the learning experience.

This interactive approach, combining theory and practice, reinforces and strengthens student knowledge in women's studies by affording students first-hand exposure to women who discuss ways in which their lives are affected by gender, race, and class. Students witness how the social construction of gender, race, and class makes a difference in communities and the lives of women. Students are afforded a nonthreatening space in which to share their beliefs while listening to those of others and often engaging in meaningful debate. A biology major, Janet,[1] described the experience as follows:

> WOW, I came to the CDC (Centers for Disease Control/internship site) and the Atlanta Semester believing that women could aspire to anything. In my own stubborn way, I was as sexist as the liberal feminists that I argued against all semester. Now that I realize that perhaps there will be discrimination along the way. Those who discriminate and those that use that as an excuse to fail are the ignorant ones. With the help of this program, I'll recognize any gender-related challenges . . . I will survive and succeed despite [them].

I like to think of the program classroom as one embroiled in creative conflict where a process of "checking, correcting and enlarging the knowledge of individuals (occurs) by drawing on the knowledge of the group" (Palmer 1987:112). Every aspect of the program broadens student awareness of social issues and how women are effectively responding to meet social, political, and economic challenges. As we engage in experiential learning throughout the program, we form within our students an "inward capacity for relatedness" and a way of connecting to the world as "committed and compassionate citizens" (Palmer 1987:109). Nowhere is this more evident than in the speakers' forum section held "In Community" as an examination of women leaders affecting social change in Atlanta.

The Speakers' Forum "In Community"

In her essay, "Out of the Academy and into the Street," bell hooks (1994a:193) describes the "segregation and institutionalization of the feminist theorizing process in the academy, with the privileging of written feminist thought/theory over oral narratives. This reproduces class hierarchy in academia. hooks also states that "the production of feminist theory is complex that it is less the individual practice than we often think, and usually emerges from engagement with collective sources."

Consistent with hooks's admonition that we move "out of the academy and into the street," we designed what is now the In Community section of the speakers' forum in order to engage with collective sources and better understand feminist theory. In late 1999, and after careful examination of our goals, Atlanta Semester faculty members began the process of designing and conducting an In Community section of the speakers' forum to strengthen our examination of leadership and social change in Atlanta, specifically from a woman's perspective. Community engagement projects (i.e., service learning) have been criticized for viewing communities of color only in terms of need while failing to recognize what members of the community have to offer (Weah, Simmons, and Hall 2000) and for "perpetuating an oppressive situation in society through failure to explore the "consequent effects of the service on the service recipient": rarely is the voice of the service recipient considered in the experience (Maybach 1996). The very language of service learning designates one entity as a provider and the other a recipient, which posits a degree of domination where one entity is clearly in a subordinate position of need. This type of relationship, which represents and emphasizes communities of color in need, minimizes the strengths of individuals, thus "further marginalizing them from the mainstream" (Maybach 1996). Rarely are racist and classist issues borne by providers made salient in order to recognize and effectively deal with power differences (Bunch 1990). The Atlanta Semester speakers' forum In Community emphasizes the strengths of women leaders while also illuminating their work in addressing community needs that are often obscured by the media emphasis on demonizing the individual as well as the community. Additionally, students are encouraged to reflect on structural, as well as race and class, issues. Many service-learning/community projects are viewed as stemming from a "white-dominated movement driven by a missionary zeal" (Weah et al. 2000) and often fail to recognize the complex nature of social issues. Discussion of issues involving the effects of race, class, and gender inequities are rarely made a part of the experience. Projects are also criticized for failing to acknowledge the root causes of need and often serving to pacify the oppressed rather than working to empower them. Carol Wiechman Maybach (1996) prescribes a "more equitable model of service learning" in which students and community members reverse roles so that the student becomes the recipient of knowledge. The primary goal of the In Community speakers' forum is to bring students and women community leaders together for the purpose of developing a partnership and expanding student understanding of ways that women's leadership challenges structures and systems that seek to oppress and disadvantage individuals and groups based on race, class, and gender. Another goal is to encourage students to think of ways in which they might participate in social change efforts. This facet of the program is also dedicated to familiarizing students with urban problems confronting women and members of their communities. Students meet with the individuals and organizations working to effect social and political change. The In Community speakers' forum has been organized to meet with women leaders working on issues involving homeless women and children, women with AIDS, recovering homeless/mentally ill women, women in transition from welfare to work and often living in poverty as well as teen pregnancy organizations and teen mothers.

The Atlanta Semester Program components, including the In Community forum, are informed as pedagogic strategy by the theories and beliefs discussed in Parker Palmer's (1987) writing and in Mary Field Belenky et al., *Women's Ways of Knowing* (1986). Palmer suggests that by combining experiential learning with traditional education, we enable students to understand that the world outside the academy is not a world apart from them. Rather, we are teaching them to intersect their life stories with the stories of women in communities that are often less advantaged than those from which many of our students come. Students enrolled in the program over its five years of existence can best be described as suburban/rural, and from a middle-class background, with 44 percent of them European-American, 39 percent African American, and 17 percent international students; none of the students are from inner-city Atlanta neighborhoods. While enrollment in the program consists only of women, we feel the pedagogic philosophy and methods utilized are also applicable to men. As represented in Palmer's work, this pedagogic strategy is a way to deepen understanding of community and connection irrespective of gender. The community becomes one to which students are connected, not simply one they have been taught about. Students begin to recognize their own implications for society's fate.

In the initial design of the Atlanta Semester, the speakers' forum was intended to bring women community leaders to the campus for the purpose of meeting with students and faculty. Students were expected to respond to the women in terms of their leadership. Very quickly we realized how students were unable to grasp the true meaning of women's leadership and social change in the absence of a community context. As a result of our early experience, we developed an examination of women's leadership and social change titled In the Community for the spring 2000 class.

In preparation for In Community, students met with Loretta J. Ross, founder and executive director of the Center for Human Rights Education based in Atlanta. Ross, an African-American feminist, is a human rights activist with a distinguished career involving human rights, women's issues, diversity issues, and hate groups/bias crimes. She was one of the first African-American women to direct a rape crisis center in the 1970s. Loretta has worked extensively from a human rights perspective with the community groups and women leaders that we met in the community: the Georgia Coalition on Hunger and the Welfare Rights Union. Ross also assisted both groups to ground their work within the human rights framework as articulated in the Universal Declaration of Human Rights. Issues involving race, class, and gender were also discussed in this on-campus speakers' forum.

While we continue to invite women leaders to the campus, our interactions have far greater meaning after completion of the In Community forum. As Sue, a psychology major, notes, the In Community forum provides important learning experiences that cannot be replicated through a book or class discussion "while surrounded by the brick wall" that often separates communities:

> The (experience) opened my eyes to the injustices and inequalities that exist in our society, and in our town. I was able to see how my ignorance kept me from assisting these oppressed groups before. (The women expressed) this desire to work and be defined by one's job. (This) changed my misconception that people receiving welfare often do so to avoid working. I learned about, and made connections between, systems like transportation, economic, domestic, and corporate. The (community meeting) was a wonderful experience that taught me things I would never have learned through a book or class discussion while surrounded by the brick wall of Agnes Scott.

Sue's reflection was in response to our meeting with women leaders at the Georgia Coalition on Hunger and women being helped by that organization, many of whom experience oppression as economically poor mothers. This student also spoke of ways in which her knowledge of women on welfare had been shaped by "censorship and manipulation by the media." This experience enabled her to make connections between systems and to assess her past failure to act in a way that could support people whose lives are not a world apart from her own. She was also beginning to see the intersection of their life stories with hers and ways that systems and structures served to divide and keep them apart. This knowledge serves as a first step in understanding women's leadership and how one might participate in social change.

The In Community forum affords students the opportunity to compare what they already know about the lives of certain women with what they experience in the community and in conversation with these women, who thus become more than mere media portrayals. Students begin to critique systems and structures. More importantly, students recognize that they can make a difference and begin to offer suggestions for political and social changes. The In Community experience causes a rethinking of a student's own values and how she came to hold such values. As Nan, an economics major, comments,

> The personal testimony that I heard really touched me. I had no idea that welfare reform is still badly needed. I must admit that I strongly supported welfare reform and thought that the lifetime 5-year limit was a great idea. The media has always left me with the impression that welfare recipients are lazy and that they do enjoy collecting a free paycheck. What I heard yesterday made me change my mind. The women on welfare do need a little extra help. I think there must be more patient government workers who are willing to assist people one on one. I think that job counseling is badly needed, but job counseling at an individualized level. I think that it would be a great idea for the center located at the "Up and Out of Poverty Now Coalition" to offer job counseling services. I was also appalled at the discussion of the Georgia state minimum wage law. I think that it is terrible to legally allow such low wages for employees. There is no possible way for a breadwinner to earn enough money to support a family or even themselves. I also cannot believe that this wage level has not been changed since the 1970's. That is just unbelievable. I am 100% for changing this law. The experiences of the day motivated me to begin thinking of ways in which I can become involved.

Nan went on to select an internship with the organization 9 to 5 Atlanta Working Women and became very involved in the equal pay campaign. While initially uncertain of her ability to become politically active, as the semester drew to a close, she became more assured of that voice within herself.

As a result of the In Community experience, a student from Ireland identified and assessed a "feminist manner" of leadership as promoting "energy and strength and effective interaction," a form of leadership that viewed people as assets rather than as problems. She described the results as "remarkable: victims empowered became victors with wisdoms that all of us would do well to appreciate." This new knowledge has the potential to shape the way in which she will act in the community with others. The ways in which we, as humans, are connected becomes apparent as we move from the classroom setting into the community. Leadership is seen not as a sacrifice but as our duty as human beings to support others. Class differences and their significance to life outcomes also becomes apparent, as voiced by Terry, a history major from an upper-middle-class African-American neighborhood in Atlanta.[2] She writes,

> Being a part of the (experience) has reaffirmed my desire to work to improve society despite the sacrifice. (The organization's leaders) did not perceive their work as a sacrifice. It was their duty as human beings to help others and this idea reminded me of the interconnectedness theme presented by Loretta [Ross, in the speakers' forum]. I recognize that I am part of a privileged class although sometimes I complain that I do not have enough. I have even felt disconnected from people around me like the women at Project South [of the Georgia Coalition on Hunger] who were struggling to survive. They continue to suffer in silence because people like me refuse to hear them. I definitely heard them last Friday and hope to carry their passion with me in my future work.

This experience is one the students will not soon forget. What we are working toward in the Atlanta Semester has its own ethical and moral course. We are attempting to create within our students a capacity for relatedness to people, events, ideas, and environment. Gloria, a very active campus leader and international relations major from Africa, describes the salient nature of systems and structures as well as stereotypes that she held prior to the In Community forum:

> The [forum] was a very inspiring experience that caused me to think further of certain issues such as homelessness, poverty and mental illness. Although I know these issues exist, the [experience] enabled me to recognize and acknowledge the fact that there are systems and structures that create the situation whereby [women and children] find themselves in a state of poverty and homelessness. This experience also helped me move away from certain stereotypes that are associated with individuals with problems of mental illness and poverty. No one chooses to be poor, homeless and mentally ill. I have always had this dream of establishing a shelter and orphanage in Ghana [my home]. My education on issues of social change and the [meetings with women community leaders] has created the determination to make that dream a reality in the near future. I believe that women and children form the majority of the world's population so there is the need to protect and improve their economic and social welfare. [In Community] made me realize that education was necessary and measures should be taken to encourage women to get an education. I had a real problem with the woman at the Coalition on Hunger who had 5 children. I

never had sympathy towards poor women with 5 to 8 children who complain about the system not helping them. I failed to realize that it is the same system that has created this vicious cycle of poverty that traps poor and helpless women in the lower class. I think that one of the reasons for the high birth rate is the lack of education. I have become more conscious of how structures and systems like capitalism, racism, and classism can render a person hopeless. I have realized that homelessness and poverty are not an illusion, and can happen to anyone at anytime. These are people suffering and we need to make the conscious effort to take strides to positively affect social change.

Following the In Community program in spring 2000 participation, students attended a symposium featuring Shakti Butler and her award-winning film titled *The Way Home*. Discussions focused on women's leadership in terms of racial/ethnic and gender constraints. Students were encouraged to reflect on their position in society in relation to the film representations of race/ethnicity and class. At the end of the In Community symposium, it is generally expected that students will make important connections among their seminar readings, lectures, and the experience of meeting with women leaders. It is also hoped that students will embrace and act upon this new knowledge in ways that will reflect our interrelatedness and a moral ethic of caring.

Belenky and colleagues (1986) describe common themes regarding effective pedagogical strategies for women, themes also described by Palmer (1987) as important to all learners for strengthening experiential learning and communities.[3] These themes emphasize the need for students to develop knowledge and learn from "first hand out-of-school experiences and to know that knowledge gained through life experience is "important and real and valuable." Additionally, Belenky and colleagues state that starting from personal experience and then moving to abstractions as well as engaging in the "powerful opportunities provided by experiential learning" and becoming active agents in their own learning are also important to women. While our experience is exclusively with women, it is not our intent to suggest that a particular way of knowing is privileged along gender lines.

Critics of Belenky and colleagues' *Women's Ways of Knowing* assert that sufficient evidence does not exist to "support the contention that there is a form of epistemological development that is distinctly associated with women to a greater degree than with men" (Brabeck and Larned 1997:261). Furthermore, "evidence from the theories of intellectual development does not support the hypothesis that women engage in a different way of knowing than do men" (p. 267). Researchers have asserted that to posit empirically unsupported assertions of gender differences reinforces gender stereotypes and privileges gender over socio-economic status, race, educational experience, or other "ways people think and make meaning." Additionally, important factors such as historical period, geographic location, societal and structural barriers, religion, and sexual orientation are also ignored (Goldberger 1996, 151). Feminist critiques of *Women's Ways of Knowing* make clear that to suggest that a "single element of identity, gender, determines one's ways of knowing play[s] into more simplified and essentialist views of gender that eras[e] both differences among women and commonalities among women and men sharing similar histories" (p. 151). Critics emphasize the importance of recognizing the "multiple situations within which people find themselves, and thereby construct their understanding of self and the world" (p. 158).

The Atlanta Semester Program recognizes the importance of multiple situations and individual factors by providing an environment in which students begin to augment knowledge of self and others. Our examination of leadership and social change through the In Community forum specifically supports students and community women where they are by recognizing their knowledge of personhood, systems, and struggles. Reflections are designed to encourage students to engage with structural issues in addition to race/ethnicity and class. Consistent with Aída Hurtado's (1996b:81) critique of *Women's Ways of Knowing* for failure to address knowledge production by women of color, we are working to further strengthen the Atlanta Semester Program by making clear that knowledge is "filtered through unequal power relations based on race" as well as class and gender. We will encourage students to recognize that the "transmission and use of knowledge . . . are not neutral . . . nor are they bifurcated by sex differences between women and men, but instead . . . are political acts" that can serve to advantage certain groups over others (p. 387). Through the In Community forum students come to recognize that "previously derogated groups are holders of knowledge that do not fit . . . traditional paradigms" and that these groups have a right to be an integral part of how they desire to utilize knowledge to strengthen their communities (p. 386).

The Atlanta Semester Program serves to support the evolution of all participants' thinking. We assist students in giving birth to their own ideas and in making their own knowledge explicit. The program also encourages students to speak in their own active voice while engaging them in conversations with other voices. It is our hope and belief that we are providing a culture for growth. After engaging in the community speakers' forum, students analyze women, culture, and society from multiple perspectives and are less likely to privilege written feminist thought/theory over oral narratives.

Internships and Research Projects

Both the internship and research project posit women as the central focus of study. Through the varied internship placements with women leaders, students learn the importance of political activism to effect social change, as well as the essential "how to." Intern sites are instructed to involve students in their leadership training activities and to assign a meaningful project that can be completed in the course of the semester—typically in a period of more than 130 hours. The internship is designed such that each student is assigned to engage with a woman in a position of leadership. The goal is to understand the challenges and rewards of leadership while also examining social change from the perspective of women and organizations. Students witness firsthand the organizational issues and policies that working women face. Many of the intern sites, such as Sisterlove, AIDS Project, the Feminist Women's Health Center, the Dekalb Rape Crisis Center, and 9 to 5 Atlanta Working Women are engaged in some form of direct community involvement that allows students to develop a greater understanding of the need for political activism to effect social change at the local level. Students interning with state government representatives learn why women's caucuses are necessary and how they affect political issues and processes. The internship and research project does not exist independent of the other program components. The program structure provides an integrated perspective for examination of women's leadership in the seminar, the speakers' forum, and the internship. In addition to seminar readings regarding women's leadership, students meet with women leaders and serve as interns to women engaged in some form of leadership (primarily in grassroots and social service organizations, but also sometimes in elected political positions). Each section of the program complements and augments the others.

Over the course of three years, data were gathered to examine the effect of this integrated perspective through implementation of a pre- and postprogram assessment regarding women's leadership. On the first day of class and at the end of the semester, students were asked to describe women's leadership. This method of assessment allows examination of the treatment effect (seminar, speakers' forum, In Community speakers' forum, and internship) over the course of the semester. Analysis of the data (50 questionnaires) revealed the following examples of descriptors most often employed to characterize women's leadership in the preprogram assessment: *inclusive, able to hear and utilize opinions of others, concerned, weighing needs of all concerned,* and *consulting with others.* From individual experiences and observations prior to the program, students describe women's leadership in ways that could be deemed traditional and gender stereotypical. The only deviations from these descriptors came from two students, one of whom characterized women as "aggressive" while the other stated that women are "quietly aggressive." Contrary to traditional descriptions of women's leadership, another student noted that "men and women exhibit similar leadership qualities; what is different is how they are treated." However, she ended her assertion by stating that "women are more sensitive and nurturing leaders." This tendency on the part of students to characterize women's leadership in traditional and gender stereotypical language in the preprogram assessment could be attributed to their socialization experiences and observations of women in society.

Unlike language utilized prior to the program, the postprogram assessment evidences academic specificity. After an intensive semester of theory and practice, student language in the postprogram assessment revealed the following descriptors regarding women's leadership: inclusive, collaborative, relational, interactive, empowering others, participatory, and transformational.

It is noteworthy that language utilized in the preprogram assessment and constructed from student experiences is not substantially different from language used in the postprogram assessment, which relies to a great extent on theoretical labels. From the postprogram assessment it is possible to indirectly conclude that women leaders in the speakers' forum, In Community speakers' forum, and at the internship sites demonstrate a leadership style that reinforces theoretical constructions of women's leadership presented in the seminar. The change in language from the pre- to the postprogram assessments reflects the reinforcement caused by various aspects of the program, including the internship.

It is also evident, in both theory and practice, that we are examining a rather homogeneous group of women leaders who are more closely aligned with a feminist representation of leadership as inclusive, transforming, participatory, and empowering of others while concerned for the feelings and needs of followers (Barnett 1993; Helgesen 1990; Mueller 1993; Rosener 1990). This style of leadership is in opposition to the representation of right-wing women leaders presented in the modern hate movement as "aggressive females, courageous young women warriors" and "as full participants in brutal practices of violence" (Blee 1988:186–89). Many of the women and organizations affiliated with the Atlanta Semester Program profess to embrace feminist ideals of respect, collectivity, and participatory democracy (Ferree and Martin 1995a). It is probable that these women are exercising leadership in a manner that demonstrates resistance to replicating the very leadership structures and behaviors that they seek to dismantle—those of unequal power relations and authoritarian command and control behavior. Even women located in hierarchical organizations speak of their leadership in terms of embracing cooperation, seeking to build alliances and relationships with care and concern for others. Irrespective of organizational structure, analysis reveals that women associated with the program demonstrate a specific style of leadership, thus strengthening and reinforcing the theory that women's ways of leading, which have previously been overlooked or discounted in traditional leadership circles, can be effective.

The Atlanta Semester Program provides a unique opportunity for continued assessment of women's leadership and of feminist organizations. We will further strengthen this process by adding depth and breadth to students' critical examination of power and authority structures (Ferree 1995) in addition to an impact analysis of the longitudinal development of local community feminist organizations (Ferree and Martin 1995a; Naples 1998a). Our assessments will continue to include recognition of race and class as significant variables.

In conjunction with the internship and other components of the program, the research projects serve as a way in which students can engage in a form of social or political activism. Researching, documenting, and communicating their findings to the internship organization allows students to become participants in social or political activism. The act of documenting and involving others in the process of examining a social issue affecting women, leadership, and social change can be viewed as a form of activism. Students often assess an issue related to the internship and/or speakers' forum. Central to the subject of the research project is the role of women. Past projects have had such titles as Bridging the Gap: African-American Women and the Tools of HIV/ AIDS Advocacy; Defining the Importance of Training and Certification Requirements for Service Providers in Battered Women's Shelters; Women in Political Leadership: A Study of Women and Leadership Styles; Women Refugees: The Relationship between Gender Identity and Sexual Violence; Equity in Health Insurance Coverage for Women. The research project integrates theoretical and experiential knowledge in women's studies while enabling the student to engage in advocating for social change.

In the forward to *Women Activists* by Anne Witte Garland (1988:ix), Ralph Nader discusses "citizen work that provides the firmament of our democracy—the unsung initiatives of deeply caring people." The Atlanta Semester Program subscribes to the need for active citizens committed to participation in society. It is my belief that students who are deeply moved by a particular need in society, perhaps as a result of participation in the program, will become activists who are capable of directing and sustaining goal-oriented action even in the absence of approval from others. It is my hope that students enrolled in the program will recognize the need for their sustained citizen involvement in issues affecting not only women but all humanity, and will strengthen their commitment to solving issues facing communities and urban centers. Nader further depicts that type of citizen as "compassionate for others, self-confident in the absence of anyone else to rely on" (p. ix). The Atlanta Semester Program in Women, Leadership and Social Change provides students with the experience, information and confidence to begin "working at their citizenship." Garland found that "personal growth comes with striving for social well-being." It is my hope that students will realize a form of personal growth that embraces a belief and confidence in one's ability to act as a result of considering both theory and practice while continuing to develop new knowledge in partnership.

Notes

1. This and all names are pseudonyms.
2. For a discussion of class and racial segregation in Atlanta see Sjoquist 2000.
3. See Goldberger et al. 1996 for a discussion of socially constructed gender differences as opposed to essential differences in men's and women's ways of knowing.

15

Women's Studies and the Women and Poverty Public Education Initiative

Katherine Rhoades, Anne Statham, and Mary Kay Schleiter

This chapter presents information about a statewide activist project sponsored by the Outreach Office of the University of Wisconsin Women's Studies Consortium. That project, the Women and Poverty Public Education Initiative (WPPEI), provides students and faculty with the opportunity to work in nonhierarchical settings on a project aimed at incorporating a fuller representation of women's voices into policy research and development. We will describe the project and its position within the Women's Studies Consortium, and then analyze our successes and some of our continuing areas of concern. To impart the role of activism in women's studies successfully to our students, we consider it important to teach not only content and theory, but also the processes involved in taking action. A key part of this preparation entails bringing "real world" applications into the classroom.

The Women and Poverty Public Education Initiative in Wisconsin

WPPEI offers one approach for doing activism in women's studies, both within and outside traditional classrooms. We have learned that helping our students address community-based issues in meaningful ways is not always an easy task. In the analysis that follows we attempt not only to present a balanced view of our work, showing both its rewards and challenges, but to also offer practical suggestions intended to help others avoid some of the pitfalls that we have encountered.

In the first ten years of its existence, the University of Wisconsin's Women's Studies Consortium attempted to rekindle women's studies activist connections by consciously adding outreach to the work of its statewide initiatives. One year after the consortium office was officially established in 1989, an outreach office was also established with University of Wisconsin Extension funding. The purpose of the outreach office was to provide Women's Studies faculty on the 26 University of Wisconsin campuses around the state with the opportunity to become engaged in issues of concern in the communities where their institutions reside. Participating faculty sought to bridge the perceived chasm between theory and practice, academe and activism.

While the campus programs continued to undertake local projects in their own communities, the outreach office organized statewide projects that provided broader opportunities for community engagement. These projects included annual statewide and regional conferences on topics of particular interest such as women and poverty; gender and environment; feminist approaches to social change; Native American issues; and major projects on infusion of material from Wisconsin Indian cultures into our curriculum and international cooperation on women's and environmental issues.

The most successful of these statewide projects is the WPPEI, which has operated in eight communities with University of Wisconsin campuses since 1994. WPPEI is a collective of academic and community women who are working to educate Wisconsin citizens about the realities of women living in poverty. In the process, we strive to dispel deeply entrenched myths and damaging stereotypes. We also work to encourage women living in poverty to insert their opinions into the welfare reform debate, and to provide the space for their leadership in these matters to be felt. Our structure entails two leaders in each of the eight communities where we work—one from among the women living in poverty, and one from the women's studies program at the local University of Wisconsin campus. (This has not always been possible in all eight sites continuously; sometimes there is only a faculty leader, sometimes only a leader from the community.) We have several statewide coordinators and research coordinators, and have managed to obtain grant money from several foundations and centers.

This project did not begin as a single classroom project. We began with the desire to influence the emerging policy debate about welfare reform, and attempted to design an approach that adhered to the feminist principles discussed above. We did not wish to speak for another group of women. We wished to work with them, furthering their own efforts, and opening a space for their voices to be heard. We did not wish to exploit their plight for our own gain, either in terms of our research or our teaching needs. Further, we did not want to appropriate their insights, experience, or understanding as our own. We also wanted to provide our students with the opportunity to become engaged in the issue of poverty and welfare reform, but we did not want this to be a coercive situation for either our students or our community partners. We realized that we would have to develop enduring relationships with women living in poverty in order to accomplish these goals. Thus, we have nurtured the groups and their leaders in the eight sites for some time, often offering them some financial compensation and opportunities for leadership expression and development. We began with regional meetings that explored the issues from the perspective of those most directly impacted by the issue of poverty and welfare reform. In this way, we were certain the agenda we pursued was not set by us alone, and that our activities would be useful to the women involved. We have monthly conference calls about what we are doing, how we are doing it, and what the results have been, and our students sometimes join us on these calls. We also have annual retreats, where we set the agenda for the next year. Our efforts have evolved into the formation of the statewide Wisconsin Alliance for Low Wage Workers, which we were funded to organize. WPPEI leaders acted as staff to this effort, as we were one of the only avenues in Wisconsin through which women most directly impacted by welfare and poverty policies have had a voice in ongoing debates. We have organized speakers' bureaus and engaged in dialogue with a range of audiences, from university students to employers to legislators and policy makers.

As a result, we have taken on many different projects. We have gathered data about women being impacted by welfare reform; formed local support groups for these women; learned to connect with local and state policy makers; produced a videotape "In Our Own Image: Not for Women Only"; published reports on our research; presented findings and papers at national and state conferences; participated in national and local forums on welfare policy; and helped shaped the ways Wisconsin's newer welfare program (W-2; the successor to the Aid to Families with Dependent Children, or AFDC, program) is administered. Our partnership model of pairing a woman living in poverty with an academic was designed to counter the issues of power and hierarchy endemic in university classrooms. Our students have worked with us on all of these projects in a variety of roles—as research assistants, speakers, videotape production assistants, group facilitators, negotiators, and peer support counselors. Sometimes our students are living in poverty, or have recently experienced poverty, but others are learning about it for the first time. Overall, WPPEI and its process raise many provocative questions, such as, Who are knowledge producers—only faculty, or others as well? Who should appropriately take action or be an "activist"? Who are our students—those in traditional classrooms, those in the community, or both? Where are our classrooms? Who are the "teachers"? How do we interact with others as learning partners in a nonelitist, nonhierarchical fashion?

Results, Implications, and Successes

As we have struggled to answer these questions, we have learned the importance of the ability to work comfortably in diverse settings, broadening personal perspectives to frame larger social processes, and understanding organizational process and leadership—for both ourselves and our students. We find that our teaching and research has benefited a great deal through our involvement in this project. For example, a woman acting as our research director, an architecture/planning graduate student who was finishing school while on AFDC, would often tell others, "Academics and activists have different personalities—and priorities." She led us to design studies that seemed sensitive and responsive to the issues of those living in poverty. Our academic participants would sometimes object to the wording on surveys because it was not rigorous or professional enough. Other WPPEI members would argue that if questions were not asked in a way the respondents could relate to, our data would be meaningless. This research director struggled with shifting power relationships as she negotiated these realms of authority and expertise. As we created something that all involved could live with, we felt we produced results that represented the perspectives of women living in poverty much better than we could have as detached researchers.

Our work was often cited by advocacy groups as the only research available that represented the perspectives of the women being impacted by welfare policy. Administrators of our state welfare program have recently begun to ask our advice about the situation of those remaining on the welfare rolls, increasingly difficult cases with multiple problems that baffle many in the system trying to deal with them. We have arrived at this point through the patient efforts of our diverse group of committed individuals, working for several years across gaps in understanding and perspective to produce a unique and inclusive product. Our students have learned much by working with us in this process. They have learned about speaking effectively to different audiences, the power of telling one's story, various ways to confront authority, methods of mediating conflict, strategies of lowering backlash and resistance, and the importance of dealing with fatigue and burnout.

In working on these issues, we are ever attentive to frequently intertwined processes of empowerment, leadership, and experiential teaching/activism as they play themselves out in our model. This work has interrupted the traditional classroom process for many of us and fundamentally changed how we see our role. For one thing, as our engagement with the community deepens, we find it becomes more difficult to distinguish between the classroom and the community. This is true for many reasons. Many of those working with us are our students, both as members of WPPEI (setting the agenda and designing the studies) and in helping gather data for our various research projects. Some have lived or currently live in poverty themselves, and they identify quite strongly with the course material and content.

Students often use their prior or current experience with poverty as fertile ground for applying the concepts we teach in our classes. They also express ambivalent loyalties, as did one student who chose to volunteer in a soup kitchen similar to one where she had been a client during a spell of homelessness. She wrote about the conflicting feelings she experienced when a fraternity held its annual volunteer day in the soup kitchen and talked among themselves and displayed patronizing attitudes toward those coming to eat, to the obvious discomfort of the patrons. This student did not want to be labeled by the fraternity members as a member of the low-status group, yet identified quite strongly with the soup kitchen clients. This merging of actual experience with critical thinking about it often provides our students with transformative skills necessary for social change. This student demonstrated sophistication in her keen awareness of the various perspectives converging on this single incident, an ability to analyze her role in it despite the intense emotional reactions she was having, and an understanding of which communication strategies would be most effective for different audiences.

As we have gained a reputation for being engaged in these sorts of projects, we attract more and more students to our classes who are community partners, in the sense that they have had past or current experience with poverty. We are also approached to work with such students on independent study projects. In some cases, these projects have involved conducting interviews, coding transcribed interviews, and other basic research tasks. Such work sometimes proves difficult for our students; some are shocked and upset by the difficulties described in the interviews. Working with these interviews has also been stressful for students who identify closely with those interviewed because of their own similar backgrounds. Recognition of the potential stress of working even in these mainstream research ways, and structuring peer support networks, has been helpful in these situations.

Some students have been given opportunities for less-traditional independent studies—working in nonprofit or activist organizations with the goal of fighting poverty. For example, one student worked to organize a campus and community contingent for a nationally organized march. Her independent study combined reading, recording observations using ethnographic methods, and keeping a journal in which she recorded what she was learning about effective political activism from community leaders. One of our recent paid staff members began working with us as an undergraduate student who was on AFDC when she did several independent study projects with Katherine Rhoades, the first author for this essay, then began collaborating on one of our major research projects, longitudinal depth interviews with women being impacted by welfare reform.

We have come to see our community partners as peers, not inferiors. We look for ways to acknowledge this and traverse the power hierarchies that traditionally divide us and prevent others' competencies from being recognized. This process has opened the space for community members to become our teachers, where teaching in a community setting provides insight into the learning process itself. It has also forced many of the academic local group leaders to look at leadership differently, as we have struggled through the dynamics of partnering with women who are in precarious economic situations. Some talk about the strain of participating in a partnership marked by such drastic material imbalances.

In creating teams across barriers of class, we have had to recognize alternative notions of responsibility, leadership, and teamwork. One woman in particular has talked about her transition from one mode of leadership to another, of coming to fully understand and implement a feminist framework. She has come to see that the blending of African-American and Latina perspectives with her own has created a stronger fabric for supporting group action toward positive policy change. For all of us, working closely with women whose lives are in delicate balance, whose priorities and commitments are necessarily different that ours, requires a reexamination of the critical aspects of leadership, partnership, and "covering for each other" (picking up the tasks when the other's life priorities come calling).

While this presents ongoing challenges, discussed below, we believe it has also resulted in a more productive and realistic understanding about what it takes to work together in multi-interest projects. In many ways, the roles have become interchangeable. Our students have become our community partners, our community partners have become our teachers, and we have become partners and coaches. As a result, we are now even more committed to the teaching model that asserts that students can help teach other, especially as they help to validate, or provide the context for, each other's experience in ways that we cannot possibly do for all students in the classroom. In preparing students to work with the project in such roles as conducting interviews, we have found that it is easier when interviewers share a personal background or experience of poverty or racism with those being interviewed. Extensive multicultural and class-sensitive training, in addition to training in listening and recognizing the need for unbiased follow-up questions, has been necessary. Our observations of missed opportunities by our nervous and naive student interviewers—who lack the experience and sensitivity to listen and interview well—and our commitment to cross barriers of class and race, are consistent themes in the classes we teach. In a class dealing with issues of class and race taught by Mary Kay Schleiter (the third author for this essay), several European-American students expressed a belief that discrimination was a thing of the past. Several African-American students used accounts of their own frustrations—difficulty in writing checks while shopping (being asked for up to five pieces of identification), or having a boyfriend frequently questioned by security guards when coming to pick a student up from her job at a bank—in order to show that their experiences were not unusual. The students hearing the stories became open to reevaluating their prior assumptions about their community. These discussions across barriers of class and race help students become more able to participate fully in their communities, and are necessary for middle-class and European-American students who wish to participate.

Another issue that underlies the experience of poverty in our society is that of gender discrimination. In another class taught by the third author, a student surprised the class by stating that a particular business where he worked had a policy, strongly promoted by a regional manager, of discriminating against women and particular racial and ethnic groups. In partial fulfillment of the research requirement for the class, the students in the class decided that they would like to gather evidence to test the possibility of job discrimination in this business. In collaboration with the local chapter of the National Association for the Advancement of Colored People (NAACP), students recorded observations of other students who applied for employment. All of the job applicants were treated respectfully during the application process, and most believed that they had been fairly treated. However, in some cases, after the applicant left the store, the application was thrown in the trash can.

Two women applicants were asked to move a heavy file cabinet as a part of the application process, a task not requested of others, and not an obvious part of the job. These findings were quietly reported to the NAACP and students wrote to the president of the corporation, which owned the business, presenting their findings and suggesting that he investigate the store himself. This level of classroom activism needs to be planned with care in order to foresee and thus avoid mistakes. The outcome for the students was to intensify their involvement in the class and give them a sense of empowerment. The intensity of the project built a strong community within the class, and this strong level of peer support created a safe space for revelation and deeper analysis. For example, one student revealed to the class that he was a Chicano, a fact he had previously hidden from all of his college classmates. His story facilitated further sharing within the class, and the students discussed other hidden statuses and aspects of their identity that they did not fully acknowledge. In this case, social class, ethnicity, and gender barriers were observed, analyzed, and overcome, allowing students to be more effective members of their communities in situations—such as that of the WPPEI project—that require that these barriers be crossed.

In another class, taught by Anne Statham (the second author for this essay), one of our local group leaders from the community was enrolled. She participated in a project to gather information about the local job center from both the perspectives of administrators and of low-income women. Her involvement was critical in helping students with little experience in this area understand fully the potential issues so that they were able to create a better research design than they might have otherwise. Another student in this group was then receiving welfare benefits and using the job center resources, so in several ways we had a merger of community partner and student. These students collected data and wrote a report that is still being used to design joint projects and programs for WPPEI.

Struggles

We have encountered many stresses, strains, and continuing struggles in executing this project. We discuss them first from the perspective of classroom practice in general, then talk about them more specifically in terms of this particular project, especially as they play themselves out for our community partners.

Classroom Practice. Our major struggle revolves around our attempts to work in an egalitarian, nonhierarchical way with our partners and students, in a way that does not exploit them or appropriate their experiences. We are constantly negotiating the various role positions entailed in the shifting relationships we form with one another, both within and outside of the classroom. Within the classroom, we struggle over not having our relationships revert to a more conventional teacher/student model that leans toward privileging the former over the latter. The dangers for students are many. We believe the instructor has the responsibility to see that students are not being harmed by—or harming—those in the community. This requires a careful balance between autonomy for students and oversight by the course instructor. If students see that the instructor will swoop in and take control in the end, they will disengage from the process very quickly. Thus, careful instruction in the beginning about possible dangers, both to themselves and others, is critical. The instructor usually needs to go onsite, to develop a relationship with those the students are working with; this is an advantage of our approach, since we have a very well-developed relationship. Ideally, a contract (formal or informal) spells out in writing what the project will entail, and is agreed to by all parties. Check-in points, where the instructor, students, and community partners discuss progress and issues, are also important.

Even so, students in our courses who have worked on various aspects of this project often find themselves caught between the contradictions of the positions involved. This could be political: they usually take one position or another, and all represent some risk for either the community participants, themselves, or the project itself. Some of them take the "expert" position of a typical course instructor and find themselves resented by the women in poverty. Others are themselves living in poverty and sometimes feel that other students in the class discount their experiences. There are others that identify with service providers or citizens in general and sometimes use stereotypes that the courses are designed to overcome.

Given the diverse dynamics, these classes demand a great deal of facilitation on the part of the course instructor. Another issue we constantly face involves that of empowering (as opposed to coercing) our students. Are we truly empowering our students? Are we asking them to do things they may resent, for their "own good"? Do they feel coerced by our approach? If so, how does this play into our efforts to provide them with fertile learning environments? Katherine Rhoades (1996) has explored this issue with one of the University of Wisconsin Women's Studies Consortium's largest programs that grants a Women's Studies major; this provides a context for understanding how this issue may play itself out for the WPPEI project. She found a great deal of ambivalence among both faculty and students about the program's success in empowering their students. One faculty member talked in glowing terms about their intentions and the necessity of trying to empower students: "[Empowerment] allows people to situate their own experiences and feelings in an historical moment and sociopolitical context—to understand how power structures those experiences. . . . It is a way to see past, or through, dominant ideology to discern the stakes some people/institutions/forms of power have in retaining our gender oppression." However, a generational peer of this faculty member had misgivings: I think 'empowerment' loads too many expectations on what a class can do. For some reason, Women's Studies students seem to expect more (politics, awareness, nurturing) from Women's Studies classes so that anything less than 'empowerment' (a loaded, 'fuzzy' term) is (and must inevitably be) a disappointment." The students expressed even more ambivalence. Few students reported feeling empowered in a more collective sense. Some of those who reported feeling 'empowered' cited utilitarian reasons—having a major that allowed a higher grade point average or required fewer credits for graduation than other majors did. For other students, empowerment meant a zone of comfort distinct from the chilly climate they experienced in other university departments. Moreover, many among the diverse group of senior students that comprised the core sample for this study viewed empowerment with suspicion or even disdain. Some explained that knowing about sexism, racism, and other "isms" had essentially robbed them of the bliss of ignorance, leaving them in the painful position of having to question all aspects of their lives within the prisms of privilege and oppression. One student commented, "I can't even order a pizza without making it a political event. Life as a feminist isn't much fun." For these students as a group, engagement with real life issues does not always lead to welcomed results.

Struggles within WPPEI. In working with WPPEI itself, we have met with mixed success in our attempts to mediate the inherent power imbalances, despite our best efforts. We try to ask hard questions about our success at empowering those we have been working with, as we believe all who do this sort of work should. We encounter this issue as we set our annual agendas, design and execute our research project, write up and disseminate our results, and develop talking points for meeting with policy makers. While we believe we have accomplished much with our written reports, public presentations, the unique and invaluable data we have gathered, and other activities that truly blend the perspectives of the various groups involved, we have encountered serious contradictions in our work, issues that must be considered in any effort to provide for engagement with the community. We find that empower-ment emerges more as an uphill struggle than as an assured outcome. For example, one of our local group leaders from the community has struggled to bring in her expertise on leadership training. She developed a leadership cur-riculum for nursing assistants in a nursing home. Yet she feels that some of the academic WPPEI members discount her expertise, and she worries others may "steal my ideas and use them without me," as has happened when she worked with other organizations. The WPPEI staff is constantly developing strategies to deal with the issue of equality—using our written communications, monthly conference calls, and annual retreats to address such issues as shared expertise and ownership and crediting of intellectual property. This example shows that such issues are important to our community partners as well as to academics, something we did not realize before we began this project. We try to speak directly and plainly with each other, in the process of reaching consensus about these issues as they arise.

Issues around equality and balance of power involve the issue of empowerment, which plays itself out somewhat differently with our community partners than with our students. The following analysis of one WPPEI participant's experience probes some of the complexities that we encounter around concepts of empowerment. We focus on a participant named Cindy, who agreed to be named as the interviewee as a way of participating in this writing project.

Dynamics of empowerment, leadership, and experiential teaching/learning in feminist praxis are embedded in Cindy's story about living as a single mother on welfare for eight years and then becoming an activist/advocate with the hope of battling the systems that once constrained her life. Her story of entering, enduring, and making attempts to leave poverty have been central to her interactions with WPPEI. As a matter of fact, despite her recent strides toward economic security, it is her story of poverty that in many ways binds her most closely to WPPEI. She summarized this well, "For WPPEI in a way I still have to be poor." Despite recent full-time employment Cindy continues to struggle to make ends meet. Although she thinks it is a good experience to retell her story of being a woman in poverty in certain situations, she also acknowledges that it "gets old" having to explain herself in these terms all of the time. She asks, "Why can't people just accept you?" She looks forward to a time that she does not have to frame herself within a "welfare mom" model. She concluded, "It doesn't bother me that I was on welfare and I do not want to forget what that was like, but it seems like my story now has to be told as leverage for getting funding for WPPEI." Cindy's dreams for the future include helping other women battle the indignities of poverty and influencing state and national policy dealing with welfare reform. She hopes one day to talk with the state governor and the U.S. president. When asked what she would say, she replied, "I will tell them my story."

In analyzing Cindy's perceptions of empowerment, it becomes apparent that "her story" has served as a transitional talisman as she has followed a path toward self-sufficiency. As an unemployed single mother she often felt that she was required to narrate her own story within the confinements of prevailing stereotypes of welfare mothers. In turn, she frequently regarded herself and her story with considerable disdain. She recalls, for example, the humiliation and anger she felt when she was required to offer the details of her life to human service workers who, in her opinion, offered little encouragement or compassion in return. As Cindy has moved toward self-sufficiency and become an even more active advocate for women and poverty reform, she has continued to embrace the power of her story as a single mother on welfare. It is noteworthy that although her story remains essentially unchanged, the meanings she attaches to it have shifted dramatically. Whereas her story once was framed in a shroud of hopelessness, it is now more apt to be wrapped in a banner of pride. Cindy now uses the emotive power of her story to energize others to join the war against those who have failed to approach issues of poverty compassionately.

Conclusion: The Full Picture of Activism

Whether we think of Cindy's role in WPPEI or our students' roles in women's studies classrooms, we know that the audiences that hear and respond to a personal narrative play significant roles in determining the effects of that narrative on the person who constructs and expresses it. Locating audiences in classrooms and in activist organizations that applaud and support a personal narrative can provide a turning point in one's perception of empowerment. When synchronism evolves between the speaker's needs and an audience's goals, a fragile hope for collective empowerment arises. We hope that this approach will make for more fruitful and successful efforts at grassroots policy creation.

We agree with Michael Apple (1993: 7) who urges researchers to engage in critical work that is conducted in an "organic way" by connecting to those progressive social movements and groups that continue to challenge the multiple relations of exploitation and domination that exist. Our research/advocacy partnership with Cindy and others in WPPEI over several years time has provided such occasions. Building on "organic" approaches to research, bell hooks reminds us that dialogue is one of the simplest ways we can cross boundaries, forge discussions, foster solidarity, and disrupt the very assumption that we can ever unequivocally meet across boundaries (1994b: 130).

Our concern with empowerment is threaded throughout our concerns about avoiding hierarchy, exploitation, and appropriation. Yet we find ourselves confronted with evidence that we may not always be successful at doing so. We have seen similar issues arise in dealing with community partners and with our students. In terms of telling stories, whether they originate with "speaking bitterness" in a women's studies classroom or with "speaking out" against social injustices in a public space beyond classroom walls, they become the symbolic substance of the empowerment process itself. Speaking about life experiences in settings that honor the speaker as well as the message spoken can provide an oasis of comfort, and including many different voices in the creation of social policy can result in a stronger more effective policy.

Even so, we remain leery of suggestions that women's studies pedagogy unequivocally "gives voice" to students or that women's studies activism necessarily yields "empowerment" to all those who commit to its causes. We argue instead that although both situations may offer the promise of personal growth—which may or may not be experienced as empowering—in part by providing a climate that openly accepts the telling and revising of stories of self that challenge larger stories of society, these situations cannot operate in total exclusion from the power imbalances that surround them. Ideally, women's studies will provide multiple locations where personal stories and other insights may shift collective meanings in productive ways, but this goal must be tempered by an awareness that some voices will be heard more easily than others. In these settings it is important to continually ask, What stories are silenced and why? What issues are ignored?

As women's studies scholars open to the possibility of diversity in perspective, one learning challenge becomes how to create spaces where individuals with similar political impulses can relate to each other with respect across differences. While we must guard against the inequalities that lurk in the wings of our actions, we must nevertheless take the risk of forging new connections between the academy and the larger communities that encircle it.

Useful Resources

Several readings have been especially helpful for students. Two autobiographies were powerful in helping students see the personal power of taking action: Anne Moody's Coming of Age in Mississippi (1976b) and Maya Angelou's I Know Why the Caged Bird Sings (1970). Three texts were very useful for helping students not familiar with the issue of poverty (and the connected issues of race and class) make sense of what they are seeing: Linda Gordon's Pitied But Not Entitled: Single Mothers and the History of Welfare (1994); Lillian Rubin's Worlds of Pain: Life in the Working Class (1992); and Carol Stack's All Our Kin (1975). Several texts were good resources for community engagement or activism; in particular, Katrina Shields's In the Mouth of the Tiger: An Empowerment Guide for Social Action (1994) and Inge Bell and Bernard McGrane's This Book Is Not Required: An Emotional Survival Manual for Students (1999).

V

Using the Web for Teaching Feminist Politics

I nternet technology is transforming feminist classrooms and feminist pedagogy. Many feminist faculty are working to integrate Internet resources into Women's Studies courses in ways consistent with our course goals and feminist values. In chapter 16, Rebecca Anne Allahyari describes her experiences teaching a women's studies internship course that interweaves conventional ethnographic method with "cyberethnography" skills. Her students were required to analyze the ways in which women's organizations present themselves on- and off-line. Students were also required to learn some basic webpage creation skills since according to Allahyari, "only with some understanding of how to create Web pages could we demystify Web page writing sufficiently to think ethnographically about the political-economy and emotion culture of activist and service organizations online."

Allahyari argues for a critical perspective on Internet technology, and like all contributors to this collection presents her course as a work in progress. All contributors share a commitment to the value of an experiential approach for helping students explore the complexities of issues raised in women's studies. They describe the compromises they are forced to make and the ways in which their courses fall short of the ideal. Obstacles abound: a paucity of potential community partners in more conservative parts of the country; logistical nightmares when classes are large; time constraints for instructors with heavy teaching loads and for students with heavy job and family responsibilities. However, the rewards are also great, especially when experiential learning projects serve to deepen students' critical consciousness and commitment to social justice.

16

Becoming Feminist
Cyber Ethnographers

Rebecca Anne Allahyari

Bridging the gap between theory and practice is essentially what this class is about. Four years of studying feminism in the realm of academia has provided me with a solid understanding of many of the issues that surround the large inclusive areas of women's rights and feminist discourse . . . Actually attempting to go into the world, and consequently the lives of many individuals that you feel are being affected by women's oppression, is very different from reading about it. It is logical that this transition should be met by the emotional processing that needs to parallel this transformation.

—Clare, white middle-class, student-intern at H.I.P.S.,
Helping Individual Prostitutes Survive

To engage in the dynamic between theory and practice, women's studies upper-level majors at the University of Maryland, College Park may take "Feminist Analysis of the Workplace" (and intern without pay ten to twelve hours per week during the semester) for twice as many credit hours as the other foundational courses.

In the spring of 2000, I taught the internship course to a group of eleven women majors, double majors, and a few pursuing the concentration in women's studies. These women were mostly in their early 20s, and all were white but for two Latinas and one African American. This distribution is fairly typical of many of UM's women's studies students except for the absence of an Asian woman or the occasional man. These students must arrange their internships prior to the beginning of the semester. Although many rely on the advice of other students, as well as the undergraduate advisors and internship reference book in the department, some use the University of Maryland online community service programs database. Many students therefore encounter their future internship setting online before visiting it, or even before talking on the phone with a staff member or volunteer. This semester I required that students think about what it means for a women's organization to maintain an online presence. Not only did we spend time thinking about websites as political presentations of organizations, but students also learned some basic webpage creation skills so that they could post excerpts from their field notes and finally their entire papers to a password-protected space. In short, I required students to bring the ethnographic method with its observational powers not only to their internship experience but also to the World Wide Web and its organizational politics.

Ethnographers—established and novice alike—find ourselves scrambling at the opening of the twenty-first century to become *multisited* ethnographers (Marcus 1995) skilled at tracing linkages between on-line and off-line social relations. In the illustrative words of one set of collaborative social scientists,

> We aim to show how the way we that we read Web sites and Internet exchanges is informed by our understanding of the links between sites, and by the awareness that comes from shifting locations, accounting for the connections between different sets of relations. This calls for both a responsible intersubjectivity and for an itinerant methodological approach that traces connections between on- and off-line milieu. (Heath et. al. 1999)

This "responsible intersubjectivity," although not avowedly feminist, resonates with feminist concerns about how shifting positionalities and personal presence shape fieldwork observations. Feminist reflections on positionality attend to the power dynamics of race, class, gender, sexuality, and nationality among participants (including in this case the student-intern fieldworker) in the setting. Fieldworkers learn that social location, positionality, and varied constructions of the participant-observer role shape their observations. For example, one student intern at the American Association of University Women (AAUW), invited midway through the semester by her supervisor to apply for a permanent staff position to begin after the semester ended, worried initially that even the application process, much less a job offer, would taint her observations. But she came to understand that her role as job applicant, followed by that of future employee, afforded her an expanded vantage point from which to observe the workings and belief system of the AAUW.

In addition to shifting positionality and relationality, self-reflexive feminist ethnographers ideally attend to the emotions of participants, emotion cultures of organizations, and emotions of the researcher (Taylor 1995). Emotions come into focus as worthy of observation, telling of motivations, and themselves con-structed by—and constructing of—particular raced, classed, gendered, sexual-ized, and nationalized sensibilities. In the internship seminar, I intended for students to go online with this complex ethnographic sensibility. I wanted our "cyberethnography" understood as the observation and analysis of organiza-tional political presence on-line, to develop not only out of observation but also out of participation based in introductory website development skills. I believed that only with some understanding of how to create webpages could we demys-tify webpage writing sufficiently to think ethnographically about the political economy and emotional culture of activist and service organizations online.

In the words of an AAUW (2000, xi) executive summary concerning pro-ducing girls conversant with information technology, "Fluency [with infor-mation technology] is best acquired when students do coherent, ongoing projects to achieve specific goals in subjects that are relevant and interesting to them." Jamie Spriggs, campus computing associate in the College of Arts and Humanities at the University of Maryland, echoed this conviction in her guest lecture to our class: "I feel really, really strongly that women need to learn this language [HTML, or hypertext mark-up language]. I see this as a really funda-mental empowerment issue." With this sensibility in mind, it seemed essential to integrate website work into our discussions and syllabus to create a femi-nist-inflected fluency among myself and the students. I therefore attempted to interweave conventional ethnographic method with cyberethnography skills. Very early on in the semester, I taught students how to take field notes, and we spent one seminar learning basic HTML. Also in keeping with this method-ological sensibility, in place of the e-mail reflector list available through the UMCP class registrations system, we communicated online via WebCT (a Web-based communication tool adopted by the University of Maryland, College Park for its faculty and students) with its elaborate, threaded Web-archived dis-cussion board. I set up weekly forums to reflect the themes of the seminar. To move students toward using this communication tool, I required after the first seminar that they reiterate their self-introduction in the discussion boards, and then that they volunteer once during the semester in pairs to post to the weekly forum eight to ten websites of relevance to our weekly theme. I asked that students visit these websites prior to class; a laptop with a projector for use in the seminar permitted us to go on-line during the seminar. Another day, Spriggs took the first half of a seminar to lead the students through a recon-figuration of their University of Maryland web accounts to allow them to upload their webpages to a password-protected course website. All this Web fluency work meant that the beginning of the semester found us talking far less about the readings than I, and I believe the students, would have liked.

Nonetheless, as students posted excerpts from their field notes—as well as the first and revised drafts of their ethnographic analyses—to the course's private website, I found their ability to think analytically about connections between on-line and off-line politics increasingly sophisticated.

In asking students to apply their self-reflexive feminist ethnographic method not only to their observations in their internship setting, but also to website organization and webpage creation, I tried to move all of us further across the much touted "digital divide." I wanted us to become self-reflexive feminist cyberethnographers, in addition to being self-reflexive feminist ethnographers of organizations "on the ground." As students worked toward this goal, they came to view their organizations through as many as three different primary but often superimposed ethnographic lenses: a web lens, an office lens, and a service or activist lens. These shifting perspectives on their organizations required learning how to fine tune observational powers in order to bring into focus the dynamics of online social change politics, the visions of change embedded in policy papers and donor and volunteer recruitment and management, and the oft-fraught interaction between caregiver and care receiver, with its nuanced social inequalities. Just as students of the ethnographic method need to acquire different methodological skills in different contexts, teachers of the ethnographic method need to make pedagogical adjustments to teach them context relevant observational and analytical skills.

Students aligned these lenses differently in their field notes and ethnographic analyses. We returned repeatedly to the following questions in order to highlight shifting perspective: How do we "see" an organization differently on the Web after "seeing" it as a participant from the vantage point of an office or a service site? How do we "see" an office or service site differently after "seeing" an organization on-line? Shifting ethnographic vision makes seamless conclusions difficult and gives experiential substance to the conclusion that our ethnographic representations can be but partial, and often contradictory. Although—as will be discussed—web analysis seemed to fuel students' disenchantment with fund-raising politics, we spent considerably more time discussing the political economy of feminist service and activism than we had in previous semesters. And, in spite of how the web work seemed to sometimes dampen the flame of political ideals that inspired these students, their commitment to social justice work remained steady.

While we invested considerable time and effort in acquiring skills necessary to write and upload pages to the web, we also learned to think more critically about the politics of being online. A former women's studies major, working at a shelter for battered women and their children, described her experience of creating the website for the shelter, My Sister's Place, with help from the HandsNet Training and Resource Center. The HandsNet website proclaims that HandsNet "empowers organizations to integrate effective online communications strategies to strengthen their programs and policies for children, families and people in need." Krissi Jimroglou, director at HandsNet, agreed to visit our seminar and asked that prior to her guest lecture, we visit online at least one traditional feminist organization, such as Emily's List, one more commercial site for women, such as IVillage, and a zine, such as Bust.com, and then analyze each in light of the following questions:

1. What are the main goals of the website?
2. To whom is the website targeted?
3. What does the website ask the user to "do," either online or offline?
4. How does this encourage/discourage activism or foster community, if at all?

The question about what a website asks us to "do" proved especially useful for analyses of women's organizations and their complex politics as we refocused our ethnographic methodological perspective to include cyberpolitics.

In writing this essay, I strove for a "responsible intersubjectivity" (Heath et al. 1999) in how I represented the students' experience of this internship seminar. I posted drafts of this essay to the course's private website and e-mailed my former students in hopes that they would provide feedback on the essay and whether it captured their experience. Web ethnographer Lucy Schuchman (2000) in thinking about what she calls "located accountabilities in technology production," writes:

> The feminist move in particular reframes the locus of objectivity from an established body of knowledge not produced or owned by anyone, to knowledges in dynamic production for which we are all responsible. Given this reframing, a central concern for feminist theorists has been the problem of ensuring the presence of multiple voices in knowledge production.

Although I received little feedback, beyond affirmation, I felt accountable to the complexity of the students' experiences as I understood them. Nonetheless, this remains more my story than I had hoped it would. I recognize the ironic resonance in my experience of writing this paper with scholarly cautions that the web should not be envisioned as a utopian community of democratic participation. I believe, however, that a nascent feminist cyberethnographic sensibility will provide students a more savvy critical perspective as the world of women's activism and service goes online.

In the pages that I follow, I explore the work of teaching a feminist self-reflexive ethnographic method in an internship course. Within this context, I pushed students to bring a race, class, and gender feminist interpretation to their organizational analysis, both off-line and on-line. The Web work enriched and complicated this endeavor. I encouraged the students to attend to the emotions of participants in the organizational settings and to their own. Their moments of satisfaction and resistance ideally became points of interrogation. What organizational forms and type of work did they experience as satisfying or frustrating at what moments? And what does this reveal about the underlying emotional and ideological assumptions about women's service or advocacy work?

Bringing the Feminist I/Eye to Women's Organizations[1]

Many of the student interns from the University of Maryland find themselves inside the Capitol Beltway not only figuratively, but literally. Interns for large organizations such as the National Organization of Women (NOW), the American Association of University Women (AAUW), the National Abortion Rights Action League (NARAL), and the Planned Parenthood Federation of America (PPFA)—and also those at smaller organizations like My Sister's Place—observe firsthand how organizations may use what Roberta Spalter-Roth and Ronnee Schreiber call "insider tactics" at the expense of explicitly feminist allegiances:

> The network of women's organizations operating in Washington, D.C., has been applauded, even by opponents, for its political sophistication and its polished use of insider techniques. As part of their insider style, organizations learned the techniques of packaging information in short and readable form. . . . They developed media campaigns, focus groups, and other sophisticated forms of constituency analysis. . . . In short, these women's organizations learned to function as interest groups . . . in the hope that insider techniques would increase their power and influence, and raise the visibility of the issues they represented. (1995:113)

Leah, a white intern at AAUW, where she worked with the Lobby Corps, a contingent of mostly retirement-age white women who volunteered once a week to lobby on Capitol Hill, noted how AAUW's use of moderate pro-women—but not explicitly feminist—language, mirrored this insider polish:

> AAUW is definitely a mainstream women's organization. A former Public Policy employee described AAUW to me as "a good, moderately progressive organization," which is a very accurate statement. AAUW is a pro-choice organization and clearly does feminist work on both national and local levels for the benefit of all women and girls. However, despite the fact that AAUW is discussed in our course book, *Feminist Organizations*, AAUW does

not identify itself anywhere in its own literature as a feminist organization. The Association's most basic mission statement is: "The American Association of University Women promotes equity for all women." . . . I believe that AAUW's reluctance to associate itself with feminism is a political strategy, rather than a reflection of their ideology. . . . AAUW definitely has more doors open to it on Capitol Hill. I have first-hand heard from many congressional staffers that they "love AAUW and that it has such a wonderful reputation."

Perhaps not surprisingly, Leah's admiration for AAUW's work faltered as she struggled with its educational elitism. She spoke poignantly in the seminar about her surprise that AAUW members must be working on a bachelor's degree or already be a college graduate. In spite of her comrades in the Lobby Corps being of her mother's generation or older, her mother, without a college degree, could not join the AAUW. Hired mid-semester to continue on at the AAUW after her May graduation, one of Leah's goals will be to "advertise AAUW more to college campuses in an effort to recruit a younger, more diverse population."

Similar concerns about insider tactics eclipsing inclusivity surfaced in the organizational analysis of Karen, a white, working-class intern at Maryland NARAL, as well:

The majority of our members are white, middle to upper class women. I was thinking of this when I was reading Nancy Naples' article, "Women's Community Activism: Exploring the Dynamics of Politicization and Diversity." . . . Maryland NARAL does deal with some class issues, such as low income women's right to state and federally funded abortions, but that is about as far from our member base as we move. What bothered me most was that I feel that abortion is every woman's issues. . . . I discussed this with my supervisor. She did not seem to understand where I was coming from. She basically told me that NARAL has very little to do with multicultural feminism, as the organization is purely issue driven. From her perspective, we did not only fight for the reproductive rights of white women; we fight for the reproductive rights of all women, regardless of race, class or sexuality. I understand where she is coming from, but I still feel like Maryland NARAL is a bit elitist.

Yet, Karen noted, later in her analysis,

When the state legislature tries to pass bills that will financially restrict lower class women's rights to choose, we attack this as a racial issue, because in many ways it is. If you are a white, middle or upper class woman and you want an abortion, you can get one. You can afford to travel; you can afford to pay large fees in hospitals. But lower class women do not have these options and we recognize that the reproductive freedom we fight for is not only for the right to choose, but the *ability* to choose.

These examples illustrate that students in large, established advocacy organizations found themselves struggling with how these organizations used insider tactics to sidestep an up-front feminist organizational identity. As a student intern at NARAL, Karen—referencing Spalter-Roth and Schreiber (1995: 115)—astutely noted in her ethnographic analysis how Maryland NARAL straddled the insider-outsider tensions particularly plaguing large membership organizations by "marketing feminist issues in the dominant language of individual liberalism, while simultaneously trying to raise collective consciousness to mobilize and to educate around structural issues." Nonetheless, students often based their assessment of organizations' feminist politics on the then disappointing litmus test of whether or not the organizations evidenced feminism by using the word or its derivatives in their mission statements, publications, and/or on their websites.

Although most organizations failed this test, our consideration of websites revealed how organizations managed inside-outsider tensions by burying their more radical politics behind a moderate home page. We spent some time in the classroom looking at the website for My Sister's Place, a "shelter for battered women and their children." The home page includes their mission statement: "My Sister's Place is an interactive community committed to eradicating domestic violence. We provide safe, confidential shelter, programs, education, and advocacy for battered women and their children. Our goal is to empower women to take control of their own lives." Beneath this, a button labeled "Click here for our Guiding Principles" leads viewers to their 11 principles, which include: "7. We believe that relationship violence stems from a systematic inequality in the distribution of power. 8. We believe violence against women is rooted in sexism. It is not only an individual's survivor's problem, but fundamentally affects society as a whole and is, in various ways, an institutionalized form of oppression." While suspicious of how the *feminist* label might shut certain doors on Capitol Hill, students realized that the same label might also be a barrier to racial and class inclusivity in women's community activism.

In the seminar, we talked about the political repercussions of characterizing women doing community activism not for sex-based inequality but on behalf of their racial and class communities as "border feminists" (Pardo 1995). An African-American student and intern at Planned Parenthood and a Hispanic-American intern at a legal clinic for the Spanish-speaking community spoke eloquently about how they believe that the very term *border feminists* might relegate feminists of color to the margins of a white-dominated feminist movement. Sandra, a Hispanic-American student and a government and poli-tics/women's studies double major, felt herself torn between what she charac-terized as "first world" feminists "usually categorized by their emphasis on achieving equality between women and men" and "third world" feminists "mainly known for seeking social justice for their communities":

> Being Latin American born and having grown up in the United States I have seen both sides of the struggle that is mentioned by both first and third world feminists. . . . Interning at CASA de Maryland has been the first full encounter I have had with the Hispanic population in the United States. The reaction I have to certain events at the office are biased by my upbring-ing and mixed heritage. I do not formally identify myself as a first or third world feminist. I am neither; if anything my observations reflect the influence of my upbringing and my struggle to find an identity in between both worlds.

Perhaps not insignificantly, La CASA de Maryland, where Sandra worked pri-marily on a campaign for domestic workers' rights, was the only internship organization without a website.

In these discussions, we strove to bring the complexity of an intersectional approach to our thinking about the online politics of race. How do interlock-ing hierarchies of class, race, gender, and sexuality produce oppression and opportunity in online organizing and mobilizing?

For example, one of the two interns at My Sister's Place noted that in the home page image—a pleasingly simple line drawing of a woman and another woman or a child, raised arms joined in a heart, the two foreshad-owed against the image of a house—as well as in the text of the website itself, race remained absent. Drawing on her knowledge of feminist theory, the stu-dent critiqued this logo as a problematic instance of what Ruth Frankenberg (1993) calls "color- and power-evasiveness." As scholars of the web have noted, "online discourse has typically kept the binary switch of race in the 'off' position" (Kolko, Nakamura, and Rodman 2000:5). In a parallel vein to Ruth Frankenberg and her critique of color blindness, E. R. Mason (2000) argues against "erase-ism" on the web:

> The blindness approach may seem innocuous in its intent, but it disempow-ers one's sense of identity more than it works towards freeing it from stereo-types. Instead of actually ridding people of social prejudices, we are pushed to simply ignore that they are there: if we do not see race, then we do not see racism, if we do not see gender, we do not see sexism, and so on.

Why would a fairly radical women's shelter engage in racial-ethnic erase-ism on its website? The insights offered by Krissi Jimroglou of HandsNet seem

Rebecca Anne Allahyari

instructive. We noted that the button in the upper-left corner of the My Sister's Place site—understood by web designers as the "privileged spot" on the page that draws the initial attention of our eyes (Spriggs 2000)—reads "Programs." Clicking on this button leads the reader to "Volunteer Opportunities," with a listing of nine such opportunities. The interns at this shelter concluded that staff intended the website not for potential shelter "residents"—many of whom are women of color—but rather to recruit the (predominantly) volunteers so essential to the workings of a battered women's shelter and crisis hotline. The site's creator, Krissi Jimroglou, estimated that with a minimum of $200 to $400 in training a staff person could create a website like that of My Sister's Place. She contrasted this website to the elaborate site of the Feminist Majority, with its daily news flashes, feminist gateway to the Internet, searchable feminist career center, and other resources. Jimroglou estimated that the Feminist Majority probably paid AppNet (credited with the creation of the site) at least $50,000 simply to design the initial site. Yet, the My Sister's Place website may serve as an effective tool for recruiting volunteers and donors.

Self-reflexive, web-savvy ethnography throws into relief feminist organizations' dependency upon volunteers and donors. For example, Monica, an African-American middle-class intern at Planned Parenthood of Maryland, analyzed differences between the websites for PPFA, the national Planned Parenthood, and PPM, the Maryland chapter:

> Both the Web sites . . . act to get Web surfers financially involved in the organizations. The PPFA Web site is at first very political with legislative updates and links to get connected to local legislators. There are also links to find a PPFA clinic near you and information about reproductive health. But on almost every page there is a link to make a donation. The most interesting view of the innovation of Web technology and money is the link to Amazon.com. If you go through the portal on the PPFA page to Amazon.com, a percentage of your purchases will be donated to PPFA.
>
> The PPM Web site is simpler and has larger text. It also has information about political activism, volunteerism, employment, and reproductive health. Surprisingly the levels of donating money to PPM are more intricate than [those of] the PPFA website. The more money you give, the more prestigious the title and recognition award. Donations come in the form of cars (patient transportation) and funding for prenatal care, abortion, and lobbying. The donation request that surprised me most was the Legacy of Choice Society. This allows one to name PPM as a benefactor of a will, trust, and life insurance and retirement plans. At first I was shocked at this level of donation. In thinking more about it, I realize that many organizations are left money from the wealthy. I realize my initial shock came from thinking about PP as a feminist organization and my dissociation of feminism and that type of financial interaction usually representative of rich, white conservatives.

The student-intern most consistently aware of the politics of money solici-tation worked in the fund-raising team at NOW; at her supervisor's direc-tion, Margaret, a white, middle-class women's studies intern, examined the Feminist Majority website to do Internet research for potential donor lists that NOW could either rent or obtain through list sharing. In comparing the Web sites, she noted,

> On NOW's Web page below the picture and the choice of categories it is again broken down by a table of contents. It takes each main category and breaks down subtitles under each. This sort of gets a little cluttered and there is a lot going on. One topic that seems to be a much bigger deal to NOW than Feminist Majority Foundation is the support section. On FMF there is one thing that says "join" to click on. However on the NOW page this subject is presented quite differently. At the top center around the pic-ture there is a section title "Support NOW" with two subtitles, "join NOW" and "NOW catalog." Then underneath the table of contents page there are several different titles listed in regards to joining. This is all on the home-page where the FMF homepage just has one little box to click on. . . . When clicking on "Support NOW" the result is very different from clicking on the "join" on the FMF page. For NOW, these different categories pop up with what seems like endless possibilities to support the organization. On the FMF page there is a segment on "How Can I Help" and "Benefits," then there is an enrollment form and that's it.

Acknowledging that "I could however just be seeing it as this way because of the way I am secluded with my one [fund-raising] team," Margaret felt increasingly cynical about feminist insider politics at NOW:

> They seem to be taken over by the insider tactics and seem to care more about the politics and the outcome in the long run than what the member is actu-ally all about. This correlates with the concept in Spalter-Roth and Schreiber's article: "these women's organizations learned to function as interest groups in the hope that insider techniques would increase their power and influence, and raise the visibility of the issues they represented" (113).
>
> NOW is using these insider tactics to give themselves more voice.

Reflecting on Margaret's experience, I recalled another student intern sev-eral years prior who worked in the fund-raising department at the National Women's Museum. She began her internship with great enthusiasm but expe-rienced the soliciting corporate donors and the organization of fund-raising as disappointingly detached from the art world she so valued. Not inconse-quentially, however, she learned a lot about how donor interests narrowed the range of art shown at the museum.

Website analysis probably amplifies the cynicism in all of us. Shifting ethnographic perspectives give complicated emotional and moral texture to our political evaluations. That is, what I think of as a felt politics illuminates how we interpret politics based on our emotional experiences, and their implicit moralities, as participants in organizational cultures. We feel politics to be right or wrong, pure or tainted, and web politics often seemed most tainted. This begs consideration of why print literature doesn't seem so tainted. Perhaps because websites are abbreviated in comparison to the voluminous print literature of even small organizations, and perhaps because soliciting donations and recruiting volunteers featured so prominently, political mobilizing overshadows the importance of political organizing, with its face-to-face interactive emotional labor. Print literature may be distributed to circumscribed audiences and as such doesn't necessarily suggest conflicting organizational goals; analysis of websites, however, reveals an emphasis upon donation solicitation and volunteer recruitment with a simultaneous burying of feminist ideals. Although the strategic distribution of print literature may reflect similar objectives, unlike a website it does not throw into relief the ongoing efforts at volunteer recruitment and donation solicitation so necessary in nonprofit organizations. In short, website analysis effectively highlights the "chameleon" adaptive technique of organizations striving to legitimate their work (Peyrot 1991), and as such generates cynicism in students.

Feminist cyberspace fieldworker Lori Kendall (1999:60) advises us that ethnographies of on-line communication should strive to include fieldwork off-line:

> In addition to taking into account larger social institutions affecting on-line participation, researchers need to consider participants' local off-line environments, as well as to explore how participants blend their on-line and off-line lives and social contexts. Individuals exist and participate in off-line social contexts both sequentially and simultaneously with their on-line participation. However, many accounts of on-line spaces, experiences, and communications ignore this, often describing on-line spaces almost wistfully as a new and discrete utopian world.

In the future I would ask students to reflect more on these matters, and most importantly, to supplement their fieldwork with questions about online politics, such as: Who designed the site? How do expenditures for the website compare to those for print media and other communication mediums? At whom is the website targeted? What do the creators hope that readers of the site will do? Do these goals overlap or differ from intentions for the print literature? Of the organizational members, volunteers, activists, and service recipients, who has seen the website and what do they think of it? How has a web presence been useful or inspiring, and how has it been a drain of resources or a disappointment?

The Insights and Satisfaction of Working One-on-One

If casting the ethnographic I/eye on the Web often results in cynicism about feminist insider politics, so too does office work often disappoint students. In contrast, one-on-one service work inspires students the most. The observational vantage point afforded by direct service work in a shelter, an outreach van, or a legal clinic for immigrants, also infuses students' field notes with a richness of detail often absent in notes detailing office work. Susan, a white student in her late twenties and hence a bit older than her classmates, made a convincing case to me that she be permitted to intern in the domestic violence unit (DVU) of a local police district, rather than in a traditional women's organization. She wrote exceptionally rich field notes detailing her observations on police ride-alongs, in the courts, and in the office of the DVU:

> Tonight I went on my first police ride-along. . . . After seeing the victim from the first call I knew that nothing short of making chalk outlines was going to phase me. . . . The kitchen was well lit and I was able to see the victim for the first time. The woman had been horribly beaten. Both eyes were blackened and one was completely filled with blood, to the point you couldn't make out her retina. . . . The woman told M. [police officer] that she had two copies of her protection order but that they were locked in a filing cabinet. M. told her that it was extremely important for her to keep a copy ON HER PERSON at ALL times in case her husband violates his order someplace other than their home. I have also been told that it was important for a victim to do that in case they wind up dead; then the police have someplace to start looking.

In her ethnographic analysis, Susan reflected that "going on the police ride-alongs is necessary to provide a framework of realism that forces me to remove the protective shroud of 'professional distance' that working in the office allots me." She added,

> The members of the D.V.U. chose their positions within the greater police department in order to effect positive change on behalf of victims of domestic violence. And, like the femocrats (Hester Eisenstein in Ferree and Martin, 1995), they wield the influence that is available to them by working within a bureaucratic structure to see to it that women are not further victimized by the system. . . . The public-position positionality views the D.V.U. much like the many feminists within Australia view the femocrats, as "mandarin," one who works for women within the government yet is

viewed as never having put themselves on the line for the feminist mission thus seen as having sold out to bureaucracy.

Susan's placement reminded all of the us of the difficulties faced by police officers sympathetic to the women's movement; her immediate boss, an African-American man, graduated with a minor in women's studies and shared many of her feminist politics. Yet, her critique of some officers' practice of making light of domestic abuse cases revealed further victimization of some women in the criminal justice system. Reading Mary Fainsod Katzenstein's work (1995) on discursive politics, or the politics of meaning-making, helped Susan to critique how some police officers talked about domestic abuse cases as "personal problems" that "got out hand" and resulted in "mutual combat."

The power of the drama of interactions between service providers and their recipients to bring alive academic women's studies' concerns became most salient among those students who moved in the course of the semester from office work to service provision—specifically from the office of My Sister's Place (MSP) into its shelter and from the office of HIPS (Helping Individual Prostitutes Survive) into mobile outreach work. Note in the following analysis how a shifting vantage point affected Ann, a white, middle-class woman, in her final assessment of the importance of the different types of work done by a shelter:

> When I first heard about MSP as a shelter for battered women, I pictured their only facility as a shelter. I also assumed that all the efforts of both the staff members and volunteers went into providing a safe residential space for women who have experienced domestic violence. Instead, MSP consists of this shelter, along with the programs described above and the administrative office. To call the organization a shelter only broadcasts the work that we do after a woman has experienced battering. It belies the work done in attempts to stop domestic violence from happening and to educate the community and raise awareness that domestic violence exists and how it hurts people.
>
> Having served different roles in the MSP programs, I have seen the immediacy and urgency of some of the work that goes on. For example, when a crisis call comes into the shelter, the current hotline worker must immediately attend to that call. If the caller requests shelter, the hotline worker refers her case to the program director of the shelter, who must quickly decide if this woman meets the requirement to stay at MSP. Therefore, it sometimes feels in the administrative offices that we get caught up in office politics, administrative work, constant phone calls to volunteers and donors, and nondirect action work. This therefore shifts the

focus, and the office climate, away from one of feminist action and a concentration on domestic violence. Though this sometimes feels like a dichotomy, I have grown to realize that the work done in the administrative office is necessary to making MSP function as a useful organization. In this instance, my internship has been good for me in showing that there is much behind the scene work that allows activism and change to happen. Though I realized that I preferred more hands-on, people-oriented work, MSP has shown me both sides of the feminist organizing coin.

Many students come to the internship course wanting to be involved in direct service work in the "front lines" of social change, distanced from the women's studies classroom with its paper shuffling and bureaucracy. For some the distinction and contradictions between service work and activist work becomes most meaningful in their internship experience. For example, student interns at My Sister's Place struggled with how shelter policies seemed instrumental in "producing the battered woman," to use the words of Karen Kendrick (1998).

A few students finished the semester feeling more attuned to policy or advocacy work than one-on-one service work. Monica, the African-American middle-class intern at Planned Parenthood of Maryland, experienced reservations similar to those experienced by other abortion clinic workers about the sexual practices of some clients (Joffe 1986). These feelings contributed to her intent to pursue policy—not service—work in the women's health field after graduation:

> I realize that my positionality affects my critique of feminism in Planned Parenthood Maryland. If I were interning in the public affairs office I would have a totally different view of how feminism works as a political platform. . . . Maneuvering through the emotional culture of the office has been an interesting experience. I have always been a big advocate for unlimited access for birth control, but it's a little daunting handing out birth control to middle school girls.
>
> It was a great experience for me to see and analyze feminism in this respect. When I first started women's studies, I thought that being in a clinic would be a great way to practice feminism in a service-oriented way. But since I've been there, I think I would rather be somewhere where feminism and activism is a bigger part of the agenda. It seems a little too easy to get lost in the little annoyances of everyday and forget the feminist ideals that brought you there. I think I'd feel more at home in an organizational or decision-making entity where I could really utilize feminist analysis to create programs.

Service work and activist work sometimes merge for students working in organizations such as HIPS. Advocating on behalf of sex workers on the street becomes a radical outreach project, with knowledge of the law and rights of sex workers necessary in interactions with police. This blurs the line between service and advocacy work or social justice and activist work, and suggests that street-level internships, while not necessarily more satisfying, nonetheless do yield more powerful emotional politics than those in conventional women's rights advocacy organizations.

For some the internship opened up possible stepping-stones down a career path (recall the student hired mid-semester for a future position at the AAUW). Angela, the Hispanic student critical of the shelter rules at My Sister's Place, nonetheless began to imagine how she might apply her psychology major with a women's studies certificate after graduation:

> I would be happy to pursue this field of work for a career. . . . For example, with my major being psychology, I can identify the need for psychological advancement in the area of [domestic violence] and other mental health issues involving women. With my certificate in Women's Studies I can very easily apply feminist theory and discourse to everyday experiences within the organization. However, the most rewarding aspect of working in a non-profit organization, such as this, is knowing that you may have made a difference in someone's life. As much of a cliché as that is, I do believe it and stand by the fact that this experience may have been one of the most important in my life.

Concluding Thoughts

> I look forward to reading the paper as I see us working through the "adolescence" of school work on the Web. It is fascinating in a way to be in on the development of such a radically different educational reform. (Elizabeth, H.I.P.S. intern, in e-mail communication to R. A. Allahyari).

Just as feminist teachers encourage students to take seriously the emotions of themselves and those we study, we should consider the emotions of our students as they encounter new ideas and ways of studying the world. I encountered far less explicit resistance—or even resentment—from my students than I expected at the beginning of the semester. Web skills provided students the means to become participant-observers in the increasingly on-line world of women's service and advocacy. Overall, the students resisted learning web skills far less than they did the rigors of taking field notes that illuminated the organizational context of service and activist work. Yet the institutional ethnographic method cautions that without considering the organizational context and value structure shaping theirs and others' emotions, their observational records may more closely resemble journals in the strictest sense than self-reflexive attempts at feminist ethnography.

Once we moved past the technicalities of reconfiguring student web accounts so that they could access the course's private website, students seemed amazed—and even exhilarated—at times by how easily they could write HTML code and hence webpages. They quickly figured out how to save files in word processing programs as HTML files, thus saving themselves a great deal of coding time. Some left the semester planning to help women's organizations with website development. Most significantly to my mind, without basic webpage creation skills, students couldn't have as effectively turned the ethnographic I/eye onto the web. I think too that students challenged to take on cyberethnography gained a far deeper appreciation for the complicated dynamic between positionality and representation. The differences in politics as they moved on and offline, in and out of service and activist work, from the street to the office, and out of the office and into the halls of congressional representatives, lent perspective on organizational politics as complex and contradictory, and ethnographic representations as partial. I do not mean to suggest, however, that students seemed stopped short in policy analyses in a stereotypical postmodern conundrum of contradictory and shifting meanings. I think rather that they offered critiques more strongly grounded in understandings of shifting political contexts.

Let me conclude by briefly introducing a set of questions inspired by a conference session at the Maryland Institute for Technology in the Humanities (MITH), aptly titled by Katie King "Terror and Possibility: Search for Enlivened Technologies," that will more explicitly guide this internship course in its future renditions. At this conference, history and women's studies professor Elsa Barkley Brown (2000) encouraged us to think more fully about *responsibility* in how individuals and organizations use the web. In a world where on-line political possibilities often receive great hype, she suggested that the differences between *political mobilizing* and *organizing* might illuminate the Web's political limits. That is, political organizations may effectively use the Web for speed in mobilizing resources and support, but not necessarily as effectively for the work of organizing. This distinction resonated for me how student-intern ethnographers seemed resentful of Web-based efforts to mobilize them as volunteer or donor constituencies. Rather, they desired to do the work of the movement through one-on-one service work, interactive organizing, or even lobbying. Does the potential speed-up in political mobilizing facilitated by the web undercut the emotionally labor-intensive work of organizing? How might we think responsibly about whether constituencies with limited Web access might be disproportionately marginalized as political work moves on-line? When does the web seem to most successfully organize activism? For whom or when does the web seem to undercut feelings of solidarity and for whom or when does the web facilitate political mobilizing and organizing by or for women?

Notes

Thanks are due to my students for their permission to undertake this paper using their feedback, and most importantly for their inspiring and self-reflective dedication to social justice work in its many manifestations. My gratitude to Jamie Spriggs for guiding my initial forays into webpage writing and teaching with digital technologies, to Krissi Jimroglou for talking with us about the social justice politics facing nonprofits online, to Katie King for sharing her thoughts about feminist teaching and technology, to Seung-kyung Kim for her reflections on teaching the internship seminar, and to Laura Nichols for her moral support of both me and the students. And, my appreciation also goes to Ellen K. Scott and Rosemary F. Powers for thoughtful readings of this paper, as well as to Melinda J. Milligan for her intellectual encouragement as I imagined writing this paper.

1. I borrow here from Dorinne Kondo's wonderfully evocative imagery of self-reflexive ethnography in her introduction to *Crafting Selves: Power, Gender, and Discourses of Identity in a Japanese Workplace* (1990). Kondo captures the coconstruction of observations and social location, identity, and field work in her imagery of the I/eye.

Resources

Student Internship Settings Websites

American Association of University Women (AAUW): http://www.aauw.org/

Helping Individual Prostitutes Survive (H.I.P.S.): http://www.HIPS.org/

Montgomery County, Maryland, Police Department, http://www.co.mo.md.us/services/police/

My Sister's Place: http://mysistersplace.com/

National Abortion Rights Action League: http://www.Naral.org/

National Organization for Women: http://www.now.org/

Planned Parenthood Federation of America (PPFA): http://www.plannedparenthood.org

Planned Parenthood of Maryland (PPM): http://users.erols.com/ppmd/whoweare.htm

Other Websites Cited Herein

Bust.com: http://bust.com/

Closing the Digital Divide: www.digitaldivide.gov

The Feminist Majority: http://www.feminist.org

Emily's List: http://www.emilyslist.org/

HandsNet Training and Resource Center: http://www.handsnet.org

Ivillage: http://www.ivillage.com/

Catie King, feminism and writing technologies homepage,
    http://www.inform.umd.edu/EdRees/Colleges/ARHU/
    Depts/WomensStudies/wmstfac/KKing/F+WT/F+WT.

Maryland Institute for Technology in the Humanities (MITH):
    http://www.mith.umd.edu/

Resource Center for Cyberculture Studies:
    http://www.com.washington.edu/rccs/

University of Maryland, College Park online community service programs
    database: http://www.umd.edu/CSP

WebCT: http://www.Webct.com/

Women's Studies 380 syllabus, University of Maryland, College Park:
    http://www.inform.umd.edu/EdRes/Colleges/ARHU/Depts/
    WomensStudies/wmstfac/rallahyari/FeministPolitics/syllabuswmst380.html

17

Conclusion:
Reflections on the Present and
Future of Feminist Praxis
in Women's Studies

Karen Bojar and Nancy A. Naples

T he articles in this collection demonstrate the diversity of strategies feminist teachers have developed for incorporating activist projects into their courses. The constraints and opportunities vary greatly from one institution to another, but one theme runs throughout all the articles: this is a very labor-intensive approach. For most of us, this work is unpaid labor, as we put in far more time than we would teaching a traditional course. Those of us in large research universities benefit from the enthusiastic support of graduate teaching assistants who frequently welcome the opportunity to put feminist theory into practice. In this context, we are also engaged in the training of a new generation of feminist activist scholars. For those of us working in community colleges, the opportunity to validate students' concerns and to provide them with the skills to fight on behalf of their communities is an unparalleled reward for our activist pedagogy.

Though it will certainly be an uphill struggle, feminist educators need to build support for efforts to include experiential/activist components in our courses. This support could take many forms, such as smaller classes; additional resources in the form of teaching assistants; additional compensation, either in the form of increased pay or released time; recognition for such work when decisions are made regarding promotion and tenure. However, academic administrators (even liberal ones) tend to be reluctant to channel resources to anything that might be considered controversial by their boards of trustees or by local political leaders, in the case of public institutions dependent on state and local funding. The compromises we make (or choose not to make) will depend on institutional constraints, local political climates, and the extent to which we ourselves are in a position to take risks.

This agenda might seem hopelessly utopian to those who teach at financially strapped colleges (which would have great difficulty providing additional financial resources) or at elite institutions (which would be very resistant to considering a commitment to experiential education when awarding promotion and tenure). Yet there are feminist goals that at one time seemed hopelessly utopian, but have been at least partially realized. If we are committed to an experiential/activist approach we need to build institutional commitment to experiential education. Certainly one of the best places to begin is in women's studies departments. Women's studies as an academic discipline has defined itself in terms of its subject matter, its methodology, and its pedagogy. A commitment to experiential education has been a major theme of feminist pedagogy; many women's studies practitioners would argue that it is central to feminist pedagogy. If we indeed have a consensus that experiential education is central to feminist pedagogy and to women's studies as a discipline, then we need to ensure that the necessary supports are in place. We also need to expand our range of community partners.

In this regard, partnerships with labor movement organizations are missing from the partnerships described by the authors in this collection (with the exception of Catherine Orr's reference to collaboration with union activists on a local living-wage campaign). In campuses across the county, many students are forging their own partnerships with unions in the antisweatshop movement and in living-wage campaigns. Women's studies practitioners can play a major role here, encouraging students to bring a feminist perspective to such campaigns and to view issues, strategies, and tactics through a gender lens.

There are many reasons why feminist activist projects and internships have not, for the most part, formed partnerships with labor unions or with feminist organizations allied with the labor movement, such as the Coalition of Labor Union Women. Historically, the labor movement has a mixed record on women's issues; prolabor feminists who work in electoral politics are often in despair at local trade unionists' willingness to endorse antichoice candidates. Finally, women's studies teachers who do not come from union families, or may never themselves have been union members, may find unions unfamiliar terrain for activist projects.

A second issue that needs further attention in experiential activist projects is that of immigration. The absence of attention to this issue is particularly troublesome given that many of our students are themselves immigrants or children of immigrants. Given the strong anti-immigrant sentiments expressed by many within our communities, it is imperative that women's studies courses and feminist activism engage in progressive efforts to counter the harassment and xenophobia encountered by these students and their families. The anti-immigrant stance, especially against those of Middle Eastern descent, has only been fueled by the events of September 11, 2001.

Writing this conclusion following the terrorist attack on the World Trade Center and the Pentagon on September 11, 2001, and the subsequent bombing of Afghanistan, we are struck by the outpouring of student activism calling for justice through peace. Many of our feminist students and women's studies colleagues are at the forefront of campus and community-based efforts to counter the racist and militaristic responses of so many others in the United States. Many of the antiracist and antiwar efforts on campuses across the country are organized in collaboration with long-standing social justice and peace organizations. This renewed collaboration between students and community groups is one bright spot in what otherwise is a very bleak landscape consisting of calls for violent retaliation and war.

As we anticipate the continued need for collective action to fight against racism, militarism, and the loss of civil liberties that will most certainly follow, we are heartened by the role that feminist analysis and activism can play in this effort. We also recognize the need to expand the range of possible partnerships we forge to accomplish these difficult goals. Furthermore, we need to pay greater attention to the role of the Internet in broadening our worldview and that of our students. In this era of technological innovation, the sources for teaching feminist politics and praxis can be drawn from a network of groups and sites around the globe. There is also much to be learned from our students and others in the communities in which we live. Experiential education as a central component of feminist pedagogy provides the framework for linking local efforts with transnational feminist politics. Here we see one of the most difficult challenges for contemporary feminist pedagogy, and one on which our effectiveness as activist educators depends.

As we try to build support for experiential education and activism in women's studies and in other feminist classrooms across our campuses, we need to continue to document and critically analyze our work. Our hope is that this collection will encourage others to add to the growing literature on teaching feminist activism, providing us with new ideas and resources, as we educate a new generation of feminists committed to feminist praxis.

Works Cited

AAUW Educational Foundation Commission on Technology, Gender and Teacher Education. 2000. *Tech-Savvy: Educating Girls in the New Computer Age*. Washington, D.C.: American Association of University Women Educational Foundation.

Ackelsberg, Martha A. 1988. "Communities, Resistance, and Women's Activism: Some Implications for a Democratic Polity." Pp. 297–313 in *Women and the Politics of Empowerment*, edited by Ann Bookman and Sandra Morgen. Philadelphia, PA: Temple University Press.

Agarwal, Bina. 1996. "From Mexico 1975 to Beijing 1995." *Indian Journal of Gender Studies* 3.1:88.

Alemán, Ana M. Martinez. 2000. "Race Talks: Undergraduate Women of Color and Female Friendships." *The Review of Higher Education* 23(2):133–52.

Alexander, Jacqui M. and Chandra Talpade Mohanty. 1997. *Feminist Genealogies, Colonial Legacies, and Democratic Futures*. New York: Routledge.

Allen, Robert L. 1995. "Racism, Sexism, and a Million Men." *The Black Scholar*. 25(4): 24–26.

Alternative Orange, Editorial Board. 1991. "Capitalism and Your Education: The Marxist Collective at Syracuse University." *Alternative Orange* 2:6–7, 15.

Alvarez, Sonia. 1998. "Latin American Feminisms Go Global: Trends and Challenges for the New Millennium." Pp. 293–324 in *Cultures of Politics, Politics of Cultures: Revisioning Latin American Social Movements*, edited by Sonia Alvarez, Evelina Dagnino, and Arturo Escobar. Boulder: Westview Press.

Amott, Teresa and Matthaei, Julie A. 1996. *Race, Gender and Work: A Multi-cultural Economic History of Women in the U.S.* Boston: South End Press.

Anderson, Mary, Lisa Fine, Kathleen Geissler, and Joyce R. Ladenson. 1997. *Doing Feminism: Teaching and Research in the Academy*. East Lansing: Michigan University Press.

Angelou, Maya. 1970. *I Know Why the Caged Bird Sings*. New York: Random House.

Aparicio, Frances R. 1999. "Through My Lens: A Video Project about Women of Color Faculty at the University of Michigan." *Feminist Studies*. 25(1):119–30.

Apple, Michael W. 1993. *Official Knowledge: Democratic Education in a Conservative Age*. New York: Routledge.

Aryabod, Shadi. 1998. "Community Action Project Report." Unpublished paper, University of California, Irvine.

Au, Ami Danice. 1994. "Group Action Project Final Report." Unpublished paper, University of California, Irvine.

Balliet, Barbara J., and Kerissa Heffernan, eds. 2000. *The Practice of Change: Concepts and Models for Service Learning in Women's Studies.* Washington, D.C.: American Association of Higher Learning.

Barbeck, Mary M. and Larned, Ann G. 1997. "What Do We Know About Women's Ways of Knowing?" Pp. 261–269 in *Women, Men & Gender: Ongoing Debates,* edited by Mary Roth Walsh. New Haven: Yale University Press.

Bargad, Adena and Janet Shibley Hyde. 1991. "Women's Studies: A Study of Feminist Identity Development in Women." *Psychology of Women Quarterly* 15:181–201.

Barnett, Bernice McNair. 1993. "Invisible Southern Black Women Leaders in the Civil Rights Movement: The Triple Constraints of Gender, Race and Class." *Gender and Society* 7(2):162–82.

Bart, Pauline B., Lynn Bentz, Jan Clausen, LeeRay Costa, and others. 1999. "In Sisterhood? Women's Studies and Activism." *Women's Studies Quarterly* 27(3/4):257–67.

Basch, Linda, Nina Glick Schiller, and Cristina Szanton Blanc, eds. 1994. *Nations Unbound: Transnational Projects, Postcolonial Predicaments, and Deterritorialized Nation-States.* Langhorne, PA: Gordon and Breach.

Basu, Amrita, ed. 1995. *The Challenges of Local Feminisms: Women's Movements in Global Perspective.* Boulder: Westview Press.

Bauman, Suzanne, and Rita Heller. 1985. *The Women of Summer: The Bryn Mawr Summer School for Women Workers, 1921–1938.* New York: Filmakers Library.

Beaud, Michel. 1983. *A History of Capitalism 1500–1980.* Translated by Tom Dickman and Anny Lefebvre. New York: Monthly Review Press.

Belenky, Mary Field, Blythe Clinchy, Nancy Rule Goldberger, Jill Mattuck Tarule. 1986. *Women's Ways of Knowing: The Development of Self, Voice, and Mind.* New York: Basic Books.

Belenky, Mary Field, Lynne A. Bond, and Jacqueline S. Weinstock. 1997. *A Tradition That Has No Name: Nurturing the Development of People, Families, and Communities.* New York: Basic Books.

Bell, Inge, and Bernard McGrane. 1999. *This Book Is Not Required: An Emotional Survival Manual for Students.* Thousand Oaks, CA: Pine Forge Press.

Bell, Sandra, Marina Morrow, and Evangelia Tastsoglou. 1999. "Teaching in Environments of Resistance: Toward a Critical, Feminist, and Antiracist Pedagogy." Pp. 23–46 in *Meeting the Challenge: Innovative Feminist Pedagogies in Action,* edited by Moralee Mayberry and Ellen Cronan Rose. New York: Routledge.

Benmayor, Rina. 1991. "Testimony, Action Research, and Empowerment: Puerto Rican Women and Popular Education." Pp. 159–74 in *Women's Words: The Feminist Practice of Oral History,* edited by Sherna Berger Gluck and Daphne Patai. New York: Routledge.

Benmayor, Rina, and Rosa M. Torruellas. 1997. "Education, Cultural Rights, and Citizenship." Pp. 187–204 in *Women Transforming Politics: An Alternative Reader.* New York: New York University Pres.

Bignell, Kelly Coate. 1996. "Building Feminist Praxis Out of Feminist Pedagogy: The Importance of Students' Perspectives." *Women's Studies International Forum* 19(3):315–25.

Blee, Kathleen M. 1998. "Reading Racism: Women in the Modern Hate Movement." Pp. 180–98 in *No Middle Ground: Women and Radical Protest,* edited by Kathleen M. Blee. New York: New York University Press.

Bobo, Kimberly A., Jackie Kendall, and Steve Max. 2000. *Organizing for Social Change.* Washington, D.C.: Seven Locks Press.

Bookman, Ann and Sandra Morgen, eds. 1988. *Women and the Politics of Empowerment.* Philadelphia: Temple University Press.

Boxer, Marilyn. 1982. "For and about Women: The Theory and Practice of Women's Studies in the United States." *Signs: Journal of Women in Culture and Society* 7(3):661–95.

Brents, Barbara, Ruby Duncan, and Elizabeth Fretwell. 2000. "UNLV Women's Studies Program Faculty/Community Associates of Women's Studies Assessment of Feminist Praxis Report." August.

Brown, Elsa Barkley. 2000. "History and Cultural Production." Paper presented at the Terror and Possibility: Search for Enlivened Technologies Conference, Maryland Institute for Technology in the Humanities, University of Maryland, College Park, April 25.

Brown, Lyn Mikel and Carol Gilligan. 1992. *Meeting at the Crossroads: Women's Psychology and Girls' Development.* New York: Ballantine.

Bunch, Charlotte. 1990. "Making Common Cause: Diversity and Coalitions." Pp. 49–56 in *Bridges of Power: Women's Multicultural Alliances,* edited by Lisa Albrecht and Ruth M. Brewer. Philadelphia: New Society Publishers.

Butler, Johnnella E., Sandra Coyner, Margaret Homans, Marlene Longenecker, and Caryn McTighe Musil. 1991. *Liberal Learning and the Women's Studies Major.* College Park, MD: National Women's Studies Association.

Butler, Shakti. 1998. *The Way Home: Women Talking About Race, Gender and Class in the United States* (Video). Oakland, CA: World Trust.

Bystydziensky, Jill, ed. 1992. *Women Transforming Politics: Worldwide Strategies for Empowerment.* Bloomington, IN: Indiana University Press.

———, and Joti Sekhon, eds. 1999. *Democratization and Women's Grassroots Movements.* Bloomington, IN: Indiana University Pres.

Cable, Sherry. 1993. "From Fussin' to Organizing: Individual and Collective Resistance at Yellow Creek." Pp. 69–84 in *Fighting Back in Appalachia: Traditions of Resistance and Change,* edited by Stephen Fisher. Philadelphia: Temple University Press.

Castillo, Ana. 1994. *Massacre of the Dreamers.* Albuquerque: University of New Mexico Press.

Cohen, Cathy J. 1999. *The Boundaries of Blackness: AIDS and the Breakdown of Black Politics.* New York: New York University.

Cohen, Cathy, Kathleen Jones, and Joan Tronto. 1997. *Women Transforming Politics: An Alternative Reader.* New York: New York University Press.

Collins, Patricia Hill. 1990. *Black Feminist Thought: Knowledge, Consciousness, and the Politics of Empowerment.* Boston: Unwin Hyman.

———. 1991. "Learning from the Outsider Within: The Sociological Significance of Black Feminist Thought." Pp. 35–59 in *Beyond Methodology,* edited by Mary Margaret Fonow and J. A. Cook. Bloomington: Indiana University Press.

———. 1998. *Fighting Words: Black Women And The Search For Justice.* Minneapolis: University of Minneapolis Press.

———. 2000. *Black Feminist Thought,* 2d ed. New York: Routledge.

Conley, Francine Heather. 1998. "The Kitchen." Performance review of *The Kitchen* by Arnold Wesker. *Theatre Journal* 50(1):125–27.

Conway-Turner, Kate, Suzanne Cherrin, Jessica Schiffman, and Kathleen Doherty Turkel, eds. 1998. *Women's Studies in Transition: The Pursuit of Interdisciplinarity.* Newark, DE: University of Delaware Press.

Coontz, Stephanie. 1992. *The Way We Never Were: American Families and the Nostalgia Trap.* New York: Basic Books.

Davis, Sara N., Mary Crawford, and Jadwiga Sebrechts, eds. 1999. *Coming into Her Own: Educational Success in Girls and Women*. San Francisco: Jossey-Bass.

Denzin, Norman. 1989. *Strategies of Multiple Triangulation in the Qualitative Research Act*. New York: Sage.

DeVault, Marjorie L. 1999. *Liberating Method: Feminism and Social Research*. Philadelphia: Temple University Press.

Dewey, John. 1944/1966. *Democracy and Education*. New York: The Free Press.

Drenovsky, Cynthia K. 1999. "The Advocacy Project on Women's Issues: A Method for Teaching and Practicing Feminist Theory in an Introductory Women's Studies Course." *Women's Studies Quarterly* 27(3/4):12–20.

DuBois, W. E. B. 1969. *The Souls of Black Folk*. New York: Signet Classics.

Durning, Alan. 1992. *How Much is Enough? The Consumer Society and the Future of the Earth*. New York: Norton.

Ehrenreich, Barbara. 1990. *Fear of Falling: The Inner Life of the Middle Class*. New York: Harper.

Eisenstein, Hester. 1995. "The Australian Femocratic Experiment: A Feminist Case for Bureaucracy." Pp. 69–83 in *Feminist Organizations: Harvest of the New Women's Movement*, edited by Myra Marx Ferree and Patricia Yancey Martin. Philadelphia: Temple University Press.

Ellsworth, Elizabeth. 1992. "Why Doesn't this Feel Empowering? Working Through the Repressive Myths of Critical Pedagogy." Pp. 90–119 in *Feminisms and Critical Pedagogy*, edited by Carmen Luke and Jennifer Gore. New York: Routledge.

Enloe, Cynthia. 1989. *Bananas, Beaches and Bases: Making Feminist Sense of International Politics*. Berkeley and Los Angeles: University of California Press, 1989.

Evans, Sara and Harry Boyte. 1986. *Free Spaces: The Sources of Democratic Change in America*. New York: Harper and Row.

Farganis, Sondra. 1994. *Situating Feminism: From Thought to Action*. Thousand Oaks, CA: Sage.

Feagin, Joe R., Hernán Vera, Nikitah Imani. 1996. *The Agony of Education: Black Students At White Colleges And Universities*. New York: Routledge.

Feminist Collections. 1999. Special issue on Academy/Community Connections, 20(3).

Ferree, Myra Marx and Beth B. Hess. 1995. *Controversy and Coalition: The New Feminist Movement across Three Decades of Change*. New York: Twayne.

———. 2000. *Controversy and Coalition: The New Feminist Movement across Four Decades of Change*. New York: Routledge.

Ferree, Myra Marx, and Patricia Yancey Martin, eds. 1995a. *Feminist Organizations: Harvest of the New Women's Movement*. Philadelphia: Temple University Press.

———. 1995b. "Doing the Work of the Movement: Feminist Organizations." Pp. 3–34 in *Feminist Organizations: Harvest of the New Women's Movement*, edited by Myra Marx Ferree and Patricia Yancey Martin. Philadelphia: Temple University Press.

Fisher, Berenice Malka. 2001. *No Angel in the Classroom: Teaching through Feminist Discourse*. Lanham, MD: Rowman and Littlefield.

Fisher, Kimberly G. 2000. "Kitchen Fights: Building a Women of Color & White Women Alliance." Unpublished independent study paper, Susquehanna University.

Forbes, Kathryn, Linda Garber, Loretta Kensinger, and Janet Trapp Slagter. 1999. "Punishing Pedagogy: The Failings of Forced Volunteerism." *Women's Studies Quarterly* 27(3/4):158–68.

Frankenberg, Ruth. 1993. *White Women, Race Matters: The Social Construction of Whiteness*. Minneapolis: University of Minnesota Press.

Freedman, Estelle B. 1990. "Small Group Pedagogy: Consciousness Raising in Conservative Times." *Feminist Studies* 5(30):512–29.

Freeman, Jo. 1995. "From Seed to Harvest: Transformations of Feminist Organizations and Scholarship." Pp. 397–408 in *Feminist Organizations: Harvest of the New Women's Movement*, edited by Myra Marx Ferree and Patricia Yancey Martin. Philadelphia: Temple University Press.

Freire, Paulo. 1970/1983. *Pedagogy of the Oppressed*, translated by Myra Bergman Ramos. New York: Continuum.

———. 1985. *The Politics of Education: Culture, Power, and Liberation*. South Hadley, MA: Bergin and Garvey.

Fuentes, Annette and Barbara Ehrenreich. 1984. *Women in the Global Factory*. Boston: South End Press.

Garber, Linda. 1998. "Student Activism." wmst-l@umdd.umd.edu.

Garland, Anne Witte. 1988. *Women Activists: Challenging the Abuse of Power*. New York: The Feminist Press.

Gelb, Joyce, and Marian Lief Palley. 1996. *Women and Public Policies: Reassessing Gender Politics*, 3d ed. Charlottesville: University Press of Virginia.

German, Lindsey. 1996. *A Question of Class*. London and Chicago: Bookmarks.

Gilbert, Melissa Kesler. 2000. "Educated in Agency: Student Reflections on the Feminist Service-Learning Classroom." Pp. 117–38 in *The Practice of Change: Concepts and Models for Service-Learning in Women's Studies*, edited by Kerrissa Heffernan and Barbara J. Balliet. Washington, DC: American Association for Higher Education.

Gilbert, Melissa Kesler, Carol Holdt, and Kristin Christophersen. 1999. "Letting Feminist Knowledge Serve the City." Pp. 319–49 in *Meeting the Challenge: Innovative Feminist Pedgogies in Action*, eds. Maralee Mayberry and Ellen Cronan Rose. New York: Routledge.

Giroux, Henry A., and Stanley Aronowitz. 1985. *Education Under Siege: The Conservative, Liberal and Radical Debate Over Schooling*. South Hadley, MA: Bergin & Garvey Publishers.

Giroux, Henry A. and Peter McLaren. 1994. *Between Borders: Pedagogy and the Politics of Cultural Studies*. New York: Routledge.

Glaser, Barney G. 1992. *Emergence vs. Forcing: Basics of Grounded Theory Analysis*. Mill Valley, CA: Sociology Press.

Glaser, Barney G. and Anselm Strauss. 1967. *The Discovery of Grounded Theory*. New York: Sage.

Gluck, Sherna Berger, with Maylei Blackwell, Sharon Cottrell, and Karen S. Harper. 1998. "Whose Feminism, Whose History? Reflections on Excavating the History of (the) U.S. Women's Movement." Pp. 31–56 in *Community Activism and Feminist Politics: Organizing Across Race, Class, and Gender*, edited by Nancy A. Naples. New York: Routledge.

Goodstein, Lynne. 1997. "When is a Women's Studies Course a 'Women's Studies' Course?" Pp. 213–32 in *Doing Feminism: Teaching and Research in the Academy*, edited by Mary Anderson, Kathleen Geissler, Joyce Ladenson, and Lisa Fine. East Lansing: Michigan State University Press.

Gore, Jennifer M. 1993. *The Struggle for Pedagogies: Critical and Feminist Discourses As Regimes of Truth*. New York: Routledge.

Gordon, Linda. 1990a. "Family Violence, Feminism, and Social Control." Pp. 178–98 in *Women, the State, and Welfare*, edited by Linda Gordon. Madison: University of Wisconsin Press.

——— (ed.) 1990b. *Women, the State and Welfare*. Madison: University of Wisconsin Press.

———. 1991. "Black and White Visions of Welfare: Women's Welfare Activism, 1890–1945." *Journal of American History* September, 559–90.

Gordon, Linda. 1994. *Pitied but not Entitled: Single Mothers and the History of Welfare.* New York: Free Press.

Gossett, Barbara J., Michael J. Cuyjet, and Irwin W. Cockriel. 1998. "African Americans' Perception of Marginality in the Campus Culture." *College Student Journal.* 32(1):22–32.

Gottfried, Heidi, ed. 1997. *Feminism and Social Change.* Urbana: University of Illinois Press.

Gramsci, Antonio. 1971. *Selections from the Prison Notebooks.* New York: International Publishers.

Grewal, Inderpal, and Caren Kaplan, eds. 1994a. *Scattered Hegemonies: Postmodernity and Transnational Feminist Practices.* Minneapolis: University of Minneapolis Press.

———. 1994b. "Introduction: Transnational Feminist Practices and Questions of Postmodernity." Pp. 1–33 in *Scattered Hegemonies: Postmodernity and Transnational Feminist Practices,* edited by Inderpal Grewal and Caren Kaplan. Minneapolis: University of Minnesota Press.

Gutierrez, Lorraine and Edith Lewis, eds. 1999. *Empowering Women of Color.* New York: Columbia University Press.

Haraway, Donna. 1988. "Situated Knowledges: The Science Question in Feminism and the Privilege of Partial Perspective." *Feminist Studies* 14(3): 575–99.

Hardiman, Rita and Bailey W. Jackson. 1992. "Racial Identity Development: Understanding Racial Dynamics in College Classrooms and on Campus." Pp. 21–37 in *Promoting Diversity in College Classrooms: Innovative Responses for the Curriculum,* edited by Maurianne Adams. San Francisco, CA: Jossey-Bass.

Hartsock, Nancy. 1983. *Money, Sex and Power: Toward a Feminist Historical Materialism.* New York: Longman.

Haywoode, Terry. 1991. "Working Class Feminism: Creating a Politics of Community, Connection, and Concern." Ph.D. dissertation, The City University of New York.

Heath, Deborah, Erin Koch, Barbara Ley, and Michael Montoya. 1999. "Nodes and Queries: Linking Locations in Networked Fields of Inquiry." *American Behavioral Scientist* 43(3):450–64.

Helgesen, Sally. 1990. *The Female Advantage: Women's Ways of Leadership.* New York: Doubleday.

Hewitt, Nancy. 1990. "Charity or Mutual Aid? Two Perspectives on Latin Women's Philanthropy in Tampa, Florida." Pp. 55–69 in *Lady Bountiful Revisited: Women, Philanthropy, and Power,* edited by Kathleen McCarthy. New Brunswick, NJ: Rutgers University Press.

Hirsch, E. D. Jr. 1987. *Cultural Literacy: What Every American Needs to Know.* New York: Vintage.

Hoffmann, Frances L. and Jayne E. Stake. 1998. Feminist Pedagogy in Theory and Practice: An Empirical Investigation, *NWSA Journal* 10(1):79–97.

Hogeland, Lisa Maria. 1998. *Feminism and Its Fictions: The Consciousness-Raising Novel and the Women's Liberation Movement.* Philadelphia: University of Pennsylvania Press.

hooks, bell. 1984. *Feminist Theory: From Margin to Center.* Boston: South End Press.

———. 1989. *Talking Back: Thinking Feminist, Thinking Black.* Boston: South End.

———. 1990. *Yearning: Race, Gender and Cultural Politics.* Boston: South End Press.

———. 1994a. "Out of the Academy and Into the Streets." Pp. 191–97 in *Getting There: The Movement Toward Gender Equality.* New York: Garroll and Graf Publishers.

———. 1994b. *Teaching to Transgress: Education as the Practice of Freedom.* New York: Routledge.

———. 1995. *Killing Rage: Ending Racism.* Penguin Social Sciences.

———. 2000. *Feminist Theory: From Margin to Center.* 2nd edition. Boston, MA: South End Press.

————, with Tanya McKinnon. 1996. "Sisterhood: Beyond Public and Private." *Signs: Journal of Women in Culture and Society* 21(4):814–29.

Hope, Diane S. 1999. "To Risk the Self." *Women's Studies Quarterly* 27(3/4):243–48.

Humm, Maggie, ed. 1992. *Modern Feminisms: Political, Literary, Cultural.* New York: Columbia University Press.

Hurtado, Aída. 1989. "Relating to Privilege: Seduction and Rejection of White Women and Women of Color," *Signs* 14 (4):6–18.

————. 1996a. *The Color of Privilege: Three Blasphemies on Race and Feminism.* Ann Arbor: University of Michigan Press.

————. 1996b. "Strategic Suspension: Feminists of Color Theorize the Production of Knowledge." Pp. 372–92 in *Knowledge, Difference And Power: Essays Inspired by Women's Ways of Knowing,* edited by Nancy Rule Goldberger, Blythe Clinchy, Mary Field Belenky, and Jill M. Tarule. New York: Basic Books.

Hyman, Colette A., and Diane Lichtenstein, issue eds. 1999. "Expanding the Classroom: Fostering Active Learning and Activism." *Women's Studies Quarterly* 27(3/4).

Joffe, Carole E. 1986. *The Regulation of Sexuality: Experiences of Family Planning Workers.* Philadelphia: Temple University Press.

Jordan, June. 1985. *On Call: Political Essays.* Boston: South End Press.

Kamel, Rachel, and Anya Hoffman, eds. 1999. *The Maquiladora Reader: Cross-Border Organizing Since NAFTA.* Philadelphia, PA: American Friends Service Committee.

Kang, Laura Hyun Li. 1997. "Si(gh)ting Asian/American Women as Transnational Labor." *Positions* 5(2):417.

Kaplan, Caren. 1997. "The Politics of Location as Transnational Feminist Critical Practice." Pp. 137–52 in *Scattered Hegemonies: Postmodernity and Transnational Feminist Practices,* edited by Inderpal Grewal and Caren Kaplan. Minneapolis: University of Minnesota Press.

Kaplan, Temma. 1997. *Crazy for Democracy: Women in Grassroots Movements.* New York: Routledge.

Katzenstein, Mary. 1998. *Faithful and Fearless: Moving Feminist Protest inside the Church and Military.* Princeton, NJ: Princeton University Press.

Katzenstein, Mary Fainsod. 1995. "Discursive Politics and Feminist Activism in the Catholic Church." Pp. 35–52 in *Feminist Organizations: Harvest of the New Women's Movement,* edited by Myra Marx Ferree and Patricia Yancey Martin. Philadelphia: Temple University Press.

Kendall, Lori. 1999. "Recontextualizing 'Cyberspace': Methodological Considerations for On-Line Research." Pp. 57–74 in *Doing Internet Research: Critical Issues and Methods,* edited by Steve Jones. Thousand Oaks, CA: Sage.

Kendrick, Karen. 1998. "Producing the Battered Woman: Shelter Politics and the Power of the Feminist Voice." Pp. 151–74 in *Community Activism and Feminist Politics: Organizing Across Race, Class, and Gender,* edited by Nancy A. Naples. New York: Routledge.

Kenway, Jane, and Helen Mondra. 1992. "Feminist Pedagogy and Emancipatory Possibilities. Pp. 138–66 in *Feminisms and Critical Pedagogy,* edited by Carmen Luke and Jennifer Gore. New York: Routledge.

Kimmich, Allison. 1999. " 'I Found Hope,' or Reflections on Theory-Practice Pedagogy." *Women's Studies Quarterly* 27(3/4):59–69.

King, Katie. 1994. *Theory in Its Feminist Travels: Conversations in the U.S. Women's Movements.* Bloomington: Indiana University Press.

Kingsolver, Barbara. 1989. *Holding the Line: Women in the Great Arizona Mine Strike of 1983.* Ithaca, NY: ILR Press.

Kolko, Beth E., Lisa Nakamura, and Gilbert B. Rodman. 2000. "Race in Cyberspace: An Introduction." Pages 1–14 in *Race in Cyberspace,* edited by Beth E. Kolko, Lisa Nakamura, and Gilbert B. Rodman. New York: Routledge.

Kondo, Dorinne K. 1990. *Crafting Selves: Power, Gender, and Discourses of Identity in a Japanese Workplace*. Chicago: University of Chicago Press.

Krajewski, Sandra. 1999. "Women's Studies: Returning to our Activist Roots and Achieving Tenure Along the Way." *Feminist Collections: A Quarterly of Women's Studies Resources* 20(3):4–7.

Krathwohl, David R. 1998. *Methods of Educational and Social Science Research: An Integrated Approach*, 2d ed. Syracuse, NY: Longman Press.

Lather, Patti. 1991. *Getting Smart: Feminist Research and Pedagogy With/in the Postmodern*. New York: Routledge.

Lewis, Magda. 1992. "Interrupting Patriarchy: Politics, Resistance and Transformation in the Feminist Classroom." Pp. 167–91 in *Feminisms and Critical Pedagogy*, edited by Carmen Luke and Jennifer Gore. New York: Routledge.

Lorde, Audre. 1983. "The Master's Tools Will Never Dismantle the Master's House." Pp. 98–101 in *This Bridge Called My Back: Writings by Radical Women of Color*, edited by Cherríe Moraga and Gloria Anzaldúa. New York: Kitchen Table.

Luke, Carmen and Jennifer Gore. 1992. *Feminisms and Critical Pedagogy*. New York: Routledge.

Maher, Frances A., and Mary Kay Thompson Tetreault. 1994. *The Feminist Classroom*. New York: Basic Books.

Marcus, George E. 1995. "Ethnography in/of the World System: The Emergence of Multisited Ethnography." *Annual Review of Anthropology* 24:95–117.

Martin, Jane Roland. 2000. *Coming of Age in Academe: Rekindling Women's Hopes and Reforming the Academy*. New York: Routledge.

Martin, Patricia Yancey. 1990. "Rethinking Feminist Organizations." *Gender and Society* 4(2):182–206.

Martinez, Elizabeth Sutherland. 1998. *De Colores Means All of Us: Latina Views for a Multi-Colored Century*. Cambridge, MA: South End Press.

Mason, Eleanor Russel. 2000. "Erase-ism.: Brillo Issue 3. Retrieved online from htrp://www.brillomag.net/No3/contents.htm (9 Mar. 2000).

Maybach, Carol Weichman. 1996. "Investigating Urban Community Needs." *Education and Urban Society* 28(2):224–33.

Mayberry, Maralee, and Ellen Cronan Rose, eds. 1999. *Meeting the Challenge: Innovative Feminist Pedgogies in Action*. New York: Routledge.

McMaster, Susan. 1998. *Silence: Poets on Women, Violence and Silence*. Kingston, Canada: Quarry Press.

Mies, Maria. 1986. *Patriarchy and Accumulation on a World Scale: Women in the International Division of Labour*. London: Zed Books.

———. 1993. "Liberating the Consumer." Pp. 251–62 in *Ecofeminism*, edited by Maria Mies and Vandana Shiva. Atlantic Highlands, NJ: Zed Books.

———, and Vandana Shiva. 1993. *Ecofeminism*. London: Zed Books, 1993.

Miles, Angela. 1996. *Integrative Feminisms: Building Global Visions, 1960s–1990s*. New York: Routledge.

Mitchell, Juliet. 1971. *Woman's Estate*. New York: Pantheon Books.

Mitchell, Stacy. 1993. "Sexual Harassment: Final CAP Report." Unpublished paper, University of California, Irvine.

Moeller, Susan D. 1998. *Compassion Fatigue: How the Media Sell Disease, Famine, War, and Death*. New York: Routledge.

Mohan, Rajeswari. 1994. "The Crisis of Femininity and Modernity in the Third World." *Genders* 19:224.

Mohanty, Chandra. 1997. "Women Workers and Capitalist Scripts: Ideologies of Domination, Common Interests, and the Politics of Solidarity." Pp. 3–29 in *Feminist Genealogies, Colonial Legacies, Democratic Future*, edited by M. Jacqui Alexander and Chandra Talpade Mohanty. New York: Routledge.

Mohanty, Chandra Talpade. 1991. "Under Western Eyes: Feminist Scholarship and Colonial Discourses." Pp. 51–80 in *Third World Women and the Politics of Feminism*, edited by Chandra Talpade Mohanty, Ann Russo and Lourdes Torres. Bloomington: Indiana University Press.

Mohanty, Chandra Talpade, Ann Russo, and Lourdes Torres, eds. 1991. *Third World Women and the Politics of Feminism*. Bloomington: Indiana University Press.

Mohanty, Chandra Talpade. 1995. "Feminist Encounters: Locating the Politics of Experience." Pp. 68–86 in *Social Postmodernism: Beyond Identity Politics*. Cambridge: Cambridge University Press.

Moody, Anne. 1976. *Coming of Age in Mississippi*. New York: Dell.

Moraga, Cherríe. 1981. "La Güera." Pp. 27–34 in *This Bridge Called My Back: Writings by Radical Women of Color*, edited by Cherríe Moraga and Gloria Anzaldúa. Boston: Persephone.

Moraga, Cherríe and Gloria Anzaldúa. 1981. Preface and Introduction. Pp. xxiii–xxvi in *This Bridge Called My Back*. Boston: Persephone.

Morris, Aldon D. 1992. "Political Consciousness and Collective Action." Pp. 351–73 in *Frontiers in Social Movement Theory*, edited by Aldon D. Morris and Carol McClurg Mueller. New Haven: Yale University Press.

Morrison, Toni. 1970. *The Bluest Eye*. New York: Washington Square.

Mouffe, Chantal. 1993. *The Return of the Political*. London: Verso.

Mueller, Carol. 1993. "Ella Baker and the Origins of 'Participatory Democracy.'" Pp. 51–70 in *Women in the Civil Rights Movement: Trailblazers & Torchbearers 1941–1965*, edited by Vicki L. Crawford et al. Bloomington: Indiana University Press.

Mukherjee, Ranu. 1999. "Community Action Project Final Report." Unpublished paper, University of California, Irvine.

Munaweera, Nayomi. 1995. "Race and Domestic Violence: Vietnamese Women at Interval House." Unpublished paper, University of California, Irvine.

Myers, Bahareh. 1995. "How to Make the Most out of Your Research Experience." Unpublished paper, University of California, Irvine.

Naples, Nancy A., ed. 1998a. *Community Activism and Feminist Politics: Organizing Across Race, Class and Gender*. New York: Routledge.

———. 1998b. "Women's Community Activism and Feminist Activist Research." Pp. 1–27 in *Community Activism and Feminist Politics: Organizing Across Race, Class, and Gender*, edited by Nancy A. Naples. New York: Routledge.

———. 1998c. *Grassroots Warriors: Activist Mothering, Community Work and the War on Poverty*. New York: Routledge.

Naples, Nancy A., with Emily Clark. 1996. "Feminist Participatory Research and Empowerment: Going Public as Survivors of Childhood Sexual Abuse." Pp. 160–83 in *Feminism and Social Change: Bridging Theory and Practice*, edited by Heidi Gottfried. Urbana: University of Illinois Press.

Naples, Nancy A., and Manisha Desai, eds. 2002. *Women's Activism and Globalization: Linking Local Struggles and Transnational Politics*. New York: Routledge.

Narayan, Uma. 1997. *Dislocating Cultures: Identities, Traditions and Third World Feminism*. New York: Routledge.

National Organization of Women. 1973. "Report of the National Organization of Women Task Force on Volunteerism." Reprinted in *Ms. Magazine*, February, 1975, p. 73.

Nguyen, Hanh. 1995. "Domestic Violence and the Vietnamese American Community." Unpublished paper, University of California, Irvine.

Noddings, Nel. 1994. *Caring: A Feminist Approach to Ethics and Moral Education*. Berkeley and Los Angeles: University of California Press.

Norris, Pippa. 1997. *Women, Media, and Politics*. New York: Oxford University Press.

O'Donnell, Sandra. 1994. "The Care of Dependent African-American Children in Chicago: The Struggle Between Black-Self-Help and Professionalism." *Journal of Social History* 27(4):763–76.

O'Leary, Catherine M. 1997. "Counteridentification or Counterhegemony? Transforming Feminist Standpoint Theory." Pp. 45–72 in *Politics and Feminist Standpoint Theories*, edited by Sally J. Kenney and Helen Kinsella.

Olsen, Lester C. 2000. "The Personal, the Political, and Others: Audre Lorde Denouncing "The Second Sex Conference." *Philosophy and Rhetoric*, 33(3):259–85.

O'Reilly, Mary Rose. 1989. " 'Exterminate the Brutes'—And Other Things That Go Wrong in Student-Centered Teaching." *College English* 51:142–46.

Palmer, Parker J. 1987. "Community, Conflict and Ways of Knowing: Ways to Deepen our Educational Agenda." Pp. 105–13 in *Combining Service and Learning*, vol. 1, edited by Jane Kendal et al. Raleigh, NC: National Society for Internships and Experiential Education.

Pardo, Mary. 1995. "Doing It for the Kids: Mexican American Community Activists, Border Feminists." Pp. 356–71 in *Feminist Organizations: Harvest of the New Women's Movement*, edited by Myra Marx Ferree and Patricia Yancey Martin. Philadelphia: Temple University Press.

Pearson, Nelda K. 1999. "Social Action as Collaborative Transformation." *Women's Studies Quarterly* 27(3/4):98–113.

Peck, Elizabeth G., and JoAnna Stephens Mink, eds. 1997. *Common Ground: Feminist Collaboration in the Academy*. Albany: State University of New York Press.

Peet, Melissa R. and Reed, Beth Glover. 1999. "Activism in an Introductory Women's Studies Course: Connected Learning through the Implementation of Praxis." *Women's Studies Quarterly* 27(3/4):21–35.

Peyrot, Mark. 1991. "Institutional and Organizational Dynamics in Community-Based Drug Abuse Treatment." *Social Problems* 38(1):20–33.

Pollitt, Katha. 1999. "Prosecuting Innocence." *Nation*, December 13. See also http://past.thenation.com/cgibin/framizer.cgi?url=http://past.thenation.com/issue/991213/1213politt.shtml.

Powers, Tenisha. 1999. "Sexual Violence against Women: Date Rape." Unpublished paper, University of California, Irvine.

Pratt, Bruce Minnie. 1988. "Identity: Skin/Blood/Heart." Pp. 27–82 in *Yours in Struggle: Three Feminist Perspectives on Anti-Semitism and Racism*, edited by Elly Bulkin, Minnie Bruce Smith, and Barbara Smith. New York: Firebrand Press.

Prochaska, James O., John C. Norcross, and Carlo C. DiClemente. 1994. *Changing for Good*. New York: Avon Books.

Reagon, Bernice Johnson. 1992. "Coalition Politics: Turning the Century." Pp. 510–14 in *Race, Class, and Gender: An Anthology*, edited by Margaret L. Anderson and Patricia Hill Collins. Belmont, CA: Wadsworth.

Reinelt, Claire. 1995. "Moving onto the Terrain of the State: The Battered Women's Movement and the Politics of Engagement." Pp. 84–104 in *Feminist Organizations: Harvest of the New Women's Movement*, edited by Myra Marx Ferree and Patricia Yancy Martin. Philadelphia: Temple University Press.

"Report of the National Organization for Women Task Force on Volunteerism." 1973. Reprinted in *Ms.*, February, 1975, 73.

Rhoads, Robert A. 1997. *Community Service and Higher Learning: Explorations of the Caring Self.* Albany: State University of New York Press.

Riger, Stephanie. 1994. "Challenges of Success: Stages of Growth in Feminist Organizations." *Feminist Studies* 20(2):275–300.

Ring, Siobhan. 1999. "Seizing Academia for Social Change." *Women's Studies Quarterly* 27(3/4):230–40.

Romanoff, Bronna, Chrys Ingraham, Patk Dinkelaker, and Jennifer MacLaughlin. 1999. "Women Changing the World: A Course in Community Collaboration." *Feminist Collections: A Quarterly of Women's Studies Resources* 20(3):42–44.

Rosen, Ruth. 2000. *The World Split Open: How the Modern Women's Movement Changed America.* New York: Viking.

Rosner, Judy B. 1990. "Ways Women Lead." *Harvard Business Review* 68(6):119–125.

Ross, Lisa. 1994. "Women With AIDS: Community Action Report." Unpublished paper, University of California, Irvine.

Rubin, Lillian B. 1976. *Worlds of Pain: Life in the Working-Class Family.* New York: Basic Books.

Ruddick, Sara. 1989. *Maternal Thinking: Toward a Politics of Peace.* New York: Ballantine Books.

Rupp, Leila and Verta Taylor. 1987. *Survival in the Doldrums: The American Women's Rights Movement, 1945–1960s.* New York: Oxford University Press.

Sandoval, Chela. 1991. "U.S. Third World Feminisms: The Theory and Method of Oppositional Consciousness in the Postmodern World." *Genders* 10:1–24.

Schniedewind, Nancy. 1983. "Feminist Values: Guidelines for a Teaching Methodology in Women's Studies." Pp. 261–70 in *Learning Our Way: Essays in Feminist Education,* edited by Charlotte Bunch and Sandra Pollack. Trumansburg, NY: The Crossing Press.

Scott, Joan W. 1992. "Experience." Pp. 22–40 in *Feminists Theorize the Political,* edited by Judith Butler and Joan W. Scott. New York: Routledge.

Shields, Katrina. 1994. *In the Tiger's Mouth: An Empowerment Guide for Social Action.* Philadelphia: New Society.

Shohat, Ella, ed. 1998. *Talking Visions: Multicultural Feminism in a Transnational Age.* New York: The MIT Press.

Short, Kayann. 1999. " 'Why Shop? Week': Shopping, Service-Learning, and Student Activism." *Feminist Collections: A Quarterly of Women's Studies Resources* 20(3):32–33.

Shrewsbury, Carolyn M. 1997. "What Is Feminist Pedagogy?" *Women's Studies Quarterly* 25(1/2): 166–73.

Singley, Carol J. and Elizabeth Sweeney. 1998. "In League with Each Other: The Theory and Practice of Feminist Collaboration." Pp. 63–79 in *Common Ground: Feminist Collaboration in the Academy,* edited by Elizabeth G. Peck and JoAnna Stephens Mink. Albany: SUNY Press.   •

Silliman, Jael, and Anannya Bhattacharjee. 1999. "Relocating Women's Studies and Activism: A Dialogue." *Women's Studies Quarterly* 27(3/4):122–36.

Sjoquist, David L., ed. 2000. *The Atlanta Paradox: A Volume in the Multi-City Study of Urban Inequality.* New York: Russell Sage Foundation.

Smith, Barbara. 1998. "Racism and Women's Studies." Pp. 95–98 in *The Truth that Never Hurts.* New Brunswick, NJ: Rutgers University Press.

Smith, Dorothy E. 1987. *The Everyday World as Problematic: A Feminist Sociology.* Toronto: University of Toronto Press.

———. 1990. *Conceptual Practices of Power.* Boston: Northeastern University Press.

————. 1992. "Sociology from Women's Experience: A Reaffirmation." *Sociological Theory* 10(1):88–98.

————. 1996. "Telling the Truth after Postmodernism." *Symbolic Interactionism* 19(3): 171–202.

————. 1999. *Writing the Social: Critique, Theory, and Investigations.* Toronto: University of Toronto Press.

Smith-Rosenberg, Carol. (1985). *Disorderly Conduct:Visions of Gender in Victorian America.* New York: Oxford University Press.

Spalter-Roth, Roberta and Ronnee Schreiber. 1995. "Outsider and Insider Tactics: Strategic Tensions in the Women's Policy Network during the 1980s." Pp. 105–27 in *Feminist Organizations: Harvest of the New Women's Movement*, edited by Myra Marx Ferree and Patricia Yancey Martin. Philadelphia: Temple University Press.

Spring, Joel. 1995. *The Intersection of Cultures: Multicultural Education in the United States and the Global Economy.* Boston: McGraw-Hill.

St. Peter, Christine. 1997. "Introduction to Women's Studies in Focus: Field-Based Learning in the Practicum Course." *Atlantis* 22(1):109.

Stack, Carol. 1975. *All Our Kin.* New York: Harper and Row.

Stake, Jayne E., Laurie Rhodes, Suzanna Rose, Lisa Ellis, and Carolyn West. 1994. "The Women's Studies Experience: Impetus for Feminist Activism." *Psychology of Women Quarterly* 18:17–24.

Stake, Jayne E., and Suzanna Rose. 1994. "The Long-Term Impact of Women's Studies on Students' Personal Lives and Political Activism." *Psychology of Women Quarterly* 18:403–12.

Stanley, Liz. 1990. "Feminist Praxis and the Academic Mode of Production: An Editorial Introduction." Pp. 1–19 in *Feminist Praxis: Research, Theory and Epistemology in Feminist Sociology*, edited by Liz Stanley. New York: Routledge.

Stern, Susan P. 1994. "Social Science from Below: Grassroots Knowledge for Science and Emancipation." Ph.D. dissertation, City University of New York.

Tarbell, Kathryn. 1999. "Community Action Project Final Project." Unpublished paper, University of California, Irvine.

Taylor, Verta. 1995. "Watching for Vibes: Bringing Emotions into the Study of Feminist Organizations." Pp. 223–33 in *Feminist Organizations: Harvest of the New Women's Movement*, edited by Myra Marx Feree and Patricia Yancy Martin. Philadelphia, PA: Temple University Press.

Tong, Rosemarie. 1989. *Feminist Thought: A Comprehensive Introduction.* Boulder: Westview Press.

Suchman, Lucy. 2000. "Located Accountabilities in Technology Production." (draft). Department of Sociology, Lancaster University. http://www.cump.lancaster.ac.uk/Sociology/SOC0391s.html [23 June 2000].

Tran, Lisa. 1993. "Women's Studies 50B Community Action Project Final Report." Unpublished paper, University of California, Irvine.

Trigg, Mary, and Barbara J. Balliet. 2000. "Learning across Boundaries: Women's Studies, Praxis, and Community Service." Pp. 87–101 in *The Practice of Change: Concepts and Models for Service-Learning in Women's Studies*, edited by Kerrissa Heffernan and Barbara J. Balliet, pp. 87–101. Washington, DC: American Association for Higher Education.

Tumino, Stephen. 1993. "About the Cover (Around the Image): The Commodification of Radicalism." *Alternative Orange* 3(1):2–16.

United Nations Development Report. 1998. New York: United Nations.

Vasquez, Ann. 1994. "Community Action Project Report." Unpublished paper, University of California, Irvine.

Waite, Sara L. 1999. "Contributions of Sisterhood Organizations at Susquehanna University: A Critical Response." Unpublished paper, Susquehanna University.

Walker, Alice. 1983. *In Search of Our Mothers' Gardens: Womanist Prose.* New York: Harcourt Brace Jovanovich.

Walker, Tobi. 2000. "A Feminist Challenge to Community Service: A Call to Politicize Service Learning." Pp. 25–38 in *The Practice of Change: Concepts and Models for Service Learning in Women's Studies,* edited by Kerissa Heffernan and Barbara J. Balliet. Washington, DC: American Association of Higher Education.

Weah, Wokie, Verna Cornelia Simmons, and McClellan Hall. 2000. "Service Learning and Multicultural/Multiethnic Perspectives." *Phi Delta Kappan* 8(9):673–76.

Weiler, Kathleen. 1988. *Women Teaching for Change: Gender, Class & Power.* South Hadley, MA: Bergin and Garvey.

———. 1995. "Revisioning Feminist Pedagogy." *NWSA Journal* 7:100–106.

Wiegman, Robyn, ed. 2002. *Women's Studies On Its Own.* Durham, NC: Duke University Press.

Wolkomir, Richard. 1999. "Will the Kitchen Please Shut Up!" *Smithsonian.* 30(6):56–58.

Women's Studies Program, University of Nevada, Las Vegas. 1997. "Assessment Plan for Women's Studies."

Woods, Harriet. 2000. *Stepping Up to Power: The Political Journey of American Women.* Boulder: Westview Press.

Zinn, Maxine Baca, and Bonnie Thornton Dill. 1996. "Theorizing Difference from Multiracial Feminism." *Feminist Studies* 22(2):321–31.

Ziv, Ilan. 1987. *Consuming Hunger.* Vols. 1, 2, and 3. Maryknoll, NY: Maryknoll World Video Library.

Additional Resources:
Reference Guides, Videos, and Websites for Teaching Feminist Activism

Prepared by Joan Ariel and Jennifer Rogers

The following bibliography is designed to assist faculty and others interested in feminist experiential learning as they seek to identify publications for curriculum development. Any published bibliography also represents but a snapshot of materials available at a particular moment in time. Use these listings as a place to begin, keeping in mind the vast quantity of resources in all formats continually produced. The publications presented below are divided into the following categories: 1. reference guides; 2. videotapes; and 3. websites. We hope that this division will facilitate access to particular types of materials useful to faculty as they conceptualize and construct courses incorporating feminist praxis.

1. General Reference Guides to Publications on Feminist Politics

Listed below are a few key resources which will be useful in identifying materials related to feminist praxis and pedagogy. This list is by no means intended to be comprehensive, but rather to give teachers and students a place to begin future investigation. If you cannot locate or access these resources on your own, ask your librarian for assistance.

Periodicals

Feminist Collections: A Quarterly of Women's Studies Resources

> Published by the office of the University of Wisconsin System Women's Studies Librarian, 430 Memorial Library, 728 State Street, Madison, WI 53706; (608) 263-5754; online at http://www.library.wisc.edu/libraries/WomensStudies/

> Contains news of the latest print and audiovisual resources for research and teaching in women's studies.

Feminist Teacher: A Journal of the Practice, Theories and Scholarship of Feminist Teaching

> http://www.uwec.edu/academic/curric/tkemp/

Since 1984, this peer-reviewed journal has addressed numerous issues related to feminist teaching including not only gender and sexism but also all forms of social injustice, including racism, classism, and homophobia. Provides a forum in which educators discuss pedagogical strategies, theorize about successes or failures, and share resources.

New Books on Women and Feminism

Published by the office of the University of Wisconsin System Women's Studies Librarian, 430 Memorial Library, 728 State Street, Madison, WI 53706; (608) 263-5754; online at http://www.library.wisc.edu/libraries/WomensStudies/

The most complete record of English-language feminist publishing available today. Published every six months, this comprehensive bibliography provides coverage of the most recent books in women's studies and women's issues. Organized into 28 subject sections, it also provides detailed author and topic indexes. Cites not only authors, titles, and publishers, but precise information needed for ordering books through libraries or bookstores—price, ISBN, references to book reviews and announcements, and addresses for small presses not found in standard sources. Also available through the *Women's Resources International* database (see below).

Women's Studies Quarterly

www.rit.edu/~wsqwww/

An educational project of the Feminist Press at The City University of New York in cooperation with the Rochester Institute of Technology. Since 1972, Women's Studies Quarterly has been "the leading journal on teaching in women's studies." Thematic issues feature vital material for specialists and generalists alike, including the most recent scholarship available in jargon-free language; classroom aids such as course syllabi; discussion of strategies for teaching; and up-to-date, complete bibliographies as well as hard-to-find or never-before-published documents and literary materials. The intersections of race and class with gender are of special concern, as are international perspectives.

Reference Books

Barrett, Jacqueline K. and Jane A. Malonis. 1993. *Encyclopedia of Women's Associations Worldwide: A Guide to Over 3,400 National and Multinational Nonprofit Women's and Women-Related Organizations.* London: Gale Research.

Bartlett, John W. 1996. *The Future is Ours: A Handbook for Student Activists in the 21st Century.* New York: Henry Holt.

Blasius, Mark and Shane Phelan. 1997. *We Are Everywhere: A Historical Sourcebook of Gay and Lesbian Politics.* New York: Routledge.

Burnham, Linda. 1991. *Women of Color: Organizations and Projects: A National Directory.* Berkeley: Women of Color Resource Center.

Button, John. 1995. *The Radicalism Handbook: Radical Activists, Groups, and Movements of the Twentieth Century.* Santa Barbara: ABC-Clio.

Carabillo, Toni, Judith Meuli, and June Bundy Csida. 1993. *Feminist Chronicles, 1953–1993.* Los Angeles: Women's Graphic.

Choi, Jung Hee. 2000. *National Directory of Women of Color Organizations and Projects: 2000 Updates.* Berkeley: Women of Color Resource Center.

Cullen-DuPont, Kathryn. 2000. *Encyclopedia of Women's History in America.* New York: Facts On File.

Fleisher, Paul. 1993. *Changing Our World: A Handbook for Young Activists.* Tucson: Zephyr Press.

Hallgarth, Susan A. and Paulette P. Tulloch. 1992. *NWO: A Directory of National Women's Organizations.* New York: National Council for Research on Women.

Harding, Thomas. 1997. *The Video Activist Handbook.* London: Pluto Press.

Kavenik, Frances M. and Angela Howard. 2000. *Handbook of American Women's History.* Thousand Oaks, CA: Sage.

Kramarae, Cheris and Dale Spender. 2000. *Routledge International Encyclopedia of Women: Global Women's Issues and Knowledge.* New York: Routledge.

Lazard, Dorothy and Mana Hayakawa. 2000. *Women of Color on the Web: An Internet Supplement to the National Directory of Women of Color Organizations and Projects.* Berkeley: Women of Color Resource Center.

Mannix, Kelly and Heather Northcott. 1999. *The Busy Woman's Guide to the Internet: Activism and Research On-line.* Toronto: International Women's Rights Project.

Morgan, Robin. 1996. *Sisterhood is Global: The International Women's Movement Anthology.* New York: Feminist Press.

Nelson, Barbara J. and Najama Caudhuri. 1994. *Women and Politics Worldwide.* New Haven, CT: Yale University Press.

Project, Censored. 1999. *The Progressive Guide to Alternative Media and Activism.* New York: Seven Stories Press.

Rao, Digumarti Bhaskara. 1999. *Women and International Action.* New Delhi: Discovery.

Shaw, Randy. 2001. *The Activist's Handbook: A Primer.* Berkeley and Los Angeles: University of California Press.

Slavin, Sarah. 1995. *U.S. Women's Interest Groups: Institutional Profiles.* Westport, CT: Greenwood Press.

Stromquist, Nelly P. 1998. *Women in the Third World: An Encyclopedia of Contemporary Issues.* New York: Garland.

Walch, James. 1999. *In the Net: An Internet Guide for Activists.* London: Zed Books.

Zimmerman, Bonnie. 2000. *Lesbian Histories and Cultures: An Encyclopedia.* New York: Garland.

Databases

Contemporary Women's Issues, 1992–present

http://www.rdsinc.com/cwi/

An excellent source for information on global feminism and women's activism around the world. Provides full-text access to over 800 sources by more than 150 organizations of many types in over 220 countries. Coverage begins with sources from 1992 and expands through the present with more than 130 periodicals and nonperiodical source publications including newsletters, pamphlets, research reports, bibliographies, fact sheets, and guides. Search options allow focusing on particular geographical region and limiting by article or publication type.

Women's Resources International, 1972–present

http://www.nisc.com/factsheets/wri.htm

This comprehensive index includes over 219,000 records drawn from a variety of essential women's studies databases, including Women Studies Abstracts (1984–present), the University of Toronto Women's Studies Database (1972–present), and many major bibliographies. Provides Quick, Advanced, and Expert search options; the Advance and Expert searches allow searching by index terms such as social activism; political activism; and community action.

2. Videotapes

Videotapes listed below explore multiple themes related to activism in the United States and around the world. The list is fairly comprehensive but by no means exhaustive. It strives for broad geographical and topical representation and, while including a few titles from earlier years, emphasizes videos produced since 1990. Brief annotations describe the relevance of the videotape to activism; fuller descriptions can be found on the distributor's website at the URL given in the citations. Academic and some public libraries should have many of these videotapes in their collections; videotapes are also sometimes available via interlibrary loan. Many of these videos are available through Women Make Movies 462 Broadway suite 500, New York, NY 10013; 212-925-0606; 212-925-2052 (fax). Website address: www.wmm.com; e-mail: info@wmm.com (for general information); orders@wmm.com (for film and videotape orders). Women Make Movies is arguably the premier distributor of feminist media and offers many videos related to feminist activism among the more than 400 titles available for rent or purchase.

After Stonewall: From the Riots to the Millennium. 1999. John Scagliotti and Janet W. Baus. 88 min. First Run Features. www.firstrunfeatures.com.

This sequel to *Before Stonewall* chronicles the history of lesbian and gay life and activism from the Stonewall riots to the end of the century and explores changes in the movement that have been prompted by AIDS.

Algeria: Women at War. 1992. Parminder Vir. 50 min. Channel Four Television; Distributed by Women Make Movies. www.wmm.com.

Addresses the role of Algerian women in the liberation struggle from the French and in contemporary politics of the country, raising critical questions about the balancing act between women's and national liberation struggles.

America Needs Human Rights. 1998. Megan Sheer. 23 min. Food First/Institute for Food and Development Policy. www.foodfirst.org/.

"Told in the voices of welfare mothers, homeless men and women, low-wage workers, seniors, veterans, and health care workers, [this video] uses a human rights framework to portray the social ills of contemporary America and lay the basis for a powerful movement for fundamental change"

—Container.

America's Victoria: Remembering Victoria Woodhull. 1995. Victoria Weston. 56 min. Women Make Movies. www.wmm.com.

In 1872, Victoria Woodhull became the first woman to campaign for the U.S. presidency. A radical suffragist, she also advocated a single sexual standard for men and women, legalization of prostitution, and reform of marriage. Includes interviews with contemporary feminists such as Gloria Steinem offering perspectives on Woodhull's importance in U.S. history.

And the March Continues. 1997. Guadalupe Olvera San Miguel. 30 min. Spanish with English subtitles. Frameline. www.frameline.org.

Combines documentary and narrative forms to present a history of the lesbian movement in Mexico from its origins to the present, drawing upon testimonies from Mexican lesbians and movement leaders.

As the Mirror Burns. 1990. Cristina Pozzan and Di Bretherton. 58 min. Women Make Movies. www.wmm.com.

Presents a unique perspective on the role of women in the Vietnam War who, instead of being innocent victims, made up over 70 percent of the guerrilla forces actively engaged in the struggle against foreign domination and, subsequently, worked tirelessly to restore peace to their land. Study guide available.

As Women See It. 1983. 30 min. each. Women Make Movies. www.wmm.com.

A unique collection of five films that address women's activism in "third world" countries: the 'Chipko' environmental movement in India; daily life in Senegal; political struggles in Nicaragua; community activism in Peru; and women's lives in Egypt.

Before Stonewall: The Making of a Gay and Lesbian Community. 1985. Greta Schiller, Robert Rosenberg, and Andrea Weiss. 87 min. Cinema Guild. www.firstrunfeatures.com.

Traces the social, political, and cultural development of the gay and lesbian community. Highlights the history of gay activism from the early homophile rights movement to the events that led up to the 1969 police raid on the Stonewall Inn, a gay bar in New York City, and the three-day riot that followed, marking the birth of the gay liberation movement.

bell hooks: Cultural Criticism & Transformation. 1997. Sut Jhally. 66 min. Media Education Foundation. www.mediaed.org.

bell hooks makes a compelling argument for the transformative powers of cultural criticism. She demonstrates how learning to think critically was central to her own self-transformation and how it can play a role in students' quest for a sense of agency and identity. Includes footage from films, music videos, and news coverage.

Berkeley in the Sixties. 1990. Mark Kitchell. 118 min. California Newsreel. www.newsreel.org.

> Academy award nominated documentary in three parts: 1. Confronting the University: The Free Speech Movement (42 min.); 2. Confronting America: The Antiwar Movement (32 min.); and 3. Confronting History: The Counter Culture Movement (45 min.). Captures the turmoil and passion of the student and women's movements, the civil rights marches, and antiwar protests.

Beyond Beijing. 1996. Shirini Heerah and Enrique Berrios. 42 min. Women Make Movies. www.wmm.com.

> The 1995 Beijing United Nations Fourth World Conference on Women and the parallel Nongovernmental Organizations (NGO) forum represented the largest global gathering of women in recorded history. NGO workshops convened by grassroots activists contributed to the growing strength of the worldwide movement to improve the status of women. Discussion guide/action kit available.

Beyond Borders: Arab Feminists Talk about Their Lives. 2000. Jennifer Kawaja. 50 minutes. Films for the Humanities and Sciences. www.films.com.

> A feminist delegation composed of author Nawal Saadawi and other renowned activists from the Middle East and North Africa gathers at the United Nations, on college campuses, and in church basements to speak out about the deterioration of women's rights in Arab states, repressive internal constraints, and intrusive Western influence.

Black Women, Sexual Politics and the Revolution. 1992. Not Channel Zero. 30 minutes; color. Black Planet Productions; Third World Newsreel. www.twn.org.

> Michelle Wallace and other black women speak candidly on issues of sex, class, and gender roles. The videotape examines how African-American women deal with issues of poverty, abortion, battering, and lack of health care and addresses how women's roles in community struggle and activism are often overlooked. Also examines media portrayals with an emphasis on the representation of black women in music videos.

The Body of a Poet: A Tribute to Audre Lorde, Warrior Poet, 1934-1992. 1995. Sonali Fernando. 29 min. Women Make Movies. www.wmm.com.

> In an imaginary biopic, a group of young women pay tribute to the life and work of Audre Lorde, black lesbian poet and political activist.

Breast Cancer: Speaking Out. 1992. KCTS/TV. 30 min. Filmakers Library. www.filmakers.com.

> Short, powerful documentary about four women with breast cancer who become activists in the cause of their own health, fighting for information, insurance coverage, and their share of federal funds.

Calling the Ghosts: A Story about Rape, War and Women. 1996. Mandy Jacobson and Karmen Jelincic. 60 min. Bowery Productions. Distributed by Women Make Movies. www.wmm.com.

> In the Bosnia-Herzegovina War, rape was as much an everyday weapon as bullets or bombs. This powerful documentary profiles two women who, raped and tortured in the Serb concentration camp of Omarska, subsequently turned their personal struggle for survival into a larger fight for justice—aiding other women similarly brutalized and successfully lobbying to have rape included in the international lexicon of war crimes by a United Nations tribunal at the Hague.

Casting the First Stone. 1991. Julie Gustafson. 54 minutes. First Run/Icarus Films. www.frif.com.

> Focuses on six women who regularly confront each other from opposite sides of a police barricade outside of the Women's Suburban Clinic in Paoli, Pennsylvania. Three believe that abortion is an inalienable right; three consider it murder. Gives equal voice to activists on both sides of the abortion struggle.

Change Makers. 1995. Consumer Research Foundation. 56 min. Direct Cinema Limited. www.directcinema.com/.

> Portrays the U.S. consumer movement since World War II, based on interviews with 25 prominent consumer leaders from the fields of education, government, and consumer activism.

Chicana. 1979. Sylvia Morales, Anna Nieto-Gomes, and Carmen Moreno. 23 min. Women Make Movies. www.wmm.com.

> Winner of two Emmy Awards, this powerful documentary traces the history of Chicana and Mexican women from pre-Columbian times to the present. It covers women's roles in Aztec society, their participation in the 1810 struggle for Mexican independence, their involvement in U.S. labor strikes in 1872, their contributions to the 1910 Mexican revolution, and their activism and leadership in contemporary civil rights causes.

Daring to Resist: Three Women Face the Holocaust. 1999. Barbara Attie and Martha Goell Lubell. 57 min. Women Make Movies. www.wmm.com.

> A compelling portrait of three Jewish women who joined the Jewish resistance to Nazism, taking a stand against tyranny and making a difference in varied ways: as a ballet dancer shuttling Jews to safe houses and distributing resistance newspapers; as a photographer and partisan waging guerrilla war against the Germans; and as a leader in an underground Zionist group smuggling Jews across the border.

Daughters of de Beauvoir. 1989. Imogen Sutton. 55 min. Filmakers Library. www.filmakers.com.

> The life story of Simone de Beauvoir, one of the leading figures of the international women's movement, is told in conjunction with the stories of some other

feminist writers and activists inspired by her work. Kate Millet, Marge Piercy, Eva Figes, and Ann Oakley discuss the influence of de Beauvoir's *The Second Sex*.

Daughters of the Golden Bengal Women in the Struggle against Poverty. 1999. Magdalena Metker. 30 min. Films for the Humanities and Sciences. www.films.com.

Depicts the growing movement of women in Bangladesh who, in defiance of repressive social customs and religious doctrines, run profitable cottage industries in their villages in order to contribute economically to their families and villages.

DiAna's Hair Ego: AIDS Info Up Front. 1990. Ellen Spiro. 29 min. Women Make Movies. www.wmm.com.

Documents the South Carolina AIDS Education Network, an AIDS prevention and sex education group for the black community, founded by DiAna DiAna and operated in her beauty salon. A provocative, funny, and informative testament to the power of individuals to make a difference.

An End to Silence: Women Grasp the Initiative. 1994. 30 min. each. TransTel.

This series provides insightful background into several different independent women's initiatives and provides compelling evidence that the actions of a small group can change society as a whole. Eleven segments: 1. Throwing Off the Masks: A Women's Theatre Collective in Nicaragua; 2. Women Think Ahead: A Farming Project Group on Sumatra; 3. Women Create Development Policies: The National Women's Union in Djibouti; 4. S.O.S.: Women against Everyday Violence: Self-Help Initiatives for Victims of Violence in Rio; 5. Solidarity Isn't Something That Happens in Books: Women of Lima Battle for Survival; 6. The Strength of the Downtrodden: An Autononous Women's Refuge in Germany; 7. Paradise Is Under Your Mother's Foot: Women in Pakistan Seek Their Rights; 8. Lufuluri, a Garifuna Survival Strategy: Women in Belize; 9. Born of Tears: The Housemaids' Union in Cuzco, Peru; 10. Why Mary Wouldn't Sell the Grapefruit: Irish Women against Apartheid; and 11. All Work and No Pay: German Women Look Back at their Past.

Environmental Racism. 1990. 57 min. Third World Newsreel. www.twn.org.

Two 30-minute programs focus on educating and organizing disadvantaged communities to act on environmental issues and conditions affecting them. Part 1 shows how techniques used during the civil rights movement can be applied to deal with issues such as urban waste dumping near poor communities, fighting for clean water and air, and toxic dumping in Africa by U.S. chemical companies. Part 2 targets issues and organizing among Native and Mexican communities in the Southwest, Latinos facing homelessness in urban areas, and indigenous Amazonians fighting against the destruction of their environment by cattle ranchers.

Eyes of the Storm: The Return of Hong Kong to China. 1997. J. Tobin Rothlein and Street Voice Productions. 52 min. Filmakers Library. www.filmakers.com.

Shot in Hong Kong during its historic and controversial return to China, this video provides a compelling look at individuals amidst a changing political system.

Legislators and political activists, including Linda Wong, a Hong Kong University student leader, share their hopes and fears as they struggle to preserve history and the memory of Tiananmen.

Eyes on the Prize: America's Civil Rights Years, 1954 to 1965. 1986. Henry Hampton. 360 min. PBS Video. www.pbs.org.

Acclaimed six-part series documenting the history of the American civil rights movement: 1. Awakenings (1954–56); 2. Fighting Back, 1957–62; 3. Ain't Scared of Your Jails, 1960–61; 4. No Easy Walk, 1962–66; 5. Mississippi: Is This America? 1962–64; and 6. Bridge to Freedom, 1965.

Faith Even to the Fire: Nuns for Social Justice. 1991. Jean Victor. 55 min. Filmakers Library. www.filmakers.com.

Documentary dipicting contemporary U.S. nuns working for social justice, even when it brings them into conflict with the established church. It follows the stories of three nuns: Rosa Martha Zarate, a Mexican nun who works and organizes Latinos in San Bernardino, California; Sister Judy Vaughan, an Irish American nun in Chicago whose pro-choice stand almost got her expelled from her religious order; and Sister Marie de Pores Taylor, an African-American nun who is a community and political activist in Oakland, California.

Fighting for Our Lives: Women Confronting AIDS. 1990. Linda Anguiano. 29 min. Center for Women's Policy Studies.

Confronting the fact that over 70 percent of the women with AIDS in the United States are women of color, African-American, Latina, Native-American and Asian-American women organize to stop the spread of HIV and AIDS in their communities.

Four Women of Egypt. 1998. Tahani Rached. 90 min. Women Make Movies. www.wmm.com.

This documentary explores opposing religious, social, and political views in modern-day Egypt through the experience of four deeply committed activists, Muslim, Christian, and atheist. Despite their fundamental differences, divergent viewpoints, and passionate arguments, their friendship endures.

Freedom on My Mind. 1994. Connie Field and Marilyn Mulford. 110 min. California Newsreel. www.newsreel.org.

Compelling and eloquent documentary of the civil rights movement and the events surrounding the Mississippi Voter Registration Project of the early 1960s in which a small group of young activists changed history. Nominated for an Academy Award, winner of both the American Historical Association and the Organization of American Historians awards for best documentary.

Gabriela. 1988. Trix Betlam. 67 min. Women Make Movies. www.wmm.com.

Documentary portrayal of the work of Gabriela, a mass organization of diverse women's groups in the Philippines founded in 1984 to bring students, nuns, artists, farm and factory workers, prostitutes, and housewives together to demand a voice in national politics.

Gay USA. 1977. Arthur Bressan. 71 min. Frameline. www.frameline.org.

Film coverage of the 1977 Lesbian and Gay Pride parades and marches throughout the United States intercut with on-the-street interviews with gay men and women about their lovers and how they came out, and other footage including lesbians marching against housework and drag queens protesting fascism.

Globalization and Human Rights. 1998. 57 min. Globalvision. www.globalvision.org.

This one-hour documentary, hosted by Charlayne Hunter-Gault and originally broadcast nationally on PBS, explores the effects of the globalized economy on international human-rights concerns and standards.

The Golden Cage: A Story of California's Farmworkers. 1989. Susan Ferriss. 29 min. Filmakers Library. www.filmakers.com.

Chronicles the experiences of Mexican farmworkers in California, tracing the history of the activist United Farm Workers union from the sixties to the late 1980s.

Golden Threads. 1998. Lucy Winer and Karen Easton. 56 min. Women Make Movies. www.wmm.com.

This documentary profiles 93-year-old lesbian activist Christine Burton, founder of a global networking service for midlife and elder lesbians.

Gotta Make This Journey: Sweet Honey in the Rock. 1983. 50 min. Women Make Movies. www.wmm.com.

Presents a documentary tribute to the radical black women's a cappella group Sweet Honey in the Rock, whose music serves the cause of social activism.

Grrlyshow. 2001. Kara Herold. 18 min. Women Make Movies. www.wmm.com.

Examines the "girly zine" revolution and culture in feminism's "third wave." Demonstrates the subversive power of feminism and new ways in which women are claiming their own voice.

Guerrillas in Our Midst. 1992. Amy Harrison. 35 min. Women Make Movies. www.wmm.com.

Profiles the activist Guerrilla Girls who, dressed in gorilla masks, demonstrate to promote greater representation of women and minority artists in art exhibitions.

Habitual Sadness. 1997. Byun Young-Joo. 70 min. Filmakers Library. www.filmakers.com.

Korean "comfort women," forced into sexual slavery by the Japanese in World War II, speak out about their past oppression and their current shared community.

Hammering It Out. 2000. Vivian Price. 54 min. Women Make Movies. www.wmm.com.

A community initiated lawsuit that resulted in hundreds of women getting trained in the building trades and working on a billion-dollar freeway in Los Angeles frames this documentary on the Century Freeway Women's Employment Project. This labor activism spotlights feminist issues of equality, identity, and changing gender roles.

Hanan Ashrawi: A Woman of Her Time. 1995. Mai Masri. 50 min. Cinema Guild. www.cinemaguild.com.

Profiles Hanan Ashrawi, former spokesperson for the Palestine Liberation Organization during the Middle East peace talks with Israel who later turned down a position in the new government in order to continue her efforts on behalf of peace and human rights. Details her personal history and activities with Jerusalem Link, a feminist alliance of Palestinian and Israeli activists, as well as with the Palestinian Independent Commission for Citizen's Rights.

Invisible Women. 1991. Marina Alvarez and Ellen Spiro. 25 min. Women Make Movies. www.wmm.com.

Women who are HIV-positive discuss how they "came out" about their infection and became politically active. Also presents political demonstrations by ACT UP that focus on issues important to HIV-positive women.

Islam and Feminism. 1991. Nighat Said Khan. 26 min. First Run/Icarus Films. http://www.frif.com/.

Documents the efforts of Pakistani women's organizations to battle the severe discrimination and inequities in Pakistan's Islamic law, which does not distinguish among rape, adultery, and fornication. Under this law, the testimony of two women is valued as equal to that of one man and a rape victim can be charged with having had extramarital sex.

Jane: An Abortion Service. 1996. Kate Kirtz and Nell Lundy. 58 min. Women Make Movies. www.wmm.com.

In the face of criminalized abortion, Chicago-based activists created Jane, the women's health group who performed nearly 12,000 safe illegal abortions between 1969 and 1973 with no formal medical training. An exploration of empowerment through collective action and service.

Kababaihan Filipina Portraits. 1989. Marie Boti and Malcolm Guy. 40 min. Cinema Guild. www.cinemaguild.com.

Documents the grassroots women's movement in the Philippines through profiles of women from various walks of life who were involved in the progressive People's Power movement for social change.

Las Madres: The Mothers of Plaza de Mayo. 1986. Susana Muñoz and Lourdes Portillo. 64 min. Women Make Movies. www.wmm.com.

> Academy Award–nominated documentary about the Argentinian mothers' movement to demand to know the fate of their sons and daughters who were among 30,000 "disappeared" during the 1970s and '80s. A powerful testimony to breaking the silence expected of women in the name of human rights.

Let's Own It! The Struggle of the Lincoln Place Tenants Association. 1998. Karen Brodkin. 31 min. Extension Center for Media and Independent Learning, University of California, Berkeley. www-cmil.unex.berkeley.edu/media/.

> Lincoln Place, a large apartment complex in Venice, California, was slated for demolition and redevelopment. This videotape, made by a noted feminist anthropologist, documents how a group of retired residents joined forces with younger residents—primarily women and single parents—to fight against the redevelopment proposal and displacement of 1,500 tenants and work toward the creation of a permanently affordable housing community.

Listening for Something: Adrienne Rich and Dionne Brand in Conversation. 1996. Dionne Brand. 56 min. Women Make Movies. www.wmm.com.

> This exchange between eminent American poet Adrienne Rich and Trinidadian-Canadian poet/filmmaker Dionne Brand, who share strong feminist and lesbian identities but are different in generation, race, and class, focuses on political activism, citizenship, and racism among other topics in a remarkable conversation intercut with readings of their poems.

Love, Women, and Flowers (Amor, Mujeres y Flores). 1988. Marta Rodriguez and Jorge Silva. 58 min. Women Make Movies. www.wmm.com.

> This beautiful and powerful documentary addresses the hazardous working conditions for the 60,000 women who work in Colombia's flower industry. Includes the testimonies of the women workers and documents, with urgency and intimacy, their efforts to organize.

Macho. 2000. Lucinda Broadbent. 26 min. Women Make Movies. www.wmm.com.

> Profiles the Men against Violence group of Nicaragua, who create new and innovative ways to confront male violence and machismo.

Made in India. 1998. Patricia Plattner. 52 min. Women Make Movies. www.wmm.com.

> Portrait of the SEWA (Self-Employed Women's Association), the famous women's organization in India that holds to the simple yet radical belief that poor women need organizing, not welfare. SEWA also corresponds to the Indian word *sewa*, meaning service.

Made in Thailand. 1999. Eve-Laure Moros and Linzy Emery. 30 min. Women Make Movies. www.wmm.com.

> Chronicles the grassroots movement of women garment and toy factory workers in Thailand to organize unions and their empowering campaign for human and worker's rights. Revealingly exposes the cheap labor of the global economy and the human cost behind the production of everyday items that U.S. consumers take for granted.

Margaret Sanger. 1999. Bruce Alfred. 87 min. Films for the Humanities and Sciences. www.films.com.

> Using rare archival footage, diary excerpts, and commentary from historians, critics, and relatives, this program documents Sanger's extraordinary life and activism in the promotion and legalization of birth control. Sanger opened the first birth control clinic in the United States and launched the research that led to the birth control pill, but also used racist and elitist arguments for eugenics to promote her cause.

Margaret Sanger: A Public Nuisance. 1992. Terese Svoboda and Steve Bull. 28 min. Women Make Movies. www.wmm.com.

> A "witty and inventive" documentary that highlights Sanger's pioneering strategies of using media and popular culture to advance the cause of birth control, effectively changing public discussion of birth control from issues of morality to issues of women's health and economic well-being.

Maria's Story. 1990. Manona Wali and Pamela Cohen. 58 min. Filmakers Library. www.filmakers.com.

> Representing a growing number of Latin-American women on the forefront of social change, Maria is a 39-year-old mother of three whose passion for social justice led her to become a leader in the guerrilla movement in El Salvador.

McLibel: Two Worlds Collide. 1997. Franny Armstrong. 53 min. Media Education Foundation. www.mediaed.org.

> A documentary of two environmental and social activists, Helen Morris and Dave Steel, who took on the McDonald's corporation, resulting in the longest trial in British history. The film examines the global food business, the implications for freedom of speech, and the power of two ordinary but principled people.

Miriam's Daughters Celebrate. 1986. Lilly Rivlin. 21 min. Filmakers Library. www.filmakers.com.

> In a kind of religious activism, Jewish feminists create new rituals (a Passover seder and a baby-girl-naming ceremony) to update traditions and make religion more responsive to women.

Miss Amy and Miss May. 1990. Cynthia Wilmot. 40 min. Women Make Movies. www.wmm.com.

Through interviews and dramatizations, portrays the lives of Amy Bailey and May Farquharson, women's and civil rights activists in 20th-century Jamaica.

My Feminism. 1998. Laurie Colbert and Dominique Cardona. 55 min. Women Make Movies. www.wmm.com.

Interviews with leading feminist activists who claim that feminism is one of the most successful and significant revolutions of the late 20th century. They link equality, gender, race, reproductive rights, sexualities, women's health, abortion, parenting, poverty, and power as interlocking platforms of the feminist global agenda.

My Home, My Prison. 1992. Susana Muñoz and Erica Marcus. 70 min. Women Make Movies. www.wmm.com.

Videotape based on the Palestinian-Arab activist and journalist Raymonda Hawa Tawil's autobiography of the same name, published in 1979 during the military occupation of the West Bank and the Gaza Strip.

My Name is Kahentiiosta. 1995. Alanis Obomsawin. 29 min. Women Make Movies. www.wmm.com.

Profiles a young, courageous Kahnawake Mohawk woman who was arrested after a 78-day armed standoff in 1990 between the Mohawks and the Canadian federal government in the Mohawk movement for self-determination. Kahentiiosta is detained four days longer than other women because the court refuses to accept her aboriginal name and she refuses to capitulate.

New Directions: Women of Zimbabwe; Women of Guatemala; Women of Thailand. 2000. Joanne Burke. 90 min. (three films, 30 min. each). Women Make Movies. www.wmm.com.

Three-part series about women's activism and empowerment in developing countries from an award-winning documentarian. Each short film spotlights the critical role women are playing as community-based leaders: providing education, inspiration, and practical assistance to other women in their countries.

Not Channel Zero. 1993. 30 min. Third World Newsreel. www.twn.org.

A portrait of the Not Channel Zero collective and their innovative activism through videotape production asserting that the revolution must be televised. The group produced over six videotapes in less than two years, focusing on topical issues concerning and affecting African Americans; these included *Black Women, Sexual Politics, and the Revolution* (1992) and *Our House: Gays and Lesbians in the Hood* (1990).

One Woman, One Vote. 1995. Ruth Pollak. 106 min. Direct Cinema Ltd. www.directcinema.com.

Documents the 72-year struggle for women's suffrage in the U.S. that culminated in the ratification of the Nineteenth Amendment in 1920. It illuminates the alliances, infighting, betrayals, and defeats that paved the way for victory in the battle for women's right to vote. Originally broadcast on PBS as an episode of the television series *The American Experience*, and narrated by Susan Sarandon.

Out at Work. 1996. Kelly Anderson and Tami Gold. 56 min. Frameline. www.frameline.org.

Documents the lives of three gay workers from 1991 to 1996: a lesbian who became politically active after being fired from a Cracker Barrel restaurant in Georgia; a gay man who worked with his union to fight harassment in an auto factory in Detroit; and a New York Public Library employee who sought health benefits for his partner.

Out: The Making of a Revolutionary. 2000. Sonja de Vries and Rhonda Collins. 60 min. Third World Newsreel. www.twn.org.

"Convicted of the 1983 U.S. Capitol Bombing, and 'conspiring to influence, change, and protest policies and practices of the United States government through violent and illegal means,' Laura Whitehorn, an out lesbian and one of six defendants in the Resistance Conspiracy Case, spent 14 years in prison. Out is the story of her life and times: five tumultuous decades of struggle for freedom and justice. Whether you agree or disagree with radical left politics, this is a documentary that will challenge you to think about what you might be willing to risk for your own beliefs" (from the catalog of Third World Newsreel).

Pain, Passion, and Profit. 1992. Gurinder Chadha. 49 min. Women Make Movies. www.wmm.com.

Activist and entrepreneur Anita Roddick of Body Shop International interviews several women in Africa who have successfully developed small-scale business enterprises in their own communities. She poses questions about how the role and status of women affects their enterprises and how those enterprises provide a means of community and economic development for women.

¡Palante, Siempre Palante! 1996. Iris Morales. 48 min. Third World Newsreel. www.twn.org.

"In the midst of the African American civil rights struggle, protests to end the Vietnam War and the women's movement for equality, Puerto Rican and Latino communities fought for economic and social justice. From Chicago streets to the barrios of New York City and other urban centers, the Young Lords emerged to demand decent living conditions and raised a militant voice for the empowerment of the Puerto Rican people in the United States" (from the catalog of Third World Newsreel).

People Power. 1989. Ilan Ziv. 53 min. First Run / Icarus Films. www.frif.com.

An exploration of the use of nonviolent activism to achieve social change focusing primarily on the fall of Pinochet in Chile, the Palestinian intifada, and Corazon Aquino's "People Power" revolution in the Philippines.

A Place of Rage. 1991. Pratibha Parmar. 52 min. Women Make Movies.
www.wmm.com.

> June Jordan (poet), Angela Davis (political activist), Alice Walker (writer), and
> Trinh T. Minh-Ha (writer/filmmaker) comment on racial discrimination and its
> effects upon American culture and make suggestions for the future. Includes his-
> torical footage of civil rights movement in the 1960s.

Positive. 1990. Rosa von Praunheim and Phil Zwickler. 80 min. First Run Features.
http://www.firstrunfeatures.com/.

> This powerful video by a noted filmmaker documents the New York City gay com-
> munity's response to the AIDS crisis and the spirit of activism generated by play-
> wright Larry Kramer, musician and cofounder of People With AIDS Coalition
> Michael Callen, and New York filmmaker and journalist Phil Zwickler. They force-
> fully speak out, and their groups, like ACT UP and Queer Nation, demand a
> response to the epidemic that has threatened to annihilate them.

Postcards from the Future. 1997. 47 min. Films for the Humanities and Sciences.
www.films.com.

> Features women activists around the world: in Kenya using simple technologies to
> save their regions desertification; in New Guinea fighting to save the people's way
> of life; in Chechnya building the new Russian peace movement; and in Brazil using
> innovative techniques in the police force to combat violence against women.

Rachel's Daughters Searching for the Causes of Breast Cancer. 1997. Allie Light, Irving Saraf,
and Nancy Evans. 106 min. with guide (28 pp.). Women Make Movies.
www.wmm.com.

> This documentary follows a group of women, all breast cancer activists who are
> fighting or have survived the disease, on a personal mission to unearth the causes
> of breast cancer. Incorporates interviews with prominent scientists, documentary
> footage from high cancer-rate areas, and investigates women's personal battles to
> stay healthy.

Raise the Roof: Demand Government Action for Human Rights. 1999. Globalvision.
www.globalvision.org.

> Produced for Amnesty International USA, this video is designed to empower grass-
> roots activists to organize for human rights causes with national and state legisla-
> tures. Features nonpartisan tips and advice from members of Congress.

Rebel Hearts: Sarah and Angelina Grimke and the Anti-Slavery Movement. 1994. Betsy Newman
and Terese Svoboda. 58 min. Women Make Movies. www.wmm.com.

> Profiles Sarah and Angelina Grimke, daughters of a wealthy slaveholding family
> from Charleston, South Carolina, who left the South to become the first female
> agents of the antislavery movement. Their passionate rhetoric and fiery speaking
> style led them to the front ranks of the abolitionist movement and set the stage for
> the establishment of the women's rights' movement.

Resurgence: The Movement for Equality versus the Ku Klux Klan. 1981. Pamela Yates, Tom Sigel, and Peter Kinoy. 54 min. First Run/Icarus Films. www.frif.com.

> A bitter two-year strike led by black women against a chicken processing plant in Laurel, Mississippi, provides the focus for this examination of two sides of a political battle in the United States: the efforts of union and civil rights activists to achieve social and economic reform, and the deeply disturbing upsurge of activity in the Ku Klux Klan and the American Nazi Party.

The Right to Choose. 2000. Charlotte Metcalf. 24 min. Bullfrog Films. http://www.bullfrogfilms.com/.

> Part 8 of a series on how the globalized world economy affects ordinary people, this video profiles activism in Ethiopia especially around the practice of forced marriage, reproductive rights, and primary education for women.

Righteous Babes. 2000. Pratibha Parmar. 51 min. Women Make Movies. www.wmm.com.

> Acclaimed filmmaker Pratibha Parmar explores the intersections of feminism, activism, and popular music through the direct, aggressive, and revolutionary work of women rock musicians like Madonna and Ani DiFranco.

Ripples of Change. 1996. Nanako Kurihara. 57 min. Women Make Movies. www.wmm.com.

> Combines powerful political analysis with a passionate personal story to document the Japanese women's liberation movement in the 1970s and its influence on contemporary Japanese society.

Rosa Parks: The Path to Freedom. 1996. Emery C. King and Patrick Maday. 26 min. Filmakers Library. www.filmakers.com.

> Profiles Rosa Parks, a quiet but forceful woman whose demand for her civil rights led to dramatic social change in the 1960s. Contains an overview of the events that took place in Montgomery, Alabama: Parks's arrest, the bus boycott, and the segregation laws that were finally overturned. It also portrays Parks's continuing commitment to social justice for all people.

Salt of the Earth. 1953, rereleased 1987. Herbert J. Biberman. 94 min. MPI Home Video. www.mpimedia.com/.

> This classic, compelling feature film recounts the true story of Chicanos in the zinc mines of New Mexico striking for better working and living conditions. When an injunction is issued against the workers, the wives take up the battle with a furious determination, leaving the husbands to care for home and children. Made largely with nonactors and presciently advocating the rights of workers, minorities, and women, the film was blacklisted during the McCarthy era as sympathetic to communism.

Scraps of Life. 1992. Gayla Jamison. 28 min. Filmakers Library.
www.filmakers.com.

> Women who survived the massive murders of the Pinochet years in Chile come
> together to demand truth and justice from the new government and sewing
> murals out of scraps of fabrics, called arpilleras, that record Chile's bloody history.
> These activist sewing circles also undertake projects to assist the poor and educate
> the country's youth.

Senegal: The Power to Change: Combatting Female Genital Mutilation. 2000. Gerd Inger
Polden. 30 min. Filmakers Library. www.filmakers.com.

> Documents the grassroots movement since 1997 throughout the villages of Senegal
> to abolish the practice of female genital mutilation (FGM). The protest against FGM
> started with an educational program set up by the United Nations in cooperation
> with a local NGO and ended in 1999 when, through the education and activism of
> these women, the parliament of Senegal passed a law forbidding FGM.

Silence Broken: Korean Comfort Women. 1999. Dai Sil Kim-Gibson. 57 min. NAATA.
www.naatanet.org.

> A powerful and emotional documentary about former Korean "comfort women,"
> forced into sexual servitude by the Japanese Imperial Army during World War II,
> now demanding justice for the crimes against humanity committed against them.
> They are not seeking financial compensation, but a measure of personal honor and
> vindication in the form of an official apology from Japan.

Sisterhood Alive and Well: The Million Woman March. 1997. Andre Walker. 30 min.
Cinema Guild. www.cinemaguild.com.

> Documents the 1997 Million Woman March in Philadelphia, in which black
> women from all over America mobilized to demonstrate their concerns for black
> America and to express their sense of unity as a movement with the power to
> influence American society.

Six Generations of Suffragettes: The Women's Rights Movement. 1999. 15 min. Films for the
Humanities and Sciences. www.films.com.

> Traces the growth of the women's movement in America through six generations
> from Elizabeth Cady Stanton to her great-great-great-granddaughter Elizabeth
> Jenkins-Sahlin, and their fights for equality in the voting booth, the classroom, and
> the workplace.

Some American Feminists. 2001. Luce Guilbeault, Nicole Brossard, and Margaret
Wescott. 56 min. Women Make Movies. www.wmm.com.

> Interviews and newsreel footage place the American feminist movement in a his-
> torical perspective. Six of the women who gave impetus to the second-wave move-
> ment (Rita Mae Brown, Margo Jefferson, Kate Millet, Lila Karp, Ti-Grace Atkinson,
> and Betty Friedan) discuss those issues that most concern them.

Some Ground to Stand On: The Story of Blue Lunden. 1998. Joyce P. Warshow. 35 min. Women Make Movies. www.wmm.com.

> Chronicles the life story of Blue Lunden, a working-class lesbian activist whose odyssey of personal transformation parallels lesbians' changing roles over the past 40 years. At 61, she reflects on her work as a lesbian rights, feminist, and anti-nuclear activist.

Spirits Rising. 1995. Ramona S. Diaz. 56 min. NAATA. www.naatanet.org.

> Portrays the evolving role of women in the Philippines from precolonial priestess to president of the republic. Includes interviews with President Corazon Aquino and prominent individuals who facilitated the "people power" movement.

A State of Danger. 1989. Jenny Morgan. 30 min. Women Make Movies. www.wmm.com.

> Probes the struggles of Palestinian and Israeli activists, most of them women, examining grassroots support, human rights and the role of Arab and Jewish women in bringing peace to the region.

Step by Step: Building a Feminist Movement. 2001. Joyce Follet and Wisconsin Public Television. 56 min. Women Make Movies. www.wmm.com.

> This exploration of front-line feminism follows the lives of eight Wisconsin women, six of whom became founders of NOW, emerging out of the labor, civil rights, and political movements of the 1940s and '50s.

Takeover. 1990. Peter Kinoy and Pamela Yates. 58 min. First Run Icarus Films. www.frif.com.

> The first documentary about homeless Americans organizing portrays the actions on May 1, 1990, when homeless people in eight U.S. cities broke locks and took over vacant houses. The takeovers inspired other homeless people to act and, in some cities, become political forces.

To Empower Women: The Beijing Women's Conference. 1999. Patricia James, Janet Linney, and Bob Purdy. 28 min. Off-Center Video. www.offcentervideo.com.

> Filmed at the Non-Governmental Forum in Huairou, China, and narrated by Bella Abzug, this video calls women to activism for worldwide women's rights and the global women's movement. Documents the efforts of women leaders attending the UN Fourth World Conference on Women to improve conditions for women in Zimbabwe, Germany, Papua New Guinea, Iran, the Philippines, Israel, the Solomon Islands, and the United States.

Troubled Paradise. 1992. Steven Okazaki. 56 min. NAATA. www.naata.org.

> Portrays the struggle of native Hawaiian activists to preserve their rich culture in the face of the numerous social and political problems facing the indigenous population.

Tuti. 1999. Riri Riza. 20 min. First Run/Icarus Films. www.frif.com.

Tuti's son disappeared during the protests that helped bring down the Suharto regime in Indonesia although he was a bus driver and did not fit the profile of most activists. Searching for her son, Tuti joins the families of other missing activists and confronts the unresponsive military establishment.

A Union in Wait. 2001. Ryan Butler. 28 min. Frameline. www.frameline.org.

Recounts the struggle of long-time partners Susan Parker and Wendy Scott, members of the Wake Forest Baptist Church in North Carolina, to have a union ceremony in Wake Forest University's Chapel in the face of university opposition and a community divided by the ensuing controversy.

Up against the Wall Ms. America. 1968. 8 min. Third World Newsreel. www.twn.org.

Short entertaining film documents the guerrilla theater tactics that early women's liberation activists used to raise awareness of what beauty pageants really represent.

The Veiled Hope: Women of Palestine (L'Espoir Voile: Femmes de Palestine). 1994. Norma Marcos. 59 min. Women Make Movies. www.wmm.com.

Palestinian women living on the Gaza and West Bank mobilize to rebuild Palestinian cultural identity. Provides an in-depth analysis of their political position as they juggle women's and national liberation struggles.

Visionary Voices: Women on Power: Conversations with Shamans, Activists, Teachers, Artists and Healers. 1992. Penny Rosenwasser. 22 min. Women Make Movies. www.wmm.com.

"Visionary Voices features a multi-racial group of women activists, artists and healers reading excerpts from their interviews in a book of the same name about healthy uses of power. The simplicity of the form of this video enhances the complexity of views expressed by these remarkable women; an inspirational work about the contribution women of color have made to the women's movement as well as how to teach without domination, organize without intimidation, disagree without degradation, relate without manipulation and practice compassion without losing focus or strength" (from the catalog of Women Make Movies).

Voices from the Front. 1991. Robyn Hutt, David Meieran, and Sandra Elgear. 90 min. Frameline. www.frameline.org.

Documentary about AIDS activism in the United States, 1988–1991, in which individual testimony makes clear the emotional and political effects of community activism. Includes coverage of demonstrations and interviews with AIDS activists seeking to change public consciousness, expose the failure of the health care system, and challenge government inaction and neglect.

Voices from the Front Lines. 1997. Eric Mann, Mark Dworkin, Melissa Young, and Howard Dratch. 40 min. Cinema Guild. www.cinemaguild.com.

> Profiles the Los Angeles-based Labor/Community Strategy Center, a grassroots political activism group that emphasizes multiracial community organizing and confronts serious issues such as corporate injustice, environmental racism, and equitable public transportation.

Voices Heard Sisters Unseen. 1995. Grace Poore. 76 min. SHaKTI Productions; Women Make Movies. www.wmm.com.

> This powerful documentary portrays the multi-issue activism of survivors of domestic violence working for justice and safety through an integrated response to services for battered women. Study guide available.

Voices of Change. 1996. Lyn Wright and Barbara Doran. 92 min. Women Make Movies. www.wmm.com.

> Five-part documentary examines individual activism and issues facing women worldwide providing insights into the realities of international feminism. Women in Guatemala, Latvia, Pakistan, and Canada discuss their work for native and worker's rights, educational equity, and the search for free artistic expression, connecting their activism to past and future familial and cultural traditions.

War Zone. 1998. Maggie Hadleigh-West. 35 min. Media Education Foundation. www.mediaed.org.

> Activist filmmaker Maggie Hadleigh-West believes that the streets are a war zone for women. Armed with only a video camera, she both demonstrates her experience of the degrading gender rules of the street, where access to women's bodies is regarded as a male right, and, by turning and confronting her abusers, reclaims the space that was stolen from her.

When Democracy Works. 1996. Scot Nakagawa and Catherine Gund Saalfield. 30 min. Frameline. www.frameline.org.

> Examines the role of democracy and the work of progressive grassroots organizers to thwart the radical right in the U.S. featuring three case studies: David Duke's campaigns for political office in Louisiana; the conservative drive to pass antigay Amendment 2 in Colorado; and the anti-immigrant Proposition 187 and anti–affirmative action initiatives in California.

Why is Preparing Fish a Political Act? 1991. Russell Leong. 20 min. NAATA. www.naatanet.org.

> This portrait of Asian-American poet and activist Janice Mirikitani addresses legacies of struggle, power, and self-determination and includes a segment on her work with the homeless at Glide Memorial Church in San Francisco.

Will Be Televised. 1991. Shu Lea Chang. 300 min. Third World Newsreel. www.twn.org.

A series of five one-hour tapes from videomakers who have become activists for social and political change in Asia. Movements in Korea, the Philippines, Taiwan, Hong Kong, and China demonstrate the struggles for freedom of expression and democracy.

The Willmar 8. 1980. Lee Grant. 55 min. California Newsreel. www.newsreel.org.

Recounts the inspiring story of eight women who formed their own independent union and went on strike in Willmar, Minnesota, to combat employment discrimination. Although they lost the battle, they won a new sense of empowerment and community.

Wilma P. Mankiller, Chief of the Cherokee Nation: Woman of Power. 1992. Nola Roeper and Mary Scott. 29 min. Roeper-Scott Video Productions. Women Make Movies. www.wmm.com.

Profiles the first female chief of the Cherokee Nation and her groundbreaking work in governance, community development, and furthering the cause of her people. Explores the delicate balance between participating in existing white power structures and maintaining personal and cultural integrity.

With a Vengeance: The Fight for Reproductive Freedom. 1989. Lori Hiris. 40 min. Women Make Movies. www.wmm.com.

Presents a compelling history of the struggle for reproductive freedom since the 1960s, reflecting the wider history of the contemporary women's movement. Interviews with early abortion rights activists, including members of Redstockings and the Jane Collective, are intercut with young women who testify to the need for multiracial grassroots coalitions and African-American activists who make connections between racism, reproductive freedom, and health care for the poor.

With Our Own Eyes. 1995. David Goodman and Denis Doyon for American Friends Service Committee. 20 min.; includes study guide. NAATA. www.naatanet.org.

Documents a visit by teenage students from the United States and Puerto Rico to Hiroshima and Nagasaki to learn about the effects of the atomic bomb and why they should care today about the bombings. Recommended for lessons in history, politics, and activism.

Women and Social Action. 1994. Cheryl Lambert. 1440 min. PBS Adult Learning Services. www.pbs.org/als/.

Twenty-four segments on 13 videocassettes: 1. Social Action and Social Change; 2. Perspectives on Women; 3. Leadership and Social Action; 4. Commonalities and Differences; 5. Gender Socialization; 6. Transforming Knowledge; 7. Families; 8. Child Care; 9. Women and Health; 10. Women, Weight, and Food; 11. Pregnancy and Childbirth; 12. Motherhood; 13. Abortion and Reproductive Issues; 14. Religion; 15. Work; 16. Sexual Harassment; 17. Low-Income Resistance; 18. Homelessness; 19. Connecting the Issues; 20. Violence against Women; 21. On the

Streets and in the Jails; 22. Rape and Self-Defense; 23. Perspectives on Social Change; 24. New Directions.

Women for America, for the World. 1985. Vivien Verdon-Roe. 28 min. Educational Film and Video Project; Distributed by Facets Multimedia. www.facets.org.

In this Academy Award–nominated film, women speak out for health, educational, and economic needs as they redefine the meaning of world security.

Women in War: Voices from the Front Lines. 1990. Pat Mitchell. 96 min. Filmakers Library. www.filmakers.com.

This two-part series profiles women who have found power under the disempowering conditions of war. Part I: Jews and Arabs in Israel and Palestine involved in the peace-making process and Nobel Peace Prize winner Mairead Corrigan working to end violence in Northern Ireland. Part II: Salvadorean women's leadership in the popular-front movements for social justice, and women activists in Boston, New York, Washington, and Los Angeles mobilizing to reclaim their neighborhoods from crime.

Women of Change. 1999. Joan Prowse. 54 min. Filmakers Library. www.filmakers.com.

A testimony to the potential strength of sisterhood across borders, this videotape profiles women whose fight for human rights often brings them in conflict with profiteering multinational companies: Canada's Josephine Grey and Mexico's Bertha Lujan lead social movements to help people out of poverty and combat oppressive working conditions in foreign-owned factories.

Women of Niger: Between Fundamentalism and Democracy (Femmes du Niger: entre Integrisme et Democratie). 1993. Anne Laure Folly. 26 min. Women Make Movies. www.wmm.com.

A compelling account of the activism of women to win their democratic rights in Niger, a traditionally Islamic country where authorized polygamy and Muslim fundamentalism present tremendous social and religious obstacles.

The Women of Summer: An Unknown Chapter of American History. 1985. Suzanne Bauman. 55 min. Filmakers Library. www.filmakers.com.

Chronicles a unique social and educational experiment, the Bryn Mawr Summer School for Women Workers where, from 1921 to 1938, 1,700 blue-collar women were introduced to humanistic and political thought, including Marxism and trade unionism. Tells the story of these women through oral histories, letters and diaries, and historical footage, and joins the 50-year reunion of the alumnae, where they reconfirm their commitment to social justice.

Women of Vieques. 2000. Sonia Fritz. 19 min. Cinema Guild. www.cinemaguild.com.

This video portrays the involvement of Puerto Rican women activists in the continuing protests against U.S. Navy use of the island of Vieques as a military training site.

Women Organize. 2000. 32 min. Women Make Movies. www.wmm.com.

A video by the Union Institute Center for Women and Organizing Documentation Project. Women community and union organizers from varied backgrounds demonstrate the diversity of feminist activism in the global struggles for racial, social, and economic justice. Described as "pedagogically and analytically sharp, and deeply moving," it covers a range of concerns including environmental issues, labor, and sexualities as well as organizational theories and debates about collective action.

Women's Health, Thirty Years of Activism. 1999. Nancy E. Stoller. Eight videotapes (ca. 90 min. each).

Panel discussions about women's health, grassroots activism, and organizations focused on women's health issues, taped in Community Studies 148: Women's Health, taught by Nancy Stoller at the University of California, Santa Cruz, in April and May 1999. Panel members are women active in community organizations. The eight sections are (1) Santa Cruz Women's Health Collective; (2) Women against Rape; (3) Reproductive Issues; (4) California Prostitutes Education Project; (5) Asian Women's Health; (6) Breast Cancer: Outreach and Activism; (7) Body Image: Four Fat Activists; and (8) California Coalition for Women Prisoners. While this series is not in formal distribution, it may be available through interlibrary loan from UC Santa Cruz.

Women's Rights since Beijing. 1996. Eulogio L. Ortiz Jr. 27 minutes. Globalvision: International Center for Global Communications Foundation, Inc. www.globalvision.org.

Charlayne Hunter-Gault anchors four segments from the PBS program *Rights and Wrongs: Human Rights Television* that address global women's activism. The first segment examines the United Nations Fourth World Conference on Women (in Beijing) and at progress made on women's rights globally and within the United States after the conference. In the second segment, Bella Abzug reflects on the growing empowerment of nongovernmental organizations and the strategies that made the outcome of the Beijing conference so successful. The third segment profiles three grassroots organizers from Bangladesh, Zimbabwe, and the United States who discuss their work and how women's issues are linked globally. In the final segment, Hunter-Gault interviews Vandana Shiva, an Indian environmentalist and women's activist.

You Got to Move. 1985. Lucy Massie Phenix and Veronica Selver. 87 min. First Run/Icarus Films. www.frif.com.

A documentary about personal and social transformation, this film records the progress of individuals who, together with Tennessee's legendary Highlander Folk School, have worked for union, civil, environmental, and women's rights in the South. It goes beyond individual issues to explore the very process of social and political change and the evolution of leadership, joyfully confirming that people can make a difference.

Yuri Kochiyama: Passion for Justice. 1995. Patricia Saunders and Rea Tajiri. 58 min. NAATA. www.naatanet.org.

> Profiles Yuri Kochiyama, an Asian-American woman and humanitarian civil rights activist who first became aware of social injustice in the United States during her time in a Japanese-American internment camp during World War II. She stresses the need for members of all races and ethnicities to work together for common goals, and for a fundamental change in political power structures.

4. Websites

This *highly selective* list of online resources represents a wide variety of websites that range from small grassroots activist organizations to large feminist organizations that serve as clearinghouses on special issues and/or provide numerous services. Included are organizations and personal websites that are nongovernmental, nonprofit, private, feminist, activist, grassroots, and provide information, entertainment, or a place to voice alternative points of view. Most sites date since 1999 except those that serve as an archival reference, such as transcripts and proceedings from the Beijing +5 Conference. These sites may aid students, teachers, activists, and would-be activists in their quest for examples of other activist work, the integration of academia and activism, pedagogical resources, funding resources, and the widely diverse online community of fellow activists. Quoted descriptions are taken from statements on the websites.

About-Face. www.about-face.org/index.html.

> "By encouraging critical thinking about the media, and personal empowerment, About-Face works to engender positive body-esteem in girls and women of all ages, sizes, races and backgrounds."

African Women Global Network (AWOGNet). www.osu.edu/org/awognet.

> "African Women Global Network (AWOGNet) is a global organization that networks all men and women, organizations, institutions and indigenous national organizations within Africa, whose activities are targeted towards the improvement of the living conditions of women and children in Africa." Site contains in-depth resources on the countries in Africa and links to African sites.

Alan Guttmacher Institute. www.agi-usa.org.

> "The Alan Guttmacher Institute (AGI) is a non-profit organization focused on reproductive health research, policy analysis and public education. To fulfill this mission, AGI seeks to inform individual decision-making, encourage scientific inquiry and enlightened public debate, and promote the formation of sound public- and private-sector programs and policies." The site provides statistics and policy papers on topics such as abortion, STDs, pregnancy, and contraception.

American Association of University Women (AAUW). www.aauw.org.

The AAUW "is a national organization that promotes education and equity for all women and girls." It is composed of three corporations: the 150,000 member Association; the AAUW Educational Foundation, which funds research on girls, action projects, and grants for women; and the AAUW Legal Advocacy Fund, which provides funds and support for "women seeking judicial redress for sex discrimination in higher education."

American Civil Liberties Union (ACLU)—Women's Rights Section. www.aclu.org.

The ACLU has a long history of fighting civil liberties violations in America. Their website contains sections on student activism, gay and lesbian rights, and women's rights, among many others.

American Federation of Labor—Congress of Industrial Organizations (AFL-CIO). www.aflcio.org.

"The mission of the AFL-CIO is to improve the lives of working families—to bring economic justice to the workplace and social justice to our nation." The site has very interesting and useful resources on working families, wage laws, and the gender gap, as well as a working women's department.

Amnesty International USA: Women's Human Rights. http://www.amnesty-usa.org/women/.

AI is a grassroots activist organization focused on freeing political prisoners, abolishing the death penalty, and ending prisoner abuse. Their site provides information on international human rights violations, recent news, and AI's advocacy for women's human rights and other activist goals.

Association for Women's Rights in Development (AWID). www.awid.org.

"AWID is an international membership organization connecting, informing and mobilizing people and organizations committed to achieving gender equality, sustainable development and women's human rights." The site has articles on 'Feminist Organizational Development,' 'Gender Equality and New Technologies,' 'Women's Rights and Economic Change,' and 'Young Women and Leadership.'

AVIVA. www.aviva.org.

"AVIVA is a free 'Webzine,' being run by an International group of Feminists based in London. [It] is an International Women's Listing Magazine which enables women all over the world to make contact with each other." The site has global news, action alerts, international resources, and lists of organizations.

AWARE—Arming Women Against Rape & Endangerment. www.aware.org.

"AWARE is a source of training, information, and support for women learning how to cope with violence. AWARE training is focused on self-defense skills that can enable you to avoid, resist, and survive situations ranging from low levels of aggression to extremely violent assault." This site offers information on courses and how to defend yourself as well as a self-defense quiz.

B.a.B.e. (Be Active, Be Emancipated). www.babe.hr/eng.

"B.a.B.e. is a strategic lobbying and advocacy group located in Zagreb, Croatia, working for the affirmation and implementation of women's human rights."

Bad Jens—Iranian Feminist Monthly. www.badjens.com.

"Bad Jens is a feminist online magazine mainly addressing readers outside Iran. It is hoped to be a step towards improving links between activists/academics inside and outside the country."

Beijing '95:Women, Power, & Change. www.igc.org/beijing/beijing.html.

"These pages are an archive of the Original IGC/APC Beijing Pages." Contains interviews, documents, and archived press releases from the 1995 UN Conference on Women.

Black Women's Rape Action Project (BWRAP). www.bwrap.dircon.co.uk/BWRAPintro.html.

Located in Britain. "Founded in 1991, we are one of the few Black women's organisations specialising in offering counselling, support and advice to Black women and other women of colour, immigrant and refugee women, who have suffered rape, sexual assault or other violence."

Boston Women's Health Book Collective. www.ourbodiesourselves.org/.

"The Boston Women's Health Book Collective is a nonprofit, public interest women's health education, advocacy and consulting organization. Beginning in 1970 with the publication of the first edition of Our Bodies, Ourselves (OBOS) and continuing for 30 years, the BWHBC has inspired the women's health movement."

The Center for Reproductive Law and Policy (CRLP). www.crlp.org/aboutcrlp.html.

"The Center for Reproductive Law and Policy (CRLP) is a non-profit organization dedicated to promoting women's equality worldwide by guaranteeing reproductive rights as human rights."

Center for the American Woman and Politics (CAWP). www.rci.rutgers.edu/~cawp.

"A unit of the Eagleton Institute of Politics at Rutgers, The State University of New Jersey, CAWP is a leading authority in its field and a respected bridge between the academic and political worlds." The site provides statistics on women officeholders and candidates, information about the gender gap and voting patterns, a list of woman PACs, and more.

Center for Women's Global Leadership (CWGL). www.cwgl.rutgers.edu.

"The Center for Women's Global Leadership (Global Center) develops and facilitates women's leadership for women's human rights and social justice worldwide." CWGL has a policy and advocacy program and the site provides information on how to get involved, related resources and articles, and publications.

Choices Campus Community. www.feministcampus.org.

A project of the Feminist Majority Leadership Alliances, provides activist tools, resources, and community support to start pro-choice activism on campus.

Coalition against Trafficking in Women.
www.uri.edu/artsci/wms/hughes/catw/catw.htm.

"The Coalition Against Trafficking in Women is a feminist human rights non-governmental organization that works internationally to oppose all forms of sexual exploitation." Site includes publications, speeches, a fact book, and activist campaigns.

Coalition of Labor Union Women (CLUW). www.cluw.org.

CLUW is dedicated to making the labor movement "more responsive to the needs of all women, especially the needs of minority women who have traditionally been singled out for particularly blatant oppression." The website includes links to progressive labor organizations and to CLUW's The Reproductive Rights Project established in 1990 to build labor/pro-choice coalitions, and to update labor union members on legal, medical, and political reproductive health issues.

Cybergrrl. www.cybergrrl.com.

Cybergrrl is a virtual women's world with information on health, technology issues, books, travel, and many other topics.

Disabled Women's Network (DAWN)—Ontario. http://dawn.thot.net/index.html.

"The DisAbled Women's Network (DAWN) Ontario is a province-wide organization for Women with all types of disAbilities. We are a feminist organization which supports women in our struggles to control our own lives."

The Electra Pages. www.electrapages.com.

"The Women's Information Exchange is the organization behind ElectraPages. In 1980, advocating the use of computers to empower the women's movement, we started the National Women's Mailing List." The site has a searchable database of 9,000 feminist groups that include conferences; government agencies; lesbian, gay, bisexual, and transgender organizations; and much more.

EMILY's List. www.emilyslist.org.

Emily's List helps Democratic Party women campaign for office by recommending viable candidates to voters, raising campaign contributions, building strong campaigns, and mobilizing Democratic women voters.

Fairness and Accuracy in Reporting (FAIR). www.fair.org.

"FAIR, the national media watch group, has been offering well-documented criticism of media bias and censorship since 1986." The site has action alerts, a "women's desk," and articles from their bimonthly magazine *Extra!*

Feminist Activist Resources on the Net. www.igc.apc.org/women/feminist.html.

Produced by Sarah Stapleton-Gray, this site is "oriented toward connecting feminists who are activists to resources on the Internet which could be of use." Covers eight activist areas from reproductive rights to global issues as well as general resources for political activists.

Feminist Conspiracy. www.transfeminism.org/conspire.

"Feminist Conspiracy is committed to multi-issue activism, which means we believe we must fight against not just sexism, but also racism, classism, heterosexism, ableism, and all other oppressions in order for women to be truly free." The organization is located in Oregon and has been involved in many activist campaigns in the Portland area.

Feminist Majority Foundation Online. www.feminist.org.

The Feminist Majority is a long-time organization that is active in women's rights campaigns. The site offers an excellent collection of resources, information for and about women, and details on how to get involved in activist campaigns.

Feminist Utopia. www.amazoncastle.com/feminism.

Colleen McEneany's site offers a wide variety of resources, links, cartoons, recommended reading, activist shopping sites, and more. It is an excellent place to spend time exploring an online feminist world.

Feminist.com. www.feminist.com.

"Feminist.com is a grassroots, interactive community by, for and about women. We aim to facilitate information-sharing among women and encourage mobilization around political issues." The site has action alerts, a list of women-owned business, and information about their antiviolence campaign.

FGM Education and Networking Project. www.fgmnetwork.org.

"The purpose of the FGM Education and Networking Project is the dissemination on-line and offline of material related to female genital mutilation, otherwise known as female circumcision. The Project seeks to form an online clearinghouse and a community for researchers, activists, attorneys, and health care practitioners to obtain information and network with others involved in similar projects."

Girls Incorporated. www.girlsinc.org.

"Girls Incorporated is a national nonprofit youth organization dedicated to inspiring all girls to be strong, smart, and bold. Girls Inc. develops research-based informal education programs that encourage girls to take risks and master physical, intellectual and emotional challenges." Site provides fact and resource sheets, tips for parents, and activism news.

Global Fund for Women. www.globalfundforwomen.org/.

"The Global Fund for Women is a grantmaking foundation supporting women's human rights organizations around the world working to address critical issues such as gaining economic independence, increasing girls' access to education, and stopping violence against women."

Global Reproductive Health Forum. www.hsph.harvard.edu/Organizations/healthnet/.

"The Global Reproductive Health Forum at Harvard (GRHF) is an internet networking project that aims to encourage the proliferation of critical discussions about reproductive health and gender on the net. GRHF provides interactive electronic forums, global discussions, distributes reproductive health and rights materials from a variety of perspectives through our clearinghouse as well as maintains an extensive, up-to-date research library."

Guerrilla Girls. www.guerrillagirls.com.

"The Guerrilla Girls are a group of women artists, writers, performers, film makers and arts professionals who fight discrimination. Dubbing ourselves the conscience of culture, we declare ourselves feminist counterparts to the mostly male tradition of anonymous do-gooders like Robin Hood, Batman, and the Lone Ranger."

Human Rights Campaign (HRC). www.hrc.org.

"As America's largest gay and lesbian organization, the Human Rights Campaign provides a national voice on gay and lesbian issues. The [HRC] effectively lobbies Congress; mobilizes grassroots action in diverse communities; invests strategically to elect a fair-minded Congress; and increases public understanding through innovative education and communication strategies."

Human Rights Watch (HRW). www.hrw.org.

HRW is dedicated to protecting the human rights of people around the world. The site has a Women's Rights Division that details human rights violations with special attention to women. They work "to prevent discrimination, to uphold political freedom, to protect people from inhumane conduct in wartime, and to bring offenders to justice."

ifeminists.com. www.ifeminists.com.

Ifeminism is individualist feminism. This site is an all-inclusive online center where people looking for a new way to approach feminism can gather online, learn, and access a wealth of information.

In Motion Magazine. www.inmotionmagazine.com/.

"A multicultural, online U.S. publication about democracy," this sites covers activism in a variety of areas including education, healthcare, civil and human rights, and globalization.

Information on Sexual Harassment. www.de.psu.edu/harassment.

Nancy Wyatt's sexual harassment site provides educators, students, researchers, and the public in-depth information about sexual harassment from a variety of perspectives. It also has sections on legal aspects, cases, links, and resources.

Institute for Women's Policy Research (IWPR). www.iwpr.org/.

"The Institute for Women's Policy Research (IWPR) is a public policy research organization dedicated to informing and stimulating the debate on public policy issues of critical importance to women and their families. IWPR focuses on issues of poverty and welfare, employment and earnings, work and family issues, the economic and social aspects of health care and domestic violence, and women's civic and political participation."

Integrating Gender Equity and Reform (InGEAR). www.coe.uga.edu/ingear.

"This web site is being developed as part of a multi-university project titled Integrating Gender Equity and Reform (InGEAR).The purpose of the web site is to provide teachers and teacher educators with access to materials that will enhance their own understanding of gender equitable classroom practices." The site offers information on scholarships, publications, and examples of curricula and teaching strategies.

International Gay and Lesbian Human Rights Commission (IGLHRC). http://www.iglhrc.org/.

"IGLHRC's mission is to protect and advance the human rights of all people and communities subject to discrimination or abuse on the basis of sexual orientation, gender identity, or HIV status." The site has a geographical map of action alerts, information on access to treatment, asylum awards, publication lists, and press releases.

International Women's Health Coalition (IWHC). http://www.iwhc.org.

"IWHC works to generate health and population policies, programs, and funding that promote and protect the rights and health of girls and women worldwide, particularly in Africa, Asia, Latin America, and countries in post-socialist transition." Site includes critical issues, publications, conferences, and country programs.

Karamah: Muslim Women Lawyers for Human Rights. www.karamah.org/.

"Karamah: Muslim Women Lawyers for Human Rights is a charitable, educational organization which focuses upon the domestic and global issues of human rights for Muslims."

Lesbian.org. www.lesbian.org.

Lesbian.org is committed to promoting lesbian visibility on the Internet. The gallery has links to other webpages, an annotated bibliography on butch/femme issues, and a guide to the Internet.

MANA. www.hermana.org.

MANA, a national Latina organization, "empowers Latinas through leadership development, community service and advocacy." There are chapters across the United States.

Ms. Foundation for Women. www.ms.foundation.org.

The Ms. Foundation funds and advocates for women and girls and has launched Take our Daughters to Work Day and the Collaborative Fund for Women's Economic Development, among other projects.

The National Abortion and Reproductive Rights Action League (NARAL). www.naral.org.

"For over thirty years, NARAL has been the political arm of the pro-choice movement and a strong advocate of reproductive freedom and choice. NARAL works to educate Americans and officeholders about reproductive rights and health issues and elect pro-choice candidates at all levels of government."

The National Center for Curriculum Transformation Resources on Women (NCCTRW). www.towson.edu/ncctrw.

"The National Center produces directories, manuals, and essays useful in curriculum transformation. [It] provides materials and information for helping faculty and administrators carry out curriculum change directed toward incorporating scholarship and research on women."

National Gay and Lesbian Task Force (NGLTF). www.ngltf.org.

"NGLTF is the national progressive organization working for the civil rights of gay, lesbian, bisexual and transgendered people, with the vision and commitment to building a powerful political movement." This site contains information on state & local organizing, federal advocacy, a wide variety of issues, and press releases.

National Organization for Women (NOW). www.now.org.

"NOW is the largest feminist organization in the nation, with more than half a million contributing members." The site contains action alerts, links, resources, news, and legislative updates.

National Partnership for Women and Families. www.nationalpartnership.org/.

"Founded in 1971 as the Women's Legal Defense Fund, the National Partnership has grown from a small group of volunteers into one of the nation's most powerful and effective advocates for women and families." The site provides information on important legislation and ways to take action.

National Women's Political Caucus (NWPC). www.nwpc.org.

"Founded in 1971, the National Women's Political Caucus (NWPC) is the only national, grassroots membership organization dedicated to increasing the number of pro-choice women in elected and appointed office regardless of party affiliation." The site has a list of events, information on membership, and forums for action.

National Women's Studies Association (NWSA). www.nwsa.org.

"NWSA supports and promotes feminist/womanist teaching, learning, research, and professional and community service at the pre-K through post-secondary levels and serves as a locus of information about the inter-disciplinary field of Women's Studies for those outside the profession." The site has links to their journal and task forces, and information on their conferences, scholarships, research resources, and more.

New York Women's Foundation. www.nywf.org.

> The Foundation is a cross-cultural alliance of women helping low-income girls and women in New York to achieve sustained economic self-sufficiency and self-reliance. The site provides the guidelines for grant proposals and information on their annual Celebrating Women Breakfast.

NOW Legal Defense and Education Fund. www.nowldef.org.

> "NOW Legal Defense's docket of 70 cases covers a wide range of gender equity issues. NOW Legal Defense also provides technical assistance to Congress and state legislatures, employs sophisticated media strategies, distributes up-to-the-minute fact sheets, and organizes national grassroots coalitions to promote and sustain broad-based advocacy for women's equality."

Ontario Women's Justice Network. www.owjn.org.

> "An online legal resource for women's organizations and individuals working on issues related to justice and violence against women and children."

Planned Parenthood. www.plannedparenthood.org.

> Provides a wide variety of resources on sexual health and well-being, action alerts, useful links, and research information.

Prostitutes' Education Network. www.bayswan.org/penet.html.

> "The Prostitutes' Education Network is an information service about legislative and cultural issues as they effect prostitutes and other sex workers. The service is comprised of information for sex workers and activists/educators who study issues of decriminalization, human rights in the context of prostitution, violence against prostitutes and women, sex workers and pornography, as well as current trends in legislation and social policy in the U.S. and internationally." Includes a link to the Whore Activist Network about sex-worker activists and activism.

Revolutionary Association of the Women of Afghanistan. www.rawa.org.

> "RAWA, the Revolutionary Association of the Women of Afghanistan, was established in Kabul, Afghanistan, in 1977 as an independent political organization of Afghan women fighting for human rights and for social justice in Afghanistan."

The Ruckus Society. www.ruckus.org.

> "The Ruckus Society provides training in the skills of non-violent civil disobedience to help environmental and human rights organizations achieve their goals." The site has online training manuals and information on their Action Camps.

Rural Womyn Zone. www.ruralwomyn.net.

> An online community for/about women living in rural communities in the U.S. and Canada. Provides e-mail lists, action alerts, resources, articles, and more.

Sisterhood is Global Institute (SIGI). www.sigi.org.

"Established in 1984, SIGI seeks to deepen the understanding of women's rights at the local, national, regional and global levels, and to strengthen the capacity of women to exercise these rights." The site contains information on SIGI events, publications, action alerts, and a variety of resources.

Society for Women's Health Research. www.womens-health.org.

The Society is an advocacy group that works to "improve the health of women through research." The site has resources on women's health care, statistics, links, sex-based biology, and more.

Transgender Law and Policy.
http://academic.brooklyn.cuny.edu/polisci/pcurrah/genderlaw/index.htm.

Paisley Currah's (Brooklyn College of the City University of New York) website provides up-to-date information and resources about nondiscrimination laws based on gender and sexuality.

UNIFEM—United Nations Development Fund for Women. www.unifem.undp.org.

UNIFEM "works to ensure the participation of women in all levels of development planning and practice, and acts as a catalyst within the UN system, supporting efforts that link the needs and concerns of women to all critical issues on the national, regional and global agendas."

United Nations Division for the Advancement of Women (DAW).
www.un.org/womenwatch/daw.

DAW "works closely with governments, its partners in the United Nations system and civil society" to advocate for improvement in the status of women by researching and implementing policies and supporting the Beijing Platform for Action. The site has information on the Beijing +5 Conference, a calendar of events, and a list of publications.

United Nations Population Fund (UNFPA). www.unfpa.org.

"UNFPA extends assistance to developing countries, countries with economies in transition and other countries at their request to help them address reproductive health and population issues, and raises awareness of these issues in all countries, as it has since its inception." There are webpages on the "state of the world population," "empowerment and the status of women," "gender, population and development," and many others.

The Violence against Women Office. www.ojp.usdoj.gov/vawo.

"The Violence Against Women Office works with U.S. Attorneys to ensure enforcement of the federal criminal statutes contained in the 1994 Act, assists the Attorney General in formulating policy related to civil and criminal justice for women, and administers more than $270 million a year in grants to help states, tribes, and local communities transform the way in which criminal justice systems respond to crimes of domestic violence, sexual assault, and stalking."

Visions in Action. www.visionsinaction.org.

Visions in Action, an international nonprofit organization, has grassroots volunteer programs that are committed to social change. They offer volunteer positions in Africa and Mexico. The site has information on the programs and the application process.

Whore Activist Network. www.whoreact.net.

This site addresses sex worker activism and activists. Includes publications; information on decriminalization; forum on racism, classism and sexism; and other topics.

Why Shop? Week. http://spot.colorado.edu/~shortk/whyshop.html.

Why Shop? Week was organized by Women's Studies students at the University of Colorado-Boulder. The site provides information on ethical consumption, businesses that exploit women, and the United Nations Fourth World Conference on Women, Beijing.

Women For Women International. http://www.womenforwomen.org/.

"Women for Women International provides women with tools and resources needed to move out of crisis and poverty and into stability and self-sufficiency." Current focuses include Bosnia-Herzegovina, Rwanda, Kosova, Bangladesh, and Nigeria.

Women in Community Service (WICS). www.wics.org.

"Partnering with government, human service and other nonprofit agencies, WICS delivers quality lifeskills, job readiness and support services to women on public assistance, women in prison, women who are homeless and public housing residents." The site has information on WICS job opportunities and how to become a volunteer as well as links to related sites.

Women, Law & Development International (WLDI). www.wld.org.

WLDI is "a non-profit, non-governmental organization committed to the promotion and defense of women's rights globally. WLDI identifies and publicizes violations of women's human rights, networks with women's rights leaders and organizations to develop common strategies for action and trains women to become women's rights advocates."

Women Leaders Online/Women Organizing for Change. www.wlo.org.

"The first and largest women's activist group on the internet—empowering women in politics, media, society, the economy and cyberspace." The site provides action alerts, feminist links, and voting guides.

Women Leading through Reading. www.litwomen.org/wltr.html.

"Women Leading Through Reading is an initiative with a twofold purpose: to raise awareness about the particular challenges women face as they seek to enhance their literacy skills, and to explore alternative ways for women to improve their literacy skills." The site has resources and materials for book discussion groups including a Best Practices Training Manual, with information on how to organize and do training for the WLTR book groups.

WomenAction 2000. www.womenaction.org.

WomenAction is "a global information, communication and media network that enables NGOs to actively engage in the Beijing+5 review process with the long term goal of women's empowerment, with a special focus on women and media." The website brings together people from around the world who are working toward women's empowerment, the passage of Convention on the Elimination of All Forms of Discrimination against Women, and the strengthening of women in government.

Women's Aid Online. www.womensaid.ie/.

Based in Dublin, Ireland, "Women's Aid is a feminist, service based, political and campaigning organisation committed to the elimination of violence and oppression against all women through effecting political, cultural and social change." Site has information on domestic violence, statistics, services that Women's Aid provides, and ways you can help.

The Women's Bureau of the U.S. Department of Labor. www.dol.gov/dol/wb.

Developed in June 1920, the Women's Bureau "is the single unit at the Federal government level exclusively concerned with serving and promoting the interests of working women. Central to its mission is the responsibility to advocate and inform women directly and the public as well, of women's work rights and employment issues." The site provides links to related sites and publications, and statistics on working women.

Women's Environment and Development Organization (WEDO). www.wedo.org.

"WEDO is an international advocacy organization that seeks to increase the power of women worldwide as policymakers at all levels in governments, institutions and forums to achieve economic and social justice." There are sections on "Gender and Governance," "Sustainable Development," and "Economic Justice."

Women's Human Rights Resources. www.law-lib.utoronto.ca/diana/mainpage.htm.

"The purpose of the Women's Human Rights Resources Web Site is to provide reliable and diverse information on international women's human rights via the Internet."

Women's International League for Peace and Freedom (WILPF). www.wilpf.org.

"WILPF works to achieve through peaceful means world disarmament, full rights for women, racial and economic justice, an end to all forms of violence, and to establish those political, social, and psychological conditions which can assure peace, freedom, and justice for all." The site has information on the groups campaigns, committees, and actions.

Women's Studies Programs, Departments, and Centers. www.research.umbc.edu/~korenman/wmst/programs.html.

The site has "links to more than 600 women's studies (including 'gender studies') programs, departments, and research centers around the world that have web sites."

WomensNet. www.igc.org/igc/gateway/wnindex.html.

WomensNet provides news from around the world about women; action alerts; and discussion forums. It is part of the Institute for Global Communications, which has other significant sites.

Women'sNet. http://womensnet.org.za/.

"Women'sNet aims to empower South African women to use information and communications technologies (ICTs) towards advancing women's equality." The site has sections on news, health, South African organizations, gender in Parliament, preventing gender violence, HIV/AIDS, the Beijing +5 Conference, and more.

Women'space. www.womenspace.ca.

Online version of a Canadian magazine that focuses on women and activism. Site also has online Feminist Heritage greeting cards and a section devoted to activist campaigns and articles.

WomensWatch. www.un.org/womenwatch/.

"WomenWatch is a joint UN project to create a core Internet space on global women's issues." It provides information on what the UN is doing to improve the status of women worldwide, regional data, and news, as well as on-line forums.

Working to Halt Online Abuse (WHOA). www.haltabuse.org.

"The mission of WHOA is to educate the Internet community about online harassment, empower victims of harassment, and formulate voluntary policies that systems administrators can adopt in order to create harassment-free environments."

Contributors

Anna M. Agathangelou is the director of the Global Change Institute in Cyprus. She is working on a book entitled *The Global Economy of Sex*, which addresses issues concerning sex and domestic workers. Her research interests include feminist pedagogies, postcolonial theory, feminist research methods, globalization, and transnational violence against women. She has published articles in *Studies of Political Economy*, *American Political Science Review*, and *Canadian Woman Studies/les cahiers de la femme*. Dr. Agathangelou also enjoys reading and writing poetry in different languages.

Rebecca Anne Allahyari is visiting assistant professor in religious studies and sociology at the University of California, Santa Barbara. At the time she began writing her chapter for this collection she was visiting assistant professor in women's studies and American studies at the University of Maryland, College Park. Her book, *Visions of Charity: Volunteer Workers and Moral Community* (2000), and her current field work among homeschooling families, reflects her interest in moral identities and everyday religious politics.

Joan Ariel has an M.A. in women's studies from San Francisco State University and an M.L.S. from the University of California, Berkeley. She is women's studies librarian and a member of the Women's Studies Steering Committee at the University of California, Irvine. She also teaches Gender and the Politics of Information, which investigates from feminist perspectives the challenges inherent in the "information age" and its embedded gender and political dimensions.

Karen Bojar has a Ph.D. in English literature from Temple University, and an M.S. in education from the University of Pennsylvania. She is professor of English and Coordinator of the Women's Studies Program at the Community College of Philadelphia, where she has taught for the past 25 years. Her publications include "Conceptualizing the Introduction to Women's Studies

Course at the Community College" (in *Teaching Introduction to Women's Studies: Student Resistance and Classroom Strategy*, edited by Carolyn DiPalma and Barbara Scott Winkler; 1999) and "Volunteerism and Women's Lives: A Lens for Exploring Conflicts in Contemporary Feminist Thought" (in *Women's Studies in Transition: The Pursuit of Interdisciplinarity*, edited by Kate Conway-Turner et al.; 1998). Currently, she is chair of the Philadelphia NOW Political Action Committee, a member of Pennsylvania NOW Political Action Committee, President of Philadelphia NOW, and Treasurer of NARAL-PA Foundation.

Melissa Kesler Gilbert is an engaged scholar for Campus Compact and an affiliated member in Sociology at Denison University in Ohio. She has published numerous articles and book chapters in the fields of women's work, feminist pedagogy, and service learning. She is currently a service-learning consultant for higher-education, providing faculty development seminars throughout the United States.

Simona J. Hill is assistant professor of sociology and anthropology at Susquehanna University. She earned her B.A., M.A., and Ph.D. from the University of Pennsylvania. Committed to higher education that enhances a person's abilities to think critically and act responsibly towards future generations, her mission is one of multiculturalism, community leadership, scholarship, and mutual empowerment.

Nancy A. Naples is author of *Grassroots Warriors: Activist Mothering, Community Work, and the War on Poverty* (New York: Routledge, 1988) which was a finalist for the C. Wright Mills Award of the Society for the Study of Social Problems. She is also editor of *Community Activism and Feminist Politics: Organizing Across Gender, Race, and Class* (Routledge, 1998) and *Women's Activism and Globalization: Linking Local Struggles with Transnational Politics* (Routledge, 2002). She currently holds a joint appointment in sociology and women's studies at the University of Connecticut. Her main research interests center on exploring the development of women's political consciousness and activism; the role of the state in reproducing or challenging inequality; and how differing community contexts influence women's resistance and political activism.

Catherine M. Orr is an assistant professor of women's studies at Beloit College in Beloit, Wisconsin. Her research interests include the history of women's studies in the U.S. academy, representations of feminism in U.S. popular culture, and the tension between activism and professionalism in the lives of leftist academics. She has published articles in *Hypatia, Women's Studies Quarterly*, and *Feminist Collections*. In addition to working on a book about activist academics, she is enjoying the the trials and tribulations of homeownership in Madison, Wisconsin, along with her two unnamed cats.

Jennifer L. Rexroat is a doctoral candidate in the Department of Political Science at the University of Illinois, at Chicago. She has completed a graduate concentration in the University of Illinois, at Chicago Gender and Women's Studies Program. Her dissertation examines the degree of feminist identification among women of low socioeconomic status and women of color. She is the author of "The Impact of Low Socioeconomic Status on Feminism" (1997). Her major fields of teaching and research interests include American politics, public policy analysis, and gender and politics.

Katherine Ann Rhoades is an associate professor in the Foundations of Education Department and Honors Program and a member of the Women's Studies Steering Committee at the University of Wisconsin-Eau Claire. Her research focuses on the implications of gender, race, and poverty on educational access and success. She is currently conducting a qualitative study of Hmong teachers and their perceptions of the process of becoming bilingual/bicultural educators.

Jane A. Rinehart is professor of sociology and women's studies at Gonzaga University in Spokane, Washington, and helped to found the Women's Studies Program at Gonzaga, serving as its director for five and a half years. She teaches courses in the sociology of gender, social theory, and feminist thought. Her publications include a coedited anthology, *Taking Parts: Ingredients of Leadership, Participation, and Empowerment* (1994); journal articles on teaching classical social theory, feminist theorizing as a conversation, and feminist pedagogy; and book chapters on feminist responses to "McDonaldization," teaching the introductory course in women's studies, and tools for curriculum innovation in women's studies.

Jennifer Rogers graduated from the University of California, Irvine, with a major in sociology and women's studies. She is currently a graduate student in sociology at the University of California, Santa Barbara.

Ellen Cronan Rose is professor and chair of the women's studies department at the University of Nevada, Las Vegas, where she teaches feminist theory and feminist praxis to undergraduate women's studies majors and minors and an introduction to women's studies course, feminist pedagogy, and the capstone course (directed readings and research in women's studies) to candidates for the graduate certificate. In a previous incarnation she published books and articles on contemporary women writers, particularly Doris Lessing and Margaret Drabble, but since 1993, her scholarship has reflected her increasing involvement in interdisciplinary women's studies teaching and administration. She serves on the Governing Council of the National Women's Studies Association as conference program chair.

Catherine Sameh is the cofounder and director of the Women's Community Education Project, the eight-year-old nonprofit parent organization of In Other Words Women's Books and Resources. She has been a feminist activist since the 1980s, focusing mainly on reproductive rights and lesbian issues.

Mary Kay Schleiter is an associate professor of sociology and chair of the Department of Sociology-Anthropology at the University of Wisconsin-Parkside. She has a Ph.D. in sociology from the University of Chicago. Her research focuses on the sociology of occupations, and careers and inequality. Her recent research projects focus on the consequences of welfare reform in the lives of women in transition from Aid to Families with Dependent Children to full-time work.

Kayann Short is a senior instructor in the Farrand Academic Program at the University of Colorado. With students in her Global Women Writers course, she has recently developed a service-learning project, Women's Coalition With Cuba, in alliance with the international women's rights group MADRE and the Federación de Mujeres Cubanas. Why Shop? Week 2001, Is The Price Right?, highlighted how consumerism fails to challenge the social and economic inequities that leave women vulnerable to violence and urged that economic policies address the real needs of women—peace, security, healthcare, education, and nutrition—rather than promote media-induced desires like perfect hair, thin bodies, and trendy clothes.

Anne Statham has been teaching sociology, women's studies, and environmental studies at the University of Wisconsin-Parkside since 1982. For nine years she was outreach administrator of the University of Wisconsin Women's Studies Consortium and is now director of the Institute for Community Based Learning on the UW-Parkside campus. In addition to her research on the impacts of welfare reform, she has done many community projects related to plant shutdowns, brownfield redevelopment, employer/employee relations, and other issues in low income neighborhoods.

Patricia Washington is an assistant professor of women's studies at San Diego State University. A sociologist by training, she uses a gendered lens to examine social stratification in the U.S. and abroad, with an emphasis on social inequalities and efforts to eradicate those inequalities. Her current research focuses on hate- and bias-motivated violence and the revictimization of lesbian and gay sexual assault survivors, with particular emphasis on the experiences of lesbian and gay sexual assault survivors of color. A second major area of research is the use of community-based service learning to advance feminist pedagogy, enhance student learning outcomes, and foster civic and intellectual engagement. Dr. Washington has written and consulted nationally and internationally on the efficacy of community-based service.

Isa D. Williams is founding director of the Atlanta Semester Program in Women, Leadership, and Social Change at Agnes Scott College. She received her Ph.D. from Emory University in Women's Studies. Her areas of teaching include women and leadership; women and behavior in organizations; and contemporary feminist theory. Isa's research has focused on factors affecting women's leadership and the sociological aspects of women and work. She was selected as a faculty delegate to travel in China and Korea for the purpose of examining women's lives and the structure of women's studies programs. In the spring of 1998, she led a student study group to the Middle East for the purpose of studying women's leadership in an international context. She was a member of an NGO delegation to the 2001 U.N. Conference Against Racism in South Africa.

Index